EAST-WEST CENTER
SERIES ON

CONTEMPORARY ISSUES IN ASIA
AND THE PACIFIC

Series Editor, Bruce M. Koppel

Chiefs Today

Chiefs Today

TRADITIONAL PACIFIC LEADERSHIP
AND THE POSTCOLONIAL STATE

Edited by Geoffrey M. White and
Lamont Lindstrom

STANFORD UNIVERSITY PRESS
STANFORD, CALIFORNIA
1997

Stanford University Press
Stanford, California
© 1997 by Stanford University Press
Printed in the United States of America
CIP data are at the end of the book

A series from
Stanford University Press and the East-West Center

CONTEMPORARY ISSUES IN ASIA AND THE PACIFIC

Bruce M. Koppel, Editor

A collaborative effort by Stanford University Press and the East-West Center, this series addresses contemporary issues of policy and scholarly concern in Asia and the Pacific. The series focuses on political, social, economic, cultural, demographic, environmental, and technological change and the problems related to such change. A select group of East-West Center senior fellows—representing the fields of political science, economic development, population, and environmental studies—serves as the Advisory Board for the series. The decision to publish is made by Stanford.

Preferences will be given to comparative or regional studies that are conceptual in orientation and emphasize underlying processes and to works on a single country that address issues in a comparative or regional context. Although concerned with policy-relevant issues and written to be accessible to a relatively broad audience, books in the series will be scholarly in character. We are pleased to offer here the second book in the series, *Chiefs Today: Traditional Pacific Leadership and the Postcolonial State*, edited by Geoffrey M. White and Lamont Lindstrom.

The East-West Center, located in Honolulu, Hawai'i, is a public, nonprofit educational and research institution established by the U.S. Congress in 1960 to foster understanding and cooperation among the governments and peoples of the Asia-Pacific region, including the United States.

Acknowledgments

LEADERSHIP has been a long-standing concern within Pacific Studies and within social science generally. As Pacific states have obtained their independence, issues of leadership have become increasingly complex and even more compelling in light of changing politics of culture and tradition. Contributors to this volume first met to address these issues at two annual meetings of the Association for Social Anthropology in Oceania, in New Orleans in 1992 and again in Kona, Hawai'i, in 1993.

We would like to thank all the participants in those sessions for contributing to this exploration of the contemporary position of traditional chiefs within the independent Pacific. In addition to the authors represented here, symposium participants included Niko Besnier, William Donner, David Gegeo, Jane Goodale, Matori Yamamoto, Richard Feinberg, Elizabeth Keating, Karen Nero, William Rodman, and Richard Scaglion. Several participants later published papers elsewhere (e.g., Besnier 1993; Boggs and Gegeo 1996; Scaglion 1996; and Yamamoto 1994; see also Feinberg and Watson-Gegeo 1996).

We would also like to thank Elisa Johnston, Anne Stewart, and Carol Wong of the East-West Center Publications Office for assistance with manuscript editing and preparation, and Laura Bloch, our editor at Stanford University Press.

Contents

Contributors

KATHLEEN M. ADAMS is Assistant Professor of Anthropology at Loyola University of Chicago. She is currently completing a manuscript on the politics of tourism and art in Tana Toraja, Indonesia, as well as a co-edited volume entitled *Home and Hegemony: Domestic Service and Identity Negotiation in Asia*. Her publications include articles in *Ethnology, Annals of Tourism Research, Cultural Survival Quarterly, Southeast Asian Journal of Social Science*, and in numerous edited volumes.

LAURENCE MARSHAL CARUCCI is Professor of Anthropology at Montana State University. He has conducted research in the Marshall Islands since 1976 and has published on a wide array of topics, including the celebration of "Christmas," World War II, aging, community and domestic violence, alcohol and tobacco use, and concepts of personal, atoll, and regional identity. He has lived for several years on Ujelang (Wūjlañ) and Enewetak (Āne-wetak) atolls, and has worked throughout the Marshall Islands, particularly Kwajalein (Kuwajleen), Rongelap (Roñlap), and Majuro atolls.

ROBERT W. FRANCO is Associate Professor of Anthropology at Kapiolani Community College in Honolulu. He has worked for more than two decades with Samoan communities in Western and American Samoa, Hawai'i, and California. He has published *Samoan Perceptions of Work: Moving Up and Moving Around* (AMS, 1991) and a wide range of articles from his ongoing research and community development work. He has been a leader in developing international Asia-Pacific curricula, and was awarded the Community Colleges in International Development International Fellowship in 1993. He now directs the KCC program on "Intergrating Service into a Multicultural Writing Curriculum."

ALAN HOWARD is Professor of Anthropology at the University of Hawai'i. He is author of *Learning to Be Rotuman* (Columbia University

Press, 1970), *Ain't No Big Thing: Coping Strategies in a Hawaiian-American Community* (University of Hawai'i Press, 1974), *Hef Ran Ta (The Morning Star): A Biography of Wilson Inia* (University of the South Pacific, 1994), and coeditor of *Developments in Polynesian Ethnology* (University of Hawai'i Press, 1989) and *Spirits in Culture, History, and Mind* (Routledge, 1996).

KERRY JAMES works in Sydney as a South Pacific consultant and researcher in the firm of Hooper James Consultants. She received her Ph.D. in Social Anthropology from University College London. Since 1990, she has held research fellowships at the Macmillan Brown Centre for Pacific Studies, the University of Canterbury; the Center for Pacific Island Studies, the University of Hawai'i at Manoa; the Pacific Islands Development Program, East-West Center; and the Research School of Pacific and Asian Studies, Australian National University, and has published widely on Tonga.

ROGER M. KEESING, at the time of his death in 1993, was Professor of Anthropology, McGill University. He was widely known for his writings in cultural anthropology and for his long-term research among the Kwaio people of the Solomon Islands. His many publications include *Kwaio Religion: The Living and the Dead in a Solomon Island Society* (Columbia University Press, 1982) and *Custom and Confrontation: The Kwaio Struggle for Cultural Autonomy* (University of Chicago Press, 1992).

PETER LARMOUR is Director of Graduate Studies in Development Administration at the National Centre for Development Studies, Australian National University. He has published widely on South Pacific politics, government, and land tenure, and is currently working on "governance" issues.

STEPHANIE LAWSON is a Fellow in the Department of International Relations, Research School of Pacific and Asian Studies, Australian National University. She has published widely on politics in the South Pacific region, focusing on aspects of democratization, ethnic conflict, the politics of culture, and nationalism. Her book *The Failure of Democratic Politics in Fiji* (Clarendon, 1991) was awarded the Crisp Medal in 1992 by the Australasian Political Science Association. Her most recent book is titled *Tradition Versus Democracy in the South Pacific: Fiji, Tonga and Western Samoa* (Cambridge University Press, 1996). Her present research interests include the politics of culture and democratization in Southeast Asia, theories of culture and nationalism, and contemporary issues in ethics and world politics.

LAMONT LINDSTROM is Professor of Anthropology at the University of Tulsa. He is the author of *Knowledge and Power in a South Pacific Society* (Smithsonian Institution Press, 1990), *Cargo Cult: Strange Stories of Desire from Melanesia and Beyond* (University of Hawai'i Press, 1993), and with Geoffrey M. White has edited two previous volumes on Melanesian cultural policy and Pacific War ethnohistory.

CLUNY MACPHERSON is Associate Professor in Sociology at the University of Auckland, New Zealand. His research interests are social and economic development in the South Pacific, relations between Pacific states in the world system, and migration within the Pacific. Within that general area he has specialized, with his wife and coresearcher La'avasa, on the Samoas and Samoan migration. Their most recent book is *Samoan Medical Belief and Practice*, published by the University of Auckland Press.

TOON VAN MEIJL is a Senior Research Fellow of the Royal Netherlands Academy of Arts and Sciences and is based at the Centre for Pacific Studies at Nijmegen. He is a graduate of the University of Nijmegen, the Netherlands, and the Australian National University, from which he obtained his Ph.D. in 1991. His doctoral dissertation, entitled "Political Paradoxes and Timeless Traditions: Ideology and Development Among the Tainui Maori, New Zealand," was based on twenty-five months of fieldwork with the Tainui Maori, the main supporters of the Maori King Movement. He is currently interested in the comparative study of kingships in the Pacific.

GLENN PETERSEN teaches anthropology, geography, and international affairs at the City University of New York's Graduate School and Bernard M. Baruch College. He has been a student of Micronesian political life since the early 1970s, and his works include *One Man Cannot Rule a Thousand: Fission in a Ponapean Chiefdom* (University of Michigan Press, 1982) and *Ethnicity and Interests at the 1990 Federated States of Micronesia Constitutional Convention* (Australian National University, 1993).

EVE C. PINSKER is Associate Director of the Neighborhoods Initiative Evaluation Project at the University of Illinois at Chicago. She did her graduate work in anthropology at the University of Chicago. She conducted field research in the Federated States of Micronesia for a total of thirty-eight months, in 1978, 1979, 1985–87, and 1990, focusing on relationships between national and local communities. She has also published on ethnic dance performance and has done field research in Chicago relating to the areas of ethnic dance and community development.

JAN RENSEL is Adjunct Assistant Professor at the University of Hawai'i. She is coeditor of *Home in the Islands: Housing and Social Change in the Pacific* (in press), and has conducted research on Rotuma and among Rotumans, in urban Fiji, Australia, New Zealand, Hawai'i, and Europe.

GEOFFREY M. WHITE is a Senior Fellow at the East-West Center and member of the graduate faculty in anthropology and Pacific Islands studies at the University of Hawai'i. His publications include *Identity Through History: Living Stories in a Solomon Islands Society* (Cambridge University Press, 1991) and, with Lamont Lindstrom, *Island Encounters: Black and White Memories of the Pacific War* (Smithsonian Institution Press, 1990).

UNITED STATES

Los Angeles

Oahu
Hawaii

HAWAII

ston

MEXICO

Mexico City

North Pacific Ocean

Clipperton

T   I

Kiritimati

Line Islands

equator

C
O
O
K

I
S
L
A
N
D
S

Marquesas
Islands

MERICAN
SAMOA

F
R
E
N
C
H

P
O
L
Y
N
E
S
I
A

Tuamotu Archipelago

Society Islands

Tahiti

Rarotonga

Austral Islands

Gambier Islands

Pitcairn
Islands

South Pacific Ocean

Easter

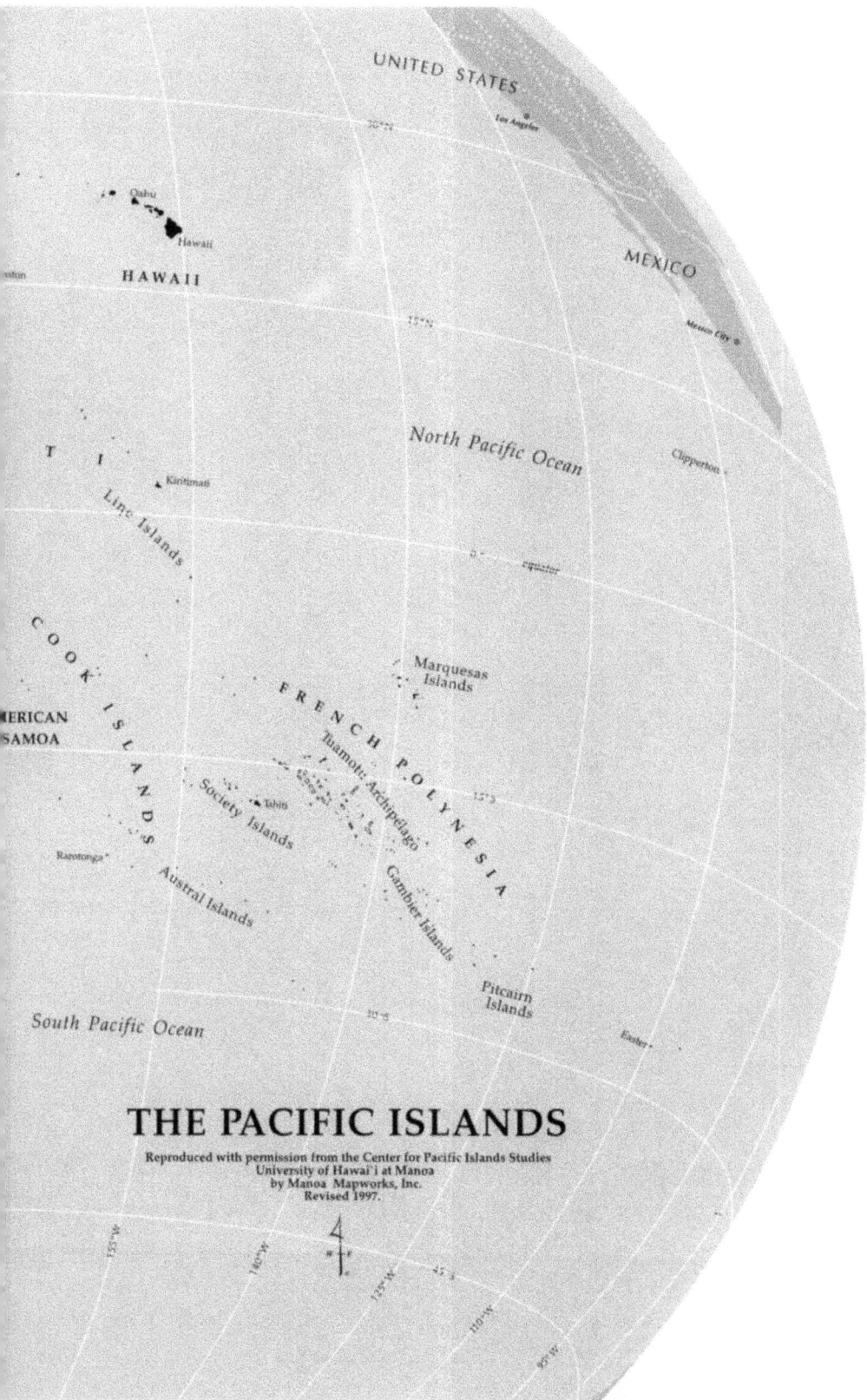

THE PACIFIC ISLANDS

Reproduced with permission from the Center for Pacific Islands Studies
University of Hawai'i at Manoa
by Manoa Mapworks, Inc.
Revised 1997.

N
W   E
S

Chiefs Today

·

1

Introduction

Chiefs Today

LAMONT LINDSTROM AND GEOFFREY M. WHITE

THE "CHIEF" has played an important role in comparative political theory, although usually he is regarded as a transitional character representing the displacement of old, traditional ways by newer, modern ones. The forces of modernity were meant to usher him (or sometimes her) from the global stage, replacing tribal or feudal styles of leadership with the universalistic, rational forms of the nation-state and its attendant bureaucracies.[1] But the grand narratives of modernization and Westernization have not worked out in quite the ways anticipated by their authors. The principles of democracy and human rights have not led to a new, homogenized world order; rather, these principles themselves have become the subject of global debate.

In the context of this debate, the "chief"—historically an icon of local tradition and identity—has become a subject of contestation and transformation, especially within postcolonial states where inherited political systems are being rethought and reinvented. The discussions that surround chiefs today in the Pacific and elsewhere reveal much about the sources of meaning and value that underwrite the legitimacy of contemporary leaders (see Feinberg and Watson-Gegeo 1996). By examining the terms of these debates in the Pacific, this volume explores the kinds of local and national narratives that are variously challenging, adapting, or otherwise transforming global visions of modern democracy.

To be sure, narratives of human progress, of the coming triumph of democracy and rationality, of the approaching end, even, of history itself, are with us still. The original mellifluous, booming tones of these promises, however, have become noticeably worried and thin. Political and economic progress, once presumed to be the natural and inevitable result of unswerving laws of history, now appears to demand constant human attention and design. Max Weber's influential typology of political legitimacy, and common theories of progressive stages of political advance, have proven too simple. The traditional chief and the charismatic leader are with us still.

Political environs of the South Pacific, although freshly populated with presidents, prime ministers, members of parliament, local court justices, and the like, continue to be ruled in many areas by "custom chiefs."[2] In some Pacific nations, the number of chiefs has multiplied considerably in recent years following the withdrawal of colonial powers from the region. Simple evolutionary models, based on European history and theory, that run from hereditary traditional leader to modern politician-bureaucrat, fail to describe the historical experience of much of the world, including the Pacific Islands. This was already apparent a century ago. Colonial states in the Pacific and elsewhere sought out chiefs where they traditionally existed, or created them where they did not, to serve as administrative functionaries, linking colonial centers with village hinterlands. Rather than fading away as obsolete, premodern political figures, chiefs were vital elements—sometimes formalized, sometimes not—within state administrative structures (see Chapters 2, 6, 10, and 12; Powles and Pulea 1988; and compare Aborisade 1985; van Rouveroy van Nieuwall 1987b; and Geschiere 1993 for the colonial history of African chiefs).

Over the last two centuries, indigenous leaders and Pacific Islands states have arrived at several inventive accommodations. On some islands (Tonga, notably), certain leading families founded chiefdoms and kingdoms that they continue to rule. In the Cook Islands, the House of Ariki Act of 1966 established a constitutional body of titled chiefs modeled on the British House of Lords (Sissons 1994). Elsewhere (e.g., the Solomon Islands and Vanuatu), new chiefly positions—including that of "paramount chief"—emerged during colonial history and have solidified in the context of national independence and the independent state's new institutional needs. Other variations exist in New Zealand, for example, where chiefs operate as representatives of tribal communities encapsulated within a metropolitan state; and in Western Samoa and Indonesia, where state leaders and chiefs possess sometimes parallel, sometimes divergent, interests.

The renewed visibility of chiefs in the context of modern nation-states is evident well beyond the Pacific. In South Africa, Chief Mangosuthu Buthelezi, president of the Zulu Inkatha party, demanded state recognition of the Zulu monarch, King Goodwill Zwelithini, as the precondition for Zulu participation in the Republic of South Africa's first democratic election. And even in the United States, surely the climax of many modernist political narratives, chiefs continue to find a voice in political affairs. As we write this, one of us lives in Hawai'i, where images of indigenous chiefs (*ali'i*) and monarchs heat up a Native Hawaiian sovereignty movement; the other works in Oklahoma, where Chief Wilma Mankiller of the Cherokees and her fellow chiefs from some thirty-four other federally recognized tribal governments rule alongside, sometimes on top of, and frequently in conflict with Oklahoma's elected city councillors and state legislators.

Positioned between local (ethnic, tribal) constituencies and the apparatus of nation-states, the "chief" stands at the intersection of local, national, and global political cultures. Just as the "chief" once occupied a strategic position in colonial systems of indirect rule, so today he finds himself mediating local realities and larger spheres of national and transnational interaction. Far from premodern relics, the chiefs of modern Pacific states increasingly figure in the rhetoric and reality of national political development. It is our contention that the renewed significance of chiefs, and the debates and disagreements that surround them, emerge from a collision of discourses of identity and power circulating in the Pacific today. In some cases these collisions produce demands for the revitalization and reempowerment of traditional chiefs; in others they evoke attempts to constrict or regulate their power. Either way, the controversies and contestations provide a window onto the course of social and political transformation in the Pacific today.

By presenting a range of cases, this book works to break up persistent and simplifying dichotomies of tradition/modernity or indigenous/Western that may be found in much of today's political rhetoric. For example, efforts by states to codify chiefly status may also subvert practices once used by communities to limit or counter the power of chiefs—practices as diverse as exile or ritual clowning (cf. Hereniko 1995; and Chapter 9). On the other hand, the introduction of democratic practices may bolster the position of chiefs, as in the case of postwar Yap, where elections in 1946 saw five of ten chiefs appointed by the former Japanese administration defeated by higher-ranking traditional chiefs (Poyer 1995).

Almost everywhere in the Pacific today, people are debating the importance of "chiefs" and the legitimacy—or illegitimacy—of current chiefly political practice. The encounter between custom and democracy—between traditional and legal-bureaucratic authority—continues to animate island politics (Crocombe et al. 1992). For example, in his keynote address to the Pacific Science Congress in Honolulu in 1991, former Papua New Guinea prime minister Michael Somare spoke on the subject of leadership in Melanesia. In that address he asserted that "traditional leadership and the democratic process are two completely different and opposite things" and called for greater recognition of chiefs and principles of indigenous leadership instead of the blind application of principles of Western democracy (Somare 1991).

To expand briefly upon the contemporary significance of chiefs for tensions between (Western) democracy and (indigenous) tradition, consider events in which the status of chief has been at issue. In Fiji, media guidelines are announced by the Minister of Information that restrict coverage of political speeches deemed racially or culturally inflammatory, including statements that might "challenge the traditional Fijian system of chiefs" (Pacnews, July 30, 1993). In Western Samoa, a village council of chiefs (*matai*) mandates the execution-style slaying of a chief for offenses against the village and its *matai*, after which twenty-eight people are sentenced to fines and prison terms by a magistrate who notes that the case reveals problems in reconciling individual rights guaranteed by constitutional law and "traditional Samoan authority personified by village chieftains" (see Chapter 2). In the Solomon Islands, a policeman challenges a group of "custom chiefs" from the island of Malaita over their role in hearing civil cases in the national capital, noting that they attempt to "judge people from other provinces using Malaita custom" (*Solomon Star* [Nov. 24, 1993]: 5). In war-torn Bougainville, where state control and local government collapsed in the wake of separatist rebellion and military suppression, "chiefs" emerged as strident voices speaking for local communities in the name of tradition. As negotiations continue to lurch forward, the role of chiefs is debated among the multiple parties involved in the conflict, including now two local authorities, a rebel army, and the Papua New Guinea national government and defense force.

In each of the above cases, the status and power of the chief have become public issues in the context of national political change and development. Like these incidents, the cases taken up in this volume chart the shifting terrain of national imagination and power in the Pacific today (see Foster 1991, 1995). Whether the nation-state is attempting to protect chiefly status, as in the case of Fiji's media guidelines, or acting to define the limits of chiefly authority, as in the case of national officials seeking to regulate local chief councils in Western Samoa and the Solomon Islands, such events mark the boundaries of national institutions. These events suggest a general strategy for the comparative study of political culture in the Pacific. By looking to the margins and boundaries of the state, we find critical events that offer strategic sites of investigation. Whether in the interfaces of central and local government, at the edges of national maps, or in diaspora communities where ethnic and national communities reconstitute themselves in the context of cosmopolitan, urban environments, chiefs are central actors in the dramas of political transformation.

As an example of one such zone of liminality, consider events during the past decade along the border between Papua New Guinea and the Solomon Islands—a border made tense, even lethal, by the crisis on Bougainville. The efforts of the Papua New Guinea defense forces to seal off a previously permeable border against the flow of medical supplies (and weapons) resulted in numerous shooting incidents and killings, including two Solomon Islands citizens killed on their own soil—an incident redressed in 1994, when Papua New Guinea paid SI$1.5 million in compensation to the Solomon Islands government. As both governments sought to improve methods of managing and policing the border, the Solomon Islands government talked of the need to involve traditional chiefs in the process. After a national delegation, including local chiefs, visited the Torres Straits to study border-management policies at the boundary between Australia and Papua New Guinea, the Solomon Islands foreign minister stated that "the involvement of chiefs in the administration and management of the border [is] very important" (*Solomon Star* [May 11, 1993]: 2). (Ironically, perhaps, chiefs referred to as "tribal leaders" in the Torres Straits declared their independence from Australia in a call for sovereignty just a few months later.)

Through a range of ethnographic studies in diverse island societies, this volume explores the often contested place of chiefs (or traditional leaders, broadly construed) within independent Pacific states today. Some contributors focus on the tribulations of particular chiefs, trapped between customary and state expectations of leadership; others examine the contemporary capacities of chiefs in broader perspective. We follow chiefs today in the three cultural regions of Oceania—Polynesia, Micronesia, and Melanesia—and one chapter (Chapter 14) reports on comparable political processes on the island of Sulawesi, in Pacific Rim Indonesia. Peter Larmour's concluding chapter reviews the common patterns and the distinctive circumstances of the chiefs and states taken up in this volume.

Chiefs Yesterday

Given that most of the contributors to this volume are anthropologists, it is important for us to trace briefly anthropology's own entanglement with definitions and constructions of chiefs in the Pacific. Historically, anthropology has had much to say about chiefs and other types of leader in the context of local political systems and, secondarily, histories of colonization and missionization (White 1991). Given anthropology's traditional orientation toward the study of difference, the emphasis has often been on describing pre-European forms, and placing them within wider systems of comparison and classification. In contrast, our interest is neither typologi-

cal nor strictly indigenous.[3] Instead, we examine contemporary constructions that draw from multiple types and categories, indigenous and foreign, local and global. More significantly, it is important to recognize that
each of the opposed terms in dualisms such as local/global or indigenous/
foreign is contingent on the other. The meaning of "tradition" emerges in
counterpoint to discourses of modernization and development. The focus,
then, is not on political types, but on discourses that work to construct,
validate, and empower local leaders as traditional or customary. To study
chiefly discourse, then, is to locate chiefs in history, to see their status as
subject to ongoing revision in response to changing circumstances. Seen
in this light, chiefs emerge in transactions of meaning between multiple
spheres of identity and power.

Pacific leaders making claims to traditional authority nowadays are
"chiefs." From Bougainville to Efate to Papeete, the esteemed title today
is "chief" (or *jif* or *chef*)—and this is the term that we, too, adopt to refer
to Pacific leaders who claim traditional authority. Islanders thus echo so-
ciologist Max Weber's language: "In the case of traditional authority, obedience is owed to the person of the chief who occupies the traditionally
sanctioned position of authority and who is (within its sphere) bound by
tradition" (1947:328). This popular usage overruns common anthropological distinctions among Pacific leadership types—especially the distinction between the chief and the bigman (and now also "great man";
see Godelier and Strathern 1991). These two terms—Polynesian (and Micronesian) chief and Melanesian bigman—together have served to delineate a major ethnographic boundary in the Pacific. Not only is the
Melanesian bigman defined through contrast with chiefs, but the contrast
drawn in Marshall Sahlins's (1963) original demarcation was evolutionarily ordered, with chiefs leading more complex political groups than do
bigmen. As a more recent invention, however, the bigman label circulates
in a narrow range of usage—a marker of knowledge of the anthropological typology of political leaders in Oceania.

Neither "chief" nor "bigman" was among the earliest terms that European observers used to make sense of Pacific leaders. Participants in Alvaro de Mendaña's voyage to the Solomons in 1568, and later Pedro de
Quiro's 1605–6 voyage, which traversed the Tuamotus and Vanuatu and
skirted the southern Papuan coastline, wrote instead of "kings" and ca-
ciques (the latter a Spanish borrowing from Arawakan sources in the Ca-
ribbean) (Kelly 1964:86, 198). Kings likewise ruled in Africa, as Farrar
(1992) has noted, until eighteenth- and nineteenth-century social evolu-
tionist theories demoted these royalty to the level of chief. In European
progressive cosmology, the true "king" properly appears only with civilization; African kings and Pacific kings from earlier seventeenth-century

reports had now to be reclassified as mere "chiefs"—this, now, the evolutionarily appropriate leadership type among barbarian peoples. In a parallel terminological move, former native kingdoms receded into humbler "tribes." In this context, references to Oceanic kings in European travel writings often exhibit an ironic tone, with regal status ascribed to the leaders of small and materially simple communities (see Theroux 1992 for a contemporary example of this type of satirical usage).

Farrar notes that the earliest applications of the title "chief" date to the end of the sixteenth century; the word "chief" "was first applied . . . to native leaders in Ireland and the Scottish highlands" (1992:272). In centuries to come, as English speakers found the opportunity to expand upon this original, internal colonialism, they applied the term "chief" pervasively in the Americas and Africa. By the eighteenth and nineteenth centuries—the period of major European exploration and colonialization of the Pacific—"chief" was the normal term to label the leaders of savage and barbarian peoples. Missionary anthropologist R. H. Codrington, writing of Melanesia in 1891, noted: "Chiefs exist, and still have in most islands important place and power, though never perhaps so much importance in the native view as they have in the eyes of European visitors, who carry with them the persuasion that savage people are always ruled by chiefs" (1891:46; see also W. H. R. Rivers's usage of "chief" in his 1914 overview of Melanesian society).

Nineteenth-century island leaders, along with their overseas advisors, were no doubt sensitive to the antiprogressive connotations of the title "chief." In those places where new state entities emerged—in Polynesian Tonga, Tahiti, and Hawai'i—victorious leaders instead claimed for themselves the title "king" or "queen": King Tāufa'āhau George Tupou I, Queen Pomare IV, King Kamehameha I. And kings imply kingdoms. This rhetoric of kings and queens asserted modernist nineteenth-century political assumptions of discrete nations encompassed within independent states. In some instances, appropriating the ritual politics of monarchy provided ways of resisting or otherwise engaging European ambitions of empire. Thus, when would-be colonizers deposed King Kamehameha III from his Hawaiian throne in 1843, a military expedition led by British Admiral Thomas intervened to restore the Polynesian monarchy. (This event is now celebrated as "Restoration Day" by advocates of Hawaiian sovereignty.) Where Pacific states failed to form, local leaders had to make do with the title "chief"—for example, the "high chiefs" of the Tupua and Malietoa families of Samoa (see Chapters 2 and 4).

Pacific kings also emerged within political movements of resistance to colonial intrusion; the best known of these is perhaps the New Zealand Maori effort to crown a king in 1858 (van Meijl 1993; Clark 1975:2).

Whereas this sort of political resistance in the 1800s produced kings and queens, similar processes of local organization in the face of today's increasingly centralized state authority are generating renewed recognition of chiefs and "paramount chiefs." Talk about kings, however, still surfaces to mark claims to special local powers. When Jimmy Stephens, leader of Vanuatu's formerly rebellious Nagriamel political movement, party, and church, was buried in 1994, he was eulogized as the "king of the Nagriamel movement," the "late head of the royal family of Fanafo" (*Vanuatu Weekly* 483 [May 5, 1994]: 2; see also Howard's 1992 description of a recent aspirant to Rotuman kingship). But the Pacific today has only one internationally acknowledged king—King Tāufaʻāhau Tupou IV of Tonga— although various claimants to the defunct thrones of Hawaiʻi and Tahiti periodically enliven political discussion in those islands. King Tāufaʻāhau stands alone above thousands of chiefs of sundry rank.

By the 1900s, as colonization and missionization accelerated in the western Pacific, some Europeans remarked that many Pacific leaders in this region did not even appear to be proper chiefs. Missionaries and colonial administrators eager to identify power structures that could assist in their efforts to manage or transform island societies commented that leaders in many of these societies led without marked systems of rank or titular authority, that they did not appear to inherit their offices, and so forth. Codrington, after identifying chiefs in various parts of Melanesia, complained that in Vanuatu, ritual societies that allowed men to achieve social importance had "introduced much obscurity into the problem of the existence of hereditary chiefs in the Banks Islands" (cited in Rivers 1914:139). In earlier writings, he also noted the effects of colonial expectations: "A trader or other visitor looks for a chief, and finds such a one as he expects; a very insignificant person in this way comes to be called, and to call himself, the king of his island, and his consideration among his own people is of course enormously enhanced by what white people make of him" (1891:46). The significant point here is not so much that chiefs are in many areas an invention of colonial expectations but that their status was emergent, fashioned in transactions with outsiders who had come to trade, missionize, and otherwise colonize.

Subsequent observers of societies in the western Pacific struggled with how to describe political systems that lacked formalized hierarchy and leaders who appeared to lack chiefly attributes and regalia. Anthropological wordsmiths devised a series of labels for Melanesian leaders, ranging from "headman," "centerman," and "strongman" to "director" and "manager," before settling on the now-popular "bigman."[4] An effect of this relabeling was to demote some Pacific leaders one further step down the ladder of social evolution. Three tiers at this point emerge: the progressive modern state, governed by civilized or rapidly civilizing kings; the tribe, ruled by chiefs; and the band, village, or kinship group, guided by some less powerful, less regal sort of self-made leader.

Sahlins's (1963) influential comparison of chiefs and bigmen did much to cement the latter term in anthropological parlance. Sahlins, drawing largely on ethnographic accounts of Bougainville Island and Papua New Guinean political systems, characterized the bigman as reminiscent of the free-enterprising rugged individual of European heritage. The bigman combines an ostensible interest in his followers' general welfare with a more profound measure of self-interest, entrepreneurial acumen, and economic calculation (1963:289). This caricature epitomizes a leader whose political status flows primarily from personal and economic ability. Whereas a true chief succeeds to an ascribed status, a bigman achieves his leadership position.[5] A politically ambitious individual accumulates both subsistence and prestige goods (e.g., pigs, shell money, yam, taro, and other foodstuffs) in order to give away this wealth. (Among other things, bigmen have acquired anthropologists in the course of their efforts at reputation-building, enlisting them in the service of circulating accounts of their accomplishments to an ever-widening audience; see, for example, works by Keesing [1983] and Strathern [1979] as examples of a new biographical genre that has grown out of such collaborations.) The bigman also manages rituals of economic redistribution, as well as exchanges in knowledge and services (Harrison 1993). By astute economic generosity and management, he secures influence over his kin and neighbors, who become his allies and debtors. People support a bigman's political endeavors and his ambitions to build his "name" because he contributes to their brideprice funds and bankrolls their ritual obligations, and because they also, as a group, share in his increasing political renown.

Today in Melanesia, though, "bigman" has lost terminological currency. Anthropology has been increasingly concerned with its various reifications, including the geographic concepts of Oceania's three culture areas, Melanesia, Micronesia, and Polynesia. Despite the fact that these categories have become ingrained in the politics and geography of today's Pacific, scholarly critics worry that they have been too crudely drawn (Guiart 1982; Thomas 1989). Furthermore, lurking just behind the tripartite division of Oceania into distinct culture areas is the binary opposition of (Polynesian) chiefs and (Melanesian) bigmen—a duality that is increasingly suspect. Island leadership patterns are varied and complex, and the term "chief" may accurately describe the qualities of leaders in many Melanesian societies, just as many chiefs in Polynesia rely on personal ability and political cunning as much as genealogical status to ensure their positions (see Chapter 13; Douglas 1979; Lutkehaus 1996).

More important, many postcolonial local leaders have now reclaimed for themselves the title "chief." A variety of local, provincial, and national councils of chiefs exist throughout the region (such as Vanuatu's Malvatumauri and Fiji's Great Council of Chiefs); no one yet has organized a National Council of Bigmen. Language groups across the Pacific have selected the word "chief" (or its cognates) as the standard gloss for indigenous terms for traditional leaders. What "chief" means, exactly, differs from community to community, as the chapters in this volume demonstrate (see, e.g., Chapters 8 and 14). In our usage, the term designates a political leader who draws his authority and influence from a discourse of local tradition.

There is an instructive progression in some five centuries of political terminology in the Pacific. This begins with "king" and moves down to "chief," then to "bigman," and now has reversed back up to "chief" (although a number of exceptions may readily be noted, e.g., Douglas 1979). And some leaders, like Vanuatu's Jimmy Stephens, have ennobled themselves and returned all the way back up to king—or alternatively, to "paramount chief" or "president," the latter title trumping even the progressive claims of the civilized kings. We explore in this volume the political circumstances that have motivated this chain of labels—forces that not only include the rise and fall of European theories of social progress, but also more importantly, reflect islanders' creative responses to increasingly centralized state authority, including their efforts to accommodate the global within the local and vice versa.

We can note three kinds of chief today. In some communities, chiefs' traditional perquisites and their state-guaranteed authority now overlap, to the degree that the chief or king stands for the nation or group as a whole. Abuse of this sort of chiefly cum state power has sometimes sparked popular protest. Chiefs in these areas represent the state, serving as its statesmen. Elsewhere, chiefs have surfaced as a mechanism of local accommodation to centralized state authority. This sort of chief mediates between central institutions and the political periphery within Pacific states. Such bureaucratic chiefs are in effect minor functionaries who sustain and advance state operations at the local level. And still elsewhere, chiefs rise up against the state, serving, in symbol and in practice, to resist central authorities. These chiefs lead to oppose the state.

Chiefly Statesmen

From colonial times onward, with the intrusion of mission and colonial authorities, Pacific chiefs have drawn from both indigenous and Western rhetorics of power. Anthropological models, struggling to represent pure indigenous types on the one hand and sociopolitical change on the other, have generally failed to represent the interpenetration of these forms. It is not uncommon for chiefs to merge their traditionalist status with the legal-bureaucratic authority of state office. If it does not always produce a new structure, the conjuncture at least becomes a cauldron for political invention.

In Tonga, the royal family continues to inherit the office of king, and thirty-three ennobled families inherit eligibility for parliamentary membership (see Chapters 3 and 4; Marcus 1989). In Western Samoa, candidates for Parliament must possess chiefly titles, and until 1990 only entitled chiefs could vote in national elections (see Chapters 2 and 4). Even though most Pacific chiefs acquire state offices by means of election or appointment, chiefly titles are an important bank of political capital. In Fiji, for example, although anyone legally might serve as prime minister or president, these offices since independence have been dominated by powerful chiefly families (see Chapter 6). This is the case as well in the Marshall Islands, where chiefs also control the nation's political institutions (see Chapter 10).

This multiplying of authority advances the political legitimacy of a state whose powers and acts thereby may be justified in both traditional and modernist terms. It is no surprise that many state leaders (who may come to office with weak or no claims to chiefly status) are eager to collect additional chiefly titles while in office, as has been the case in Vanuatu and the Solomon Islands (see Chapter 11; cf. Vaughan 1991:319 for Africa). Pacific politicians sometimes even share their enthusiasm for chiefly titles with their peers from beyond the islands. Numerous anthropologists working in Samoa and elsewhere, for example, proudly reveal such honors bestowed upon them. More dramatically, a Reuters item from September 7, 1995, reported the following:

Australia's urbane Prime Minister Paul Keating, who wants his country to be part of Asia, will be crowned a paramount chief of the Oro people when he visits Papua New Guinea next week. . . . Keating, who collects empire clocks and favours Italian designer suits, will be sworn in as a paramount chief of the remote Oro mountain people in a primitive jungle ceremony that involves spear-brandishing warriors and bare-breasted women.

The statesman-chief can stand for the nation, symbolizing its productive union of tradition and modernity. However, although a double authority may amplify the legitimacy of a nation's leadership, it opens to challenge a state's modernist and traditionalist claims alike. On the side of the modern, critics may decry outmoded tradition's contamination of bureaucratic rationality and democratic politics (see Chapter 6). A "democracy movement" in Tonga, for example, presently castigates the state's political system as archaic and undemocratic because of the domination of decision-making by the royal family and titled nobility. Such a system is easily reframed as a quaint but ill-advised survival of outmoded feudalism. Critics also condemned as undemocratic Western Samoa's former chiefly limitations on the poll, leading to a national referendum on the issue (see Chapter 2; cf. Mensah 1990 and Vaughan 1991 for parallel worries about chiefly threats to democracy in Africa).

Alternatively, political critics may condemn leaders' claims to traditional authority on the grounds that the state's exploitation of such authority vitiates its authenticity. Chiefs who become involved in politics are no longer true chiefs. Their customary duties and reciprocal relations with followers dry up or are made difficult by their dual status as state leader and custom chief. Gift exchanges are supplanted or transformed by transactions in consumable commodities. Social devices that once ensured reciprocity between a chief and his community and that limited chiefly aggrandizement now no longer adequately function.

Customs of ritual clowning in Pacific societies that once functioned as reminders of chiefs' dependency on followers, for example, today have only diminished efficacy in tempering chiefly practice. Recent events and political developments in Fiji, Tonga, and Samoa indicate that greater social distance now separates many chiefs from common folk. Ensconced in constitutional politics, living in towns or cities, engaged in the pursuit of power and money, many chiefs (both traditional and modern) perhaps could benefit by employing a clown or jester as part of their households. In the evenings, villagers might arrive with a comic sketch in which they could play out their frustrations and needs, and perhaps occasionally parody the oppressive face of authority (Hereniko 1994:21). But most chiefs who take on state office are detached from traditional devices, such as clowning, that manage chiefly/community relations. Their command of the state's apparatus subverts their customary authority. Howard and Rensel (Chapter 7), for example, report on a series of disputes on Rotuma, where people have accused chiefs of misusing their traditional and official authority to acquire unfair business advantage and misappropriate public funds (see also Chapter 10, on chiefly businessmen in the Marshall Islands whose economic and political success subverts their ritual status; and Chapter 14, on comparable conflict among the Toraja).

The alliance of legal-bureaucratic and traditional authority is a complicated and uneasy political exercise. On the one hand, a double-barreled legitimacy is a powerful weapon that justifies both state governance and those select individuals who rule. On the other hand, the traditionality of state leaders and institutions can impugn their modernity, and vice versa.

Chiefly Bureaucrats

The larger community of Pacific chiefs occupies humbler corners of the fabric of contemporary Pacific politics. Most states do not restrict high office or limit access to the polls solely to the chiefly class. Everyone is equal in the eyes of the law. But this modernist legal fiction uneasily overlays extant local political systems that continue to generate chiefs (or *jifs* or *ariki*). Maintaining a process that began in the first moments of colonization, Pacific constitutions have in several ways attempted to incorporate chiefs into state systems. National governments continue to explore ways in which local authority systems might be blended with the sorts of administrative structures and practices demanded by the modern nation-state.

Miles, for example, writes of "the search for appropriate models" (1993:31) for the participation of chiefs in the administrations of Niger, Nigeria, and Vanuatu. The political problem here is that developing states must make work for chiefs. This must be, however, the right sort of work—something that takes advantage of chiefs' traditional status and local authority but that will not disturb the sometimes unsteady authority of central governments. Miles suggests five possible, safe, and useful "modern functions" for traditional rulers within modern state apparatuses: (1) to broker incoming projects and deals for local economic development; (2) to boost the authority of state leaders by ennobling them on regular occasions with sundry traditional titles; (3) to police the hinterlands, overseeing "low-level" conflict resolution; (4) to serve as ombudsmen between their communities and the state bureaucracies (see Ayeni 1985); and (5) to rouse community solidarity and provide local administrative services in situations where central governments are ineffectual or even disintegrating.

Chiefs, in sum, are to serve the state as its middlemen and its brokers (see Rodman and Counts 1982). They advance a state's political authority and programs, developmental or otherwise, into the nation's hinterlands. From a political functionalist perspective, chiefs extend the reach of the state into the remoter areas of the nation at the same time as they improve citizens' access to state bureaus and programs. For example, Prime Minister Maxime Carlot Korman appointed the president of Vanuatu's National Council of Chiefs to advise the nation's new ombudsman (a position called for constitutionally but only filled some fourteen years after independence). Vanuatu thus looks to find useful work for chiefs as counselors for state bureaucrats.

Chiefs in migrant "colonies" away from home islands can also provide important political and judicial services in those communities, including those in Pacific towns such as Port Vila (see Chapter 11), as well as in distant metropolitan cities such as Auckland, Sydney, Honolulu, or Los Angeles. Two councils of Samoan chiefs, for example, presently assemble in Hawai'i (see Chapter 4).

Pacific states have variously recognized traditional leaders and combined them into councils or houses of chiefs, granting them a range of bureaucratic functions (see Chapters 6, 8, 9, 10, 11, and 12). The constitutions of Fiji and Vanuatu, for example, establish national councils of chiefs that convene periodically. These councils, as well as individual member chiefs, possess a range of officially designated powers running from the administrative to the judicial to the merely advisory. The status of national bodies of chiefs varies greatly from one state to another, depending upon the nature of national integration and administration on the one hand, and the predicament of local leaders on the other. The Parliament, or *fono*, of Western Samoa is in effect the national council of chiefs that commands greatest legislative powers in the Pacific, insofar as only individuals with chiefly, or *matai*, rank may be elected to that body (Chapter 2). In Fiji, the Bose Levu Vakaturaga, or Great Council of Chiefs, found its powers considerably expanded in the aftermath of the military coups that invoked the protection of tradition as a major objective. The 1990 constitution grants veto powers over all parliamentary law that affects Fijian interests (*Pacific Islands Monthly* [July 1993]: 36–37). In Vanuatu, conversely, members of the Malvatumauri only have the right to advise the nation's elected parliament on matters regarding land and *kastom* (see Chapter 11). And Petersen (Chapter 9) reviews debates during the Federated States of Micronesia's constitutional convention to encharter a chamber of chiefs—a charter subsequently defeated in the popular referendum that ratified other articles of the constitution.

In many Pacific localities, there is an uneasy balance between chiefs, who have both traditional and bureaucratic power, even if only advisory or otherwise limited, and the civil servants (local council members, government secretaries, town councillors, etc.) who are charged with regional administration (see Chapter 7; Lutkehaus 1996). James (Chapter 3) describes one Tongan village where the authority of a town officer filled a vacuum created by the absence of titled nobility. Macpherson (Chapter 2), on the other hand, remarks that Western Samoa's Village Fono Act of 1990 allows "every village *fono* [council of local chiefs] to exercise any power or authority in accordance with the customs and usage of that village." This act specifically reserves local governance for the traditional leadership of Samoan villages. As mentioned earlier, the collected *matai* of Lona village in 1993 vigorously asserted their jurisdiction over local governance by sentencing to death and then shooting a fellow chief who had outraged local sensibilities in various ways. Macpherson (Chapter 2) notes that though the Samoan state might be willing to entrust local administrative and judicial duties to village chiefs, that state itself is enmeshed in global political networks and thus is subject to external pressures to protect individual human rights, as construed by dominant modernist political doctrines. Elsewhere in the Pacific, states are more jealous of their legislative and judicial powers, and there coexist dual systems of civil authority and customary village leadership that operate in parallel.

Pacific states have attempted historically to bend traditional local authority to central colonial or national ends by inviting chiefs to serve as local administrators (unpaid, in many places). Chiefs are charged with keeping order, with running lower-level local courts or moots while alerting state police and courts to weightier offenses, and with advising higher state functionaries and institutions (including national parliaments, island councils, etc.). Not all traditional leaders, however, are willing to take on the role of state middleman, broker, or even ombudsman; and those who do may find themselves abandoned by their communities and ill rewarded by their governments. Howard and Rensel (Chapter 7) analyze the difficult position of Rotuman chiefs, who are caught between their bureaucratic duties for the Fijian state and local traditional expectations of chiefs that they are increasingly unable to meet (for African parallels to troubled Pacific chiefly bureaucrats, see van Rouveroy van Nieuwall 1987a, 1987b; Goheen 1992).

Chiefly Oppositions

Miles's fifth chiefly political function (noted above) is to stand in for state authorities when these break down or otherwise fail to deliver social services, and to sustain people's feelings of national identity and solidarity. There is a debate in the African literature, for example, about whether traditional authorities (chiefs who were previously retired and marginalized) might be recalled to step in and fill the administrative void left by contracting or collapsing central state governments (Geschiere 1993).

Some Pacific chiefs have been even more forward than this. They have proposed to lead their people even before a state has withdrawn from a region, and have worked, moreover, to quicken that withdrawal. Several cases have been previously mentioned: the case of Chief/King/Prophet Jimmy Stephens and the Nagriamel rebellion on Espíritu Santo; the Bougainville Island Council of Chiefs' support of the secessionist Bougainville Revolutionary Army's attacks on Papua New Guinea government forces (*Solomon Star* [Apr. 10, 1992]: 8); and a declaration by Torres Straits custom chiefs who are seeking "independence from Australia" (*Solomon Star* [Sept. 24, 1993]: 3).

Both the strengthening and the weakening of a state's centralizing powers may also encourage an advancement or multiplication of chiefs at the local level. Local, customary authorities can take on new functions, fending off deprecations of the state, or representing one region in competition with other regions for the state's resources. The last two decades have seen a surge of "paramount chiefs" in various regions of the Solomon Islands, for example, as villages combine into larger unities, in part to stake claims to state resources vis-à-vis neighboring provinces (see Chapters 12 and 13).

The chief, as an authority both of tradition and by tradition, and as head or figurehead of a political community, often comes to represent the common identity and aspirations of that community—particularly should the community be entangled in larger national entities (cf. Rappaport 1990; White 1991). Chiefs today carry this special symbolic charge in Hawai'i and New Zealand, where island communities are encapsulated within large metropolitan states. Hawaiian sovereignty activists, for example, passionately call forth the name of Queen Lili'uokalani, the last of the Kamehamehas, who was deposed by U.S. interests in 1893. The queen's capacity to symbolize Hawaiian unity and political opposition to the American state is crystallized in histories of her overthrow and confinement by the foreigners—histories that now circulate globally in books and video documentaries recounting the usurpation. If Hawaiian sovereignty advances, however, the function of chiefs to personify identity may be pushed to another level, animating claimants to chiefly titles from all the islands of the archipelago that Kamehameha's armies vanquished a century and a half ago. Such internal divisions were foreshadowed by the "theft" of a sacred ancestral casket from the Bishop Museum in 1994 and its secret return to the island of Hawai'i—a removal challenged by some Hawaiian leaders from the island of Oahu.

The situation is more complicated in New Zealand, where numerous chiefs, paramount chiefs, and tribes proliferate, in part to accommodate, in part to oppose, the evolving political initiatives and programs of the state. Van Meijl (Chapter 5) reports that nearly 200 Maori organizations in 1989 applied for the status of tribal authority in response to government plans to devolve the Department of Maori Affairs, transferring its resources and responsibilities to such tribal authorities. Maori chiefs here stand in opposition to the state, but they stand also in opposition to one another, and thereby obstruct the political designs of pan-Maori movements.

Chiefs Tomorrow

Pacific chiefs are not antique survivals from pre-state political formations. They are, rather, animated, defined, and in some cases produced by the contemporary politics of modern nation-states—states through which wash the swells of an intensifying world economic and political system (see Bergendorff 1993). The evolutionary narrative of a progression from traditional to legal-bureaucratic authority, and from chiefs to kings to presidents, has proved only a romantic political fable. The agenda for global modernization has become clouded with suspicions that universalist models of economic development carry within them unrestrained individualism and materialism. A parallel cultural struggle is evident in the political arena, where Western ideals of democracy and human rights are challenged as code words for reproducing Euro-American values in the international sphere. Nowhere are these tensions more clear than in the young democracies of the Pacific, the last region to be colonized and brought within the sphere of global capitalist economic activity.

In Africa, whose nations began to achieve independence at the zenith of the modernizing 1960s, the last days of chiefs once appeared to be at hand. Many commentators, as well as national constitution writers, allowed traditional leaders scant role in the political operation of the newly independent nations (Davies 1990). But thirty years on, in many nations of that continent (including Angola, Burundi, Rwanda, Somalia, and Liberia), chiefs and other traditional leaders continue to enjoy greater authority and stability than its fragile central governments (Sanders 1983; Vaughan 1988).

In the Pacific, where most nations came to independence some years after the African states, political elites in general have been less hostile toward custom. Tradition in general, and chiefly authorities in particular, have been less frequently posed rhetorically as an outdated menace to the modern state. If anything, the rhetorical deployment of traditions and chiefs in the Pacific is just the opposite—invoked by modern leaders such as Michael Somare (see Somare 1991) as a way of challenging discourses of modernity that seem continually to privilege the knowledge and position of former colonial masters.

In contrast with the African situation, the small scale of many Pacific nations ensures greater isomorphism between the parallel systems of traditional and state governance. In many places, a community of chief and followers is also a state-established precinct or province wherein the chief is the legal, or effectual, local authority. In Tonga, the traditional system of paramount chief and followers overlaps completely the modern political apparatus of head-of-state and national citizenry. In the course of establishing these traditional/modern isomorphisms, the chief becomes significant as an index of the level of political integration and legitimacy enjoyed by a nation-state. Thus, in the United States and elsewhere, institutionalized chieftainship has been put forward in court as one of the criteria used to determine the legal status of indigenous groups as "tribes" deserving certain rights and protections under the law (Sturtevant 1983, cited in Clifford 1988).

But the political future of chiefs in the Pacific will not be secured solely by their traditionality or by determined efforts to unite ancient customs with current political practice, but by their modernity as well. The chief and the tribe both are in large part effects of the nation-state (see Chapter 15; van Binsbergen 1987). "Ironically, paramount chiefs are good to Westernize with" (Chapter 12; see also Chapters 13 and 10). Pacific chiefs continue to originate customary and local political practice, but this custom and these localities have for a century or more been encapsulated within colonialist and nationalist state structures, just as these state structures are increasingly absorbed by the global political system. And these larger political structures, both national and international, that today circumscribe traditional political arenas also motivate island chiefs and define for them available roles as state minister, local justice, joint-venture capitalist, or rebel traditionalist. From today, the Pacific state's future will dictate that of the Pacific chief. In whatever scenario, the end of the twentieth century for Pacific Islands societies bears witness to the conclusion that the past has a future after all.

2

The Persistence
of Chiefly Authority
in Western Samoa

CLUNY MACPHERSON

The Missions and the Chieftaincy

The continued influence of the chieftaincy in Western Samoa was guaranteed by the nature of the Samoans' earliest contacts with Europeans.[1] The foundation of what was to become a symbiotic relationship was laid by the pioneer missionary John Williams of the London Mission Society in 1830. In Tonga, while en route to Samoa on his first visit, Williams met a chief named Fauea whom Williams believed to be the son of a principal chief of Samoa and who apparently described himself as a near relation of Malietoa (Moyle 1984:54). Fauea, his wife, his child, and a friend joined the ship in Tonga, and Williams, aware of the potential value of the man's assistance, wrote in his diary, "We were glad to find such a person at Tonga to accompany us in our voyage hoping he would prove of use to us in our intercourse with his people" (ibid.:54). On the voyage to Samoa, Fauea advised Williams on how to contact and treat the Samoans to avoid alienating them and impeding the work of the mission. This counsel un-

Fa'afetai to Iosefa Maiava, presently of the United Nations Development Program Apia and lately of the University of Hawai'i, for the conversations that set me thinking about the chieftaincy in contemporary Western Samoa. This would have been a better paper if Iosefa had written it. *Fa'afetai fo'i* to Associate Professor Bill Hodge of the School of Law at Auckland University for the legislation, to Dr. Tim O'Meara of the University of Melbourne for his thoughtful commentary on an earlier draft of the paper, and to John Hellesoe of the National University of Samoa for comments.

doubtedly contributed to the subsequent success of the mission. Williams was indebted to Fauea for general advice and thanked God for Fauea's counsel (ibid.: 80).

Williams's indebtedness to Fauea did not end there. Fauea also promoted the London Mission Society's mission to the first groups of Samoans encountered, and Williams was "much delighted with the manner in which he was introducing the object of our voyage" (ibid.: 68). Fauea, a significant chief in his own right, introduced Williams to one of the most influential chiefs of the time, Malietoa Vai'inupo of Savai'i, who became responsible initially for the protection and later for the sponsorship and success of the London Missionary Society's missionary activity in the Samoas.

Neither Williams nor later missionaries had reason to challenge the power and influence of the *matai* of Samoa directly. Indeed, the first encounter reflected the asymmetrical nature of power. Williams assured Malietoa that he did not seek any property and asked him to permit teachers to live and teach the word among his people and to protect them as they did so, to provide a house for the teachers and to allow his people to worship, and to allow the teachers to instruct his people in reading and writing. In return for this assistance Williams held out the possibility of teachers coming from England to continue the work. He also strongly advised Malietoa to bring an end to the war with Upolu. Malietoa apparently readily agreed to all but the last request, the only one that directly challenged his authority. On that matter Malietoa noted that "he could not do away with the present but after this fight would endeavour to prevent a like occurrence": hardly an unequivocal assurance (ibid.: 74).

Missionaries' motives for cooperating with the chieftaincy were diverse. Though chiefs' powers were considerable and derived, at least in part, from association with spirits, the chiefs were not priests, and their willingness to embrace the *lotu*, albeit on their own terms, meant that their power was not seen as an impediment to the introduction of Christian belief, as it had been elsewhere in Polynesia. Williams, for instance, noted with some relief that the Samoans did not "pay the servile homage to their chiefs that the natives of some of the islands do." He also observed that there were "a very few chiefs at the Samoa's old Malietoa & one or two others who are considered paea [*pa'ia*] or sacred whose feet are kissed & after whom water is sprinkled & who on certain occasions are fed by another person but the body of the people by no means pay that servile respect to the chiefs which is done at many Islands" (ibid.: 238).

Though chiefs held great power in Samoan society, it was essentially secular, political power, which Williams and others quickly realized could be effectively employed in the service of the mission. Although missionaries noted the existence of some "heathen chiefs" or "Devils" (ibid.: 149) who initially resisted the *lotu,* they were also well aware that as these *matai* embraced the *lotu,* they, too, became firm allies and made their followers available for instruction. This fact made the missionaries more determined to persuade these chiefs to embrace the faith.

Williams's appreciation of the influence of chiefs in Samoan society was apparent in his reports of the Samoan mission. His diaries are probably the earliest accounts of the role and influence of chiefs in Samoan society. His initial accounts of encounters with Fauea, the principal chief Malietoa, Malietoa's younger brother Taimalelagi, and Matetau of Manono are principally descriptive. Later, however, Williams ventured some generalizations on the chieftaincy. These constitute the baseline accounts of the significance and influence of chiefs in Samoan society.

Throughout his accounts, Williams made clear distinctions between chiefs (*ali'i*) and their talking chiefs (*tulafale*). He noted that "the people generally are divided into distinct classes, principal chiefs or allies (*ali'i*), warriors Tulaafales (*tulafale*) or tillers of the ground, Tradesmen, Fishermen, & Cooks" (ibid.: 249–50). Williams pointed to the combination of birth and property that established the principal chiefs.

Chieftainship is I believe hereditary yet a chief must with his noble birth possess property otherwise the simple circumstance of his being of high birth will not secure him much respect. Tis property here that constitutes the gentleman. Any person possessing property can be raised to the rank of Chief. A person wishing thus to be raised goes to a principal Chief and makes him a handsome present. The Chief then bestows on him some great name which if he has the property to sustain the dignity of will secure for him a corresponding degree of respect. Several of the principal chiefs who are now in possession of the greatest authority are not of high birth. (Ibid.: 250)

Williams's account went on to outline the role and relationship between the *ali'i* and the *tulafale:*

Warriors [whom Williams had earlier noted were *tulafale*] are held in great estimation by the Chiefs. They supply them with every thing and will not allow them to work or to plant. Tulaafales [sic] are the persons who possess the greatest property of any class of individuals in the Islands. They are a kind of master farmer. Each chief has two four six, or more Tulaafales to supply him with taro bread fruit &c two or more times a day and at the end of so many months he pays them in cloth or mats. Consequently the Tulaafale's become the richest persons in the country for the Chiefs give them nearly all they can obtain & depend on them in return to supply all their wants. (Ibid.: 250)

The mats, which provide the basis of this symbiotic relationship between *ali'i* and *tulafale,* were collected by a series of visits, or *malaga,* the object of which was "to collect *siapo* [bark cloth] & mats which is the currency of this country" (ibid.: 251).

Williams's interest in the chieftaincy was not, however, purely anthropological. He realized that the chiefs' power was the key to the successful introduction of the new faith to the Samoans. The chiefs commanded the political influence necessary for the introduction of the faith. When chiefs accepted the faith, they did so on behalf of the family they headed. By converting the *matai* of a district or village to Christianity, missionaries could quickly "win the souls of entire villages for the Lord." Furthermore, the chiefs were able to guarantee that their families and villages were made available for the continuing instruction necessary to the installation of a "more deeply rooted faith."

Chiefs also commanded physical capital, labor and organizational resources. Missionaries' acceptance of the chiefs' continued control of these resources arose in part from their need for access to these resources to create capital assets for the extension of mission activity within and beyond Samoa. At the "village" level, this meant the provision of land and buildings such as churches and residences for the pastors and teachers. The chiefs also provided food, as well as plantation and household labor, for the missionaries and teachers. At the "national" level, this meant the provision of land and buildings for the theological college at Malua (1845) and the ancillary buildings such as the printery, also at Malua.

At the "international" level, the chiefs' willingness to generate funds was the key to the extension of the activities of the mission beyond the Samoas. The Samoan mission field generated both personnel and resources for the London Missionary Society's activities in the western Pacific. Samoan pastors trained in the Malua Theological Seminary in Upolu, Samoa, served the mission with distinction from 1846 on as far west as Papua New Guinea (Gunson 1978). Funds raised from the annual *Me* or "mission meetings," copra, and coconut-oil production were essential to the extension and support of the mission's activities in the western Pacific.[2] The chieftaincy's continued support and influence were crucial in the organization of all of these activities.

To focus exclusively on the missionary objectives and activities in Samoa is to risk overlooking the Samoans' objectives and activities in embracing and protecting the missions. The chiefs were not passive reactors to the missions' activities. Though their motives can only ever be imperfectly understood, there are clues to the reasons for their responses to the missions. Malietoa's interest in Williams and his teachers is a case in point. The timing of Williams's arrival was fortuitous. Williams arrived at the end of a period of civil war during which various families had sought to extend their authority over all of Samoa. Malietoa Vai'inupo, Williams's host, had triumphed over some of his principal rivals but had not been able to extend his authority over Samoa. An *aitu*, or spirit, Nafanua, the goddess of war, had led Malietoa to believe that his eventual authority over Samoa would come from the heavens (Meleisea 1987:13). The arrival of Williams's ship, under sail, off Malietoa's village, Sapapali'i, Savai'i, was seen by Malietoa as the fulfillment of Nafanua's prophecy. Malietoa's interest in the *lotu* may have owed as much to his concern with the possibility of extending secular power over Samoa as it did to any sense of moral need on his part. Furthermore, the songs composed and sung by Malietoa's family to Williams's party on the first visit referred to Williams and his associate Charles Barff as "two great chiefs" (Williams 1838: 341), which suggests that Malietoa may have regarded the English as no more than chiefs and their associates, entitled to the same respect as other *malaga* or visiting parties led by chiefs.

The possibility that the chiefs used the *lotu* for their own ends gains support from other sources. When Williams returned to Samoa in 1832, he found that the eight Polynesian teachers whom he had left on his first visit had not been allowed to move out and to take the gospel to all of Samoa. They had been divided between Malietoa and his brother Taimalelagi. Meleisea notes that this seems to indicate "that Malietoa intended to monopolise this new source of sacred power" (1987:13), for as he notes later, "Nor . . . did the Samoans embrace Christianity lightly. They did so with deliberation for the most materialistic of reasons" (ibid.:17).

Other chiefs apparently also came to share Malietoa's belief in the potential benefits of embracing this new source of influence. When chiefs (including, incidentally, a number Malietoa's rivals) were not provided with missionary teachers by the London Mission Society, they sought the services of pastors and teachers from other sources. As Meleisea notes, "Chiefly competition for access to the new religion, probably with the hope of controlling and benefitting from it, introduced sectarian rivalry into Samoa" (ibid.:13). Thus, the early Wesleyan mission presence in the Satupaitea district in Savai'i was due to the efforts of the powerful local *matai*, Lilomaiava, Tuina'ula, and Malietoa Talavou, to obtain the advantages associated with the mission from their Methodist connections in Tonga to the south. The Catholic mission presence was similarly due to the efforts of a small number of chiefs in villages in Falealupo Savai'i and Apia, who had not secured missionaries from other sources, to avail themselves of this new form of authority (Franco 1976:9).

The chiefs' interest in and willingness to support the missions' activities and to protect their pastors and teachers, for whatever motive, meant that they were an aid rather than an impediment to the missionaries. A natural alliance developed between the chiefs and the missions.[3] This was a lucky coincidence for the missions. Had they confronted a hostile chieftaincy with their limited resources, their chances of any effective evangelization would have been very slim indeed.[4]

The missions' dependence on the chieftaincy meant that the character of their programs was significantly influenced by the need to retain the chiefs' support. As Gilson noted, because the missions grew so rapidly, there were never sufficient funds to support the number of teachers placed in Samoa. The teachers, therefore, were necessarily dependent on their "hosts" for support. "Perhaps this was fair enough, but it was also expected that the teachers should solicit and enjoy the 'kindness' of their hosts without compromising the work of the mission. This was impossible" (Gilson 1970:102). This set of facts prevented missionaries and teachers from acting in ways that might have been seen to undermine their allies' power within Samoan society.[5]

However, as Meleisea has noted, though the chiefs remained powerful figures within Samoan society,

Christianity, as propagated by the nonconformist missionaries, transformed the nature of chiefly authority . . . the results of Christian teaching were that the sacred powers which had been attributed to them and which were largely the source of the political authority of these chiefs, were weakened. Missionaries and later the Samoan clergy largely replaced the *ali'i pa'ia* as the holders of sacred power. The belief persisted . . . that the authority of all *matai* was divinely sanctioned, but by Jehovah, rather than Tagaloa-a-lagi. (Meleisea 1987:13)

Though contact with Christianity may have altered the basis of chiefly authority, it did not displace the chieftaincy. As Meleisea notes,

Overall, Christianity had a levelling affect. It replaced the ideological justification for attributing great power to a few great chiefs and re-defined chiefly power as a secular political authority, reducing the crucial distinction between *ali'i* and *tulafale*. . . . The idea that high chiefly titles carried great prestige did not disappear with Christianity, but the holders of high titles and those who aspired to such honours had to seek new ways to acquire prestige to maintain the rank of their titles, in the church, in government and through economic means. (ibid.:14)

The formal relationship that developed between the mission and the chieftaincy early on has continued to the present. To this day, the powers of the two remain separate. In the major denominations, no chief may be a pastor and no pastor a chief at the same time. The early pattern was established by Williams and later European missionaries for what might have been considered, at least in part, expedience. Later, as the Samoanization of the mission proceeded, the acceptance of the importance of the chieftaincy continued, even though the motives for acceptance of the increasingly Samoan pastorate may well have changed.

Commerce, Consuls, and the Chieftaincy

As commercial and diplomatic interest in the Samoas intensified, a new group of Europeans started to take an interest in Samoan chieftaincy. Their motives were somewhat different from, and indeed often in direct conflict with, those of the missions. Though Williams had argued that missionary activity prepared the way for commerce to raise funds among commercial interests in England (Gilson 1970: 138), the missionaries generally opposed commerce. Indeed, any challenge to their control of the trade in copra oil and copra would have interrupted the supply of funds that they needed to extend the work of the mission into the western Pacific.

Commerce was represented by the missionaries, with some justification, as a real threat to the order and industry that they sought to promote among the Samoans.[6] The missions were probably also at least as concerned that their influence might be eroded by the presence of wealthy foreigners, who could use wealth and marriage into prominent families to extend their influence beyond trade and into politics, a sphere shared largely by the Samoans and missions.

But missionary opposition to nonmissionary commerce was not entirely the product of self-interest. Missionaries were well aware of cases of fraudulent trade practices in which unscrupulous traders had exploited inexperienced new traders; of cases in which the development of a trade in liquor and arms had been manipulated in various ways to alienate land; and of cases of forced labor and "blackbirding" elsewhere in the Pacific where commercial interests were not controlled, or at least checked, by other forces.

Ironically, as Gilson notes (ibid.: 186), missionary reports of the character and extent of the transformation of Samoan society occasioned by their activities tended to encourage foreign settlement. Certain *palagi* (European) settlers, such as J. C. Williams and George Pritchard, who enjoyed a credibility born of their associations with the mission, encouraged foreign settlement, from which they hoped to benefit personally. Pritchard, for instance, claimed that "hundreds of thousands of acres of the most fertile soil [were] lying waste" in Samoa and that people familiar with the island had estimated "that Upolu alone would support Five Millions and leave plenty of land for the natives" (Pritchard, cited in Gilson 1970: 186). Pritchard, it is said, hoped to gain both economically and politically from the encouragement of settlement, but as Gilson notes (ibid.: 186), he probably only compounded his problems in the process.

Realizing that settlement was inevitable and that the Samoans could and would engage in commerce when they considered it in their interests, the missionaries sought to control rather than prohibit it (Gilson 1970: 140–43). This led to various attempts to institute a scheme to control immigration to ensure that settlers would be "people of piety and good moral character" who would accept the laws of the islands (ibid.: 158). The proposed scheme was not to work, and it was not long before immigration started to produce a new challenge to the chieftaincy.

The new settlers found on arrival that missionary accounts of the Samoas had exaggerated the extent of the transformation in this South Seas El Dorado. Far from a highly disciplined and pliable indigenous population, the settlers found the governance of Samoa in a state of anarchy that prevented them from pursuing their program, which, according to Gilson, had as its minimum objectives "the destruction of organised Samoan resistance to foreign economic penetration, and the preservation of peace and order, that life and property might be secure and the Samoans freer to develop the 'civilised' tastes and habits conducive to the growth of industry and trade" (ibid.: 188). Among the colonists' proposed solutions to the dilemma was the "Hawaiian solution." This entailed the creation of a kingdom in which power and authority was concentrated in the hands of a monarchy chosen, of course, with the benefit of the enlightened and dispassionate counsel of the settlers. This was necessary to get the central state structures needed to guarantee internal order and to engage in ordered, formal external relations, both of which were prerequisites for ordered and profitable commercial activity.

The monarchy was chosen, Gilson argues, because it was familiar to European settlers; it was considered a "success" in Hawai'i; it was supposed to be "natural" to Polynesians, and it was supposed to be a form of governance through which Europeans could hope to gain and exert influence on developments in Samoa (ibid.: 188). It represented a potential threat to the chieftaincy because it involved replacing one basis of central authority in Samoa, the *tafa'ifa*, with another in which Europeans chose and installed the most apparently pliable contender for the kingship without respect for the dynamics of Samoan authority. Successful intervention in this area would have disturbed the fluid balance in the Samoan polity. The commercial interests were not, however, to have their way as easily in Samoa as they had elsewhere in the Pacific.

The obvious basis for such a development would have been to support the most influential contender for the paramountcy, or *Malo,* and to strengthen it at the expense of the power of the less influential party, or *Vaivai.* In Samoa this course of action has inherent risks because of the volatile nature of coalitions. Such a strategy might have succeeded in the early 1830s, when the forces led by Malietoa Vai'inupo were clearly dominant. But by the 1840s, when the settlers had started to consider the possibilities, such a course was no longer readily available. Missionaries had, for theological, practical, and political reasons, encouraged the early rehabilitation of the *Vaivai*, and the power differentials, on which such a strategy might have built, had been eroded. In fact, the erosion had proceeded to the point at which the *Malo* and the *Vaivai* were about to engage in another struggle for control, and many Europeans, fearing the consequences of backing the wrong side, were forced to remain largely neutral.

Not all did so, however. For ideological and political reasons, various Europeans sought to intervene to prevent a "futile" and potentially inconvenient if not dangerous war between the *Malo* and the *Vaivai*. As Gilson noted, "Europeans thus presumed to act as mediators and peacemakers, in which roles missionaries were joined by naval officers. By their interference, however, they only helped to prolong the conflict and to prevent the conclusive settlement of the issues that had occasioned it" (ibid.: 190). At least in the meantime, Samoans were to determine the way in which the chieftaincy would develop. Europeans were denied any effective role in shaping the role of the chieftaincy.

Deprived of the immediate prospect of achieving political control through influencing the reform of the domestic government, the Europeans considered other avenues that would have represented even more serious challenges to the chieftaincy. Amongst these was a call to various powers to institute imperial control and to impose, by force if necessary, the reforms necessary for "peace and prosperity." For a variety of reasons, none chose to exert control in Samoa, and in fact, as Gilson noted, "So unresponsive were the Powers that none would even give its official backing to efforts being made towards the reconstitution of government in Samoa" (ibid.: 192).

In the event, the war that broke out in 1848 continued inconclusively until 1857. The conclusion of the war saw Europeans, anxious to obtain land and the conditions necessary to make money, pursuing the possibility of a "Hawaiian solution" again. But because the war had been exhausting and inconclusive, the Samoans showed little inclination to reestablish the *tafa'ifa* on which such a solution might have been built.

In the 1860s, the demand for cotton grew, and Samoa was seen as a good site for commercial cotton-cropping. The settlers renewed a demand for land on which to plant cotton, and this might have led to considerable pressure on the consuls to exert influence on the chieftaincy to release land. But just as the pressure was mounting, a series of factors combined to force Samoans to release land voluntarily. Drought and bushfires reduced the amount and range of food available to the Samoans, and they were forced to sell land and to make wage labor available to augment food supplies. Though this allowed Samoans to make land available on their own terms, it also resulted in Europeans obtaining a significantly larger

stake than they had earlier, making them more determined to influence
the course of events in Samoa. This voluntary alienation of land also prevented a confrontation between emboldened settlers and a chieftaincy
weakened by a protracted and inconclusive war.

The newly landed settlers still had little prospect of imposing their
wishes on the Samoans directly. Having failed to install a "monarchy,"
the settlers could, at best, hope to persuade the chieftaincy of the advantages of domestic political reform. This, they had hoped, might be built
on Samoan *itu malo* or districts, and might involve the established polities
within these areas promulgating and enforcing codes of laws for these districts. The districts might, it was hoped, be combined in a confederation
to achieve some consistency across them. The chieftaincy, then, remained
central to the settlers' hopes of obtaining even this more limited domestic
political reform. Some minor progress was made but, as settlers should
have known, the districts were not the most stable platform on which to
build political reform. Samoan district politics were volatile and were
driven by factors that were not well understood by the settlers, who were
therefore not able to exert very much influence.

By 1869, despite some early optimism about the prospects of reform,
the Samoans were headed again for war, and the settlers' hopes and aspirations were again forced to the edges of the Samoan political agenda.
Without external interest in, or support for, their concerns, they were
forced to accept a neutral position to avoid association with either side and
the possibility of later retribution by the victors.[7] The Samoan chieftaincy
remained well and truly in control of Samoan political development.

But the *Faitasiga* war that was to follow—a civil war that broke out
over confederation (see Gilson 1970:262–70)—also defused some of the
pressure for reform, which was intended to ensure supplies of land and
labor. In order to secure armaments, Samoans were forced to sell large
areas of land, to which Goddefroy und Sohn and the Central Pacific Land
and Commercial Company were able to claim title. Land was alienated
on an even greater scale in the second phase of the war, between late 1871
and 1873.[8] By the war's end, 350,000 acres had been claimed by Europeans. The Europeans saw the prospect of the emergence of a landless class
of people who would, out of necessity, provide the labor force necessary
to exploit their new landholdings.

Their dreams of cheap land were to be shattered because many of these
sales were shown later to be defective transactions. Much of the land had
been alienated by people who were not entitled to do so; Gilson estimated
that only about 1 percent of the sales, covering some 2,000 acres, were not
disputed (ibid.:288). The Samoan government that emerged after the war
refused to confirm title in many cases, and there was little that settlers

could do except press for reforms that would have guaranteed the sanctity of such contracts.

Settler dreams of cheap labor were also shattered. Samoans, noting that the work was more suited to donkeys than humans, showed little inclination to labor on settlers' plantations. Between wars and cycles of ceremonial visiting (*malaga*), many Samoans were reestablishing their plantations to permit them to return to war and visiting. The labor demands generated by these activities meant that surplus Samoan labor was not available on the regular basis that settlers required to plan production. Eventually the settlers, unable to separate Samoans from their land and create a source of landless labor, were forced to secure more expensive indentured labor from Melanesia and later China.

A real prospect for reform and the emergence of a unified central government came after the war in the person of an American, A. B. Steinberger. Steinberger, claiming official backing from Washington, promoted a government at Mulinu'u that garnered considerable support from Samoans because it was clearly focused on their concerns and appeared to advance their interests. A high degree of unity was apparent, and Steinberger came to enjoy the power and influence that Europeans had for years hoped to achieve through central government.

Unfortunately, Steinberger's pro-Samoan agenda and policy, and his growing influence among Samoans, triggered more of the petty jealousies that had typified the consuls' relations with one another. The suspicion that Steinberger's influence would favor Samoans' interests at the expense of those of settlers, and that his influence would be used to advance the interests of the United States ahead of other European interests, led the consuls to undermine the Steinberger government. Steinberger's deportation to Fiji in 1876 spelled the end of the most promising attempt to exert influence on the Samoan chieftaincy and, through this, on Samoan political developments.

Worse still, the consuls' meddling alienated many Samoans who were cooperating with Steinberger. The consuls found that the Mulinu'u government, smarting from the removal of Steinberger, was not about to cooperate. Gilson noted that they were granted rights to extraterritorial jurisdiction over foreigners, but only reluctantly. Their more significant demands

that the constitution be amended to allow the consuls to participate in the government were turned down flat along with proposals that certain existing provisions be observed or implemented, for example, by the appointment of a king and establishment of a land commission. The general granting of land claims . . . the *Ta'imua* [lawmakers] and *Faipule* [deputies] refused to entertain in any form and they often proved unwilling to take up European reports of Samoan "offenses.". . .

In brief, this was, in most ways which mattered to foreigners, a government of inaction, if not obstruction. (Gilson 1970:334)

With the prospect of influence—indeed, even cooperation—with the Mulinuʻu government fading, the Europeans turned to another rival government, the Puletua, led by Malietoa Laupepa and based in Aʻana. They hoped to back Malietoa Laupepa and his government until they were both strong enough to grant concessions and willing to do so out of gratitude for European support. It proved to be a bad move, for the Puletua forces were soundly beaten in Faleʻula in 1877 by the Mulinuʻu government's forces, and the Europeans then had to deal with a government that they had sought to undermine.

The Samoans granted Britain, Germany, and the United States each most-favored-nation status and left them to compete with one another. This ensured that the three, each suspicious of the other's ambitions, would be unable to exert unified pressure for transformation of Samoan government. But this could not guarantee the survival of the Mulinuʻu government, which fell to a combination of external and internal pressures in 1879.

Ten years later, in April 1889, the colonial powers, determined to settle on an arrangement that would provide the basis for orderly cooperation and eventually control of the Samoan state, convened a three-power conference in Berlin that produced the Berlin Act, which in turn lasted until the creation of a condominium conferred in the Treaty of Berlin in 1899. The Berlin conference persisted with the belief that a king was necessary and insisted on the effective right to appoint by determining which of the Samoan appointees was acceptable. The arrangements for the kingship would, as Gilson notes, eventually destroy the condominium (ibid.:416). The Berlin Act concentrated on establishing certain formal, central institutions such as the kingship, but left much of the rest of Samoan social organization effectively untouched (ibid.:415). But even as the foreign powers seemed finally to be gaining control of the central government, Samoans continued to control village and district government more or less as they always had. More significantly, they retained ownership of their land, which effectively guaranteed their independence of foreign control.

The first challenge to the condominium's power to appoint came in 1893, when the condominium provided support for their candidate Malietoa Laupepa to put down the rival forces of Mataʻafa. But no sooner was one challenge put down than another emerged, usually, as Gilson notes (ibid.:396–433), during the hurricane seasons, when the naval support on which Laupepa depended was absent. Between 1893 and 1900, the only control the condominium achieved beyond the followers of its king was achieved during those periods when warships were available in Samoa to support him.

By the turn of the century, it could be said that seventy years of European settlement had made relatively little impact on Samoan social organization in general and the role and status of the *matai* in particular. The Europeans' failure to establish effective control over Samoan politics had denied them much real influence beyond the Apia area. In fact, as Boyd notes (1969: 121), the Westerners' presence promoted rather than prohibited fragmentation in a polity already prone to disunity. For much of the period, the Europeans had been little more than spectators at events played out around Samoan interests and rules. They had not succeeded either in alienating significant areas of Samoan land for their use or in producing a landless population to provide the cheap labor to exploit that land. Samoan land and population remained firmly under the control of *matai*.

German Colonial Power and the Chieftaincy

When Germans took control of the islands of Upolu, Savai'i, Manono, and Apolima as part of a treaty settlement on March 15, 1900, the Samoans were faced with a single power determined to extend its influence and control at the expense of that of the Samoan polity. The Samoans' situation was made more difficult because they could no longer exploit the competing aspirations and mutual suspicion of the three powers and divide them among themselves. But the greatest obstacle they would face was the man whom Germany appointed governor of Samoa, Wilhelm Solf. He was an educated man and, as Hempenstall notes (1978: 33), was unlike the typical Colonial Department administrator. He did not set out to transform the economy for the exclusive benefit of German interests. On the contrary, according to Hempenstall, Solf was aware of Samoan ethics and history and had analyzed Germany's role in Samoan development. He was thus determined to protect the integrity of Samoan society (ibid.: 53). Furthermore, though his program involved significant changes in the relations between Germany and the Samoans, he was not set to achieve these either immediately or by force. Instead, "he brought to Samoa a natural respect for the intrinsic value of exotic cultures and a readiness to deal with Samoans on their own terms. Above all, he renounced force as a means of implementing policy. 'All radical measures are evil. Time and goodness and justice are the best means of governing in Samoa,' was his firm conviction" (ibid.: 32–33). Solf also brought valuable personal assets to his position, assets that the Samoans respected in a leader, including rhetorical skill, an imposing presence, and a paternal manner (ibid.: 33).

Solf would need all of these qualities to carry out his program for Samoan development because he could not depend on force. He had at his disposal only a group of thirty young Samoans, the *fitafita*, who were used primarily for administrative activities, plus the occasional services of naval vessels should things have come to an issue of force. For the most part, his program's success, at least with the Samoans, would depend on his ability to engage them politically and to deliver continued economic prosperity.

Solf had seen the consequences of the Samoan political system's tendency to segment and was determined to take control of the process and exercise a greater degree of control than had been possible under the condominium. The kingship, which had so often been a cause of dispute, was to be replaced by an administrator, and the Samoan government was to be relegated to an advisory role. Though he was committed to transforming the kingship and the roles that the *tulāfale* (orators) of Tumua and Pule played in national government, Solf did not seek to change either the role that chiefs played in local government or their control of land or labor. In the event, both his program and his resolve were tried early in his administration.

By 1901, certain key Samoan chiefs, including Lauaki Namulau'ulu Mamoe, had sensed Solf's plan to limit their power and had looked for opportunities to confront him. But Solf was also well aware of the power imbalance and avoided a physical confrontation, which the Samoans would almost certainly have won. But the imbalance extended beyond force: the economy of Samoa was heavily dependent on the Samoans' copra production, which represented over 50 percent of the total production of copra, and on their increasing purchasing power. The consequences of passive resistance, in the form of a retreat from cash-cropping and non-payment of head taxes, could have been as serious as those of active resistance. Even after a strike in 1902 organized by Lauaki and the deputies, no penalties were doled out by the administration, to avoid alienating the most powerful chiefs (ibid.: 38).

The first confrontation occurred in 1903, when Solf deported two chiefs, one for sedition and the other for inciting to murder. But even as he was deporting them, Solf was protecting the Samoans against the demands of European settlers for legislation forcing Samoans to provide compulsory labor for their plantations. While it was clear that he had little time for the European planters' demands, Solf's move was also forced by his awareness of the consequences of confrontation with the Samoans,

knowing as he did that the people were quite capable of effective counter action: at the very best, copra cutting would cease, white traders would be boycotted, and the people would revert to subsistence agriculture. Since the export/import economy depended on Samoan production and consumption, the financial ruin of European business would inevitably follow. At worst the Samoans might rise in armed rebellion. (Ibid.: 40)

The next confrontation between Solf and the chieftaincy came in 1905, with the Samoan determination to establish a cooperative known as the Oloa movement, or the Kamupani, to control the purchase, sale, and shipping of Samoan copra and to avoid the exploitation to which Samoan sellers had been subject at the hands of unscrupulous European traders. Behind the most obvious economic motives of the leaders of the Oloa movement, however, Solf saw more sinister political and economic ambitions: a determination to raise support and funds for the *Malo* among Samoans and to challenge the Europeans' power by breaking their monopoly of commerce.

Governor Solf, believing he had dealt with this challenge, embarked on an overseas visit. His departure, however, produced an opportunity for advocates of the stalled Oloa movement to move to reestablish it. The acting governor, Erich Schultz, was no more anxious than Solf to confront the movement head on, but he was aware of the need to move to establish the administration's control. He imprisoned two of the group's leaders in the Vaimea prison, but before an official request for their release was considered, other chiefs freed the two as a gesture of Samoan independence and solidarity (ibid.: 46).

When Governor Solf returned, he took advantage of growing internal dissension to foment antagonism among the various Samoan factions. In these circumstances, he was able to publicly humiliate the faction's leaders and to demand that the *Malo* vacate Mulinu'u. By so doing, he publicly destroyed the semblance of Samoan autonomy. He installed an appointed twenty-seven-member Council of Faipule composed of "loyalists and those too influential to dismiss" (ibid.: 47), which met only twice a year in Mulinu'u. Even with the upper hand, Solf was careful not to push the Samoans to a point that could provide the grounds for a new unity, which might lead to an active challenge that he could not win. This restraint included allowing his nemesis Lauaki to remain in Samoa while other chiefs were deported.

Between 1905 and 1908, rising copra prices and the establishment of fair trade practices brought increased prosperity for the Samoans, who were producing on average 66 percent of the world's copra and enjoying the benefits of rising copra prices. During the period, Solf was able to exercise his influence indirectly and had no reason to interfere with the day-to-day economic and political affairs of the hinterland or the organization of production by the traditional chieftaincy.

But in 1908, when Solf went on leave, Lauaki, who had been biding his time, sought to unite Samoans behind a bid to reestablish the authority of Tumua and Pule, which Solf had so efficiently destroyed. With general support within Samoa, he planned to engineer a confrontation on Solf's return in which he would publicly demand moves to restore the authority of various symbols and institutions of Samoan independence. He hoped to force Solf to deny his demands and thereby produce unity among the Samoans.

Acting Governor Schultz became aware of Lauaki's plan. He persuaded Mata'afa Iosefo, a key figure in it, to apply his influence as *ali'i sili* ("highest chief") to discourage his supporters from taking part in the demonstration. The confrontation did not take place, and Lauaki was publicly undermined. Solf returned and sought to press home victory over Lauaki, but in an apparent (and uncharacteristic) misjudgment, he pushed the Samoan into a situation from which he was bound to fight back to save face. Lauaki organized the Mau o Pule, a nationalist movement that sought the removal of colonial forces from his power base in Savai'i, and, initially at least, his charisma and oratory won him considerable support.

Governor Solf now

found himself in an unenviable position, faced with a developing opposition front of *Tumua* and *Pule*, with the masses at their heels, while he lacked any sort of military support with which to assert his authority. . . . Solf could not simply break the movement by imprisoning its leader. Lauaki had been careful to organise *o le mau* along the lines of a legitimate, *fa'a Samoa* form of protest and opposition. Direct suppression would have been construed by the majority of Samoans as tyranny and injustice. (Ibid.: 58)

Lauaki was also apparently reluctant to use force against the Europeans but was able to exploit his political skills and the availability of force to extract a conditional pardon for his challenge to Solf's authority from a reluctant Governor Solf in front of crowds of armed supporters in the village of Vaiusu, about 4 kilometers from Apia. Solf had granted the pardon on the condition that Lauaki return to Savai'i and defuse the tension he had created. But Lauaki's belligerence had created other problems for Solf, who found himself encouraged by both *Tumua* leaders and European settlers to take a more active offensive against Mau o Pule forces. Lauaki, possibly sensing his advantage, continued to mobilize support in Savai'i until early February 1909, when Solf, concerned with the turn of events, called Berlin for military support that would allow him to retake the initiative.

Six weeks later, Solf had a naval force and 680 sailors and marines at his disposal and was able to change his tactics. But even then he was unable to pursue a military solution because, as Hempenstall noted (ibid.: 62), he wanted to avoid driving Lauaki's forces to the bush, where the Europeans were at a serious disadvantage, and where in time the loyal Samoans might join with Lauaki's cause to fight for independence from colonial rule. Solf decided instead to deport Lauaki and some of his key allies. It was a risky move, since Lauaki had already warned Solf that deportation and death were the same thing. In the event, however, Savai'i districts, faced with a full-scale military offensive and the prospect of protracted civil war, withdrew their support and isolated Lauaki and his followers. Lauaki and nine chiefs and their families surrendered and were taken immediately to exile in Saipan. Ironically, in a move intended to show his displeasure with districts that had supported the Mau o Pule Solf sacked their officials, fined their chiefs, and distanced them from the administration. The move forced many Samoans back to subsistence production and strengthened the authority of the chieftaincy, which retained control of this sphere of activity.

Solf's resolve to respect and work with Samoan institutions was, perhaps surprisingly in the circumstances, undiminished. He continued to believe that power and "goodwill in respecting the holy traditions of the Samoans" (ibid.: 66) would preserve peace. Eighteen months later, he had devised a way of removing the instability that followed from the tension between competing claims for the paramountcy. It was left to his successor, and former deputy, Erich Schultz, to carry out the final acts in which the Kaiser as *tupu sili* ("highest king") was to replace the remaining *ali'i sili* at his death with two *fautua*, or advisors, representing each of the royal families. Schultz continued with Solf's policies, and increasing Samoan agricultural productivity and the resultant prosperity maintained an uneasy peace until 1914, when World War I broke out and ended the Germans' control of Samoa.

It might be said that Solf and Schultz successfully disempowered and then dismantled the elements of the paramountcy that had generated the continuous instability in Samoan politics. It is also true, however, that both accepted and utilized other elements of the Samoan polity to achieve their ends. No attempt was made to disempower the district and village chiefs who managed social and political order and economic production. These chiefs played a significant role, as both producers and consumers, in the production of the colony's wealth, and were indispensable elements of German colonial policy. They were left in control of the vast majority of their land and labor, and they retained the authority that allowed them to manage these. Thus, at the close of the German administration of Samoa, although the most visible national chiefs within the Samoan polity had been neutralized, a large number of district and village chiefs had been largely unaffected. In fact, freed from the social and economic costs of periodic calls to arms in support of the royal families, these lesser chiefs were able to exploit their control of the land and labor to extend their hold over Samoan social and economic life.

New Zealand Colonial Power and the Chieftaincy

New Zealand assumed military control in Western Samoa at the outbreak of World War I. This control was confirmed formally in a League of Nations mandate in December 1920. On the surface, the new administration posed no apparent threat either to Samoan social organization in general or to the chieftaincy in particular.

The early administration was characterized by a lack of interest on the part of the New Zealand government, press, and public. As Boyd noted (1969:129),

the New Zealand Parliament showed little inclination to play any part in Samoan affairs. Rather, it was disposed to follow Sir Apirana Ngata's advice that the Samoans should be left to enjoy themselves in their own way, not because it was believed that this was a sound principle, but because it was beginning to realise that New Zealand had no vital interests at stake.

The New Zealand government settled for a form of administration that the Germans had established.[9]

The problem of national government resolved, the New Zealand administrator set out on a novel course of action intended to establish a more effective basis for village social, political, and economic development. The intent was to use "the indigenous institutions of local, native government, district and village *fonos*, in an attempt to decentralise its functions still further and establish a complete chain of authority from the villages, through the districts, to the *Fono o Faipule* and so to the Administrator" (Keesing 1934:150). This move formally acknowledged the importance of these village bodies, but in an attempt to transform certain aspects of village social organization to facilitate economic development. Early targets of this strategy were customs and practices that the administrator, General George Spafford Richardson, saw as "brakes on production": the land-tenure system, the system of ceremonial visiting (*malaga*), fine-mat exchange, title-succession ceremonies (*saofaʻi*), elaborate ceremonial marriages and funerals, and village cricket. As Boyd noted, "Richardson's zeal for Western progress was unequalled except by the first generation of evangelical missionaries" (1969:138).

Three years into the program, overt resistance to Richardson's program of "reform" started to appear. It was a consequence of Samoans' resentment of his attempts to interfere with custom and practice and of growing awareness of the long-term consequences of reforms—specifically, the "Tongan" land-tenure system and local self-government system, both of which eroded the *pule* (authority) of the *matai*. This resistance emerged, or rather reemerged, as the Mau movement, led by O. F. Nelson. Winning support for a national movement in a society prone to political segmentation required a new strategy. Boyd described this as "a political organisation of the congress type commonly found during the early phase of militant nationalism. . . . This organisation took the form of loosely knit village committees of *matai* grouped around a large nuclear working committee of up to sixty to seventy high-ranking title-holders, in almost daily contact with Nelson" (ibid.: 156–57). The Mau's tactics were a combination of Samoan techniques—widespread formal consultation and public commitment to consensus—and Western ones—national boycotts, civil disobedience, mass demonstrations, press campaigns, petitions, and deputations. In the event, one of the mass demonstrations was to result in a confrontation with New Zealand forces and the tragic loss of life that finally drew attention to Samoan grievances (Field 1984). The death of Tupua Tamasese, a high chief and leader of the Mau movement, was regarded as martyrdom and provided a new focus for the Mau, but it also forced its leadership to take stock of the situation and to consider the possibility of the use of further force.

The administrator, Colonel Stephen Shepard Allen, determined to press his apparent advantage, demanded the surrender of some Mau members and was humiliated when some 1,500 people took to the bush, pursued by his meager force of 150 marines. This highlighted yet again the difficulty of exerting any effective pressure for political or social reform on the more numerous and organized Samoans. By this time, doubts were surfacing in Wellington about the wisdom of leaving as complex a matter as Samoan politics in the hands of military people. A new administrator, Alfred Turnbull, was appointed to pursue a more conciliatory policy of necessity. It was not until a Labour government was elected in New Zealand in 1935 that the Mau's grievances were acknowledged and accommodated in Wellington.

The Great Depression, however, diverted the New Zealand government's attention from Samoa, and as long as Turnbull could keep a political lid on events in Samoa, he was left to do so. Turnbull proposed various plans for establishing formal village self-government and clarifying and delimiting the powers of *matai*, but these were largely ignored by a disinterested New Zealand government, which, Boyd notes, "virtually abdicated its authority in the villages and districts to the *ali'i* and *faipule*, and had little to do with the lives of ordinary people" (1969:184).

By 1944, however, the Samoans were tiring of the lackluster administration and, sensing that international opinion was turning their way, were
pushing for immediate self-government based on principles of Samoan
custom. The Samoan nationalist leaders noted in submissions to a visiting
New Zealand governor-general that the purpose of the mandate was the
preparation of Samoans for self-government, and that in the thirty years
of New Zealand administration, little progress had been made. The New
Zealand government was forced to respond to these new concerns.

The formal device chosen by New Zealand was a United Nations trusteeship agreement, which bound New Zealand to guarantee an orderly political advancement for the Samoan state and which, it was supposed,
would relieve the pressure for immediate self-government. But even this
was not to be fast enough for an increasingly frustrated Samoan elite, which
was already preparing to submit plans for immediate self-government to
the visiting United Nations delegation.

Guy Powles, New Zealand's high commissioner to Western Samoa, decided that New Zealand had to take the initiative if it was to have any
effective role in the process that was to follow. Unlike administrators before him, Powles saw this not as a matter of expedience but, according to
Boyd, as "something which [New Zealand] owed the Samoans for her
past failures in the political and educational fields" (ibid.: 222). He drew
up a plan for self-government that he presented to Samoan leaders for
consideration. Their principal objection was that universal suffrage would
undermine the authority of the chieftaincy.

The New Zealand government turned to new sources for advice and
was lucky to find at its disposal the Pacific historian Dr. J. Davidson, a
Fellow of St. John's College, Cambridge. Davidson would be the man
who, with Francis W. Voelcker and Guy Powles as high commissioners,
would work with the Samoans between 1947 and 1962 to establish the
framework for an independent state built on Samoan customs and practices. It was Davidson's approach, outlined in considerable detail in his
Samoa mo Samoa (1967), that guaranteed that Samoan social organization and custom would form the basis of the constitution and organization
of the Independent State of Western Samoa. A working committee was
appointed to discuss the modification of Powles's plan and to draft a set
of propositions to be put to a constitutional convention. After an extended
discussion, the eight proposals were circulated shortly before being put to
the convention. The constitutional convention took place at Mulinu'u in
November and December 1954.

The constitutional convention presented its proposals, which were
overwhelmingly supported by Samoans in a plebiscite supervised by the

United Nations. In general terms, it guaranteed the continued importance of the *matai* in Samoan social organization when it stated in the preface that the leaders of Western Samoa declared that Western Samoa was to be an independent state based on Christian principles and Samoan custom and tradition. But it was far more explicit in later sections.

The Constitution of the State of Western Samoa simply cemented in place the centrality of *matai* in modern Western Samoan society. At the highest level, this meant that holders of two of Samoa's four highest (*tama'aiga*) titles, Tupua Tamasese Mea'ole and Malietoa Tanumafili II, were made the joint heads of state. Their tenure was confined to the term of their natural lives (Article 5), and provision was made for the election of their successors (Article 18), but these people had to be inter alia qualified to be a member of parliament (Article 18.2[a]), which of course meant that the highest office would for the foreseeable time belong to a *matai*.[10]

Of more practical significance was the fact that the representatives of forty-five territorial constituencies created in the constitution were to be *matai*. Thus the prime minister, eight cabinet ministers, the council of deputies, the speaker and his or her deputy, and all backbench members were to be holders of titles. Only two members representing the individual voters could be elected without titles. Thus effective power was placed in the hands of *matai*, who were elected in turn by other *matai*. Furthermore, tampering with the institution of the *matai* was apparently barred by the constitution, which stated in Article 100 that "a *matai* title shall be held in accordance with Samoan custom and usage and with the law relating to Samoan custom and usage."

The constitution reinforced the basis of *matai* power, continuing control of customary land. It did so by explicitly preventing the permanent alienation of approximately 81 percent of the total land area of Western Samoa, which is defined as customary land (Article 102). It then created a Lands and Titles Court, which was to have jurisdiction in disputes over *matai* titles and customary land (Article 103), arguably two of the most important assets in Samoan society. Furthermore, the court was structured in such a way as to ensure that *matai* played a central role in it. Decisions on lands and titles were to be made by *matai* on the basis of what they supposed at any time to be Samoan custom and practice.

It seemed, then, that on the eve of independence, Samoans could reasonably claim to have maintained intact much of their social organization, despite 130 years of attempts by missionaries, commercial interests, and colonial powers to transform it. The Samoans' anxiety to enshrine elements of this organization in a constitution reflected their determination to protect it from further attempts at encroachment. Among the elements most completely protected was the chieftaincy.

Independent Western Samoa and the Chieftaincy

When Western Samoa became independent in 1962, few would have envisaged that the sections of the constitution and electoral legislation that provided for a system of representation in which only *matai*, or title holders, could stand for seats in the House of Representatives and in which only *matai* were enfranchised[11] would, in a relatively short time, be altered by an independent Samoan parliament.

Most Samoans accepted the principle of *matai* enfranchisement[12] but had more difficulty with the limits that it imposed on individuals who had been accustomed to influencing events. *Matai* suffrage also confined effective political power to a finite group of people: those with titles. This had two sets of consequences, individual and collective. Those individuals who wished to influence the selection of candidates, and to enjoy the various spoils that came with the possession of a vote, had to have a title. Those families who wished to achieve more influence in district and national politics had to have enough votes to exert their influence. The constitution had in fact "frozen" the total amount of political influence in time.

The ever-ingenious Samoans were not to be thwarted by a mere constitutional nicety. For a time there was a scramble to create new titles to enfranchise more people and to exert more influence in, and to take advantage of, the electoral process. This resulted in the creation and registration of new titles, many of which were frivolous and were created solely for electoral purposes.[13] The election to these titles of minors and others who would not normally have held power was a device to ensure that their votes were readily controlled by those who had "installed" them. The process, which effectively devalued all titles (Powles 1986:198), shocked many Samoans and led to a 1969 amendment to electoral legislation aimed at limiting the number of recognized titles to those which existed before independence, effectively disenfranchising approximately 2,000 newly created titles (Meleisea 1992:60–61).[14] This legislation successfully stemmed the creation of new titles and limited the possibilities of influencing the electoral process by this means. In an attempt to regain the initiative, Samoans who had been disenfranchised by the new legislation began to split titles (Powles 1986:210). Thus, a single title could be held simultaneously by a number of holders, among whom one would be the senior holder.

The practice of splitting titles was not new: there had been coholders of titles previously. What was new was the dramatic increase in the number of people holding a given title. Titles that had traditionally been held by a single person were quickly split among as many as fifteen coholders. The extent of title-splitting varied from constituency to constituency: from under 50 percent to over 300 percent between 1961 and 1979 (ibid.: 201). Though the move was intended initially as a device to subvert the Electoral Act, many of those who now found themselves holding titles were reluctant to accept that their rights were confined to the periodic exercise of the vote.

A number of Samoans were concerned with what they saw as the "devaluation" of the prestige of titles, the "dilution" of the power associated with titles, and the emergence of a new set of problems connected with succession to multiple titles. This growing concern was mirrored in international forums, and led to a constitutional challenge in 1982. As Powles noted, however, "When constitutional challenge finally came in 1982, the dissatisfaction revealed was not that of untitled villagers but mainly of part-Samoans caught disenfranchised as a result of the move by so many individuals to take chiefly titles" (ibid.: 209). Powles further observed: "Coming 20 years after independence, the *Olomalu* litigation [i.e., the constitutional challenge] is significant in highlighting how seldom chiefly authority has been before the courts, thus reflecting both the complacency by the leadership and acceptance by the population generally that the Constitution was drafted to permit the *matai* system to flourish" (ibid.: 211–12). The solution to both problems was seen to be the introduction of universal suffrage.

The Electoral Amendment Act of 1990

The amending legislation was passed into law in 1990.[15] It retained the provision for *matai* representation in Parliament (Section 5.1), but it enfranchised all adult Western Samoan citizens (Section 16.1[a] and [b]). The former provision was intended to retain the status of titles, and the latter was intended, at least in part, to halt this process of devaluation by reducing incentives to split titles for electoral advantage (Meleisea 1992: 60–66).

Because of the legal and political significance of the universal suffrage, people have assumed that it reflects the decline of the chieftaincy in contemporary Samoan social organization. This, however, is to miss the import of the act. Universal suffrage was paradoxically an attempt to preserve the status and significance of the chieftaincy, by preventing the devaluation that was resulting from the proliferation of multiple holders and the corrosive intrafamily disputes that accompanied this proliferation (ibid.: 65–66).

The Village Fono Act of 1990

Anyone who doubts the Samoans' continuing commitment to the chieftaincy ought to consider another piece of legislation, the Village Fono Act of 1990, which, despite reservations expressed by the Samoan Law Society,[16] was quietly passed into law in July 1990, some five months before Parliament was asked to vote on the amendment to the Electoral Act. The Village Fono Act effectively increased the power and influence of the chieftaincy in the area in which it is most important: the village.

The chieftaincy, in council, had traditionally enjoyed the right to govern village life and to punish offenders and their families. Since independence, a number of Samoans had challenged the power of the chieftaincy to regulate village social and economic organization. Certain traditional rights of the collective, such as the right to banish offenders from the village, and the right to control commerce, were being challenged in courts on the basis that these violated individual rights guaranteed in the constitution. The successful prosecution of certain of these cases against the judgments of *fono* was a source of concern to the chiefs, who saw this as the beginning of the encroachment of the courts into their traditional jurisdiction (Powles 1986:206). They sought a means of entrenching their rights in law and limiting further erosion. This led the Village Fono Act of 1990.

The Act allowed every village *fono* to exercise any power or authority in accordance with the customs and usage of that village (Section 3.2). It established that any past and future exercise of power and authority by any village *fono* with respect to the affairs of its village that is in accordance with custom and usage is validated and empowered (Section 3.2). In addition to powers and authority conferred in this act, every village *fono* was to enjoy such other powers, authorities, and functions as may be conferred by any other act (Section 4). Even more remarkable is Section 5.1, which confers to every village *fono* powers set out in the following subsection, "*notwithstanding that such powers may not in a particular village form part of its custom and usage.*"

The subsection specifically included the power to make rules for the maintenance of hygiene in the village (Section 5.2[a]) and for governing the development and use of village land for the economic betterment of the village (Section 5.2[b]); and the power to direct any person or persons to do any work required to be done pursuant to rules made in accordance with powers granted or preserved in Section 5.2(a) and (b). People who fail to obey any rule or direction made or given in accordance with powers granted or preserved in this section are guilty of village misconduct and liable to be punished by his [sic] village *fono* (Section 5.3).

The sanctions available to the *fono* to enforce its collective will are remarkable. Section 6 states:

Without limiting the powers of Village Fono preserved by this act to impose punishments for village misconduct the powers of every village fono to impose punishment in accordance with the custom and usage of the village shall be deemed to include the following powers of punishments:—(a) the power to impose a fine in money, fine mats, animals or food; or partly in one or partly in others of those things; (b) the power to order the offender to undertake any work on any village land.

There are provisions for appealing the judgments of the village *fono*. Every person adversely affected by a decision, including a decision as to punishment, has the right of appeal to a court (Section 11.1).[17] The court may hear and determine the appeal in one of three ways. It may allow the appeal and quash the decision of the *fono* (Section 5[a]); it may dismiss the appeal (Section 5[b]); or it may refer the decision back to the originating *fono* for reconsideration. The court may not impose any punishment or penalty or substitute one punishment or penalty for another. The most interesting provision in this area is that there is no right of appeal from a decision of a *fono* after reconsideration.

Given the extent of the powers that Parliament had conferred upon the chieftaincy in the Village Fono Act of 1990, it is perhaps easier to understand why the members of Parliament, who are of course *matai*, might have been willing to make concessions on suffrage. It is also much more difficult to argue that the introduction of universal suffrage was a symbol of a declining Samoan commitment to the chieftaincy and a break in the continuity of *matai* authority.

IN WHITE settler colonies in the Pacific Ocean and around the Pacific Rim where settlers overwhelmed native inhabitants and destroyed the native mode of production and the social order associated with it, chieftaincies were early victims. In such cases (for example, in New Zealand), various forms of chieftaincy have been reestablished. In other Pacific social formations, settlers were for various reasons never able to exert the power necessary to destroy the indigenous modes of production and the associated social orders. In these circumstances, indigenous chieftaincies have continued to hold power despite extended periods of contact. This, I have argued, was the case in what is now Western Samoa.

The missionaries found it unnecessary to destroy either the Samoan control of production or the associated social order. Their goals could be effectively achieved with relatively minor changes in both areas. The commercial settlers would have liked to have eliminated both, but they were unable to do so because they were outnumbered by the Samoans, lacked the support of the states from whence they came, were disunited as a group, and could not understand Samoan politics well enough to exert effective control in the political arena.

The first formal (German) colonial administration might have transformed both the modes of production and governance of the state. The administrators chose to limit the power of the two royal families, whom they considered responsible for the political instability that prevented the development of the colonial economy. They chose at the same time to leave intact the precolonial mode of production and the chieftaincy's authority. The chiefs' control of land and labor were to be harnessed to generate growth in the colonial economy. Thus, while Governors Solf and Schultz significantly diminished the importance of the highest and most visible levels of the Samoan chieftaincy, the substantial but less visible village and district chieftaincy retained a considerable degree of its control of resources throughout the administration.

The second colonial power, New Zealand, assumed responsibility for the administration of Samoa at a time when the responsibilities of colonial powers were clearly prescribed and overseen by international bodies that were not kindly disposed to wholesale attempts to transform indigenous institutions. The Samoans were thus able to preserve the chieftaincy through this period and to ensure that the significance which they attached to the institution was understood at constitutional conferences and embodied in the constitution of the Independent State of Western Samoa.

In the period since Western Samoa attained independence in 1962, Samoans have moved to consolidate rather than to reduce the power of their chiefs. Legislation that at first glance seemed to diminish the power of chiefs, the Electoral Amendment Act of 1990, may in fact have been put in place to ensure the preservation of the chieftaincy. Legislation that provides for the exercise of the power of the chiefs in the villages, the Village Fono Act of 1990, has extended and formalized this authority. Control of the communal land is the real basis of the chief's power. Although, as O'Meara (1987) has noted, evidence of de facto private ownership of land is emerging in some villages, it is not clear that this is widespread in Western Samoa. Thus, though the chiefs who hold power today may be very different from their predecessors in significant ways, neither they nor those who elect them show any signs of abandoning the institution. Thus it should not surprise one to find that the following passage on the *matai* system was written recently by one of Samoa's most educated female *matai*, Dr. Aiono Fana'afi Le Tagaloa:

The accusation of undemocratic [practices comes] from westerners and western-educated Samoans who seem unable and unwilling to see that the *fa'amatai* culture of the Samoan is a perfect and logical manifestation of the will and authority of the people. In that respect, the *fa'amatai* [a series of customs and practices associated with *matai* status] is a truly democratic system of government, perhaps more democratic than the much vaunted democracy of the west that has remained an ideal. That ideal may inspire . . . but, in reality, it has not been developed as the *fa'amatai,* the ideal social organisation most appropriate and relevant to the Samoan people and their culture in the past, present and future centuries. (1992:131)

Dr. Aiono Le Tagaloa's statement touched in passing on the role of "Western-educated Samoans" who challenge the legitimacy of the *matai* system. It is worth noting that this is a large group that is growing steadily as the children of Samoan migrants are raised and educated outside of Samoa in communities as far apart as Seattle and Melbourne. According to Dr. Le Tagaloa, it is this group, which is often critical of the *fa'amatai,* to whom the Western Samoan is looking for the professional and middle-management skills desperately neeeded for national social and economic development. It is significant that the shortage of human resources is created in the first place by the exodus of those Samoans born and raised in Samoa. As Asenati Liki notes in her study of expatriate Samoan professionals, although some leave for professional reasons, others leave precisely because of the *fa'amatai* (Liki 1994).

As Western aid withers, the inexpensive and uncritical sources of overseas expertise dry up, and the government will be forced to look ever more seriously to expatriate Samoans for these skills. This group is unlikely to place its skills at the disposal of a system that they distrust or with which they disagree, as research has already shown (Macpherson 1985). The return of a significant number of such people, with an influence born out of the scarcity of their skills, would produce an articulate advocacy of a counterposition. A challenge to the legitimacy of the *fa'amatai* may yet be the cost of economic development.

Epilogue

As this chapter was being edited, a set of events unfolded in Samoa that might ironically do to the power of the chieftaincy what missionaries, colonial powers, and others could not. On September 26, 1993, in the village of Lona, in the Fagaloa district of Western Samoa, a chief, Nu'utai Mafulu, was shot twice in the head in front of his home and in view of his wife and five children by *taulele'a* (untitled men) acting on instructions from the *matai* of the village. The deceased's house had been stoned for an extended period earlier in the day; and the shooting was followed by the burning of his house, shop, bus, and a private vehicle.

The deceased, who had lived for some twenty years in New Zealand, had returned to Samoa in 1990 and had on various occasions refused to accept the directives of the *fono matai* to end the sale of alcohol from his store in the village or to pay fines that the *fono* had imposed on him for these breaches. The *fono matai* had then directed villagers to boycott his bus and store. The matter came to a head when Mr. Mafulu physically challenged the right of a *matai* to ring the village bell that signaled evening curfew.

The commissioner of police, while describing the event as "barbaric" and assuring the public that justice would be done in this matter, was careful to avoid a general criticism of the role of *fono matai*. Commissioner Tanielu Galuvao noted that the spheres of village council and police in the maintenance of order were complementary, and that in this case the village appeared to have overstepped the mark and to have exceeded its *pule* (*Samoan News*, Radio New Zealand, Sept. 30, 1993).

The commissioner said that the village had undertaken to deliver the offenders into police custody on October 1, 1993, and that it was preferable for the village to do this. If, however, as a Samoan television news reporter noted (Radio New Zealand, Sept. 30, 1993), the village chose not to do this, the police would face serious difficulties in identifying and capturing the defendants. In fact, when police officers went to the village the following day, they confronted a crowd armed with guns and knives. The police commissioner may well have appreciated Governor Solf's dilemma as he was forced to take a low-key approach, "playing by the Samoan oratory and customs." Since then forty-one men, including thirteen *matai*, have been arrested and charged with a variety of offenses. Thirty-six pleaded guilty, but five high chiefs have pleaded not guilty and have been remanded at large.

A Samoan barrister and solicitor, Aeau Semi Epati (National Radio, Radio New Zealand, Oct. 1, 1993), noted that the Village Fono Act of 1990 could be used as a defense by the village for its actions in this case. The Act formally bestowed on village *fono* rights that they had exercised in practice but had never before been granted by law. The Act, however, did not proscribe these powers or the areas in which they could be exercised, which meant that it was not at all clear that the village had exceeded its *pule*, since it was not at all clear in the legislation where its *pule* ended, if indeed it did. Since under the Act the power of the *fono* was limited only by the customs and usages of the villages, it might be possible to point to precedents in custom that could establish that in the past, offenders had been killed for challenging the *pule* of the *fono*. Epati pointed out that where challenges to *matai* authority were involved, the defense would try to show that "there was an element of provocation; that the people acted stupidly but in the honest belief that their society was threatened" (*New Zealand Herald* [Oct. 1, 1993]: 30). Epati noted that the logic of the case for Samoans was that if people felt unable to live under the *pule* of the duly-constituted governing body of the village, they could and should remove themselves to another place in which the rules were more acceptable.

The first twenty-eight cases tried saw people charged with arson, stone-throwing, and willful damage. All pleaded guilty. In mitigation, Mr. Enoka Puni, acting for the defendants, argued that all had committed the offenses because the village *fono* ordered them to do so and threatened those who refused with banishment from the village. Twelve men between the ages of 36 and 65 were sentenced to twenty months in jail, eighteen months of which were suspended on the condition that each defendant pay the deceased's family NZ$381 and carry out 100 hours of community service. Another five men were sentenced to ten months in prison, nine months of which were suspended on the condition that each defendant pay the deceased's family NZ$76 and perform seventy-five hours of community service. The remaining eleven men charged were given two years' probation, on the condition that they perform 350 hours of community service and surrender their travel documents.

These cases were relatively straightforward, since all had pleaded guilty as charged. None of these defendants sought to mount a defense based on the rights apparently conferred by the Village Fono Act of 1990. It may well be that the five *matai* who have pleaded not guilty will adopt elements of this defense. If one such defense were to succeed, it would presumably have a significant impact on the outcomes of the other cases. But irrespective of the cases' outcomes the attention of the Samoan nation has been focused on the continuing influence of the chieftaincy. Even if these events lead to changes in the law of the land, they may not lead to changes in the conduct of village affairs, for as Commissioner Galuvao told the *Samoan Observer*, "Most people thought the law of the land was the *matai* law" (*New Zealand Herald* [Oct. 1, 1993]: 20).

Early predictions that the crime would throw the significance of the Village Fono Act into sharp relief and would lead to swift attempts to amend the legislation have proven premature. Many Samoans in both New Zealand and Samoa, while shocked by the case in point, also take the view that if people cannot accept the *pule* of the *fono matai*, they ought to live on freehold land in Apia or outside Samoa. People have a choice, and as one young educated man noted,

This must surely serve as a warning that if people want to live and make money in a village they must be prepared to accept the authority of those elected to manage the village. If they are unable to do so they should live under an authority which they can accept. They should not expect an institution to change to accommodate them. The village was there before them and will be there after they have gone.

Other influential Samoans have remarked that the appearance of anarchy is a consequence of outsiders' ignorance of the way things were done and why. A Samoan barrister noted that the villagers were careful to confine their actions to the person who had challenged the authority of the *fono* and that they had avoided injuring the deceased's wife and children to ensure that the matter did not involve other families or villages. A member of Parliament for the district in which the act had occurred noted that a cousin of the deceased had shot the victim out of a concern to protect the *fono* from further embarrassment by the family, and to ensure that the violence was contained within the family. Another lawyer noted that the fact that the village was able and willing to deliver the offenders to the police is evidence of their authority and willingness to cooperate with the state, since they could have resisted the police request with a good probability of success. The wife of a parliamentarian noted that the event was unique, occurring only because the pastor was away from the village and was unable to intervene on the deceased's behalf. These and others apparently have not found in the event in question reason for substantial revision of the Village Fono Act.

Even if Samoans are reluctant to act, however, they may be forced to do so by increasing external pressure. With allocation of a shrinking pool of foreign aid being linked to recipients' human rights records,[18] states that cannot guarantee certain basic human rights to their citizens may have to choose between access to aid funds or defense of such principles as the rights of the chieftaincy. Given the general reluctance toward and practical difficulties of constraining the power of the chieftaincy, the next few years will prove interesting and more than a little challenging for the state, which seeks to rein in the chieftaincy. Governor Solf would undoubtedly appreciate the irony.

Rank and Leadership in Tonga

KERRY JAMES

WHEN ASKED, "Who are the chiefs in Tonga?" Tongans unhesitatingly answer, "The king and the nobles are our chiefs"; that is, they refer immediately to the highest-ranking people: the monarch, other members of the royal family, and the nobility ('eiki nōpele), almost thirty of whom are presently installed in their titles and estates.

Reflecting the immense power of the central government, the category of "chief" now also includes the eleven cabinet ministers personally appointed by the king to office for life. They are among the most powerful men in the land and, like the nobles, are given the courtesy title of "the Honourable." In their case, the qualified term 'eiki minisitā shows that the honor has been bestowed by political appointment and not by birth. Four of the cabinet ministers serving at present, however, are also hereditary nobles (nōpele), and another one is the heir to a noble title; of the others, one has a matāpule (ceremonial attendant) title and others have close blood ties with nobles or aristocrats.

It is increasingly apparent that not all of the "chiefs" are regarded as effective leaders by the people, especially the nobles who neither sit in Parliament nor take an active interest in the well-being of the people on their estates. Nowadays, positions of leadership are increasingly being assumed by a range of people who are prominent in the fields of education, church and public administration, and commerce. The newer-style leaders face some problems having their authority widely recognized as legitimate, partly because the older forms of status attribution still remain so visibly prominent in the society.

The parallels between civic and household order are pronounced insofar as both are strongly heirarchical. Family relationships are organized: ideally by age, in favor of seniority, and by gender, females having precedence over males of the same generation. The father is the head of the nuclear family; his wife and children are subordinate to his authority. Properly, he should take into account the wishes of his sisters in the management of both his immediate and the wider family, especially those of his "eldest sister," because she is believed to be, in a special sense, the "chief" of her brother's family (James 1992:92). Similarly, the head or "chief" of the Free Wesleyan Church is the president, to whom all other ministers are subordinate, although they, in turn, as *kau taki 'o lotu* (church leaders), direct the people in church matters; the "chief" of a funeral is a specially designated person, called the *fahu*, usually a senior female related through the deceased's father's side, and so on.

The strength of the present system, as Marcus has remarked, lies less strictly in the imposition of chiefly values than in their dissemination throughout society so that each segment of kin and household organization essentially replicates the internal organization of the aristocratic structures of kindred. What appear to have been solely *'eiki* customs of kinship rank are now followed by an emancipated population and have come to represent Tongan culture and tradition. Now, every male household head (*'ulumotu'a*) is the chief in his own family (Marcus 1977:214). The idea of social precedence based on birth and descent is central to Tongan social organization, and politics. No matter what personal feelings people might have toward their superiors, the "chiefs" of Tonga are accorded the etiquette betokening deference, respect, and love: some of the attitudes that are part of the notion of *'ofa*, a concept that is as central to Tongan as it is to other Polynesian cultures. Indeed, the displays of submissiveness associated with differences in rank are among the most enduring characteristics of Tongan life and have become so thoroughly established as to be a point of pride in the Tongan character (Campbell 1992: 6, 26).

If asked to elaborate the notion of chiefliness, Tongans move from ideas of rank and focus more on *pule* (power or governing authority). They will mention the *pule'anga* (the modern government), the *pule kolo* (village chief), the *faifekau pule* (leading church minister), or, perhaps, the *faiako pule* (school principal). They may speak of the *kōvana* (governor, of each of the Ha'apai and Vava'u island groups), or *minisitā* (minister of the crown). These last two terms are derived from English and denote introduced roles. All these are "the people in front," the *kaumu'a*.

Proposals by members of the prodemocracy movement in Tonga have centered upon the need to make the nobles and government ministers, who together dominate Parliament, more responsible and popularly accountable for their actions. The reformers are mostly members of an emerging middle class frustrated by the ceilings placed on commoners' political and economic ambitions by privileged establishment figures. They profess also to speak in the interests of the mass of semisubsistence growers. However, a convention held in Nukuʻalofa in November 1992 on issues concerning the constitution and possible moves toward greater democracy brought protests from people who feared the king's position might be compromised. One antireformist spokesman said:

> We are not happy about the plans for the convention and the stated reasons behind it because we really love and respect our King, the Royal Family, the Nobles of the Realm, and Ministers of the Crown, as well as Christianity and its leaders of the future. . . . The King rules the nobles and the people and . . . his body is sacred. . . . We are frightened that this authority might be taken away. (*Tonga Chronicle* [Nov. 5, 1992]:3)

Despite the inequities of a system that places political and economic power in the hands of a few, most Tongans, including most prodemocratic reformers, want to retain the unique institutions that remain precious emblems of cultural heritage and identity (Marcus 1989:190–91). As more commoner Tongans become wealthy, achieve success in business, and acquire numerous overseas connections with kin and commercial partners, the retention of chiefly privilege in Tonga becomes increasingly onerous if it clashes with the commoners' ambitions, or merely irrelevant if they have become independent and escaped from the sphere of nobles' influence. Yet, even so, many would agree with the statement made by the brother of the secretary to cabinet: "I wish that we will never lose our chiefs, disregarding how bad some of them are. It is something that we are used to. It is what makes us different from others" (*Matangi Tonga* [July–Sept. 1993]:40).

Part of people's hesitation regarding political and institutional change (quite apart from the affront to tradition represented by any proposed alteration to the chiefly establishment and to the constitution) is that they are unsure where else to turn for guidance, or what the untried commoner "radicals" might have in mind as an alternative to the present rule by nobles and the few commoner government ministers. Many people are sympathetic to the aims of the reformers but do not accept the individuals as candidates for leadership of the country. Their uncertainty resonates with that of Fijians on the eve of independence and self-government in Fiji, which was so eloquently described by Ratu Mara, the then–prime minister, who is currently the president of the recently formed Republic of Fiji.

> Undefined constitutional changes conjure up all sorts of political perils in the mind of Fijians. . . . It is probably the inherent reaction of island people to run to shelter when the winds of change gather force. In this context the only shelter the Fijians know is the present constitution, as the government has not been explicit in its

proposed constitutional change. They should be pitied rather than condemned for preferring the devil they know to the one they do not know. (Ratu Mara, quoted in Lal 1992:187)

Chiefs and Aristocrats

In Tonga's highly rank-conscious society, the term *'eiki* (collectively, *hou'eiki*) refers to anyone of a superior rank to oneself in the family or community. The term *'eiki* is often used synonymously with "chief." But its older meaning, which has been glossed as "chiefly aristocrat," emphasized the element of aristocratic rank derived from birth rather more than the secular powers that the titled chiefs exercised over mundane affairs (Bott 1981:10). Most of the nobles today are no longer effective leaders because they are less closely associated with their people and less incorporated in local communities than were the titled chiefs who ruled before the constitutional changes of the last century.

In order to understand how this change has taken place, it is necessary to "locate the chiefs in history." The Tongan monarchy, supported by a few great aristocratic titles with which it has closely intermarried, seems at first sight to be an example of Polynesian cultural continuity in which the chiefs of yesterday have become the rulers of today. The discourse that works to maintain and validate the Tupou dynasty and the "natural leadership" of its nobles makes rhetorical use of this theme. But these institutions and the relationship between them came about only in the last century—as part of a transaction of identity and power surrounding the rise to prominence of Tāufa'āhau, a ranking Ha'apai warrior chief who became King George Tupou I—and have continued to undergo revision in response to changing circumstances. Inevitably, the responses have seemed to some people to be too rapid, and to others, too slow or inappropriate.

Before the constitutional changes of 1875, power rested with local chiefs, who ruled groups of people from their extended families and others who lived and worked on their land. These groups of supporters were called the chief's *kāinga*. Unlike the discussions held by the *matai* (titled heads of the families) in Samoan villages (Chapter 4), the powers of the local chief in Tonga were, in theory, delegated from a higher, more powerful chief. Offenders were not brought to public trial as in Samoa, but in Tonga were dealt with by the chief, whose powers were, in practice, absolute and arbitrary. His punishments could include execution, carried out immediately by either himself or one of his powerful henchmen (Lātūkefu 1974:10).

Several chiefs were able to consolidate immense power over their lo-

calities. By the beginning of the nineteenth century, some had stopped contributing valuables to the highest-ranking title holder, the semisacred Tu'i
Tonga, for his *'inasi*, or annual ceremony of "first fruits," and were asserting their independence in other ways (ibid.:23). Local autonomy was
turned in some instances to selfish and cruel ends, and was threatening the
unity of the Tongan polity. When the Wesleyan missions arrived in the
1820s, the powers of all three of the most high-ranking dynastic titles,
those of the Tu'i Tonga, the Tu'i Ha'atakalaua, and the Tu'i Kanokupolu,
appear to have become merely nominal and ceremonial. Mission reports
of the 1820s suggest that the chiefly lines had become so disorganized that
neither a Tu'i Tonga nor a Tu'i Kanokupolu was actually in office at the
time. The Tu'i Ha'atakalaua had ceased to be a focus of power as early as
the beginning of the previous century, since appointments to his office
were made only intermittently and often from among members of the Tu'i
Kanokupolu family (Lātūkefu 1974:22; Campbell 1992:24). It appears
that the holders of the three highest titles had become remote and largely
ineffectual figures.

Rivalries were common between the chiefs, especially after the entry of
Christian missionaries into Tonga. Conflict flared between the chiefs who
welcomed the new religion and its ministers, and those who bitterly opposed them. The struggles were not primarily religious wars, but struggles
for supremacy among contenders for the high titles. The conflicts nevertheless became closely influenced by the new sources of power that the
foreigners (*papālangis*) brought. Missionaries largely provided literacy,
spiritual enlightenment, and political advice, but marooned sailors, escaped convicts from New South Wales, and beachcombers provided firearms and fighting men. Later, traders and an increasing number of other,
mostly Anglo-Australian, settlers in Tonga took an active part in Tongan
political wrangles.

The decisive victor in these struggles was Tāufa'āhau, a remarkable
warrior and politician, who rose from the chiefly ranks of Ha'apai, the
middle group of islands of the Tongan archipelago, to claim supremacy
first over Vava'u, the northern group, and finally over Tongatapu, the
main island in the south. Proclaimed in 1845 the first king, Tupou I,
Tāufa'āhau quickly sought to break the power of the chiefs who opposed
him. With the advice of the Wesleyan missionaries to whose faith he had
converted, and whose *mana* (believed supernatural force) he found to be
a richer source of power than that of the old religious system, he promulgated a series of legal codes that forbade the chiefs to arbitrarily seize the
possessions of their people or to extract from them numerous customary
labor services (*fatongia*) as they had been wont to do.

The legal constraint on chiefly powers issued in 1862, known as the
Emancipation Edict,[1] aroused opposition from chiefs who realized they

had lost more from their conversion to Christianity and their espousal of
the new system and king than they had first imagined. One of the leading
chiefs, Tungī, asked ironically what would happen to them. "We cannot
fish, we cannot till the land, we cannot do anything for our living." Indig-
nantly playing on the word *fatongia* (the enforced labor the chiefs could
no longer legally command), Tungī asked, "Why don't you just take the
ngia and leave us the *fato*?" Here, *ngia* refers to *ngeia*, the prestige derived
from power. In effect, Tungī was saying: Take the penumbra of power but
leave us the *fatongia*, the labor of our commoner people, for us to live on
(Lātūkefu 1974:173).

The Institution of the Nobles

Having begun to destroy the basis of the old chiefly powers, the king then
created in effect a new landed aristocracy that, he thought, would owe its
loyalty, because it owed its existence, to him. By the constitution of 1875,
a limited number, only twenty, were selected from the hundreds of traditional chiefs to be the nobles of Tonga. Large tracts of land located in
parcels throughout the kingdom were attached as *tofi'a* (hereditary estates) to these noble titles, and smaller estates were given to six *matāpule*
(ceremonial attendant) titles. In each case, the title was to pass in each
generation strictly according to male primogeniture. The constitution also
provided for every adult man the right to claim land from his (now noble)
chief's estate.

Like earlier legislation, these moves were designed to limit the powers
of former chiefs and raise the status of ordinary common people. Tupou I
appointed another ten traditional chiefs as hereditary nobles in 1880. His
successor, Tupou II, appointed another two noble titles, and Tupou III
(Queen Sālote) created one more, making the total of thirty-three noble
titles that exist today. There are usually fewer than thirty-three nobles installed in office at any one time. Some titles are vacant because a legitimate
heir has not been produced. In other cases, the union of lines has resulted
in some titles becoming fused; for example, the direct descendant of the
Tuʻi Tonga is Kalanivalu-Fotofili, while the king's youngest son today
holds three prestigious noble titles: Lavaka, Ata, and ʻUlukālala.

The New Nobles

On what basis were chiefs selected to become Tonga's *nōpele?* The new
term, derived from the English "noble," signifies an important break with

the traditions of the *'eiki*. As the king made clear in his closing speech to the 1875 Parliament that ratified the constitution, the basis for selecting the nobles was not their high rank but their strength. Chiefs with a large number of supporters living under them were more likely to prove troublesome to the king's new government than those of higher rank with fewer supporters. The new nobility thus straddled the old order of rank and the new order of status now acquired from the central government personified by the monarch. Some of the newly created nobles were *sino'i'eiki* (literally, having "the body of an aristocrat"), which meant that they were of extremely high birth rank. They were people who ultimately could trace a fairly close consanguineal tie with the Tu'i Tonga's family, preferably one that passed solely through women to a senior sister of the Tu'i Tonga. These criteria reflected ancient beliefs concerning rank and its transmission through females. Formerly, control over chiefly *kāinga* was probably exercised jointly by the senior female and the senior male chiefs, as "sister" and "brother," of the ruling family (Wood-Ellem 1981, 1987). When no suitable male was available, women could be installed as titled chiefs. This was not the desired practice because it was believed that males should exercise secular authority over family and *kāinga* matters while the aristocratic women wielded a mystical potency. Nevertheless, the great warrior 'Ulukālala, during the internal conflicts of the early nineteenth century, when he was increasing his power over Tongatapu, appointed his "aunt" (probably, his father's sister) Toe Umu as the chief over Vava'u in the north (Martin 1827 vol 1:137). Other examples of female chiefs have been well documented (Gunson 1987). The practice of allowing only men to succeed to noble titles confirmed a male bias that undoubtedly was inherent in Tongan chiefly arrangements but reflected more the need perceived by Tupou I, influenced by his principal Wesleyan missionary advisor Shirley Baker, to conform to European ideas of what a modern constitutional monarchy should be.

The new Tupou dynasty was anxious to deconstruct the old mystique of rank and to absorb its residual semidivine associations by means of a series of strategic marriages with descendants of the Tu'i Tonga. The great majority of the *hou'eiki* (the former chiefly aristocrats) of old Tonga were not given noble titles and entered the last quarter of their nation's nineteenth-century history with only the same legal status as commoners (Campbell 1992:169). The former chiefs who were not ennobled are sometimes known as *'eiki si'i*. Their names may still be respected locally, especially if, as is frequently the case, their descendants have distinguished themselves in educational or church spheres. But they have no corporate identity or importance as a category in national affairs. Today, to emphasize claims to birth rank that stem from the pre-Tupou era is considered not only bad-mannered but potentially subversive (Marcus 1989:204). The individuals who are considered eminent because of their family heritage might be referred to as *motu'a* (elder), *tauhi fonua* (keepers of the land), or *ivilahi* (men of personal skill and power) rather than *'eiki*.

Thus, of the thirty titles ennobled by 1880, a few were held by great aristocrats and more by less aristocratic but extremely powerful chiefs. Today, there are very few, perhaps six or seven, great aristocrats among the nobles. One of them is the present prime minister, Baron Vaea of Houma, who shares with the king a common grandfather, Tupou II. His wife, Tuputupu, is extremely highborn, and their eldest daughter has further consolidated their rank (and that of the royal family) by her marriage to the king's youngest son, Lavaka-Ata-'Ulukālala.

Few other present-day nobles, however, have claim to great birth rank, and many are not considered to be aristocrats at all. Those who have acquired wealth and influence through their skills and achievements and their incumbency of high government position may be regarded as *pule* (leaders) or *'eiki* (chiefs) of a great many people. Those who have little besides their titles and estates, however, are best termed "gentry" (Marcus 1977:218), because what power they possess lies primarily in their control of land and the commoner tenants who reside on it. If all their land has been allocated and registered by individuals, even this power has markedly diminished, and they are regarded more and more merely as members of the emergent middle class (Fonua 1993).

In addition to the great variation of rank and power that exists today among the thirty or so hereditary nobles, the older term *'eiki* has itself been extended as a title of respect to all eleven ministers of the Crown, irrespective of whether they are commoners or nobles. At last count, five were legally commoners, five held noble or *matāpule* titles, and one other is heir to a noble title, but all are referred to as *'eiki minisitā*—in English, "Honorable Minister."

As has been noted in several places, Tonga's successful resistance last century to the imperial ambitions of major cosmopolitan powers was based on significant self-transformations that assumed the appearance of Western models (Marcus 1977:216). The institution of a constitutional monarchy and the preservation of a number of major traditional chiefs in the form of a Western-style landed aristocracy contradicted the alternate image of a still-savage people led by chiefs, and confirmed Tonga's ability to handle its own affairs in a modernist way. The loyalty of the new nobles, however, remained neither strong nor consistent during the reigns of succeeding monarchs, Tupou II and Queen Sālote Tupou III, each of whom tried to reconcile the warring interests of powerful nobles with each other, with monarchical interests, and with the interests of the state. The nobles' and royal family's retention of control over much of Tonga's land, together with their disproportionate representation in Parliament, governmental committees, statutory boards, commercial corporations, and other significant areas of Tongan life, has sustained their character as a powerful elite and has had decisive effects on development.

In modern Tonga, rank is attributed more on the basis of connection to the present royal family than to links with the former great aristocrats. Some nobles still assert significant authority over the people of their estates, rather in the style of the old chiefs over their *kāinga*, but others do not. This situation has come about as the result of several factors, among which the nobles' role in the distribution of land and their preferential relationship to other scarce resources are still key.

The Control of Land

The Land Act of 1882 made every Tongan male taxpayer 16 years and over eligible to receive both a town and a garden allotment from either the government or the estate of his noble. The allotments then passed to the eldest male descendant in perpetuity, as long as rent was paid to the noble and tax was paid to the government. This move was calculated to remove the commoners' dependence on the chiefs for their livelihood and to replace it with fealty to the king and government, with which the allotments were formally registered. In 1915, however, amendments to the Land Act returned a measure of power to the nobles by making it necessary henceforth for commoners to receive the permission of the noble before they could register an allotment from his estate with the Ministry of Lands (Campbell 1992:128).

The requirement of a noble's approval made applicants for land feel obliged as in former times to give the nobles the best of their crops and frequent days of labor in gratitude for allocations of land. If the noble were displeased with a farmer, he could promise the land to someone else, who, in turn, had to try harder to please him. By law, the delays of the estate-holding noble can be overruled by the Minister for Lands, but he, too, has always been a noble, and few villagers would go to one powerful noble with a complaint against another. Some nobles have delayed registration of allotments for years in order to retain access to the goods and services of the people living on their land (Maude 1965:105; Lātūkefu 1974:211–12; Needs 1988:56–58).

Allotments have become progressively harder to obtain as the number of eligible males in the rapidly expanding population has increased. As a result, the abuse of noble privilege with regard to land has come increas-

ingly under fire from prominent church and social leaders. By 1996, most
of the land in the kingdom had been allocated to individual smallholders,
although some of it is still not registered by them. Once a man registers an
allotment, he becomes, in effect, a "little noble" in terms of his individual
control of it, especially since legislation passed in the late 1970s has allowed commoner allotment-holders to lease part or all of their hereditary
allotments (James 1995b). Yet most noble landlords still have particular
advantages compared with most commoners because of their larger estates and greater political influence. The abuse by some of them of their
privilege, through their continued demands for gifts and services from the
people traditionally bound to them, has been a major cause of Tonga's
nobility being labeled derogatorily as "feudal" and anachronistic. But the
abuse of poorer people by those in positions of power is done for the most
modern of reasons: the desire for money and personal gain. The cultural
continuity with the past gives nobles a "double-barreled legitimacy" for
positions of authority in the kingdom but can also impugn the claim for
modernity that is their only possible validation for continued salience and
survival.

Other reasons for the social distance between nobles and people include the physical distance between their places of residence, differences
in lifestyles, and the generally one-sided nature of their relationship. The
preconstitutional chief's extraction of tribute was frequently backed by
the threatened or actual use of force. The other side of the relationship,
however, was an obligation to protect the members of their *kāinga* in
battle and to care for them in peacetime. The cessation of warfare and
legislation limiting the powers of the new nobles has allowed many of
them to accept privilege without the functions and obligations to safe-
guard their people. They are, in a very real sense, civil-service chiefs, who
are paid an allowance by the government and seek only to further their
interests in relation to the center of power.

"Fitness to Lead"

Queen Sālote, during her reign from 1918 to 1965, strongly encouraged the education of members of the noble families so that there would
be a "unity of rank and fitness to lead" (Campbell 1992:128, 136). The
Education Act of 1927, for example, provided scholarships for study overseas at both the secondary and the tertiary level. The queen and her con-
sort, Tungī, personally paid the fees for many boys to attend Tupou College and for girls to go to Queen Sālote College. In addition, the queen's
eldest son, the present king, was to be a shining example to other aristocrats when, in 1942, he became the first Tongan to obtain university de-

grees, in arts and law, from the University of Sydney. He returned to Tonga to become the Minister for Education and, thus, a member of both the cabinet and the privy council. In these roles, he developed further educational opportunities for nobles and commoners. In 1949, he became premier. The prince's Western education was intended specifically to prepare him for modern government. The fact that from that time on Tongan government took a more vigorous role in promoting progress and modernization may be attributed to his influence (ibid.: 162).

In spite of this encouragement, many nobles with high office in the kingdom continued to rely on rank as their major qualification and acquired only comparatively low levels of modern education. Commoners of talent, on the other hand, mostly the descendants of *'eiki si'i*, the preconstitutional chiefs who had not been made nobles, quickly took advantage of the educational opportunities that opened up at home and, increasingly, overseas. The first men to go to Fiji for training in medicine and in the church tended to be drawn from these families (ibid.: 128, 136). The way was not easy for them as their families had little cash income, but they struggled to acquire an impressive array of modern skills.

The nobles of the present king's generation might have been slow to accept the need for education, but when they saw commoners beginning to overtake them through achievement, they made sure that their children were trained. Twenty years ago, it was observed that "many noble heirs are becoming educated and preparing for the competition among a new *élite*, where traditional status is only one component and a partial, not determining, advantage" (Marcus 1977:222). No longer can it be said, as then, that "the *poto* or educated noble [is] . . . still largely a phenomenon of the future" (ibid.). The king's three sons have each had years of secondary and tertiary education overseas, and two of them graduated from European military establishments. Several heirs to noble titles have achieved good degrees in education, law, economics, or political science from universities in Australia, New Zealand, the United States, and Britain.

Young nobles with modern educational qualifications tend to move up quickly within bureaucratic hierarchies. Their rapid elevation within the state structures is almost always welcomed. Most highly educated commoners in bureaucratic office see the leading positions as Queen Sālote did: as the appropriate roles for nobles, as long as they have the relevant training and experience. What is deeply resented but rarely occurs nowadays is the blatant advancement of incompetent people of rank over commoners who have not only high educational qualifications but also years of bureaucratic service. The appointment in 1991 of a 32-year-old noble heir to the office of Minister for Labour, Commerce, and Industries, shortly after the successful completion of his economics and law degrees at the University of Auckland, accordingly raised no ire, though it was noted in some quarters with a characteristic irony that the young man also happens to be the son of the queen's sister, and, coincidently, is married to the king's niece, a daughter of the monarch's younger brother, a former prime minister. The main reservation expressed over the young heir's appointment was concern whether, after his years overseas, he was sufficiently Tongan in his dealings with ordinary people and, perhaps more important, with the older, more experienced political campaigners in the government. It was felt by some that, after having been away for so long, he would find it difficult to readily become part of the complicated personal networks of patronage and obligation that make up the dynamic of Nuku'alofa's inner government circles.

The Pull of the Urban Center

Other young overseas-educated nobles now inheriting the titles left by their more traditional fathers are finding that though they may be eminently eligible for high government office in Nuku'alofa, partly because of their ability to relate well to their European counterparts in foreign countries, they may well lack the support of their tenants. The young nobles continue to play the roles of landlord and figurehead for the estate's tenants, but their leadership roles have been eroded by the differences between generations, which make for problems of communication, which are, in turn, exacerbated by the fact that so many nobles live in the capital, Nuku'alofa, and not on their estates.

Despite efforts at decentralization and the provision of money-making incentives for development in Ha'apai and Vava'u, there is an increasing sense that Nuku'alofa is not only the seat of administration and power, but also "where it all happens" in terms of opportunity. Nobles prefer to mix with their social equals or betters and with Europeans and other expatriates rather than with their own people. They may visit their estates only infrequently, at which time their tenants go to great trouble and expense to entertain them (c.f. Hau'ofa 1987:11–12).

Some problems stem from age and generational differences. Emigration has taken away younger people, leaving behind the elderly, who do not welcome working programs put forward by a young noble not very well known to them. The Honorable Luani, who was 28 years old when invested with his title in 1987, is one young noble who has found it difficult to implement projects on his estates. "I would set out a plan . . . but then [the villagers] come along saying that was not how it was done when my father was alive," he remarked (Fonua 1992b:14). Luani remembered how his father would call on his people to come and work. He continued,

"Now it is different, there will be only a few turn up and they are not very keen" (ibid.). Villagers' independence from their noble landlords is most evident in places where all the land from the estate has been allocated and registered by the tenants, as was intended by Tupou I's 1882 Land Act. Luani went on, "The land was our power base, and we used to have the respect of the people because we owned the land, but now . . . there is no good reason for them to remain our obedient partners in the villages" (ibid.).

Luani lives permanently in Nuku'alofa, where he works. He attends church every Sunday in the village on his estate in Tongatapu, to keep in touch with his people. He finds it harder to convince the people of Tefisi in Vava'u of his interest and loyalty, since he visits his estate there only irregularly. "But I have a relative who is my representative there," he said (ibid.). The Honorable Fusitu'a, speaker of the legislative assembly, whose estates lie in the far northern outlier of Niuafo'ou, also maintains that his younger brother, who resides on his land, is well able to take care of matters in his absence, and that he himself does more good for his people by being in Nuku'alofa, where they come to consult with him on matters involving government ministries (ibid.).

Local Government and Leadership

The noble's presence by proxy is inadequate, however, for the day-to-day running of village affairs. It should be made clear that not all nobles are absentee landlords. Notable exceptions are the king's youngest son and his wife, who live with their young family on the estate belonging to his Ata title at Kolovai, in Tongatapu's western district. Two of the king's brother's sons also live with the people of their father's estate around the village of Pelehake. These young families have started rather a trend for other young couples from noble families to leave Nuku'alofa, which is crowded and noisy, to maintain permanent or holiday residences in the countryside. While it might be merely fashionable for them to follow the lead of the young royals, the relationship with their families' retainers has no doubt prospered from the more frequent contact.

Where either the noble is not in residence or his authority is on the decline, however, the other contenders for local leadership become more noticeable. Of these, the 151 town officers and 23 district officers, who report directly to the premier's office, are most likely to be officially, although not always effectively, responsible for the administration of village activities.

The local government structure has developed slowly in Tonga since

first being defined in 1903. Local officers have the authority to make rules
for the governing of "village plantations and other necessary matters relating to the welfare of the people of his [sic] village." The noble or *matāpule* holding a hereditary estate may also make regulations in the same
way for the people who reside on his estate (Fonua 1992b:14). But today,
government officials often bypass nobles when they want work carried out
in the villages. For example, said Luani,

When the government wants a village to prepare a *pola* [a large quantity of food]
for a state feast, traditionally they would approach the noble, who would together
with the town officer organise the preparation of the *pola*. But now they just go
straight to the town officer, and my only involvement is when they ask me at the
end of the feast to thank the people for preparing the *pola*. (Ibid.)

Once it was virtually unknown for the nobles' requests to be refused,
or deference not shown to them. Yet Luani has called attention to the
growing "anti-nobles sentiment." "I have heard of a noble being the last
person to be served in shops, and derogatory remarks being made against
nobles. I don't know for sure how this anti-nobles sentiment came about,
but I suspect that it is due in part to some nobles abusing their authority
and being dishonest to their people" (ibid.). I was told of an incident in
the late 1980s when a notoriously greedy noble had asked his tenants to
bring him pigs and foodstuffs from their plantations to feed his large number of guests. The tenants refused publicly, saying angrily in front of his
household and guests that they had given him more than enough and were
themselves going hungry because of his lack of concern for them. Other
less dramatic incidents have occurred where the people have listened silently, then simply not carried out the orders given to them.

THESE THEMES, frankly aired in the Tongan periodical *Matangi Tonga*,
are also apparent in the observations I have made over the last fourteen
years on a small island in Vava'u, the main northern group of the Tongan
archipelago. The island, which I shall call Falahola, is part of a small noble
estate held by successive generations of men with little rank, education, or
influence. Traditional and conservative, they lived quietly for the most
part on their land without holding any positions of power at the seat of
central government. The last of these country gentlemen died in 1971. His
successor, who returned from the United States when he acquired the title
in 1974, preferred to live in the capital. He took little interest in the administration of daily affairs on the island, although he was not above meddling in its land matters. His premature death in 1977 is believed on the
island to be due mainly to his malpractices with regard to land. He left no
legitimate issue, and the title reverted to the Crown, where it remained for

fifteen years until 1992, when his sister's son, a young Nuku'alofa man, was appointed. The present noble shows an interest in the people and has delighted them by organizing a successful rugby team made up of island men. He is also building a large house in Vava'u's main town, Neiafu, and has indicated his desire to rebuild his house on Falahola and, perhaps, live there. The more cynical, educated islanders living off the island feel that the people will give more to him than he will provide for them. Nevertheless, the islanders are delighted to have a noble once again.

Events from the 1980s, however, when I first began my visits, illustrate what happens when there is no noble around whom to focus mundane activities. The village, which had won a prize for being Tonga's most beautiful when the present noble's grandfather's sisters and daughters were there to encourage the women to sweep their yards and to plant scented and decorative flower borders, had become dirty and untidy. There was little overall organization of daily work apart from the informal household, fishing, or gardening groups. The two *matāpule* of the two former nobles were still alive and were much respected in the community; their opinions were sought on several matters of concern to the village. The younger brother of the present noble's grandfather also resided there. The gracious wife of one of the *matāpule* was also respected. Known to be closely related to one of the former great nobles of Vava'u, she was "chiefly" in the eyes of the people. By the end of the 1980s, however, all these elderly influential people had died, except for one *matāpule* who was by then very old and ill.

While the presence of the traditional leaders diminished, the influence of the town officer became more pronounced. His ability to assume greater local initiative in the relative power vacuum on the island coincided with a time, in the late 1980s, when the powers of local government officers were being revived throughout Tonga. The officers have been called upon to implement programs designed to protect the environment by cleaning villages and surroundings, and to help with other development projects.

Falahola's town officer was asked to encourage the village men to protect a giant clam nursery that was located near the island as part of a national marine resources replenishment scheme, and to request that the women keep the village clean and tidy. In 1989, after a fence to keep pigs out of garden lands was built with foreign aid funds, the town officer encouraged men, especially the more restless young men without land of their own, to prepare new plots to grow subsistence crops. He and other senior men led by example: they cleared and prepared strips on the large piece of good arable land registered in the name of the noble, which had been lying untouched since at least the mid-1970s, working together in the traditional agricultural pattern of *toutu'u*, a form of communal labor where every man works at the same time on his own garden strip within the same plantation. I asked how the town officer dared to use the land belonging to the noble without permission. People laughed and said, "He's strong. The other men will hide behind him if there is trouble from the new noble!"

The idea did not really catch on because the islanders prefer fishing to organized horticultural work. The town officer was clearly the first among his peers rather than a man who had the authority to force his fellow islanders to work. Well into his 60s and an islander born and bred, he had served consecutive terms of office amounting to over fifteen years. The people respected him and found him to be always honest in his dealings with them.[2] When they chose to follow him, it was because they liked him rather than because of his government position, and he was always careful to ask his fellow islanders to do things rather than to order them. When he died in the early 1990s, the office was assumed by his son, without waiting for an election to take place. The informality and the tendency for islanders to organize their own affairs was given dramatic expression when the new town officer used a heavy spanner to beat two young men who had been neglecting their family duties and, finally, came drunk to church. In different surroundings, the youths might well have taken legal action for the severe corporal punishment he inflicted on them. But, I was told, "all the people of the island, even the parents and the sisters" of the youths, made a point of telling the town officer that they wholeheartedly supported his action.

'Eseta Fusitu'a, a top bureaucrat who is working to make the role of local government officers even more active, agrees with the Hon. Luani that some of these officers are closer to the people than some of the nobles. But, she said, this is merely part of the modernization process that was set in motion when the constitution was proclaimed in 1875. She added, "Since it appears that there are leadership problems in the villages it may be wise to redefine the role of the town and district officers" (Fonua 1992b:15). However, she did not elaborate the ways in which the officers' roles might be redefined so as not to clash with that of the noble estate-holders.

I doubt that there will be serious trouble between the town officer and the new noble in the small estate of Falahola. But the possibility of friction will depend to a much larger extent now than in recent former times on the attitudes and actions of the newly installed noble toward his people. They will welcome him because respect for the noble of the village and island is what they remember as being the old way and still believe to be correct Tongan behavior. But if he is rude or exploitative, he will encounter an ambivalent response: respect will be given to the title, but little or no personal respect will be given to him.

Tongans are more likely to express lack of affection and respect for superiors in passive rather than confrontational ways. A comment made about another local noble woman is illustrative. Married to a Vava'u noble whose title is not nationally prominent, she frequently asks women from Falahola and her husband's village to her home in Nuku'alofa for visits of many months when she has guests to entertain or has to contribute food, goods, or hospitality for important state occasions. The village women dutifully leave their own families and their production of essential handicrafts in order to run her house, clean, cook, and serve. When she visits her husband's village in Vava'u, she is waited upon with food and traditional wealth items as marks of the people's respect for her rank; but, I was told by a local teacher,

The people don't really like her, because they know she doesn't truly care for her husband's people. She's selfish and only wants what she can get. They will give her respect (*faka'apa'apa*); but, if they really loved (*'ofa*) her, they would run down to the wharf with mats and tapa and songs of welcome when she comes to visit, crying with joy to see her arrive from the boat. But nobody goes to meet her. They just wait in the village until she drives in before they even say hello.

Alternate Role Models

Tongans look increasingly for guidance in worldly matters to relatives who have been overseas, many of whom are highly educated. The head of the national maritime training college who has a master of science degree from a university in the United Kingdom, for example, was asked during a lengthy kava session with Falahola men for his opinions about the pro-democracy movement, the 1987 military coups in Fiji, the behavior of the "radical" people's representatives in the Tongan Parliament, and, to his surprise, the "proper" way to choose the ceremonial *fahu* (the position of preeminence usually given to a senior female on the deceased's father's side) at a funeral. The men discussed at length the various possibilities open now in a very mobile society. The prevailing mood of the discussion was one not of regret for passing cultural ideals, but of how best to strike compromises between propriety, etiquette, and practical reason in the world of today, a world in which the family's *fahu* often lives far from her brother's descendants and is largely unknown to them.

Increasingly, people are adjusting the "correct" forms of precedence and deference to be shown to social superiors with the constraints imposed by modern life. Stepping into leadership roles left vacant by many of the nobles are a growing number of commoners, who are leaders in the church or in business or education, and who earn a form of respect and a personal following through their individual efforts. But, because of the deference still accorded to rank and title in Tongan society, the newer people filling leadership positions often lack legitimacy in the eyes of the people. Their assumption of authority is tentative and ambiguous, fraught with social contradictions, and tempered by the tension surrounding commoners who "get above their station" (fie 'eiki). Frequently, national groups and associations have nobles as patrons and chairpersons, while commoners make up the committees and carry out most of the work. Villagers are increasingly exercising degrees of organizational skill but are always careful to disavow any leadership role for themselves because, they say, leadership belongs to the nobles and other social superiors. "I am only helping" or "I am here only to serve" are the sentiments expressed again and again by many extremely capable commoners. As a result, there may well be said to be "a leadership crisis," especially at the local level, in the villages, in Tonga today (Fonua 1992b:14–15).

The Legitimation of Authority

The social forms that accompany the pervasive notions of hierarchy tend to be replicated in relation to some of the newer "chiefs," people with power and resources. Accordingly, relations with major foreign-aid donors have on occasion been ritualized as the petitioning of commoners to their chiefs. One foreign emissary, for example, was granted a matāpule (ceremonial attendant) who, in the Tongan manner, formally received the requests for aid and the gifts that frequently accompanied the requests. The matāpule also spoke on behalf of the ambassador when requests for project aid were granted. The requests and grants had to pass through formal, official channels, but the forms of asking and receiving were publicly "Tonganized." The ritual may have restored a sense of control and dignity to members of the Tongan elite who had themselves become in this context like commoners, petitioners and recipients of material advantage from a richer, external source of favor.

By continuing to honor particular relationships and statuses, modern Tongans are upholding the principles of their civil and political society as these have been codified over the last century and a half into "custom." But it would be a mistake to accede to the stereotype of "traditional hereditary leaders" in the case of Tonga, because title holders were always chosen, by an electoral college of family members, as much if not more for their personal achievements as for their birth rank. Nowadays, the title must pass to the oldest legitimate son. Nevertheless, the usurpation of the ascriptive position of the elder by the achievements of the younger sibling remains common in Tongan society, reflected in myths and stories referenced to the culture before European contact. It was the 1875 constitution that rigidified the more flexible former system.

It is therefore ironic that Her Royal Highness Princess Pilolevu, herself a businesswoman of note, could speak of "the wrong way" in which members of the business community are being placed above others in the family because they are better able to afford the food for feasts and funerals, air travel for relatives, and gifts. The princess said, "People should be taught that, even if people in positions of respect can only give a little, their gift is the appropriate one, not the rich person's gift. We should adhere to the old cultural values."[3] The vitality of the Tongan culture, however, may be seen in the fact that, despite some family tensions, the rights and privileges customarily given to senior kinship statuses tend to pass to those with the wherewithal "to get things done" in today's world. Accordingly, the opinions of younger people, who have lived overseas and acquired wealth and skills, frequently carry more weight in family matters than they should in terms of their seniority (James 1983:236).

HOWEVER, the buck has to stop somewhere, and in Tonga it stops with any perceived threat to the dignity or position of the monarchy. By the late 1970s, the estate holders' abuse of power had sparked a popular protest that resulted in a conference on land matters (S. Fonua 1975). In the 1980s, several of the more "radical" people's representatives in Parliament began to question the expenditure of public monies by government ministers. They spearheaded a growing "prodemocracy movement," which calls for broader popular representation in government and greater accountability of government ministers to the people.

The so-called radicals are the most active in parliamentary debates, speak more in parliamentary sessions than any other representatives except the Speaker of the House, write for newspapers, give interviews freely, and attend kava parties throughout the kingdom, particularly in Tongatapu, where they explain what is happening in government, and how the constitution is being interpreted or overlooked in certain contexts. Several of them are active in other spheres in which they are able to influence opinion: for example, one is a youth, sports, and church leader; others are businessmen and heads of nongovernment organizations; another was a lecturer who actively debated with students at the University of the South Pacific's extension center in Tonga.

The popular representatives are closely observed as models for action. It is difficult to find a Tongan term for them and the other leaders who are coming to the fore: for example, the term *kau taki*, sometimes used to refer to the newer commoner leaders, connotes those who lead as one does, say, an animal such as a horse. The fact that modern Tongans do not easily find a term for these newer people of influence suggests the anomaly and ambiguity of their role. It would be wrong, moreover, to interpret the prodemocracy movement as a "grass-roots" movement of popular protest. Most less-educated Tongan people distrust the movement because they do not fully understand it and have not had it adequately explained to them; they are afraid that it represents a threat to Tonga's chiefly and monarchical heritage. Campbell has rightly described the movement as more akin to a "bourgeois revolution," featuring "the typical requests of a new elite for less hereditary privilege and a sharing of power," than to a truly "populist" movement (Campbell 1992:222). At the same time, 'Akilisi Pohiva, the most outspoken of the reformers, emerged as a populist leader in the 1996 elections.

As the protests and public demonstrations against the government have continued, many of the newer leaders, including Pohiva, have themselves been increasingly criticized for their bad manners and verbal assaults on social superiors, and even for lining their own pockets with parliamentary salaries and perquisites. In addition, a division has grown wider within the reformers' ranks between those who would like to see greater democracy and those who merely want reform of abuses within the present system. In 1994, a political party called the People's party based on the prodemocracy movement was formed. Its creation was marred, however, by public acrimony between the leading activists: 'Akilisi Pohiva and Futa Helu wanted the term "democracy" to appear in the party's name, whereas most others are not sure that a Western-style democracy is in the nation's interests. Underlying this split is a less-publicly stated but nevertheless fundamental disagreement about religion. Pohiva and Helu, whose notions of democracy are based on the study of Greek philosophy, are well known as atheists, but most other reformers are not, nor do they want the new People's party to have such a label in a nation in which Christian and other churches are powerful and play important roles (James 1993; 1994: 195; 1995a; 1996).

The formal position of most reformers today is one of moderation: they want to see abuses of privilege checked and a greater representation of the people in Parliament, including the cabinet, but without an implied threat to the institutions of hereditary nobility or the monarchy. They rely a great deal on the new mass media published in Tonga to educate the populace and on the power of the law to carry the day. The antiestablishment rhetoric can run high, as in an editorial in a "radical" newssheet, *Kele'a*:

Our monarchical government is bound to fall. . . . Since 1987 there have been four impeachment motions of some of the ministers debated in the house . . . most of the ministers and nobles representatives looked at those parliamentary exercises as tools against their personal and vested interests. They never seemed to treat those impeachment exercises as means of improving and maintaining the integrity of His Majesty's government and of promoting the confidence of the people in the system. (*Kele'a* 7, 4 [Oct. 1992]: 1)

However, the same issue also printed part of a cabinet paper prepared by the deputy prime minister, the Honorable Dr. Langi Hu'akavamei-liku, which advocated that ministers should get no salary for attending sessions of the legislative assembly. Significantly, *Kele'a* headed the paper "A Good Thinking Minister," presumably because Dr. Hu'akavameiliku ended by saying, "In these trying times it is up to us to provide leadership and if necessary make the sacrifices that would maintain the good image of the Monarchy and benefit those whom we serve" (ibid.: 7).

MOST TONGANS still regard the royal family, nobles, and ministers of the Crown as their "chiefs." But today only a relative few of them are effective leaders. It has become increasingly difficult for people, particularly educated and successful middle-class commoners, to respect the actions and character of some privileged individuals. At the same time, many of the traditional roles are seeming less relevant in a national context in which the achievement of moneyed wealth and business success is becoming more important. Unless the nobles carve out niches for themselves in the private sector, particularly the commercial world, and demonstrate their modern relevance and integrity, they could well find their functions increasingly reduced to ritual and ceremonial spheres.

It will not happen in the immediate future, however. Commoners have only partly stepped into roles left vacant by the removal of older notions of chiefliness and by the unwillingness or inability of most modern nobles to provide effective leadership. Church leaders may be regarded in certain contexts as chiefs, as are ministers of the Crown, several of whom are nobles, in matters of state bureaucracy. Local government officers in some cases have become more effective village leaders than are the titular heads, the estate holders of the village. Notable figures in education, commerce, politics, church, and government bureaucracies increasingly step into the power vacuum that is created when traditional authority figures abnegate their roles and fail to provide care and guidance. The position of commoners who take on leadership roles is ambiguous, however, and fraught with the possibility that they are "getting above their station" (*fie 'eiki*) because of their personal lack of traditionally legitimated authority.

The activities of the "influentials" in Tonga suggest the degree of intellectual ferment that is there at present. The proreform debate, which was strongly middle class in its genesis, is gradually filtering to other strata of the society by means of both mass media and personal appeals of the reformers, but it is by no means as intense as it was in the early 1990s, nor as focused on issues of democracy as understood in the West. Pohiva remains strongly outspoken, but the views of the other People's Representatives in Parliament are more moderate.

The overall message of the reformers seems clear: if the abuses of power are halted, the Tongan people will be glad to continue to honor those they believe should lead the nation. At the same time, they resent the curbs that are placed on newer activities and on the people these activities bring to the fore. The cultural entrepreneurs—business leaders, farmers, educationalists, and churchmen, as well as the People's Representatives in Parliament who favor reform—do not want to replace their unique system; they want only to be able to trust and respect it.

The Kingly–Populist Divergence in Tongan and Western Samoan Chiefly Systems

ROBERT W. FRANCO

PRIOR TO 1800, the chiefly systems of western Samoa and Tonga branched out from four and three divine lines, respectively. Since the mid-nineteenth century and sustained European intrusion into western Polynesian politics, the western Samoan chiefly *matai* system has maintained hierarchical connections to four paramount titles (the *papa* titles), while designating authority (*pule*) to an increasingly wider range of chiefs who reside within and outside of Western Samoa (western Samoa is a geographic term, whereas Western Samoa refers to the independent nation). In Tonga, over this same period, the three paramount lines have been merged into one monarchical line in the person of King George Tāufaʻāhau Tupou IV; an elite group of chiefs has been elevated to noble status, and a vast number of middle- and lower-level chiefs have been relegated to nearly unmarked status within and outside of Tonga.

In the process of European colonialism and modern integration into a global system, the chiefly systems of Western Samoa and Tonga have diverged significantly. Since Western Samoa's independence in 1962, the *matai* system has become more "populist," providing access to *pule* for a greater number of individuals, mostly males. Tonga's chiefly system has become "kingly," allowing for the centralization of power in a monarchy and a body of nobles who head the modern nation of the Kingdom of Tonga (after Marcus 1989).

This chapter has two major objectives. First, I shall describe the local and regional quality of the chiefly systems of western Samoa and Tonga prior to European contact, the state of these systems at independence, and the global factors that influence these systems today. To meet this objective I will rely heavily on the works of Tongan scholar Sione Lātūkefu, especially his *Church and State in Tonga* (1974), and Samoan scholar Malama Meleisea and his *The Making of Modern Samoa* (1987).

Second, I shall discuss the impact of the kingly–populist divergence for Samoan and Tongan overseas communities. This divergence, combined with the exigencies of postcolonial immigration policy, causes distinctly different outcomes in terms of the strength and complexity of connections to the home islands. In addition, it results in two different bases for reckoning and perpetuating cultural identity in the overseas communities. This analysis is based on fieldwork in Samoa and Tonga, two decades of working with Samoan and Tongan communities in California and Hawai'i, and collaboration with researchers in Australia and New Zealand.

A Pre-European Context: Genealogical Connections in a Regional System

Hundreds of legends and proverbs record marriages and the chiefly lines of Samoa, Tonga, and Fiji previous to 1800. For example, Salamasina, the first Samoan to hold all four paramount (*papa*) titles, was the daughter of Vaetofaiga, who married the Tu'i Tonga (*Tu'i* connotes a kingly status in western Polynesia). A high-ranking title, Tonumaipe'a, was brought to Samoa from Tonga by Fa'asega, whose Samoan mother married Tu'i Tonga Niumatou (Meleisea and Schoeffel Meleisea 1987:41). In general, when looking at the three royal Tongan lines, the Tu'i Tonga was more strongly connected to the Tu'i Manu'a family of eastern Samoa, while the Tu'i Ha'atakalaua and Tu'i Kanokupolu lines had stronger marriage alliances with Upolu chiefs.

Meleisea and Schoeffel Meleisea (1987) list ten legendary connections between Samoa and Tonga, and another ten between Fiji and Samoa. Kaeppler (1978) also delineates the political and economic basis in the marriage triangle of Fiji, Samoa, and Tonga. She concludes that Samoa primarily gave wives and Fiji mainly gave husbands to Tonga.

In the late eighteenth century and through most of the nineteenth century, the Samoan and Tongan chiefly systems were linked by marriage. Other factors, such as Methodist missionary activities and the "alleged" imperialism of Tongan King Tāufa'āhau George Tupou I also connected the two political systems in the late nineteenth century (Campbell 1990; Gunson 1990).

Kingly Chieftainship in Tonga

In 1820, Tāufaʻāhau George Tupou, eager to reunite Tonga after a forty-year period of civil war, ascended from a small disputed inheritance in central Haʻapai. He conquered all of Haʻapai in 1826 and secured the inheritance of Vavaʻu in 1833. In 1839, Tupou promulgated the Vavaʻu Code, which took a "bold step . . . toward limiting the power of the chiefs" (Lātūkefu 1974:122).

In 1845, Tāufaʻāhau inherited the Tuʻi Kanokupolu title, gained control of Tongatapu, and proclaimed himself king. Seventeen years later, with the Emancipation Edict of 1862, it was enacted that "all chiefs and people are to all intents and purposes set at liberty from serfdom; and all vassalage, from the institution of this law; and it shall not be lawful for any chief or person, to seize, or take by force, or beg authoritatively, in Tonga fashion, any thing from any one" (clause 34.2; see Lātūkefu 1974:173).

While pursuing these domestic policies, Tupou I remained active in regional politics. Genealogical considerations and Methodist missionaries engaged him in Samoan politics, while "alleged imperialism" occupied his relations with Fiji (Campbell 1990; Gunson 1990). In the 1850s and 1860s, Tupou was implicated in manuevers with his cousin Maʻafu to gain control of eastern Fiji from Cakobau, a powerful ruling chief who claimed dominion over all of Fiji. Cakobau wrote a letter to Tupou suggesting that he (Cakobau) be allowed to rule in Fiji, and that Tupou be content to rule Tonga. To this letter George Tupou I replied: "You say that I am to govern Tonga—and you will govern Fiji. What Fiji is it that you speak of? Do you rule in Thakaundrovy? Do you rule over the Windward Islands? Do you rule at Mathauta? Or do you rule at Rewa? And as it regards Bau, that you have given to Britain. So what Fiji is it that you govern?" (Campbell 1990:166).

The Vavaʻu Code and the 1862 Emancipation Edict served to level the power of chiefs, and the constitution of 1875 served to elevate the Tāufaʻāhau line to monarchy. The constitution asserted the primacy of hereditary principles of title investiture within the monarchy and throughout the entire country. According to Lātūkefu (1974:210), by creating a hereditary law of succession, King Tāufaʻāhau George Tupou I was able to avoid the conflicts between factions with which Samoa was beseiged for several years. This warfare involved two rival Malietoa factions.

The constitution also produced a new, elevated level of hereditary chiefs who would be called "nobles." These nobles were chosen based on the numerical strength of their supporters, and were given tracts of land to be their hereditary estates (tofiʻa).

Working with his primary British advisor, Shirley Baker, Tupou set out to model his kingdom after Great Britain. He appointed thirty traditional chiefs as hereditary landed nobles, as well as six ceremonial attendants (matāpule), who were also given hereditary estates. These appointments had the effect of lowering and leveling all the mid-level chiefs, creating what Marcus (1989:203) has called a "submerged aristocracy" existing "in the shadows of the official chiefly establishment."

In 1918, Queen Sālote, as Tupou III, merged the vestiges (the last Tuʻi Tonga had died in 1865) of the three royal lines in her marriage. Soon thereafter she set out to create Tonga's official historical genealogy. Marcus relates (ibid.:201–2): "Salote also cultivated a politics of kinship and arranged marriages through which she upgraded the status of selected titleholders by linking them to the royal line of one of its collaterals . . . under Salote, the official chiefly system reached a pinnacle of mystification during recent times."

George Tāufaʻāhau Tupou IV succeeded Queen Sālote in 1965, and Tonga celebrated its full independence on June 4, 1970. For the last twenty-five years, Tonga has been opened to diffuse modernizing influences, and newly formed Tongan immigrant communities in New Zealand and the United States have been directing substantial monetary remittances around the king and nobles directly to commoner kinsmen at home.

Throughout the 1980–95 period, Tongan immigration accelerated, with new and larger communities forming in Australia, New Zealand, American Samoa, and the United States. Remittances remain significant in Tonga's balance of trade, and attempts by the king and his nobles to gain greater access to these resources have been resisted by Tongans overseas.

Populist Chieftainship in Western Samoa

A Samoan proverb, E tala tau Toga ae tala tofi Samoa, relates that Tongan stories are about warfare, while Samoan stories are about divisions (Meleisea and Schoeffel Meleisea 1987:29). Another proverb states O Samoa ua taʻoto, a o se iʻa mai moana aua o le iʻa Samoa ua uma ona ʻaisa, meaning Samoa is like an ocean fish cut into sections (ibid.:29). According to one account, the island of Upolu was divided by Pili, son of the sky god, Tagaloa-a-lagi, among his children, with further divisions recognized within Aʻana, Atua, Tuamasaga, and Savaiʻi. The Samoan emphasis on divisions requires an explicit recognition of multiple versions, and what follows is a simplified and contested account.

Samoan oral traditions and genealogy suggest a centralization of political authority around the sixteenth century, with power shifting from Manu'a in the east to Upolu and Savai'i in the west (ibid.: 3 1 – 3 2). About this time, two brothers, Tuna and Fata, descended in the junior lines from the Pili, drove the Tongans from Samoa. The Tongan chief's last words as he hastily escaped the onslaught were "Malietoa, malie tau," meaning "Fair warrior, fairly won." This exclamation resulted in the creation of a new high title, Malietoa, from which all Malietoa-related titles are descended. These Malietoa titles thus trace their origin to the service of outwarring the warrior Tongans. By contrast, the two senior lines descended from Pili were *Tu'i*, that is, kingly by virtue of their ability to trace their descent through Pili to the sky god, Tagaloa-a-lagi.

The descendants of Malietoa intermarried with the sacred chiefs, Tonumaipe'a, Tuia'ana, Tuiatua, and Tui Tonga (ibid.: 32), and Salamasina became the heir of all four *papa* lines—Gato'aitele, Tamasoali'i, Tuia'ana, and Tuiatua. During the time of Salamasina, the famous orator groups Tumua and Pule took over the decision-making role in major title succession. For example, Tumua orators, resident in Leulumoega (A'ana district) and Lufulufi (Tuamasaga district), bestowed the Tamasoali'i and Gato'aitele titles. Other orator groups throughout Samoa confer *ao* titles, which "stand at the top of a large 'family tree' or genealogy as the senior title . . . these high titles and the orator groups are like a fishing net, the strings of which link together all the families, the villages, and the districts of Samoa" (ibid.).

From the 1860s onward, representatives of British, German, and American governments struggled mightily to understand the Samoan chiefly system. They searched in vain for a political center, with each district having different high titled chiefs. During the first half of the twentieth century, while the country was under German and then New Zealand administration, the four *papa* lines continued to have the greatest *pule* in Samoan politics. In the period immediately following World War II, Samoan leaders were outraged to discover that Western Samoa had been placed under United Nations trusteeship, and they moved to establish self-government based on Samoan traditions (*aganu'u a Samoa*) and the Samoan way (*fa'a Samoa*).

As Western Samoa moved closer to independence, census figures indicated that almost "90 percent of the population was living according to *fa'a Samoa*, under the leadership of a *matai* (Meleisea 1987: 212). At independence, the Tu'i lines—that is, the A'ana and Atua chiefs—were headed by

Tamasese Mea'ole and Tuimaleali'ifano. The Malietoa lines of Tuamasaga district and Savai'i were headed by Malietoa Tanumafili II and Fiame Mata'afa. Tamasese and Malietoa were named joint heads of state, recognizing their virtual equivalence, while Mata'afa became prime minister.

The Western Samoan constitution went into effect on January 1, 1962, and Meleisea observes:

> The Constitution provided something for everyone: a matai franchise and traditional land tenure for the traditionalist; and parliamentary democracy . . . for the modernist. It gave Samoa a form of government which assumed that traditionalist institutions based on hierarchies governed by collective personal and family loyalties could live side by side with a legal system based upon a set of abstract principles of justice whose primary premise was the rights of the individual. The framers of this dual system were clearly of the opinion . . . that traditional institutions would gradually and gently die in the face of progress. (Ibid.: 211–12)

The constitution allowed for *matai*-only franchise and *matai*-only representation in the Parliament. By the late 1960s, it was apparent that title holders were splitting (*vaelua*) or sharing (*nofolua*) vacant titles in order to garner votes for Parliament from these newly titled *matai*. In 1960 there were 4,954 registered titles in pre-independence Western Samoa; by 1972, the total had increased to 9,043. Some titles had been split or were shared by as many as twenty holders (see ibid.: 201, 204). In recent years, much of the political debate in Western Samoa has centered on the issue of *matai*-only franchise, which many felt was primarily responsible for the continuing proliferation of titles up until 1988.

Meleisea argues that title creation and title splitting

> threaten the very foundations of fa'a Samoa . . . in two ways. The first is the obvious devaluation in prestige suffered by a title with multiple incumbents . . . the second threat is far more serious. . . . Where a single title, with a single estate of land appurtenant to it is held by a number of incumbents (in some cases over twenty) the probability of endless contests in the Courts as to which incumbent has *pule* (authority) over the estate is very real . . . increasingly large areas of land remain the subject of controversy, with access and use rights to it the subject of dispute between numbers of *'aiga* (families). (Ibid.: 234)

Aiono Fa'anafi Le Tagaloa has been one of the staunchest supporters of the *fa'amatai* (matai system) during these debates and the plebiscite that resulted in universal suffrage in Western Samoa in 1990. She argues (1992: 130–31):

> The proliferation of *matai* is not degrading to the *fa'amatai*. Rather, it could be seen as the Samoan culture's special reaction to the imposition of the European decision-making process of balloting, on its consultative process of *soalapule*. . . . The fa'amatai culture is a perfect and logical manifestation of the will and author-

ity of the people. In that respect, the *fa'amatai* is a truly democratic system of government.

Aiono argues convincingly that the *matai* system has been influenced by global pressures acting upon the dualities within the national constitution. But the global system has been influencing the *matai* system in other ways as well. Many *matai* residing in New Zealand and the United States return to their title villages whenever significant decisions need to be made. In addition, many *matai*, with varying degrees of success, attempt to assert political leadership in overseas communities. Further, many *matai*, both in Western Samoa and abroad, are very active in initiating, controlling, and distributing remittance resources. As Meleisea notes (1987:203), "Emigrant *matai* are at least notionally heads of *'aiga* [extended families] in Samoa (and overseas), and even though their role in Samoa may be a token one, the recognition of their titles is considered both a reward (or an incentive) for the financial contributions they are expected to make."

Samoan and Tongan Overseas Communities

By 1995, after nearly half a century of global migration and circulation, the *fa'a Samoa* connected families in Western and American Samoa to well-established overseas communities in Australia, New Zealand, Hawai'i, and the United States mainland. At least 325,000 Samoans reside in all these locales, with about half of this movement-system population residing in Western Samoa.

Each of these Samoan communities has a different character: Western Samoa is a traditional cultural and political center. American Samoa is also a cultural center as well as the dynamic center of the overall network. The most established and visible Samoan overseas community is in New Zealand. The Samoan community in Hawai'i is well into its third generation of hosting eastbound and westbound visiting groups (*malaga*). The Californian Samoan community is growing rapidly and is politically mobilized. Most Samoans in Australia spent some time in New Zealand before taking their next trans-Tasman step to Sydney.

The Sydney to Samoa to San Francisco movement system, although attenuated, is held together by frequent visiting of kin-, church-, and sports-sponsored *malaga*, and resilient cultural values such as *fa'alavelave* (mutual support in times of need), *fesoasoani* (helping out to meet temporary resource shortfalls), and *tautua* (service to the family and chiefs). (For greater elaboration of these cultural connections, see Franco 1987, 1991, 1993.)

Historical connections, emerging from Samoa's colonial experience, also contribute to international network formation and maintenance. In 1899, the Treaty of Berlin, signed by American, German, and British representatives, imposed a political boundary between eastern Samoa (primarily the islands in the Manu'a group and Tutuila) and western Samoa (primarily the islands of Savai'i, Upolu, Manono, and Apolima). Separate deeds of cession for Tutuila in 1900 and Manu'a in 1904 established the Territory of American Samoa. Western Samoa was a German territory from 1900 to 1914, and a New Zealand territory from 1914 through 1961.

American Samoans began their major movements away from home in 1951, after the closing of the World War II military base at Pago Pago. Today, American Samoa is the only American territory designated "unincorporated and unorganized." The territory stands on the utmost periphery of the American political system. However, as American nationals, American Samoans can move freely without immigration restriction into and back from the fifty states.

Western Samoans also have relatively good external movement options. New Zealand, recognizing, at least in part, its continued responsibility for the economic development of its former territory, has provided preferential labor-market access to Western Samoans, through the Treaty of Friendship signed in August 1962. Today, a large number of American and Western Samoans migrate and circulate in a relatively free and open manner.

As mentioned earlier, Samoan *matai* residing overseas frequently return home to participate in important village discussions. But Samoan communities are connected to the matai system at home in other ways as well. In Western Samoa, the *papa* and *ao* titles remain at the top of a historically rich and complex status hierarchy. Near the broad base of this hierarchy are titles that have been divided (shared and split) many times, and these lower-ranking titles provide the initial point on the path (*ala*) for moving up the hierarchy. Samoans overseas often perceive their opportunities for moving up in the traditional chiefly hierarchy as greater than their opportunities for moving up in the new host societies. Thus, their remitting remains a form of service to their chiefs and families, and this service is central to their cultural identity as a Samoan, rather than as an American or a New Zealander.

The Samoan proverb *'O le ala i le pule le tautua*, meaning that the route to authority is through service, explicitly links service and authority. Many Samoan men who serve their families and chiefs well over the course of their working career expect eventually to become *matai*, and Samoans overseas in the United States clearly see their substantial remitting as a form of *tautua* (see Franco 1991). Some overseas Samoans continue to remit because they think a chiefly title awaits them due to their years of long-distance *tautua*.

Meleisea, in his analysis of Samoan remitting from New Zealand, arrives at a similar conclusion (1991:1–6):

Samoans migrants tend to remit money for two purposes; the first applies to those whose family assisted the individual to migrate to earn money to fulfill an agreed upon goal. . . . The second type of obligation is to send money as needed in order to support the public financial obligations of the the family and its *matai*. . . . Both these forms of obligation are referred to as *tautua*. . . . *Tautua* is one of the most important criteria taken account of when choosing a *matai* to head an extended family . . . perhaps most migrants want to retire in Samoa in order to be with their families and hopefully as a recognition of their *tautua* from New Zealand, have a title conferred on them and settle down for the rest of their days.

Leulu Felise Vaʻa develops a similar argument concerning the connections between family members and *matai* in Western Samoa and their overseas kin (1993:351): "Samoan migrants are unlike others because migration is not seen as the cutting of family ties but as one means of helping the family. Even though they may be living in New Zealand, USA, Australia or elsewhere, Samoan migrants retain their rights to family lands and titles back home. Remittances are a means of maintaining and enforcing those ties."

It is important to bear in mind Meleisea's poignant remarks in the previous section concerning title proliferation in Western Samoa and related land disputes, which often result in land not being used productively by anyone. The aspirations of the long-distance remitter are not always met. In the future, it is likely that the number of land and title disputes will increase, unless, of course, more Samoans begin to perceive better opportunities for upward mobility and comfortable retirement in the new host societies. Meleisea is rightfully concerned that land and title disputes may become "the legacy of the century" after independence (1987:234). Samoans overseas with *matai* titles must frequently return home to argue their side of a case within the village council and perhaps before the National Land and Titles Court. It is difficult to go home so often, for such long periods of time, and still maintain a career promising upward mobility and a comfortable retirement in the new host society. A Hawaiʻi-based *matai* discussed how he stays connected to political developments in Western Samoa: "I have to take at least two trips a year to Samoa for the church and for the *faʻalavelave*. I have to maintain a good attendance record, and then I have to make arrangements with my employer. Many other *matai* here also have to return to Samoa frequently for *faʻalavelave*. They have difficulty balancing the *faʻa Samoa* and the requirements of work here" (Franco 1991:341). These *matai* are circulating between two worlds, wondering where they will spend the rest of their days.

In creating this international movement-system, Samoans have been able to move through rather permeable national borders. By contrast, for Tongans the borders have been far more restrictive. The Kingdom of Tonga, due to the strategies of King Tāufa'āhau George Tupou I, was never formally colonized by a Western power, and this history of political independence has resulted in Tongans having no preferential immigration treatment from New Zealand, Australia, or the United States. Still, Tongans have also been moving away from their home islands of Vava'u, Ha'apai, and Tongatapu since the early 1950s. Although the islands of Tonga did not provide a major staging base during World War II, many Tongans experienced wage labor for the first time during the war, and this contributed to their desire and ability to move overseas.

In the fifty years of Tongan overseas movement, Tongans have also established communities from Sydney to San Francisco. At least 134,000 Tongans reside in Australia, New Zealand, Tonga, American Samoa, Hawai'i, and the mainland United States. Most of Tongan emigration is voluntary. However, relative to Samoan movements, a much higher proportion of Tongan return migration is involuntary, coming in the form of deportation from the United States, New Zealand, and Australia.

Enclaves of Mormon Tongans can be found along the "Tongan corridor" from Liahona in Tonga to Australia, New Zealand, Hawai'i, California, and Utah. Within Tonga, total membership in the Mormon Church is greater than 30,000—approximately 30 percent of the national population. Nearly 10,000 Tongan Mormons live in the United States (Stanton 1993:32). As much as 25 percent of the overall Tongan movement-system population may belong to the Mormon Church. Compared to the Samoan case, Mormonism plays a greater role for Tongans in international network formation, in part because this is the one "corridor" available to them.

Tongans continue to remit substantial sums of money home, but these remittances are kept distinct from the kingly–noble political system. Unlike Samoans viewing their populist *matai* system, Tongans do not see the kingly–noble system connecting them to resources, prestige, and a comfortable retirement in the homeland.

Tongan commoners at home and abroad clearly perceive increasing social distance between themselves and the kings and nobles. 'Amanaki Talahi in his concise biography entitled *His Majesty Tāufa'āhau Tupou IV of the Kingdom of Tonga* (1989) contrasts commoner and noble status within Tonga:

How is the word commoner to be defined? In Tonga, it means an ordinary person who is at the base of the social hierarchical pyramid of the populace. He or she has no "chiefly blood" and is not even related to the nobility. The male commoner may be installed by a noble to become "talking chief," in other words a puppet of the noble. He would carry out orders from the noble. This is the closest relationship that a commoner can get into with the nobility, in social and political as well as economic affairs. (Ibid.: 10)

Two poems by Konai Helu-Thaman (1974) provide a stark contrast between the status of a commoner abroad and a noble at home in Tonga:

They Won't Leave

I am sad just thinking
About my fellow countrymen
On the run again
Packed like sardines
Into a one-room apartment
Eating fish heads
And left-overs from plush hotels
Where they wash dishes
In their spare time.
Second class citizens
Their relatives are:
Smoking cheap cigarettes
Bleeding from drunk-inflicted wounds
Hiding behind mould overcoats
Ready to marry anybody before their visas expire;
Get a green card
Then divorce the wife
For incompatibility.

My Sister

My sister is married
To a noble's son;
He has lots of land
And a big black car;
She is getting a washing machine
An electric egg-beater
And a Kelvinator refrigerator.
But she also wants
A son and three daughters
And lots of invitations to government functions,
As well as a fifty-foot tapa
To pile on top of her bed:
My sister expects too much.

Both 'Amanaki and Helu-Thaman allude to the significance of known and perpetuated status. 'Amanaki refers directly to "chiefly blood" and its importance in determining noble status. Helu-Thaman presents a sister married to a noble's son, a known heir to noble status. She also presents the sister's desire to have a son, a known heir to noble status.

In an article in the prodemocracy journal *Matangi Tonga*, Epeli Hau-'ofa remarks: "Tupou I was not the heir, but he proved himself through conquest that he had the leadership quality, and so he became Tui Kanok-upolu. But, unfortunately, when he came to power he introduced heredi-tary titles which put an end to competition, the method which had en-abled him to become king" (Hau'ofa 1992:12). Today in Tonga, this quality of known and perpetuated status stands in clear contrast to the Samoan focus on service as the route to authority. Where Tonga today has a known and perpetuated hierarchy, with the king and nobles at the apex, and commoners, at home and abroad, across a very broad base, Samoans, at home and abroad, are serving, competing, and disputing to gain a foot-hold within and move up the status hierarchy. Tongans abroad know their chances for moving up are greater in the new host societies; Samoans are not so sure. Their Samoa-focused "moving up" competes with their ability to move up in the new host society. In Samoan overseas communities, cultural identity is an expression of active, connected service to home and family, with a vision that this service will enable a return to Samoa in the future. In terms of cultural identity, Samoans never really left Samoa.

In Tongan overseas communities, cultural identity is rooted in the po-sition and person of the king. Even severe critics of the king "would never want to see the monarchy go" (Helu 1991a:5). Tongans remain justifiably proud of the fact that the Tongan kingdom has withstood colonial inter-ference and manipulation to survive into the late twentieth century. As Tongan scholar Futa Helu states (ibid.): "Tonga is unique in the Pacific. She is the sole survivor of the many South Seas kingdoms, all of them swallowed by the colossal wave of imperialism which swept across the Pacific in the seventeenth and eighteenth century." When King George Tāufa'āhua Tupou IV visits Tongan overseas communities, he is held in tremendous reverence, and his visits provide significant focus for Tongan cultural and national identity, and community solidarity. Cultural identity for Tongans overseas is rooted in a glorious national past, and an active and deep concern for the welfare of their families, whose status is known and perpetuated in Tonga.

FOR BOTH Samoans and Tongans overseas, then, cultural identity is shaped by their connections to and concern for kinsmen at home. How-ever, the kingly–populist divergence has resulted in a divergence in the basis for reckoning and perpetuating cultural identity. For Samoans, a far-reaching net of chiefly and familial rights and obligations, a net connecting political entities with relatively permeable borders, supports and entangles individuals in a Samoan identity shaped by the possibility of a future return home. For Tongans, their known and perpetuated commoner status makes their voluntary return unlikely. Their cultural identity is shaped more by the past, by the position and person of the king, known and perpetuated into the future.

The Tui Tonga exclaimed "Malietoa, malie tau," "Fair warrior, fairly won," and thus originated the Malietoa title, and the assertion of the active, serving, competing principle of Samoan chieftainship. In 1875, Tupou I instituted hereditary status because he was aware of the conflicts surrounding Malietoa in Samoa. He became the Tui Kanokupolu, king of the Tongan line most closely connected to Samoa. Today, the known and perpetuated status of the Tongan monarchy and nobility contrasts sharply with the populist and hierarchical vitality of the Samoan *matai* system. This kingly–populist divergence, combined with the exigencies of postcolonial immigration policy, plays a major role in shaping the cultural identity of Samoans and Tongans wherever they may reside. Today, King George Tāufa'āhau Tupou IV's eldest son, the crown prince and heir to the throne, remains unmarried. The king's second and youngest son, true to the ancient tradition of Tongan-Samoan intermarriage, has married the daughter of Western Samoan High Chief Malietoa. Thus, the youngest son's children, born of both Tonga and Samoa, are close heirs and comprise a long line of succession to the Tongan throne. What will be their legacy in the century after independence? Will the known line of succession be perpetuated?

Regionally, this marriage is a reassertion of the connections between the chiefly systems of Tonga and Samoa. However, on the evolving global stage, the kingly–populist divergence in these chiefly systems is resulting in very different connections between communities at home and abroad. Samoans abroad remain networked into the economic, political, and identity dimensions of their *matai* system. Though Tongans abroad reckon substantial cultural and national identity from the person and position of the king, they are disconnected from the political and economic opportunities available to the king and the nobles. The royal marriage is a source of tremendous cultural and regional identity for Samoans and Tongans, though its economic and political manifestations remain to be seen.

The Reemergence of Maori Chiefs

"Devolution" as a Strategy
to Maintain Tribal Authority

TOON VAN MEIJL

IN THE COURSE of colonial history, the New Zealand Maori people have been encapsulated in a liberal-democratic nation-state, which has increasingly assumed the ultimate control of their lives. Although the Maori people have consistently aspired to seek redress of their historic grievances, the most urgent one of which concerns the loss of sovereignty, the intensity of their political ambitions has fluctuated periodically. At present, the Maori demand for self-determination is stronger than ever before.

The contemporary revival of Maori aspirations to political, economic, and cultural autonomy within the New Zealand nation-state emerged approximately twenty-five years ago. Initially it was inspired by the black American civil-rights movement. The Maori considered the black American goal of "liberty" to resemble their claims on self-determination. Interestingly, however, the Maori, as well as other Fourth World peoples facing foreign majorities on their own lands, not only reinforced their political objectives under the impact of the black movement in the United States, but also adopted the strategy of politicizing culture from the black American minority. The maxim "Black is Beautiful" echoes among Native Americans, Australian Aborigines, and New Zealand Maori in terms of a revival of traditional culture.

Not surprisingly, traditional culture is invariably revalued in support of demands for self-determination. In New Zealand, for example, the Maori are compelled to justify their pursuit of sovereignty in a culturally specific manner because of their encapsulation within the modern nation-state. Since the sharing of a common colonial past plays an important role in uniting Maori tribes vis-à-vis their European counterparts, the desire to manage and control their own society is often validated by means of arguments couched in terms of traditional culture. Thus, Maori culture and its traditional customs have become political symbols substantiating the demand for self-determination within the New Zealand nation-state (Van Meijl 1990; Sissons 1993).

The political motivation of the reinterpretation, if not "reinvention," of culture and tradition influences the way traditional culture is shaped and reshaped. Maori traditions are reified and essentialized, while, paradoxically, their objectification and reconstitution take place principally in opposition to a stereotypical representation of European values, largely because a major goal of the discourse of tradition is to counter European domination.

In this chapter, I illustrate this proposition by discussing recent attempts at rehabilitating the traditional tribal organization of Maori society. I shall demonstrate that the model for the contemporary reorganization of Maori tribes is based on a simplified inversion of European forms of hierarchy. In addition, I argue that the current revitalization of Maori tribes has effectively been initiated by paramount chiefs who aim at reinforcing their traditional authority, among other things, by attempting to regain control of the many Maori people living in urban environments. I elaborate this argument by reviewing the policy of devolution of the Department of Maori Affairs to tribal authorities, which was introduced by the Labour governments in the late 1980s. In spite of widespread disapproval of this policy by large sections of the Maori population, who dreaded the disestablishment of the Department of Maori Affairs, often considered the only buoy for Maori people in the rough waters of modern New Zealand society, the government policy of devolution was supported by most Maori paramount chiefs, who appreciated it as an opportunity to strengthen and extend their tribal authority. To clarify my analysis of the contemporary situation, however, I begin with a brief historical introduction to the sociopolitical organization of traditional Maori society.

The Tribal Organization of Maori Society

The sociopolitical organization of precolonial Maori society was arranged along the corresponding dimensions of kinship and chieftainship (Van Meijl 1995a: 306–8).[1] The social organization of pre-European Maori society was largely based on kinship, and its root principle was descent from (a) common ancestor(s). The dimension of kinship, however, was intimately connected with the dimension of chieftainship. The position of chiefs in the hierarchical order of political organization corresponded to the structure of kinship groupings.

The basic unit of Maori society was the "subtribe" or *hapuu*, a group of kin that occupied a common territory and defined itself by descent from an apical, often eponymous ancestor. Subtribes, in turn, were made up of several extended families or *whaanau*, which ranged through three or four generations and usually consisted of a man, his wife, their children, and often grandchildren.

As several extended families constituted a subtribe, several subtribes made up a group linked together by descent from a relatively remote founder-ancestor. Groups at this level were called *iwi*, a term that nowadays is usually translated as "tribe." The concept of tribe is problematic, however, because it suggests a coherence that probably exceeded the affinal ties within *iwi* (Metge 1986:37). The composition of tribes was not only rather disjunct but also flexible, and as corporate groups *iwi* might well be a postcontact development (Lian 1987:455–61; Sutton 1990: 684–87).

The highest level of the tribal organization of Maori society was formed by the *waka* or "canoe," consisting of various "tribes" that had emerged from ancestors who had reached the shores of New Zealand on the same canoe. However, no cooperative form of government existed among them. *Waka* were loosely structured confederations of tribes that might have been galvanized by postcolonial developments as well (Buck 1949:336). They shared only a slight bond of union, often more sentimental than political or economic (Firth [1929] 1959:155–56).

As mentioned above, the political position of chiefs in precolonial Maori society paralleled the hierarchical configuration of tribal groupings. Chiefs of higher rank drew together a multitude of lower-ranking chiefs and their followers. The paramount chief was the *ariki*, and in his pedigree the senior lines of all tribal genealogies converged. Hence he was recognized as the head of the tribe.[2] The chief of the subtribe, or the *rangatira*, ranked lower than the paramount chief since he descended along junior lines. The head of the extended family was the *kaumaatua* or "elder," recognized on account of his offspring as well as his age, wisdom, and life experience (Winiata 1956).

In representations of the relationship between a chief and his (rarely her) people, consultation and consensus were important principles (Douglas 1979:21). A great emphasis was placed on reciprocity as the main feature of kinship relations. For that reason, too, it can be argued that, on the one hand, the sociopolitical organization in "traditional" Maori society was hierarchical in a Dumontian sense. In contradistinction to the classic pyramidal model of a hierarchically stratified society, the sociopolitical structure of Maori society was segmented into a hierarchy of tribal groupings and chiefs, with lower-ranking units and their chiefs being encompassed at higher levels, yet retaining their independence (Walker 1987:155-56). This form of hierarchy as encompassment explains how, on the other hand, the power of chiefs was far from absolute as their structural authority was inverted in an ideology constructed by autonomous, lower-ranking groupings whose junior chiefs were aiming to balance the power of their superiors in the encompassing hierarchy. The coexistence of a hierarchical organization and an antihierarchical ideology emphasizing reciprocity between chiefs and their tribes contributed to making the power of Maori chiefs relatively limited in comparison to the absolute rule of chiefs in the highly stratified and centralized societies of Hawai'i, Tonga, and the Society Islands (cf. Sahlins 1985a). Contrary to chiefs in those other Polynesian societies, Maori chiefs had to achieve and actualize the potentiality of power ascribed to them by birth, while they were also restrained because all lower-ranking kinship groupings and their respective chiefs remained autonomous, which allowed them to upgrade their inferior position in a populist ideology, primarily constructed to balance and counter the absolutist potential in the office of paramount chiefs.[3]

Restructuring Tribal Organizations

In the 1970s the tribal organization of Maori society was formally still intact, but had little impact on social practice.[4] Dispossession of tribal lands in the course of colonial history has resulted in a situation in which most tribes continue to exist only as nominal organizations without an infrastructural foundation and concomitant influences on social classification and interaction. Accordingly, Maori chiefs were still distinguished from people of lower rank, but their chiefly titles no longer entailed any authority on matters of influence, except perhaps in the ceremonial field. The dwindling authority of Maori chiefs was, in turn, compounded by a wave of urbanization after World War II that brought about fundamental changes in modes of self-identification among the estimated 80 percent of the Maori population that is currently abiding in urban environments. Nowadays most Maori people no longer identify themselves in terms of their tribal affiliation, but favor a pantribal, national identity as Maori. As a result, the influence of tribal organizations and their chiefs has been waning as well.

In the 1980s, however, both tribal organizations and chiefly authority reemerged. Tribal organizations, characterized by chiefly hierarchical mechanisms of power, have been revitalized as powerful interest groups in the political arena of New Zealand. The recent reinforcement of tribes has principally resulted from a new government policy of "devolution." In New Zealand, devolution is commonly defined as the process of identifying specific administrative functions that should be retained at the center of government, with all other functions being devolved as far as possible. Devolution is distinguished from decentralization, which involves a mere transferral of executive duties: devolution involves a transfer of decision-making power, which is constrained but not so restricted as to allow Maori tribes to make trivial choices while leaving all important decisions to the government (Hawke 1988:28). In colloquial language, devolution is often defined as "empowerment of people," or, in Maori, *he whakahoki te mana whakahaere ki te iwi* ("The return of decision-making power to the people").

While the concept of "devolution" has become incorporated in political discourse only since 1987 (see below), the idea for the empowerment of Maori tribal organizations in its most recent form dates back to at least 1982. In that year the Tainui confederation of tribes on the central North Island of New Zealand launched a comprehensive development program aimed specifically at regaining the political autonomy that they had lost in the course of colonial history.[5] The Tainui development plan was based on a proposal to use the remaining blocks of tribal land still held in communal ownership for development through corporate financial planning, investments, marketing, and training. In order to facilitate tribal planning and development, however, it was considered essential to eradicate the existing "government" structure of organization and, alternatively, to revitalize the Maori tribal structure of organization (Mahuta and Egan 1983).

The government structure of organization, embodied mainly in the Department of Maori Affairs, was argued to have been imposed from above to annihilate Maori tribal organizations. From the viewpont of the Tainui leadership, the Department of Maori Affairs had been lacking an appreciation of Maori underdevelopment since its establishment in 1840. It was argued that the department aimed solely at maintaining the Maori people in a position of dependency on a complacent bureaucracy. In contrast to the government structure of organization, streamlined from the top downward, it was claimed that Maori organizational structures are built up from the bottom. They are argued to be based on kinship rather than "governship,"[6] and they are supposed to allow people at the "flax-roots" level to retain their independence. Subtribal groupings, for example, appoint or elect representatives to organizations at the tribal level, such as Ngaa Marae Toopu ("the assembled *marae*" or "communities"), a platform of all Tainui communities (see also Van Meijl 1994:292–93).

In the course of colonial history, however, the tribal structure of organization had perforce become rather inactive. Insufficient land had remained to be cultivated, while the necessary finances for development had never been available. For that reason, it was now proposed to strengthen the traditional network and restructure it into an effective organization to implement development policies. Contrary to "government structures of organization," the Tainui organizational structure was to be streamlined from the bottom, from the *marae* communities.[7]

The Tainui confederation of tribes is made up of 120 subtribal *marae*. In the course of the 1980s these have grouped together into eleven "management committees" made up of elected representatives from the participating *marae*, and a number of subcommittees to assess needs in a specific field, such as education, health, and economic development. The management committees were supposed to create more effective cohesiveness for policy development and a greater unity for action, while each *marae* was allowed to retain its independence. It was hoped the management committees would enhance Tainui's credibility in negotiating with central and local government about a redirection of what the leadership labeled "negative funding" for the purpose of social and economic development. The concept of negative funding was based on the argument that hundreds of millions of dollars were spent on education, unemployment benefits, health care, prisons, and so forth, with little or no positive returns for the Maori people. The negative funding simply maintained bonds of dependency between the Maori people and the government, and these had to be severed in order to strengthen the Maori economic base and create permanent jobs (Van Meijl 1995b).

From the outset, the potential success of the Tainui development strategy depended on the goodwill of the New Zealand government to devolve some of its services and funds to the control of Maori tribes. The expectations, therefore, reached a high when New Zealand had a change of government in 1984. The new Labour government led by Prime Minister David Lange seemed more willing that any previous government to "fix the Maori problem."

Experiments with Devolution: "MANA" and "MACCESS"

Immediately after the elections, the new government called two summit conferences to address Maori concerns and to allow Maori people to put forward their own solutions. In October 1984 the Minister of Maori Affairs convened the Maori Economic Development Summit Conference, at which Maori tribal organizations from all over New Zealand argued for two basic principles to be accepted: Maori control of Maori resources, and Maori objectives on Maori terms. In March 1985 the Maori employment caucus set up at the 1984 conference was reconvened by the Minister of Employment during the Employment Conference. This second summit further endorsed the call from Maori tribes for control of resources and delivery through tribal authorities. The need to address Maori unemployment and achieve parity on all levels was discussed, and it was proposed to institute special employment and training programs. Two major affirmative-action programs were introduced (see Van Meijl 1995b).

In 1986 the government initiated a program called MANA Enterprises aimed at broadening the Maori economic base by the creation of new businesses and the expansion of existing ones. A special pool was created for funding small businesses to provide Maori people with more jobs through the development of viable Maori enterprises. Each tribal authority was responsible for vetting applications before they were submitted to the national Board of Maori Affairs. To acquire funding, usually at flat interest rates significantly lower than current commercial interest rates, proposals had to accord with strict guidelines.

In addition, the government created job-skill training programs. In 1987 a development scheme called ACCESS was set up to assist people who were at a disadvantage in the labor market to acquire skills to increase their chances of finding employment. The bulk of the budget for Access training programs was distributed through a general system administered by councils made up of community representatives, but part of the Access pool funds were apportioned to Maori authorities with the legal status of trust boards, incorporated societies, or charitable trusts. The training programs offered under this system were called Maori Access, or MACCESS.

Maori tribal authorities celebrated both Mana Enterprises and Maccess training programs as unprecedented experiments with devolution of government funding. Maori tribal organizations argued that for the first time in colonial history, they were allowed to administer substantial budgets and to manage significant projects, all for the benefit of Maori people. The results of Mana and Maccess were, nonetheless, ambivalent. Various businesses failed due mainly to a dramatic downturn in the economy and the lack of management skills, while several enterprises did not meet the required standards of accountability for public funds. Training programs were frequently criticized for surreptitiously subsidizing unskilled labor and exploiting unemployed youth. It all provided grist to the opposition and the media, who made Mana and Maccess very controversial in New Zealand public discourse. In Maori circles, the proclaimed successes of Mana and Maccess were contested as well. In order to elaborate the critique of Mana and Maccess from within Maori communities, it is necessary to take a brief look at the implementation of the development programs in one tribal district, in this case the Tainui district.

The Implementation of MANA and MACCESS
by Tainui Tribes

The highest administrative body of the Tainui tribes is the Tainui Maori Trust Board (hereafter TMTB). The TMTB is a statutory authority established by Parliament in 1946 to administer an annual grant in lieu of claims regarding the confiscation of lands in the 1860s.[8] Since initially the grant amounted to no more than £5,000 per annum, there was little to be administered by the Tainui Trust Board in its formative years. Only since a development plan was introduced in 1983 has the TMTB been taking a more proactive role in tribal management and other issues. The overall aims and objectives of development were, however, formulated in such a way that the newly founded management committees were unable to manage with them. The development strategy was not only formulated in too abstract a manner, but, more importantly, the management committees had no resources to initiate any projects. The introductions of the Mana Enterprises loan scheme and the Maori Access Training Programs, therefore, were chiefly responsible for bringing momentum to the development process (Van Meijl 1990:100–101).

Mana and Maccess offered the TMTB and the management committees the opportunity to further the objective of human resources development. The funding that now became available enabled the board to activate the tribal organization in its restructured form as well as to establish a new administrative infrastructure. A "Development Unit" was set up specifically for the purpose of administering the Mana and Maccess programs. Interestingly, however, the management structure of the Development Unit did not correspond with the ideal of Maori forms of organization as outlined in the Tainui development plan. As a consequence, the Development Unit also failed to implement a policy on so-called Maori terms (ibid.: 106).

The structure and operation of the Development Unit departed from the Maori model of organization because it was not managed by elected representatives of the management committees. Instead, it was staffed by people who had been appointed directly by Tainui chiefs. Further, and concomitantly, the Development Unit did not restrict itself to channeling and coordinating decisions made at the level of local communities; rather, it fostered a structure of centralized control. It stipulated tough conditions for the implementation of Mana and Maccess by the management committees. In addition, the Development Unit followed strict procedures regarding the distribution of funds, which were mainly allocated on the basis of (cost-)competitiveness and standards of accountability. Thus, the Development Unit not only practiced a different policy than it preached, but also disavowed its objective of facilitating interaction within the Tainui network of tribes. After all, the principle of (cost-)competitiveness in the allocation of funds discouraged the management committees from communicating about their first experiences with the implementation of development projects with their fellow tribesmen in other regions.

For the management committees operating, managing, and administering training programs and new business enterprises, the central authority of the Development Unit was difficult to accept. The main dispute between the Development Unit and the management committees concerned the procedure of funding the community projects. The Development Unit refused to block-fund the programs and phased the remittance of the budget, or "drip-fed" the management committees. The administrators running the programs found it impossible to operate on the basis of "drip-feeding" and could not understand the Development Unit's policy in this regard, as block-funding was one of the major issues in the national debate on devolution. The TMTB was among the first to argue against "drip-feeding" by the government, yet now subjected its own management committees to that very practice.

Thus, interestingly, a parallel relationship existed between the government and the TMTB, on the one hand, and the TMTB and its management committees on the other (see Van Meijl 1994:295). The Trust Board argued for devolution of government funds and control from the center of the New Zealand administration to the tribal authorities. Ideally the Trust Board regarded itself as a mere mediator between the supposedly autonomous subtribal management committees and the government devolving the funds to the people running the projects. In practice, however, the Development Unit of the TMTB established itself as a powerful bureaucracy centralizing the decision-making regarding the implementation of Mana and Maccess programs within the Tainui area.

The question to be raised here is to what extent the Development Unit's policy of centralized control of the administration of management committees was due to the politically unfavorable climate for the inauguration of devolution to Maori tribes. After all, the opposition and large sections of the New Zealand population continuously expressed utter disapproval of the Labour government's experiments with devolution, mainly on grounds of skepticism about Maori competence to administer public funds. Was the TMTB perhaps sympathetic to those public concerns, and did the board consequently concentrate more on meeting public standards of accountability than on acknowledging each tribal management committee's autonomy?

By the same token, it might be suggested that the Development Unit's authoritarian attitude toward the management committees emanated from the fact that the TMTB was still obligated to account for all details of its operation to the government. The Development Unit had yet to establish a reputation as a professional and reliable development agency. For that reason, too, it was often argued that Tainui authorities were given little opportunity to develop a "tribal" system of management. Was it a result, then, of the board's continuing dependence on the government that it willy-nilly adopted many government rules in its management of the subtribal committees?

In this context it must also be noted that the management committees were juridically answerable to the TMTB, since the legal conditions of devolution enabled only statutory authorities to apply for Mana and Maccess funding, and the Trust Board was the only statutory authority in the Tainui area. Internally the legally imposed hierarchy between the TMTB and the management committees was "officially" overturned by the setting up of a committee, with a substantial representation of community members, which under tribal law was authorized to make all decisions about the spending of the budget of the Development Unit. In practice, nonetheless, the managers of the Development Unit were unmistakably the most influential administrators in the Tainui area, allowing the Mana and Maccess committee only to endorse their policies in retrospect. As a result, many people involved in the operation of management committees did not really appreciate the advantages of the first experiments with the devolution of government funds and decision-making power to tribal authorities. In their opinion, devolution had not entailed the empowerment promised to Maori communities. The *marae* and their management committees were certainly enjoying some positive results of devolution, particularly with the Maccess training programs, but they resented the power and control of the Development Unit and its tough administrative procedures before releasing funding.

Not surprisingly, the criticism leveled at the management of the Development Unit centralizing control of Mana and Maccess also reflected on the new administrative structure of the Tainui tribes, which were supposed to be governed not from the "top down," but from the "bottom up":

I have my doubts about the Tainui tribal structure. I don't see that it is specifically Tainui, not even that it is specifically Maori. I think it is just as bureaucratic as any

European structure. From my point of view it is an ordinary replication of government structures. Only the power center has moved from Wellington [the capital
city of New Zealand] to Ngaruawahia [the town where the tribal headquarters of
the Tainui people are located]. (Author interview with management committee
member, Oct. 29, 1987)

In this quotation, the reference to Ngaruawahia provides an important
lead to answering the question of why the reception of Mana and Maccess
by those involved in the management committees was rather ambiguous.
For the people affected by the implementation of devolution most con-
cretely, the introduction of Mana and Maccess programs had induced no
fundamental changes. Many therefore expressed disappointment that the
people at the grass-roots level were barely benefiting from devolution. The
disillusion of devolution was compounded by the fact that it had resulted
in a situation in which the lower levels of the Tainui tribal alliance were
fighting the chiefly authorities at the highest level of the confederation.
Thus, devolution had shifted the battlefield from government authorities to chiefly authorities. Indeed, the experiments with devolution were
largely managed and monitored by a chiefly elite and their close compan-
ions from a central office near the tribal headquarters, which reinforced
the "traditional" division between "aristocrats" of chiefly descent and
"commoners" of lower rank.[9]
    While in the course of colonial history the influence of tribal chiefs on
the daily lives of their tribesmen of junior descent had been devalued, devolution now provided Maori chiefs with the (partly financial) means
again to support their traditional positions of prestige. The statement by
the management committee member quoted above illustrates that proposition. His remark about the transfer of power from Wellington to Ngaruawahia alluded to the increased authority of chiefs as a result of devolution. Thus, internally the conflict about the distribution of Mana and
Maccess funding was clearly regarded as resulting from a reinforcement
of chiefly authority. Was the drive for devolution of government funding
toward tribal authorities perhaps a political strategy of the chiefly elite to
regain some of their waning influence? Before this question can be addressed, the progression of devolution after the introduction of Mana and
Maccess must be outlined.

Devolution of the Department of Maori Affairs

Until the Labour government was elected to office in 1984, New Zealand
was arguably the country with the most centralized administration and
the most regulated economy in the Western world. As part of the austerity

programs that the Lange government implemented for economic reasons in the 1980s, several government departments were forced to review the organization of their administration, which resulted in a decentralization, and to some extent a devolution of central government functions regarding health, social welfare, education, justice, labor, and housing, as well as Maori Affairs.[10]

After the introduction of Mana and Maccess, the new Labour government set up the Devolution Implementation Committee on Maori Development to examine the possibility of a progressive transfer of responsibilities from the Department of Maori Affairs to tribal authorities. In addition, it was to make recommendations on how to upgrade the tribal capacity to devise and operate government programs across the entire range of community needs.

Interestingly, a prominent Tainui leader was appointed chairman of the committee. He was a direct relation of the Maori queen, the highest chieftainess of all the Tainui people. The Maori queen is of the fifth generation descending from the Tainui chief Potatau Te Wherowhero, who in 1858 was elected from a number of paramount chiefs to be crowned first Maori king. Thus, a Maori monarchy was established by various Maori tribes to unite themselves into a political confederation under the authority of one leader, to be labeled "king." The main purpose of the Maori King Movement was to secure the land and Maori sovereignty against the increasing number of British settlers in New Zealand (cf. Van Meijl 1993).

Potatau was the paramount chief of the Waikato Maori, who were living in the valley of the Waikato River, which constituted an important artery connecting all Tainui tribes. Potatau was crowned as first Maori king because his tribe was in control of the prosperous trade with European colonists. For that same reason, however, the colonial government had great difficulties accepting the Maori King Movement. It considered the coronation of Potatau a reinforcement of his strategic position of influence. In order to undermine the trade monopoly of the Waikato Maori, therefore, the British governor of New Zealand was commissioned to terminate the empire of the Maori king. After a few years the conflict resulted in a war about the control of the political and economic situation, at the end of which the British proclaimed victory and confiscated almost all land of the Waikato Maori tribe. Since that moment the Waikato tribe, the descendants of King Potatau, have been seeking redress of the confiscations of their land. Until today (see note 8) this historic struggle for land has been largely responsible for the continuing existence of the Maori King Movement, since it has kept a strong bond of unity among the affected (sub-)tribes. A major consequence of this consistent policy for a return of the confiscated lands has been, however, that other tribes, who have been able to maintain significant sections of their land, have with-drawn their allegiance to the Maori King Movement. As a result, the sup-port of the present Maori queen is restricted to the Waikato tribe and, to a lesser extent, the associated Tainui tribes of Hauraki, Ngaati Haua, and Ngaati Maniapoto.

In view of the limited political recognition of the Maori queen, it can be argued that the ultimate aim of the contemporary development pro-gram for the Tainui people concerns not only the improvement of their socioeconomic and cultural well-being, but also the reinvestment of the office of the Maori monarchy with some real power and authority, as well as the reunion of the Tainui tribes under the authority of the Maori queen. This becomes even more apparent when it is realized that the development plan was designed by a close relation of the Maori queen. And when he launched his program "to guide the Tainui people into the twenty-first century," the dismantlement of the Department of Maori Affairs was for-mulated as the only option to stimulate and support the development pro-cess. In fact, the so-called management committees were set up in antici-pation of the devolution of the Department of Maori Affairs.

In order to effectuate the development program, the Tainui leadership approached the government as early as 1982; but until a Labour gov-ernment was elected, it received no positive response from any govern-ment department. In 1984, then, the Tainui people were pleased to see appointed a new Minister of Maori Affairs, who appeared more sympa-thetic toward the confederation's proposals. The relationship between Tainui and the Minister of Maori Affairs also improved because, coinci-dentally, the new minister was of Tainui descent. He was of the Ngaati Maniapoto tribe, and for many years he had represented in Parliament the Maori people of the Western district, including many Tainui people. For the success of the Tainui development plan, however, it was most impor-tant that the new Minister of Maori Affairs had been an advisor of the Maori queen for a long time. Now that he was appointed Minister of Maori Affairs, he, in turn, selected a close relation of the Maori queen, the brain behind the Tainui development plan, to become one of his main advisors. Thus, it cannot have been accidental that initially the Labour government at least considered adopting the Tainui proposal for the com-plete devolution of the Department of Maori Affairs. For the same reason, the close relation of the Maori queen was probably invited to chair the Devolution Implementation Committee on Maori Development, a cabi-net committee that was briefed to investigate how tribes could best be invested to deliver services of the Department of Maori Affairs to their communities.

It was not long after the Devolution Implementation Committee had been appointed that it concluded that as a government bureaucracy, the Department of Maori Affairs was incapable of dealing efficiently with Maori problems. However, rather than proposing a reconstitution of the department, the committee advocated a reallocation of all its resources to the direct control of all tribal authorities. The committee even designed a model suggesting that a proportion of 15 percent (roughly equivalent to the percentage of Maori people in New Zealand) of the budget of all government departments should be placed in Maori hands.

It goes without saying that the government was unwilling to accept advice suggesting that significant resources of mainstream government departments be placed under Maori control, particularly because the news headlines were constantly screaming about alleged mishandling of Maori development money from the Mana and Maccess schemes. The government therefore dissolved the committee barely three months after it was set up, and resumed direct responsibility for the devolution policy.

In April 1988, the government published a controversial discussion paper on the matter: *He Tirohanga Rangapu; Partnership Perspectives* (Maori Affairs Department 1988a). In this paper it was proposed to transfer the programs of the Department of Maori Affairs to other government departments before making their delivery available to tribal authorities on a contract basis. At the same time, the Department of Maori Affairs was to be replaced by a new Ministry of Maori Policy that would have a control function similar to the Treasury. This proposal differed from the Implementation Committee's model in the sense that tribal authorities would still have to go through the established bureaucracy to obtain control of the delivery of government services.

The government proposal for devolution of the Department of Maori Affairs was not well received by the bulk of the Maori population.[11] This induced the Minister of Maori Affairs to embark on a consultation tour of around fifty principal Maori *marae* in all regions of the country. The minister took great pains to explain his *Partnership Perspectives*, but the response he received was almost without exception hostile. A respected elder of the Te Arawa tribe informed the minister that his people were "weeping for the loss of our Maori Affairs." The woman speaking on behalf of the Ngati Porou tribe told the minister rather directly that her people would never accept losing the Department of Maori Affairs, whatever the reasons for its abolition might be: "No Way!!! You got a cheek!!!" The elders of the Ngaati Kahungunu tribe were also forthright in their condemnation of the minister's proposal. They argued that whatever *Partnership Perspectives* said about other government departments being capable of servicing Maori needs, the reality was different. In their view there could be no doubt that the Maori Affairs staff was best able to meet

the needs of the Maori people. In addition, they argued that the partnership proposed would most likely contain a dominant partner and a sub-
servient one, where instead it should be like a marriage, with both partners equal.[12]

The Minister of Maori Affairs not only was criticized by tribal elders
for his plan to abandon the Department of Maori Affairs, but also was
accused of enabling only tribal authorities to enter into contracts with
government departments. Since the 1930s many Maori people have mi-
grated to urban environments, and they no longer feel represented by
tribal authorities. In consequence, they claimed a proportional percentage of resources from the department in order to deliver social services to
the Maori "proletariat" living in towns and cities. Since approximately
80 percent of the Maori population is based in urban environments,
Maori organizations in cities with significant concentrations of Maori
people advocated to distribute the budget of the Department of Maori Affairs not on a tribal but on a regional basis. Their main argument to review the tribal orientation of the devolution policy was the presumption
that by acknowledging only tribal authorities and bypassing urban organizations, the government aimed at assimilating most Maori people, who
were no longer represented by tribal authorities, into the European majority of the New Zealand population.[13]

In sum, then, the Minister of Maori Affairs was given a clear indication that most Maori people could not accept the devolution policy,
mainly because the Department of Maori Affairs would be phased out,
which in urban environments in particular was widely interpreted as a
final move toward assimilation. Only a limited number of tribal groupings
applauded the opportunity that the new Ministry of Maori Policy would
offer in monitoring the operations of other government departments and
ensuring that they would deliver adequate services and sufficient funding
to Maori people. The Tainui Maori Trust Board was one of the few tribal
councils that responded positively. It commended the government's initiative to offer the preconditions necessary for its own development strategy
to succeed. At the same time, the board interpreted the government's proposal not as an economy measure, as most people did, but as a positive
gesture based on the recognition that the existing delivery system for government services had failed to fulfill Maori needs (Tainui Maori Trust
Board 1988).

The question to be raised, however, is to what extent the response of
the TMTB to the government's proposal for devolution of the Department
of Maori Affairs might be considered representative for the Tainui people.
The Trust Board's submission to the government was largely written by
Tainui chiefs and their assistants, after which it was presented to the Min-

ister of Maori Affairs before it had been endorsed by the Tainui Trust Board (cf. Van Meijl 1990: 102). The board did eventually approve of the chiefs' submission on behalf of the Tainui tribes, but decisions taken by the TMTB are, in fact, rarely representative of what Tainui people tend to think. After all, (sub-)tribal representatives on the TMTB never opposed the policies advocated by the Maori queen's representative on the board. In that sense, the TMTB was not the democratic tribal organization it pretended to be. Instead, it was more like a council that was retrospectively advised of the activities undertaken by Tainui chiefs.

In spite of the TMTB's favorable response to the government's proposal of devolution, the feelings about the policy predominating among most Tainui people did not deviate significantly from those expressed by Maori people from other tribes to the Minister of Maori Affairs on his consultation tour. In other words, anyone visiting any Tainui *marae* could not but gather the impression that most Tainui people were just as skeptical about the devolution proposal as other Maori people. The main objection also concerned the abolition of the Department of Maori Affairs, which in spite of all against it was still considered an invaluable source of support for Maori people fighting government bureaucracies. By the same token, many Tainui people were hesitant whether they were properly prepared to take over the tasks hitherto accomplished by the expert staff of the Department of Maori Affairs.

The skepticism among Tainui people at the grass-roots level about their ability to take over the tasks of the Department of Maori Affairs was no doubt confirmed and compounded by the criticism of Maori accountability expressed in the media. To reassure Tainui communities, Tainui chiefs were therefore forced to emphasize that since the setting up of the management committees, the confederation was well prepared to accept the responsibility for devolution. In order not to lose its credibility with the government, the TMTB, of course, could not argue otherwise, but what is interesting here is that it had to take pains to convince its own rank and file. The subtribal management committees were perfectly aware of the problems involved in developing an organization capable of managing and administering a few miscellaneous training programs, something they felt was hampered rather than stimulated by the Development Unit of the TMTB. I would argue, therefore, that for political reasons Tainui chiefs had to reiterate time and again that their tribes were prepared "to take up the challenge," whereas the leadership at the lower levels of the administrative structure knew that in reality they were not. In view of the opposition against devolution, as well as the incertitude and confusion about it, I shall now examine why the government proceeded with its policy and how it managed to do so.

Tribal or Regional Authorities

In November 1988, the Department of Maori Affairs released a new policy statement on devolution: *Partnership Response* (Maori Affairs Department 1988c). The main change in policy concerned a gradual phasing out of the Department of Maori Affairs, instead of its immediate abandonment. It was now proposed to restructure the department and change it into an Iwi Transition Agency to support *iwi* (tribal) authorities with the establishment of an operational base. The main thrust of the devolution policy announced in *Partnership Perspectives*, however, was maintained. Contrary to its good intentions and promises to its (Maori) electorate, the Labour government essentially opted to circumvent the criticisms of the disestablishment of the Department of Maori Affairs by the vast majority of the Maori population.

The Labour government argued that many Maori people were taking its devolution policy as a fait accompli, whereas *Partnership Perspectives* only concerned a discussion paper preceding a more definite bill still to be drawn up and introduced in the Houses of Parliament. That the government did not significantly adjust its preparations for legislation and only proposed to ease down the abolition of the Department of Maori Affairs was presupposed to make no difference. More importantly, however, the government disregarded most submissions rejecting the devolution policy, because it assumed the virulence of Maori criticisms had principally been prompted by government negligence to consult with the Maori population before announcing its policy. In Maori society, chiefs and other authorities are obligated to consult with the people whom they are supposed to represent, even though the principle of consultation is active within the context of a chiefly hierarchical organization (Van Meijl 1994).

Apart from the miscommunication between the government and the Maori people, however, there are clear indications that the Minister of Maori Affairs had been more amenable to the advice of Maori chiefs than to the submissions he received on the *marae* during his consultation tour. In spite of 700 submissions disapproving of the disestablishment of the Department of Maori Affairs, the minister was only willing to prolong temporarily the existence of a government authority dealing with Maori issues and delivering services to Maori communities. He could only get away with this uncompromising view because behind the scenes he was supported by a great number of influential paramount chiefs, who in the course of 1989 also began to speak openly against the broad lobby to discontinue the devolution of the Department of the Maori Affairs.

The Minister of Maori Affairs regularly consulted with Maori paramount chiefs about important policy issues, and occasionally he convened meetings to deliberate with them about structural policy changes. This mode of interaction between the minister's office and a representation of Maori paramount chiefs had been common practice for a long time. The devolution proposal caused this practice to be modified, however, since the minister was forced to extend his consultation of Maoridom and embark on an unprecedented tour around all principal *marae* of the country. This, in turn, inspired the ministerial advisory council of paramount chiefs to convene an independent conference in order to discuss the planned devolution of the Department of Maori Affairs. They revived a defunct Maori tradition by inviting all high-ranking chiefs by the sending of a *maanuka* ("tea-tree") stick, a pre-European way of calling chiefs together, to gather for the first national meeting of chiefs since 1935. In the press it was announced that the gathering was organized to discuss the problems facing the Maori people in the modern age (*New Zealand Herald* [Oct. 31, 1988]), but few doubted that devolution was the first item on the agenda. The very moment of convening the historic conference evidently betrayed the chiefly concern that in view of the extremely hostile reception of the devolution proposal, the minister would be persuaded to preserve the Department of Maori Affairs. This would hamper the opportunities of tribal chiefs to enhance their traditional authority. Most paramount chiefs were clearly anxious to see the devolution proposal implemented.

The influence of chiefs on the government policy of devolution became most apparent in the course of 1989, when the dismantlement of the Department of Maori Affairs was imminent and the community response to it got out of control. The government introduced the Maori Affairs Restructuring Bill, which established the Iwi Transition Agency, replacing the Department of Maori Affairs for a period of five years, after which tribal authorities were hoped to be capable of managing the programs hitherto delivered by the government department. Subsequently, the government introduced the Runanga Iwi Bill, which enabled the empowering of *iwi* (tribal) authorities to administer government programs formerly run by the Department of Maori Affairs. The latter bill aroused a discussion about what constituted a tribal authority. Which tribal or chiefly authorities should be empowered to manage and administer community development programs?

In anticipation of government legislation to enable tribal authorities to deliver social services, many Maori groups and organizations legalized their status by, for example, registering under the Charitable Trusts Act. Thus, they hoped to increase their chances of becoming recognized as a tribal authority under the forthcoming Runanga Iwi Bill. The government had indicated they would select only twelve or fifteen tribal authorities, but in approximately twelve months nearly 200 Maori organizations applied for the status of tribal authority. Among these organizations, there was a marked distinction between urban and rural groups.

In rural areas many local communities refused to surrender their autonomy to some tribal authority at a higher level of their traditional hierarchical structure and applied for legal recognition of their independence. By the same token, many tribes were reluctant to recognize supertribal authorities as the principal statutory authorities to which they would be answerable about the implementation of devolution programs. In the Tainui area, for example, the tribes of Ngaati Maniapoto and Ngaati Hauraki applied for the status of tribal authority since they did not wish to account for their operations to the TMTB, which until then was the only statutory authority in the Tainui district. Both Hauraki and Maniapoto considered this dependency on the Trust Board as highly problematic: they had no representation on the board because neither had been affected by the confiscations, and the board was initially established to administer the compensation for those (sub-)tribes whose land had been confiscated. In order to avoid legal subjection to the TMTB with respect to devolution programs, the Hauraki tribes as well as Ngaati Maniapoto went to the government to set up their own Maaori Trust Boards (cf. 1988 Maori Trust Boards Amendment Bill).

The resulting division of the Tainui tribes naturally reflected on the symbolic unity that throughout the history of the Maori King Movement was claimed to be accomplished under the banner of the Maori monarchy's flag. Although the royal family was of Waikato descent, their kinship connection with other Tainui tribes had contributed to their recognition as pantribal monarchs by tribes such as the Ngaati Maniapoto and Hauraki. However, the loss of land, which historically had provided the King Movement with the inspiration to persist, had had a more dramatic impact on the Waikato tribe than on any of the others, as the Waikato had virtually been wiped out, whereas the Hauraki and Maniapoto had scarcely been affected by the confiscations. Whether the latter, therefore, felt as closely associated with the Maori monarchy and the TMTB as was claimed by some monarchist chiefs was highly contentious.

Thus, a ramification of the devolution policy was a division of the Tainui confederation into a number of tribal authorities. Contrary to its aim of strengthening the authority of paramount chiefs, the devolution policy sparked the need to confirm by law the limited power of paramount chiefs over tribes to which they did not belong but to which they were only related. This tendency to tribal division into an unlimited number of autonomous tribal organizations was paralleled in urban environments.

In urban areas, pantribal organizations were set up in order to be able to demand a share in the devolution of the Department of Maori Affairs. Although Maori customary law prescribed tribes and their chiefs to provide hospitality to guests and even to host immigrants, Maori migrants who had moved to cities in the recent past were prepared to accept the "hospitality" and, consequently, to recognize the authority of local tribes and their chiefs only with respect to ceremonial matters, not with regard to the management and administration of government resources.[14] While local tribes in cities such as Auckland and Wellington called upon their traditional duty "to look after their guests" in order to claim responsibility for the share of devolution programs to be delivered to all Maori people in those cities, including the many Maori people, who as part of the urbanization wave, had come to live on their traditional territories, Maori migrants claimed the right to represent themselves by registering as "tribal authorities."

Interestingly, the innovative pantribal associations of Maori people in urban situations also identified their organization as "tribal" and used the traditional Maori terminology to indicate that they were, for example, Ngaati Poneke, literally "the descendants of Wellington." Paradoxically, however, the main reason why pantribal organizations set up their own "tribal authorities" in New Zealand cities and some towns proceeded from their strong criticism of the tribal basis of the devolution policy. Most people living in urban environments no longer wished to be represented by tribal organizations and therefore claimed their own share of the devolution programs (see also Maaka 1994:326). Tribal organizations and authorities, on the other hand, were hoping that the implementation of devolution would stimulate their lost relatives to return to where they were thought to belong, that is, to the *marae* communities on the tribal territories in rural New Zealand. They argued that the tribal structure was one of the most salient characteristics of Maori society, which did not allow any alternative basis of sociopolitical organization to replace the tribal basis of organization, or even to be introduced alongside the tribal organizations.

The political and ideological motivation behind this argument of tribal authorities was obvious. As mentioned above, only a minority of people at the grass-roots level still identifies in terms of tribal background, and tribal organizations have nowadays relatively little influence on day-to-day interactions of most Maori people living in cities. For that same reason, most Maori chiefs were in favor of devolution, which would revamp tribal organizations and concomitantly enhance their authority and influence. The question whether the implementation of devolution should be tribally based was by no means uncontroversial, however, since the aim

of the significant lobby of Maori spokespersons and organizations emerging in New Zealand cities was to divert the process of devolution once it had
become irreversible, and to claim at least some of the government funds and
decision-making authority for regional groups and organizations representing pantribal communities in nontribal, usually urban environments.

As a result of the devolution policy, then, Maori society became deeply
divided: between lower- and higher-ranking tribal organizations on the
one hand, and between (predominantly) rural-based tribal organizations
and urban-based pantribal organizations on the other. The intense division of Maori society raises the question whether it had perhaps been a
deliberate government tactic to divide Maori interests by encouraging
tribalism and to cut spending. In that case, the chiefly strategy to either
persuade or at least support the government to devolve the Department of
Maori Affairs had worked against its aim to reinforce the tribal organization of Maori society to such an extent that it would encourage urban
Maori communities to return to their roots, which would provide them
with a more supportive cultural environment to build up a successful future in New Zealand society.

ALTHOUGH it cannot be ascertained whether the policy of devolution of
the Department of Maori Affairs had been induced by one or more Maori
paramount chiefs, or whether most Maori chiefs only became enthusiastic
about devolution after the idea for it had been launched by the minister,
it shall be clear that the argument about chiefly interests in the disestablishment of the Department of Maori Affairs reinforcing the tribal organization of Maori society and, concomitantly, the authority of traditional
chiefs is not entirely speculative. Any ambiguities about the political position of paramount chiefs regarding the devolution policy of the Labour
government were definitely taken away toward the end of 1989, when
influential chiefs called a historic national conference of unity. The abundance of circumstantial evidence about the position of chiefs and their
thoughts as well as influence on the government policy of devolution becomes rather conclusive in light of their rear-guard offensive at the *Hui
Whakakotahi*, convened at Ratana Pa in August 1989.

The conference to establish unity among the Maori people was called
by the Ngaati Tuuwharetoa paramount chief, Sir Hepi Te Heuheu, who
was supported by the Maori queen, Dame Te Atairangikaahu, and the four
Maori members of Parliament (*New Zealand Herald* [Aug. 14, 1989]).
The organization of the conference had not primarily been sparked by the
policy of devolution. It was intended to discuss most important political
issues, including the many land claims that had resurfaced after the election of the Labour government, which had opened up an avenue toward

settlement of historic Maori complaints. During the Labour government, Maori people saw an unprecedented possibility to seek redress of a number of long-standing grievances, the resolution of which was to be speeded up, however, when the government began rating extraordinarily low in the polls and public opinion about Maori issues was becoming extremely hostile. Even though it was disputable whether the momentum of political change concerning Maori matters could ever be reversed again, Maori people did not wish to take the risk of losing a unique opportunity to settle some of their far-reaching claims.

Unity had ranked high on the agenda of tribal gatherings since the 1850s, but toward the end of the 1980s it was principally debated in the context of devolution, which had brought to light a deepening division among Maori people. Whereas in the past, tribal traditions had inhibited unity to be accomplished, for example, in the form of the Maori King Movement, since the large-scale migration to urban centers tribal divisions were compounded by the segregation of tribally and nontribally oriented sections of the Maori population.

Interestingly, the progressive rift between tribal and pantribal groupings came to overshadow the historic divisions between traditional tribes at the *Hui Whakakotahi*, which was entirely dominated by a difference of opinion regarding devolution and the question of whether government resources should be distributed on a tribal or a regional basis. The relatively modern division between rural and urban Maori organizations became particularly obvious when at the conference a resolution was accepted to set up a unified Maori Congress to represent Maori people in negotiations with the government about ways to settle all land claims without bankrupting the country's treasury as well as about the implementation of devolution. The Maori people could not agree, however, on the organizational structure of the Maori Congress, whether it should be set up on a tribal or a regional basis. Traditional tribes represented by their paramount chiefs were all in favor of devolving the Department of Maori Affairs to the administration of their tribal organizations, whereas pantribal, usually urban-based organizations advocated a distribution of government resources on a regional basis.

In the course of discussion at the *Hui Whakakotahi*, the real agenda of the conveners of the unity conference became apparent. They had created a platform to try to persuade all Maori people to accept the tribal basis of the government policy of devolution. The rationale behind their political preference was clarified as well. Paramount chiefs first legitimized their view favoring the empowerment of tribal organizations and their authorities with reference to tradition: from time immemorial Maori society had been organized on a tribal basis, and consequently the proposed introduc-

tion of regional organizations was dismissed as inauthentic and as too
deeply influenced by government structures of organization. Second, the
paramount chiefs implicitly accused Maori people living in the cities of
betraying their fellow tribesmen and tribeswomen, who felt abandoned
and, as a result, ill equipped to uphold the *mana* (prestige) of their *marae*
and the cultural heritage associated with them. In that context, hope and
belief were expressed that a strengthened organization and operation of
traditional tribes would motivate Maori people living in urban environments to return "to their roots." Finally, it was claimed that Maori migrants were not entitled to set up their own organization within the territories of traditional tribes, who, according to customary law, were supposed "to cater for their guests."

Against Sir Hepi and his supporters arguing for a tribal-based structure
of organization stood those in favor of the creation of regional authorities.
They were led by the head of the Mana Motuhake political party, the well-
reputed opinion leader Matiu Rata. Rata proposed to set up seven Maori
regional authorities, each to be elected by voters on the Maori electoral
roll in its region. The regional authorities were to administer and manage
devolution programs to be delivered to those Maori people living in urban
environments who were no longer associated with a traditional tribal organization. Rata never envisaged that the regional organizations would
replace tribal organizations; instead, they were meant to be complement-
ing the tribal authorities. In the Maori Congress, too, the regional authorities were proposed to balance the tribal authorities, with three or four
representatives from each region and four or five respected elders or chiefs
from each tribe (*New Zealand Herald* [Aug. 14, 1989]).

The most conspicuous characteristic of the proposal to set up regional
authorities involved its democratic element.[15] The uncompromising proposition of tribal authorities and paramount chiefs was criticized for being
undemocratic insofar as it postulated the traditional right to represent
people who could no longer identify in terms of their organization. In addition, the experiments with devolution in the form of Mana and Maccess
programs had raised the awareness of what chiefly authority involved in
practical terms. Many people had come to realize that tribal structures of
organization were in practice not streamlined from the bottom up, as, for
example, Tainui chiefs had maintained in the justification of their tribal
strategy for development. Instead, the experiments with devolution in the
Tainui area and elsewhere had made it painfully apparent that the theoretical model for the implementation of devolution on a tribal basis was
based more on an inversion of European forms of hierarchy to validate
the necessity of devolution to Maori tribes than on an adequate reflection
of traditional Maori sociopolitical practices, in which chiefs laid down
the law.

It shall not be surprising that the issue of whether to organize the Maori Congress on a tribal or a regional basis remained unresolved at the *Hui Whakakotahi*. Eventually, the issue was left to be sorted out by a working party of twenty tribal elders, which still today has not come up with a solution potentially able to satisfy everyone. It demonstrates the intensity of the division between predominantly rural-based, tribal organizations and urban-based, nontribal groupings. Although rural and urban, tribal and nontribal sections of the Maori population have gradually separated over the past fifty years, the depth of the division between them has only been brought to light by the controversial proposal to devolve the Department of Maori Affairs to traditional tribal organizations.

In the meantime, the devolution policy of the Labour governments of the 1980s has been reversed by the National party, which was elected to the office of government in October 1990.[16] The National government set up the Ministry of Maori Development (*Te Puni Kokori*), which has replaced both the Iwi Transition Agency and the Department of Maori Affairs (*New Zealand News U.K.* 2294 [Jan. 22, 1992]: 10). As a result, the Department of Maori Affairs continues to exist as it did before, albeit under a different name and with a different logo, while tribal organizations have been made relatively powerless again, with a budget at the same level that they had before the Labour government introduced the Mana and Maccess programs. Thus, tribal organizations and chiefly authorities have only achieved that their traditional institutions have been restructured and equipped to address contemporary political and economic issues. Their most important aim, to instigate their relatives living in urban environments to return to their tribal bases, has not been reached. Tribal authorities did, however, elicit the establishment of pantribal organizations in cities, which at present seem to have anchored themselves firmly in the wide spectrum of Maori politics. Indeed, the proposed devolutionary process aiming at empowering Maori tribal organizations ultimately secured a greater vigor and recognition of urban pantribal organizations, perhaps even at the expense of their chiefly-dominated and rural counterparts.

Chiefs, Politics, and the Power of Tradition in Contemporary Fiji

STEPHANIE LAWSON

THE POLITICAL SALIENCE of "tradition" and "culture" has become a major focus in many recent academic debates over issues ranging from various expressions of ethnic nationalism to the legitimacy of state boundaries and questions of sovereignty, the rights of indigenous peoples vis-à-vis those of later settlers, the problems of cultural minorities, and the assertion of distinctive national identities by many non-Western states. Because of the implications of these issues for the organization of political power within the state, they are becoming increasingly important for theorists of democratic politics, especially in relation to the challenges they present for the universal applicability of normatively oriented Western models and concepts of democratic rule. At the very least, these challenges have stimulated a more reflexive approach to the study of democracy in a comparative context and an appreciation of the variety of forms that democratic rule can take. And at a more general level, few would now question the value of social diversity and of the rich cultural traditions found in all parts of the globe. In this respect, the idea of cultural relativism has had an important role to play in countering manifestations of rampant ethnocentricity, especially of the "Euro" variety.

In the South Pacific, as in other parts of the world that were subject to European colonial occupation and subjugation, a renewed celebration of "tradition" or *kastom* has been an important factor in countering the negative images surrounding the worth of colonized peoples and the intrinsic value of their own cultural practices. The celebration of cultural diversity and the spirit of revival in the postcolonial (and postmodern) world, however, needs to be tempered with a critical regard for the way in which cultural relativism and the reification of "tradition" may be used for politically instrumental purposes—purposes that may have a great deal less to do with the spiritual well-being of marginalized or formerly colonized peoples than with the particular interests of indigenous elites, some of whom have been especially vociferous in their attacks on "Western" concepts of democracy and political rights.

Issues concerned with "tradition" in the South Pacific are focused largely on the position of chiefs, who, as White (1992:75) points out, are now the ubiquitous symbols of "custom"—representing "the indigenous and the traditional in contrast with the foreign and the modern." Similarly, Marcus (1989:189–90) has noted that the promotion of cultural identity in a number of contemporary Polynesian societies, especially in the relatively large-scale chiefly hierarchies characteristic of Tonga and Samoa, has been sustained by the self-conscious preservation of chiefly sacredness. The political salience of issues concerning chiefly status in Fiji achieved special prominence after the military coup of 1987 and the subsequent redrafting of the constitution. Here, chiefliness was promoted emphatically as the authentic expression of Fijian "tradition," and therefore of identity for the indigenous people of the islands. Moreover, Fijian tradition is often construed generally in opposition to certain aspects of that ill-defined entity known as the "West," and specifically in opposition to the large population of Fiji Indians, as well as people of other ethnic or racial groups (including other Pacific Islanders), whose biological make-up is deficient in patrilineally acquired, indigenous Fijian genes (see Fiji 1990).[1]

This construction has some very obvious implications for political legitimacy and authority, especially with respect to the exclusion of the non-indigenous population from an effective share of political power under the new constitution of the "Sovereign Democratic Republic of Fiji." But it may also operate to marginalize those indigenous Fijians who cannot establish the requisite links with, or gain the patronage of, the prevailing chiefly establishment. Though membership in the political elite is not restricted exclusively to bearers of chiefly status, the patronage of the chiefly establishment has been a crucial factor to date. The extraordinary success of the commoner Sitiveni Rabuka in attaining first the presidency of the Party of the Chiefs (officially titled the *Soqosoqo ni Vakavulewa ni Taukei,* or SVT), then the prime ministership following the general elections in 1992, and again in 1994 after a "snap election,"[2] owes much to the patronage of important elements of the chiefly elite.

The major purpose of this chapter is to examine the nature of the claims made on behalf of "tradition" in Fiji, especially as it relates to chiefly power. In doing so, I concentrate largely on the national political sphere, which has been dominated by Fiji's eastern chiefly establishment, rather than on expressions of traditionalism at regional or more localized political levels—which do not necessarily mirror national-level discourses.[3] Nor do I look closely at how the Fiji Indian communities have responded to the politics of Fijian tradition, a subject that is worthy of much more extended analysis than could possibly be provided here.[4] In concentrating on the wider national sphere of Fijian politics, I also hope to illuminate the way in which the generalized value of tradition in Fijian life is held up against a notion of the "modern," which in turn clearly implies "Western." In political terms, the legitimacy of traditional elements of authority is contrasted positively with Western conceptions of democratic rule. As an essential background to this discussion, I next examine briefly the notion of tradition and its ideological rendition as traditionalism, and then how tradition has been constructed in Fiji, especially in relation to the notion of historic continuity.

Tradition, Traditionalism, and the Problem of Continuity

Tradition in its simplest sense denotes "anything which is transmitted or handed down from the past to the present" (Shils 1981:12). Although there is no explicit normative understanding attached to this basic meaning, it is nonetheless accompanied by a clear sense that what has been handed down through the generations in the form of practices and beliefs enjoins respect, loyalty, and a duty on the part of the present generation to preserve and pass on the basic elements of the tradition (see Williams 1976:21). As I have argued elsewhere (Lawson 1995), this is the point at which there can develop normative support for a reified concept of tradition, without necessary reference to the content of any given tradition of practice or belief. Further, when the preservation of tradition becomes an end in itself, "tradition" acquires a politicized dimension that produces an ideology of traditionalism.

It has also been argued that traditionalism, understood as "the normative theory of the importance of tradition," emerges only when a tradition has been impaired or lost (Friedrich 1972:114). These dynamics are certainly part of the story, but traditionalism must also be recognized as a strategy capable of being deployed when those who hold a privileged position by virtue of the tenets of a tradition, either individually or as a group, perceive that this position is under threat. This has been one of the most fundamental issues in the politics of tradition in Fiji, and is vital to a proper understanding of the military coup that overthrew the elected government in 1987 and effectively restored the chiefly elite to power in the aftermath (see Lawson 1990). A further important aspect of the issue is, as suggested earlier, the way in which Fijian tradition is constructed as a homogeneous entity and placed in opposition to "the West"—and "Western democracy"—an aspect that will be explored here in relation to the notion of continuity.

The idea of tradition described above conveys an explicit assumption of continuity between past and present. This can be contrasted with perceptions of sudden and drastic change, which is seen to represent a rupture between past and present. In Fiji, as in other parts of the Pacific, the most commonly perceived rupture obviously occurred with European contact and the subsequent imposition of colonial rule, with its alien institutions of government, whose "trickle-down" administrative effects touched virtually every aspect of social and economic life. Although it is almost axiomatic now to reject "fatal impact" theses that depict this rupture in terms that imply a largely static view of precontact societies lacking their own dynamics for significant internal change, there can be little doubt that European contact and colonialism produced some marked discontinuities in virtually all spheres of life, and on a scale never before experienced. There is no point in denying, for example, that the sudden and forcible welding of heterogeneous communities, such as those which existed in Fiji in the late nineteenth century, into "national" political entities under the control of a European colonial government was anything other than a severe rupture.

On the other hand, there were clearly many elements of precontact or precolonial life that continued or that were transformed more gradually under colonial rule. And indeed, official colonial policy in places like Fiji, far from promoting the "modernism" or "rationality" often associated with Western political, legal, and bureaucratic institutions, was oriented much more toward developing national institutions and political practices that embodied a range of reputedly traditional elements so as to maintain continuity and stability in a classic conservative mode of government. This was part of the logic behind such institutions as indirect rule, which were designed, among other reasons, to maintain what were thought to be existing structures of sociopolitical authority.[5]

It is evident, then, that although European contact and colonization produced some significant discontinuities, the conservative British style of colonial government sought to uphold traditional rule rather than to undermine or displace it. In Africa, for example, the administration of British colonies was largely in the hands of officials who themselves "came from a country with a long tradition of common law, a respect for inherited position, and dominated by a Burkean belief in gradualism" (Colson

1975:83). The same spirit, together with a strong sense of paternalism, pervaded the early colonial administration of Fiji. Evolutionary ideas of political development and progress, however, also enjoyed varying degrees of popularity and influence in the colonial office. These, combined with the flourishing of a more liberal (and less paternalistic) approach to colonial rule, stimulated support for some kind of responsible government, and reforms along these lines were introduced by stages in the later colonial period, especially as Fiji moved toward independence.

Initially, however, the British Crown Colony systems were exceptionally rigid, with barely a hint of responsible government in their structure or practice; even then, representative positions in legislative councils were at first reserved almost exclusively for Europeans. Although these practices were considerably liberalized during the course of colonial rule, the general colonial experience in places like Fiji provided little in the way of "preparation" for the later introduction of fully responsible democratic government in the constitutions bestowed at independence. Rather, colonialism virtually created and nurtured in Fiji a "national" chiefly elite that was to become the very embodiment of a conceptually unified Fijian "tradition," antipathetic to democratic principles of political participation and inclusion, and arguably the most powerful force in postindependence Fijian politics. And, as noted in the introduction to this volume, the politico-legal apparatus of the modern nation-state of Fiji now operates to protect the status of chiefs.

The chiefly elite and its supporters have, of course, been vociferous in defense of Fijian "tradition" against the incursions of those Western values associated with important aspects of democratic theory and practice. In the particular context within which the Fijian chiefly elite has been required to defend its privileged position, namely, that of a "plural society" characterized by the presence of a large nonindigenous population, the principle of equal voting power implicit in the idea of universal adult franchise has been specifically targeted. Thus the new constitution of the Sovereign Democratic Republic of Fiji effectively defines different groups of Fiji's citizens according to biological descent, places them in separate "communal" electoral categories, and then accords these categories differential electoral entitlements. Although the situation in Fiji is hardly as repressive or as repugnant as South Africa's former pariah regime, or the old "Jim Crow" system in the United States, these constitutional provisions nonetheless represent a form of political apartheid in which "separate" is indeed inherently unequal.

In defending the new constitutional arrangements, "alien" Western concepts of democratic politics have been clearly framed in opposition to Fijian "tradition"—with the latter standing for a natural continuation of authentic indigenous political values. Furthermore, one of the justifications for elevating the political position of indigenous Fijians and their chiefly leaders over that of "aliens" rests on the claim that, since the chiefs of Fiji ceded the islands to the British Crown in 1874 on behalf of all Fijians, then at independence, Fiji should have been returned to the descendants of these same people. Again, this can be seen as an attempt to establish continuities with the precolonial past in order to underscore the political legitimacy and authority of present incumbents, and to exclude "aliens" from the sanctifying mantle of tradition.

As suggested above, the significant position maintained by chiefs in contemporary Fijian politics owes much not only to the existing sociopolitical structures that prevailed in precolonial Fiji, but also to the nature of British colonial government, which, although at times influenced by some liberal progressivist and rationalist ideas, was most strongly imbued with the ideals of classic Western conservatism in its formative stages. These ideals, like earlier schools of anthropology, extolled the virtues of unique cultural entities—such as the indigenous Fijians were assumed to comprise. Moreover, the very assumption of "a people" comprising "a single cultural entity" leads easily to a position whereby this entity can be reified, stereotyped, and romanticized in terms of "tradition."

I have elsewhere discussed at much greater length the interesting similarities between traditionalist discourses in the South Pacific and those of classic Western conservatism (similarities that many anthropologists have little familiarity with), including their shared antipathy to democratic politics with its ascending thesis of government—where legitimate political power is conceptualized as ascending "from below," that is, from "the people." This is opposed directly to the preferred conservative thesis of descending power—where political authority is legitimated "from above" and exercised through what is assumed to be a "natural," even God-given, hierarchy.[6] It should be noted as well that conservative ideas, which are also strongly opposed to rationalist politics and other modernist notions, have by no means vanished from "the West," even though their explicit forms of expression have changed (see Lawson 1996a; also Honderich 1991). Attention to these issues, and especially to the similarities between conservative European and non-European discourses, also suggests that homogenized stereotypes of, say, "the West" as modern, rational, and thoroughly imbued with (liberal) democratic values is superficial at best and can lead as well to very misleading contrasts, dichotomizations, and the gross overstatement of Difference between "the West" and "the Rest" (see Lawson 1996b).[7]

To return specifically to Fiji's colonial history, one of its most notable features is the extent to which chiefs from a particular geographical area of Fiji came to predominate in virtually all spheres of government and administration during the late colonial era and on into independence. This gives important clues to the historical location of chiefs in particular discourses that operated "to construct, validate, and empower" (see Chapter 1) a special sector of chiefly rulers in Fiji. The homogenized, idealized, and ideologically powerful version of Fijian "tradition" that has been evident in contemporary Fijian political rhetoric is tied closely to this group of chiefs, and a brief account of early developments is therefore important in understanding present configurations of political power, authority, and legitimacy.[8]

The Colonial Origins of Chiefly Power in Contemporary Fiji

By the time Fiji became a Crown Colony of Great Britain in 1874, extensive contact between Fijians and European traders, missionaries, and "beachcombers" had been established in the eastern areas of Fiji—notably Rewa, Lau, Bau, Cakaudrove, and Macuata. European contact with the western regions had been much more limited, and so it was inevitable that the earliest colonial administrators found eastern Fijians more accessible and a great deal easier to deal with. Furthermore, of the twelve high chiefs who had signed the Deed of Cession to Great Britain, eleven were from the east, including the most powerful Fijian of the period, the Bauan chief Ratu Seru Cakobau, as well as his archrival Ma'afu, the Tongan invader of Lau.[9] The style of chiefly rule that predominated in the east accorded readily with British conceptions of hierarchical authority, too.[10] And for Fiji's first substantive governor, Sir Arthur Hamilton Gordon (later Lord Stanmore), the sociopolitical structure of the eastern chiefly system seemed to resonate with his own romanticized views of Scottish clan organization. Gordon also had some familiarity with colonial methods of indirect rule, having become acquainted with its practice by the Dutch in Java. His initial contacts with the eastern chiefs and their readiness to cooperate with the new regime, together with his preconceived notions of the benefits of indirect rule through established indigenous sociopolitical structures, and his paternalistic commitment to maintaining the "traditional" Fijian way of life as far as possible, led Gordon to establish a Native Administration (subsequently renamed the Fijian Administration) that incorporated many easterners in its structure.[11]

This integrated system of officials and deliberative bodies was obviously meant to reflect indigenous patterns of authority. In devising appropriate rules and regulations, Gordon received much of his advice from the auditor-general, John Bates Thurston, who urged the preservation of the status and privileges of hereditary rulers in any new administrative system (Great Britain 1887, enclosure in no. 11:40). Accordingly, hereditary chiefs were appointed to many of the freshly created official positions. The twelve provinces set up by the colonial administration, for example, were headed by native governors with the title of Roko Tui, while districts within the provinces were headed by another level of hereditary chiefs who were given the title of Buli (see Fiji 1883: reg. no. 1; and Gordon 1878–79:179). The need to impose uniformity on the system throughout Fiji, however, meant that many local sociopolitical structures were completely subsumed under the new grand design, which drew largely on those systems characteristic of the east. This was evident in some of the titles given to the various offices. The title of Buli, for example, had been used by minor chiefs in Bua, whereas Roko Tui was originally a title bestowed on the heads of priestly lineages in Tailevu and Rewa (see Scarr 1970:4). In addition, the "official" Fijian language adopted by the government was an eastern (Bauan) dialect that had been used by missionaries for biblical translation.

Of the deliberative bodies that complemented the hierarchy of office-bearers, the highest was the Council of Chiefs (also known as the Great Council of Chiefs, or Bose Levu Vakaturaga). There was no real precedent for a national body of this kind because there was no sense in which Fiji had comprised a single political unit or entity before colonization. Rather, the eastern regions were largely made up of chiefly states (known as *matanitu*), each of which was in turn comprised of smaller units, whereas the western areas had no sociopolitical units on the scale of the *matanitu*, and their localized structures were characterized by a relatively low degree of hierarchical stratification and organization. Certainly, the western units had no chiefs of the status enjoyed by leaders such as Cakobau and his counterparts in the other eastern provinces. This has led to the (now rather contentious) characterization of the west as more Melanesian in its sociopolitical structure, while the east is said to resemble Polynesian structures.[12]

In any event, although the strength of Fijian chiefly influence within this structure fluctuated throughout the colonial era, which saw periods of more direct methods of rule, eastern chiefly authority remained a prominent feature of the administration throughout the period. Furthermore, the Fijian members of the colonial legislative council (which gradually broadened its membership as it developed some semblance of responsible government) were drawn almost exclusively from chiefly ranks. Indeed, universal adult franchise for indigenous Fijians (as well as for women of all ethnic groups) was not introduced until the early 1960s, before which

Fijian representation was drawn exclusively from a list of nominees provided by the Council of Chiefs. Even after this time, the Council of Chiefs
retained the right to nominate two members of the legislative council.
When Fiji became an independent nation in 1970, it did so with one of the
east's highest chiefs, Ratu Sir Kamisese Mara, in control as prime minister
and another, Ratu Sir George Cakobau, as governor-general. Writing in
the mid-1980s, Routledge (1985:220) noted that

the Prime Minister, Ratu Sir Kamisese Kapaiwai Tuimacilai Mara, bears names
that were famous in traditional times. Head of the Vuanirewa, he holds the titles
of Sau, Tui Nayau and Tui Lau and is thus heir to the Fijian paramount line in the
Lau islands and the Tongan line established by Maʻafu. His wife, Adi Lady Lala,
is the Rokotui Dreketi. . . . Both, in addition, are direct descendants of the first
Cakobau, as are also Ratu Sir George Cakobau, present Vunivalu of Bau and former Governor-General, and Ratu Sir Penaia Ganilau, kinsman of the Tui Cakau
and present Governor-General.

Routledge further points out (ibid.) that with the accession of this
group of chiefs to the top positions of political power in the postcolonial
era, a strong appearance of continuity between the pre-1874 political order and the contemporary order was established. The monopoly by these
chiefs of all the highest political positions was maintained until the general
elections of 1992, with the exception of the very brief tenure of the Ba-
vadra government in April–May 1987. Following the second military intervention in September 1987, and up until the 1992 elections, Mara remained prime minister in the interim government while Ganilau made the
logical switch from governor-general to president of the new republic. But
the man who led the coups in the name of Fijian tradition, and who is now
the elected prime minister, is a commoner, albeit from the eastern province of which Ganilau was paramount chief. Thus Routledge's prediction
that Mara's departure from the prime ministership would probably represent the end of an era in which high political office was combined with
high traditional status has been partially fulfilled (ibid.:221). It is unlikely,
however, that the presidency will be occupied by anyone other than a hereditary chief of high status in the foreseeable future, especially since the
new constitution gives exclusive power to the Council of Chiefs to make
appointments to this position (Fiji 1990: sec. 21).[13]
    National institutions like the Council of Chiefs, as well as the entire
system of native administration, together with the Fijian land-tenure system, which was developed at the same time and which also drew predominantly on eastern structures, clearly belong to that category of colonial artifacts that served the essential purpose of imposing uniformity on
the otherwise diverse and heterogeneous peoples who occupied the Fiji
islands at the time of colonization. The new homogenized structures,

which persist to this day, together comprise what some refer to as the "neotraditional" order (see especially Macnaught 1982), a term that acknowledges the undeniable impact of postcontact influences and colonial political organization while at the same time it implies a clear continuity with the past.

Assertions by, or on behalf of, the chiefly elite about the traditionality and antiquity of these institutions sweep aside almost a century of colonial history and its impact on Fijian political organization, and locate the origins of some colonial institutions in the remote, and definitely precontact, past—a past that can be represented as a more pure, pristine, or uncontaminated repository of genuine Fijian tradition. The current constitutional position of colonial constructions such as the Council of Chiefs, for example, has been justified on the basis of its "*age-old* authority and functions on traditional and customary matters" (Fiji 1989:24; emphasis added). Furthermore, perceptions of the council's present role accord with the homogenizing ideology that gathers together all Fijians under the overarching mantle of chiefly authority: "Being the forum in which Fijian chiefs deliberate on important matters affecting Fijian people, it [the Council of Chiefs] has become the collective voice of the indigenous Fijians" (ibid.:30).

Writing in general terms about Oceanian nationalist ideology, Babadzan (1988:211) has emphasized the tendency of this ideology to reduce, as a matter of urgency, a plurality of identities to a grand unity by appealing to a hypothetical common tradition—a tradition that must be considered pure and not hybridized through Western contact. This purity is in fact a necessary condition for the efficacy of its function in opposing the West. Precisely the same urgency has been evident in appeals for unity amongst Fijians, and the representation of a single Fijian voice by the Council of Chiefs, for the nationalistic effort requires the reduction of diverse Fijian identities to a singularity that is more amenable to political control, and more suitable as a construct against which the "alienness" of "others," especially Fiji Indians, can be defined. Of course there is no single "Fijian tradition," nor is there a single "Fijian past." But acknowledgment of a plurality of pasts, which correlates with the actual plurality of precolonial indigenous communities in Fiji, is far less suitable for the myth-making associated with contemporary political exigencies. The viability of a myth is best assured through the assertion of a singular Truth embodied in a singular, continuous Tradition. In Fiji, the identification of that singular tradition in contemporary politics, and the particular past with which the requisite degree of apparent continuity is established, is connected very firmly with the eastern chiefly establishment, and Fijian "tradition" has therefore been most powerfully expressed in the idiom of eastern chiefly legitimacy.[14]

. . .

DEVELOPMENTS of the kind described above testify to, among other things, the utility of "tradition" as a politically instrumental tool deployed in the creative and selective fashioning of the past in the present to suit particular agendas and interests (see Linnekin 1992:251). This prompts the inevitable question of "authenticity" or "real tradition" as opposed to "invented tradition"—issues that have been much debated by anthropologists in recent years.[15] I have not been concerned to enter into that specific debate here, but one of the issues raised by Thomas (1992) in the general exploration of the "invention of tradition" phenomenon provides a suitable focus for the conclusion to the present discussion.

Thomas suggests that if conceptions of identity and tradition form part of a broader field of naming, and therefore of categorization, the interesting question that emerges is not *how* traditions are invented, but rather *against what* traditions are invented. In the context of chiefs and politics in contemporary Fiji, much of what passes for tradition, or at least the rhetoric associated with tradition, has been constructed and expounded in explicit opposition to some Western values. And because the purposes of this rhetoric have been, for the most part, to exclude Fiji Indians from the sphere of political legitimacy (as well as to fend off external critiques of the regime), while at the same time shoring up the dominance of the chiefs within this sphere and maintaining the solidarity of Fijians as a supportive bloc, the conceptual targets for contextual delegitimation are the notions of political equality and liberty, inclusion and participation, that are inherent in most versions of Western democratic theory (if not always in political practice). We therefore find the values of Western democracy targeted as contrary to the whole ethos of Fijian "tradition" in which "liberty exists only within one's social rank and equality is constrained by a fully developed social hierarchy."[16]

Finally, while chiefs in Fiji may no longer hold all the top political offices, they nonetheless control some of the most important formal political institutions as well as the powerful symbolic resources associated with "Fijian tradition." And those who aspire to such offices will be required, at least in the foreseeable future, to articulate their political agendas in harmony with perceived chiefly values and interests. The language of nationalist chauvinism, made possible by the presence of a large number of "aliens," has also served to sharpen the contours of Difference required for the construction of a singular Fijian national identity, while at the same time strengthening the force of appeals to the reified conception of tradition, which, as an ideological instrument, has sought to deny the legitimacy of alternative channels of political expression for nonindigenous Fijians and many ordinary indigenous Fijians alike.

Ritual Status and Power Politics in Modern Rotuma

ALAN HOWARD AND JAN RENSEL

LIKE THEIR COUNTERPARTS in other Pacific societies documented in this volume, chiefs on Rotuma—an isolated Polynesian island in the Republic of Fiji—are in a difficult position. Caught between a lingering traditionalism and the demands of developing the island's standard of living to the satisfaction of its inhabitants, they find themselves subject to relentless criticism. Debates over the roles of Rotuman chiefs do not conform to a simple dichotomy of tradition versus modernity, however. While in the context of "modernization" chiefs are icons of a distinctive Rotuman cultural tradition and identity (and are universally honored for the roles they play in dignifying ceremonial occasions), they are also men uniquely embedded in localized histories that motivate their actions and inform interpretations and evaluations of their behavior. The result is often a confounding of local intrigue and the politics of development, as the case study we present illustrates.

The situation of Rotuman chiefs is further complicated by the ambiguity of their position within a postcolonial, post-coup context in which Fijian chiefs have assumed a central political role as defenders of indigenous rights (see Chapter 6). Whereas the roles of Fijian chiefs have increasingly been defined and consolidated at the national level, discussion of Rotuman chiefs' roles has been muted, more a matter of gossip than of formal discussion. The responsibilities and prerogatives of Rotuman chiefs have therefore been evolving in the form of contested responses to ad hoc circumstances rather than through purposeful debate. These circumstances have weakened the political foundations of chiefly authority on Rotuma and rendered chiefs vulnerable to angry critiques.

In some respects the foundations of chiefly authority on Rotuma have always been problematic. Unlike chiefs in the more stratified Polynesian societies (e.g., Hawai'i, Tonga, Tahiti, Fiji), Rotuman chiefs were much closer to the people than to the gods. Their legitimacy relied more on populist support than on supernatural sanctions.[1] Though expected to show some degree of forcefulness (i.e., manifestations of *mana*, "potency"), Rotuman chiefs were constrained by an ethic of reciprocity in which the people provided labor and material support, while chiefs ensured their people's welfare through displays of generosity.[2] Rotuman myths clearly portray chiefs who were too demanding—who took more than they gave—as the conceptual equivalent of cannibals (Howard 1986). The behavior of Rotumans toward their chiefs over time is consistent with this mythical charter, continually demonstrating both passive and active resistance to chiefly excess.

In this chapter we examine the historical circumstances that have led to the dilemmas confronting modern chiefs on Rotuma, and provide a case study that illustrates the complexities of the contemporary situation. The case study focuses on a series of events over the past few years in which the chief of one district became embroiled in a web of political and economic intrigue spanning local and national levels, leading to an attempt to depose him and install another chief.

Historical Overview

Rotuma is located 465 kilometers north of the northernmost island in the Fiji group, and only slightly closer to Futuna, its nearest neighbor. A fertile volcanic island of 43 square kilometers, Rotuma is surrounded by a fringing coral reef of varying width and productivity. Local food production supports basic subsistence: Rotumans cultivate a range of starchy staple crops, fruits, and vegetables, and raise pigs, chickens, goats, and cows in addition to the fish, shellfish, and seaweed they obtain from the surrounding waters. For more than a century the island's primary export has been copra; periodic efforts to develop other products have been plagued with problems of storage, shipping, marketing, and management. Wage opportunities on the island have increased over time but remain limited, and remittances from migrant relatives in cash and kind are important to upgrading living conditions and raising aspirations.

Although culturally and linguistically distinct from Fiji, Rotuma was incorporated into the British Colony of Fiji following cession to Great Britain in 1881. At the time the Rotuman chiefs agreed to the move, apparently anticipating advantages from being cast into the same category

as Fijian chiefs, whom they saw as exercising considerably more authority than themselves. Thus, shortly after cession, Commissioner Charles
Mitchell reported in a letter to the governor of Fiji: "As far as I can judge
it appears to me that the chiefs found their control over the people slipping
from their hands and imagined that if Great Britain took over the island it
would reverse this and place them in the position that Fijian chiefs occupy
to their people" (dispatch dated Oct. 12, 1881; Outward Letters). However, the position of Rotuman chiefs vis-à-vis their people and the colonial
government was quite different from that of their Fijian counterparts,
leading to a different power structure.

Rotuman and Fijian Chiefs: A Comparative View

It will be useful at this point to compare the powers of a Rotuman district
chief with those of a Fijian *yavusa* chief, for it was on their understanding
of the latter's status that British administrators based their expectations of
the former. In its idealized (colonial) form, Fijian social structure was conceived as a series of three agnatic descent groups. In order of inclusiveness
these were known as *yavusa, mataqali,* and *itokatoka.* The *mataqali* that
composed a *yavusa* were ranked according to the seniority of founding
ancestors, presumed to be related as siblings. The *mataqali* founded by
the eldest son provided the *yavusa* chiefs (Geddes 1959). Within this organization, *yavusa* chiefs held authority over each *yavusa* member by virtue of real or fictive kinship seniority over them.

In contrast, chiefs on Rotuma are customarily chosen from among the
bilineal descendants of ancestors who held a title (*as togi*).[3] Rotuma is
divided into seven districts, each with a *gagaj 'es itu'u,* "district chief," as
its leader.[4] Districts are subdivided into *ho'aga,*[5] clusters of households
composing cooperating work groups under the direction of a *fa 'es ho'aga,*
"hamlet or village chief," who is responsible for organizing labor on ceremonial occasions and when district work needs to be done. Though district headmen[6] are always titled, *fa 'es ho'aga* may or may not be. On the
other hand, some men take titles without assuming a leadership position.
This suggests a conceptual separation between pragmatic leadership and
the ceremonial roles of chiefs.

At ceremonies, titled men have special rights and responsibilities not
afforded untitled men. They eat from special tables (*'umefe*) symbolizing
their status. They are honored in kava ceremonies at which their titles are
called out in rank order. Titled men are also expected to give speeches on
behalf of their kinsmen, and to be more generous than other men when
presentations of food and valuables are required.

Titles "belong" to the descendants of previous title holders, who form a cognatic descent group (*kainaga*) known by the house-site (*fuag ri*) name associated with relevant ancestors. When formal custom is adhered to, the choice of successor to a title is made at a meeting of the *kainaga*. In most districts three or four *kainaga* claim rights to a title eligible for district chief. Collectively these are referred to as *mosega*, "a bed," with the implication that the claimants are descendant from the same original source. Eligible *kainaga* are thus related to each other as putative siblings. Ideally, district chiefs should be chosen successively from each branch of the *mosega* in turn, but in practice the process is highly politicized. The second-ranking title in each district is that of *faufisi*, whose holder serves as the district chief's "right hand." He customarily acts as head of the district when the *gagaj 'es itu'u* is away. Lesser titles are bestowed on those occupying other special roles, such as head fisherman and messenger.

One ordinarily holds a title until death, but if someone is particularly remiss in his role or otherwise earns the enmity of his *kainaga*, he may be pressured to give up the title. Whether *kainaga* have a right to take back titles once given is currently a matter of debate.

Superficially viewed, the roles of Fijian *yavusa* chiefs and Rotuman district chiefs were very similar prior to colonization. Like his Rotuman counterpart, a *yavusa* chief organized activities in his district, was an arbitrator of disputes, and was ceremonially honored through precedence in kava ceremonies. Both received first fruits from their subjects. But there were also significant differences. For example, *yavusa* chiefs were ritual leaders by virtue of direct descent from deified founding ancestors, and their political power was backed by supernatural sanctions of a more direct nature than those relied on by Rotuman chiefs. And since Fijian chiefs were chosen by primogeniture, drastically limiting potential successors to a title, they were treated with deference from birth. From childhood on they were trained to superordination while their peers were socialized to subordination. On Rotuma, in contrast, with any link to an ancestral chief conferring eligibility, no one was apt to receive the privileges normally afforded a Fijian chief's elder sons. The individual selected by his kin to become chief was unlikely to have enjoyed any special recognition before that time.

These differences resulted in chieftainship of quite different characters in the two cultures. Ideologically, chiefs in both societies held comparable authority, but Fijian chiefs generally exercised a social psychological dominance over their subjects, whereas Rotuman chiefs did not. Put into cultural terms, in Fiji the powers of office were conceived as embodied in the proper individual; in Rotuma they were invested in the title rather than the man.

The Colonial Era

Fijian social organization was well suited for indirect rule, and the British made the most of it. The chiefs, by virtue of their dominance, provided ready-made channels for administration. They simply added to their indigenous roles the rights and duties allocated to them by the colonial administration, and these were generally accepted by the people without much hesitation. The perceived success of this strategy (in other colonies as well as in Fiji) initially encouraged duplication of the design in Rotuma, but without appreciation of differences in the nature of chieftainship. The intentions of the colonial administration were made clear from the outset following the Rotuman chiefs' offer of cession. In a speech in October 1879, the acting governor of Fiji, William Des Voeux, announced, "It will be the same in Rotuma [as in Fiji] should the Queen consent to take you under the shelter of her throne. Thus through you [the Rotuman chiefs] we shall govern the people of the land, to you we shall look for aid in guiding and controlling them."[7]

That there was going to be some difficulty implementing this administrative scheme was quickly recognized by Hugh Romilly, who was sent as deputy commissioner to Rotuma in 1880 with the news of Queen Victoria's acceptance of the cession petition. In an address to the Rotuma Council of Chiefs, Romilly expressed his concern for the lack of deference shown the chiefs by their people:

The Council of Chiefs will remain the same. I promise to be guided as far as possible by your experience and advise. I have observed however with pain that some of your chiefs are not treated with proper obedience and respect by your young men. In some instances you have found it difficult to get even small things done by them without grumbling on their part. If I am to introduce English law here I can only do it through the chiefs and it is absolutely essential that you should insist on the strictest obedience from the people you have under you. I do not know on whose side the fault is but I am perfectly certain you can command respect and obedience if you choose to do so. Without it you can give no assistance to me in carrying out the law. . . .

There will be a law made . . . to punish disobedience but it would be infinitely better if you could govern your peoples without having to bring them to me for punishment.[8]

Although encouraged by Romilly's pledge of support, the chiefs soon found themselves in an untenable position. The limits of their prerogatives came to the fore when, immediately upon cession, 103 Rotumans submitted a petition for re-cession of their island from Great Britain. The petition noted that the chiefs had ceded the island "without consulting them, the landholders of the country" (Outward Letters, Oct. 12, 1881). Deputy

Commissioner Mitchell concurred that the offer of cession had been made without the people's consent. "This the chiefs had no right to do," he noted, "as the landholders here occupy a very independent position, the relations between chiefs and landholders being very different from what they are in Fiji" (ibid.). By the time the colonial government responded to (and refused) the petition several months later, the petitioners had changed their minds (Outward Letters, Oct. 20, 1882). But the position of Rotuman chiefs remained problematic.

Subsequent commissioners expected the chiefs to act authoritatively but refused to enhance their actual power, while the Rotuman people ridiculed their abortive attempts at dictatorship. The chiefs evidently assumed that they would be granted arbitrary powers that could be used to their own advantage, but the commissioners were only willing to back them to the point of enforcing English law and established Rotuman custom. For their part, the people did not express resentment over the imposition of most English-derived laws, nor did they openly dispute the authority of English commissioners. According to one of the early commissioners: "I have repeatedly heard the people say we do not wish our chiefs to be placed in authority over us. We will obey the regulations made by the government but not the rules made by the chiefs." [9]

Although most of the chiefs resigned themselves to the situation, one did not. Albert, chief of Itu'ti'u, continued to press for official support, only to be continually rebuked. Finally, after an incident in which he incited his district to disobey the commissioner's orders, he was publicly censured by the Council of Chiefs (see Howard 1966 for details). Albert's humiliation made it clear to all that the chiefs' political power under colonial rule was in fact negligible. Officially the chiefs were made advisors to the resident commissioner (and after an administrative reorganization in the 1930s, the district officer); unofficially, they were relegated to the role of intermediaries between the commissioner and the people in their districts. They were often criticized by their constituents for making unpopular demands on behalf of the commissioner, and by the latter for failing to gain the compliance of their subjects.

Although its ceremonial significance continued to provide some incentive for Rotuman men to aspire to chieftainship, this was more than offset by contradictory role demands. As a consequence, competition for chiefly roles waned, and the traditional rules governing succession, flexible as they were, gave way to a lax toleration allowing almost any adult male to fill a vacancy. Contributing to the devaluation of chieftainship was the active part most commissioners played in choosing "the right man for the job." It became commonplace for the people in a district to nominate several candidates and permit the commissioner to make the final selection. [10]

Furthermore, the commissioners showed little hesitation in deposing men who failed to meet their expectations. Exasperation with the state of Rotuman chieftainship reached a climax during the 1930s, when William Carew was district commissioner. He wrote to the colonial secretary:

I would suggest for His Excellency's consideration the passing of a Rotuman Regulation penalizing the chiefs for omissions of duty, and their people for disregard to their orders on district matters.

It is also suggested that each future chief should be installed with a considerable show of Government ceremony and he be supplied with a Badge of Office whereby all then should know and respect him.

The Rotumans as a whole, are practically devoid of Race and Tradition, consequently a chief could never acquire the standing of a Fijian Roko, but he could at least be constituted as a sort of Super-Buli, to be feared and obeyed by his people.[11]

Carew's suggestions did not receive the support of his superiors and were not acted upon.

The problem for the resident commissioners, it seems, was that they saw Rotuman political institutions as neither fish nor fowl. *Gagaj 'es itu'u* did not have the kind of authority they associated with chiefdoms such as that in Fiji, but the system also lacked elements crucial to their understanding of democracy. They were determined to resolve the issue one way or the other. Whereas some, like Carew, opted to reinforce the status of chiefs (without, of course, giving up any real power themselves), others, like A. E. Cornish, instituted moves toward democratic representation on the council. In 1939, with the approval of the governor of Fiji, Cornish introduced a reform whereby a chief would be elected for a period of three years in the first instance, after which the members of the *kainaga* who had elected him would vote for a new chief, or reelect the old one if they considered him satisfactory, provided he had proved satisfactory to the government. The first chief appointed under this rule failed to get reelected by his people and subsequently complained to the government on the grounds that the new procedures violated Rotuman custom. By this time Cornish had died, and following an investigation the traditional custom was reinstated (Sykes 1948).

A few years later, J. W. Sykes, sent to Rotuma to investigate administration of the island, among other matters, proposed abolishing the Council of Chiefs and replacing it with an elected council (ibid.). Sykes's recommendation was not implemented, in large measure because it was opposed by H. S. Evans, the district officer appointed to Rotuma the year after the report was issued.

However, in 1958 a compromise was reached, and the council was reconstituted to include one representative from each district, elected by secret ballot, in addition to the chiefs.[12] Its name was changed from the Rotuma Council of Chiefs to the Council of Rotuma. Its role, to advise the district officer and communicate his rulings to the people in the districts, remained the same. This situation prevailed until Fiji obtained independence in 1970.

Repercussions of Political Changes in Fiji

Following independence, it did not take long for a crisis to develop concerning the powers of chiefs versus those of district officers. Under the colonial administration, the district officer had been *gagaj pure*, "the boss." His authority had come from the governor, whom he represented, and ultimately from the British Crown. With independence, the basis of his authority became ambiguous. The district officer at the time of independence was an educated Rotuman who had his own ideas about how Rotuma should be governed. According to informants, he intruded into the process of chiefly selection on several occasions and simply picked the person he favored, without regard to the customary rules of succession. When the chiefs complained to the newly formed government about his high-handedness, they met with immediate success. The prime minister himself came to the island and personally ordered the district officer's removal, replacing him with an experienced clerk.[13]

This action completely reversed previous responses to Rotumans' requests that district officers (or district commissioners before them) be disciplined or removed. It signaled the beginning of an entirely different relationship between the district officer and the Council of Rotuma. Whereas previously the council had been merely an advisory body, it was now empowered as a genuine legislative organization. The district officer was relegated to the role of advisor and administrative assistant to the council. This meant that council members, chiefs and district representatives alike, were finally in a position to exercise real power for the first time since cession. The council, charged with overseeing local affairs, receives a government subvention that has increased substantially in recent years, from $F52,000 in 1984 to nearly $F135,000 in 1992, as well as annual self-help grants that amounted to $F10,000 each year from 1989 to 1992.[14] As a result, the attractiveness of the role of district chief has increased considerably, and competition for vacancies has intensified (Howard 1989).

The military coups of 1987 required Rotumans to reconsider their relationship with Fiji. Especially distressing for many was Fiji's withdrawal from the British Commonwealth, since it was to Great Britain and not to Fiji that the Rotuman chiefs had initially ceded the island. Led by a charismatic part-Rotuman karate master who lives in New Zealand, a number of dissidents refused to recognize Fiji's continued political sovereignty over Rotuma. In defiance of the chiefs, who had decided that Rotuma should remain with Fiji, the dissidents selected a new set of representatives (one per district) from among themselves, and declared Rotuma independent. Initially these representatives were called "chiefs," but later, when defending themselves against criticism, they denied intending to replace the traditional chiefs and instead declared themselves "ministers" in "the only legal Cabinet in Rotuma representing the welfare and interest of Rotumans living here and abroad." [15] The movement tapped an undercurrent of Rotuman concern over levels of support from the Fiji government. The government regularly provides infrastructure and support personnel on Rotuma for health services, education, public works, communications, etc., perpetuating the priority given to public welfare by the colonial powers. But many island residents have repeatedly expressed feelings of frustration over perceived neglect, citing, for instance, irregular shipping and poorly maintained roads, as well as a lack of attention to economic development.

In this instance, however, the dissident leaders were ultimately charged with sedition, tried in court and found guilty, but assessed only small fines and put on probation. After reviewing their claims, the chief magistrate issued a decision affirming Fiji's sovereignty over Rotuma, based on his assessment of historical data.[16]

The dissent expressed by the independence movement appears to have drawn as much from discontent with the chiefs as from skepticism over Fiji's willingness and ability to meet the aspirations of the Rotuman people. The dissidents charged the chiefs with corruption, with serving their own self-interests, and (echoing their ancestors of 100 years earlier) with failing to consult their people in deciding the island's fate. These complaints were neither new nor restricted to the dissidents; they were simply levied in a more politically charged, and expanded, arena.

The post-coup political rhetoric in Fiji may well have exacerbated the situation by rendering the place of Rotumans in the republic even more problematic. The reconceptualization of *taukei* (Fijian) "people of the land,"[17] the expanded role given Fijian chiefs, the redistribution of seats in a reconstituted Parliament, all have raised questions concerning Rotuma's (and Rotumans') position vis-à-vis Fiji and the role of Rotuman chiefs within the emerging structure. The Constitutional Review Committee, in grappling with these very issues, has kept them in the limelight, stimulating public expressions of opinion that might otherwise have remained private. It should be pointed out that the functioning of the Rotuman Council has not directly been affected by the coups, and the governance of Rotuma has not materially changed despite structural changes at the national level.

Rotuma's relationship with Fiji has affected the authority of Rotuman chiefs indirectly, however, through the access to educational and occupational opportunities it allows Rotuman migrants.[18]

Outmigration and Chiefly Authority

After an initial decline following contact, the Rotuman population experienced explosive growth beginning in the 1920s, increasing from a total of 2,235 Rotumans in 1926 to 8,652 in 1986. But the number of Rotumans residing on Rotuma in 1986 was nearly the same as it had been fifty years earlier (2,554 compared to 2,543), with migration draining off the net population increase. Fiji census reports over the past several decades document a dramatic shift in the distribution of Rotumans, with an ever-increasing proportion recorded away from their home island. According to the 1986 census, 70 percent of Rotumans lived elsewhere in Fiji, with 46 percent concentrated in the Suva area (Howard and Rensel 1994).

No one currently presumes that chiefs from the home island can exercise authority over Rotumans in Fiji. The chiefs formally abrogated that possibility in 1946, by refusing a request from the migrant Rotumans to appoint someone to be their "headman." The Fiji Rotumans expressed the view that someone appointed by the Council of Chiefs would be more respected, but the chiefs suggested that the migrants choose their own leader (Minutes of the Rotuma Council, Oct. 10, 1946).

At home, chiefly authority has been undermined by the fact that emigrant Rotumans have, on the whole, been extraordinarily successful in Fiji. They are considerably overrepresented in the upper echelons of business enterprises and governmental agencies. Many emigrants have accumulated real power by virtue of their positions and networks among Fiji's cosmopolitan elite. A good many take an active interest in developments on Rotuma, and may offer assistance in helping to see plans formulated by the Rotuma Council materialize. However, the chiefs see threats to their political control in these overtures, and regard them with ambivalence. They know they need assistance to get support for their projects, but they want Rotumans in Fiji to pay obeisance to them. They anticipate quick compliance with their demands, and expect preferential treatment when they come with requests. They welcome initiatives by Fiji-based Rotumans but demand control of implementation.

Emigration has also affected symbols of status. In days past, a chief's home was the main indicator of his rank. It was the biggest and best in his district, and was built and maintained by communal labor. The chief's house served as a receiving center for visiting dignitaries and was an important symbol of the district's prosperity and organizational ability. In recent years, however, modern-style houses requiring significant capital investment are being built by persons without titles. Motorbikes and automobiles are also accessible to anyone with the money to pay for them. Chiefs can only participate in this competition for prestige items if they have ready access to cash, and most do not. A significant proportion of the money for these commodities comes from abroad, in the form of remittances from emigrants. In addition, some Rotumans who are employed on the island can afford to invest in prestigious housing and transportation by drawing on their wages or bank loans.[19] But the chiefs are paid only a small stipend for their council duties. Hence they are strongly tempted to use public funds to pay for personal privileges or to support a more elegant lifestyle. In a number of instances serious charges have been made concerning mismanagement of public funds by individual chiefs within their home districts, and collectively as a council. The loss of a chiefly monopoly over status markers following in the wake of commercialization, education, and emigration is a widespread phenomenon and poses similar dilemmas throughout the Pacific and beyond.

We now present an account of recent events, centered in the district of Oinafa, that illustrates the ways local and national levels interrelate to shape the dynamics of modern Rotuman chieftainship.[20]

The Leadership Crisis in Oinafa

When Howard visited Rotuma in 1959–60, the chief of Oinafa was a man with the title Tokaniua. Although in his declining years at that time (he was 81), Tokaniua was still highly respected. People described him as kind and caring, and he performed his duties with a quiet dignity that reflected the moral authority he held. All three villages in the district—Lopta, Oinafa, and Paptea—were united in their support of Tokaniua. There was little evidence of any factional dispute threatening the political harmony of the district.

Shortly after Howard left Rotuma at the end of 1960, the aging Tokaniua turned over the reins of chieftainship to a younger man in his district with the title Kausiriaf. Though the new chief never gained the level of respect enjoyed by Tokaniua, he managed to carry out the responsibilities of his position with general support from the Oinafa people until the mid-1970s, when he was accused of embezzling funds from the Rotuma Cooperative Association and the Methodist Church. By then, however, the role of chief had changed dramatically as a result of the termination of Britain's colonial rule. The Council of Rotuma was now empowered as a policy-making body; thus, for the first time since cession, the chiefs were in a position to exercise real political authority. The empowerment of the council also gave chiefs a central role in overseeing Rotuma's modest but steadily increasing budget allocation from the Fiji government.

Business on the island was controlled throughout the colonial era by two firms: Morris Hedstrom and Burns Philp. Following World War II, however, the Rotuma Cooperative Association (RCA) was founded, and after several years of struggle it took firm root. By 1968 it was strong enough to force the firms out of business, thus gaining a monopoly on the island's commerce.

Kausiriaf was an active member of the RCA and was appointed an internal auditor. His son-in-law, Tarterani, kept the RCA shop in Oinafa village. When the shop experienced a serious shortfall in the mid-1970s, Kausiriaf allegedly doctored the books to disguise the deficit, which amounted to several thousand Fiji dollars. When this was discovered, he allegedly embezzled money from the Methodist Church to pay back the RCA. Eventually Kausiriaf and Tarterani obtained funds from relatives in Fiji to restore what had been taken, but both were dismissed from their positions. Kausiriaf then went to the RCA's central committee to apologize formally. His *faksoro*, "apology," was given in high ceremonial fashion, involving a sacrificial pig, kava, and fine white mats. He went *hen rau'ifi*, "with leaves around his neck," symbolically offering his life to atone for his offense. This is a rare event in Rotuma, and is usually reserved for instances in which a life has been taken or blood spilled. For a chief to come *hen rau'ifi* and ask forgiveness is of great consequence in the context of Rotuman culture. It is virtually inconceivable for the offended party to refuse acceptance of an apology so presented.

But Wilson Inia, the guiding light for the RCA's success,[21] refused to accept the chief's apology. He argued that *hen rau'ifi* was a custom relevant to interpersonal offenses, as when one party injured another, but that it did not apply to business matters, where money was involved. He said that embezzlement cannot be undone that way.[22] When Kausiriaf's father, who holds the title Sakmen, heard about Inia's refusal to accept the apology, he was outraged. He sent a letter to the RCA demanding that the Oinafa RCA copra shed and shop, which were on his land, be removed immediately.

Soon afterwards, in 1977, a brother of Kausiriaf, holding the subchiefly title Toa'niu in the district of Juju, went to Suva to seek financial support to begin a rival cooperative society. The new co-op was to be named Raho, in honor of the legendary founding ancestor of Rotuma Island. For help in securing a loan, Toa'niu approached a third brother, Atfoa, who held a high position in the Fiji government. Atfoa greatly admired all that Wilson

Inia had done for Rotuma, and agreed to help his brother only with reservations. He said he favored healthy competition but was concerned about the motives of the founders. He urged them to forget their personal grudges and to work for the best interests of the Rotuman people. He obtained a loan and installed Toa'niu as Raho's manager. Atfoa attempted to monitor Raho from Suva, but could not control the everyday operations of the fledgling company.

Kausiriaf, his father, and his brothers (the Varea family, see figure) had counted on other malcontents joining their group, but they were disappointed. People on the island were well aware of the new cooperative's beginnings in Kausiriaf's predicament, and even though he did not take an active hand in founding Raho, this hardly inspired confidence. Amidst accusations of mismanagement, Raho played only a minor role in the island's economy until it was reorganized in the late 1980s (see below).

Kausiriaf's esteem within Oinafa suffered additional setbacks as a result of disputes over land and suspicions that he continually diverted district funds for his own personal benefit. For example, it was rumored that he had used USAID funds granted to the district for communal projects to build a costly addition to his house.

The Generator Dispute

When we arrived for fieldwork in 1988, hard feelings prevailed in the district. Within Oinafa village a dispute had arisen over a formula for paying electricity bills. A generator had been purchased with funds raised by the Oinafa Club in Fiji, supplemented by a grant from a government self-help program. Since meters were not installed at house sites, the issue of how fuel and maintenance costs were to be distributed among households became a focus of debate. Two factions developed. One, supported by Kausiriaf, advocated a flat rate be paid by each household, regardless of use. The other, led by a man named Eliesa, advocated payment according to the number of light fixtures and power points. At a village meeting during which the issue was discussed, the debate became heated, and angry words were exchanged. Kausiriaf was away from the island at the time, and the meeting was chaired by the *faufisi*, the second-ranking chief in the district, who holds the title Sautiak. As the debate heated up, Sautiak allegedly accused Eliesa, who also held a title at the time, of not carrying his weight in village affairs and insulted his title. As a result, Eliesa renounced his title and, along with one of his supporters, isolated himself from village affairs for more than two years. Eliesa and his supporters disconnected their houses from the reticulated village electrical system and bought their own generators. They steadfastly refused to participate in

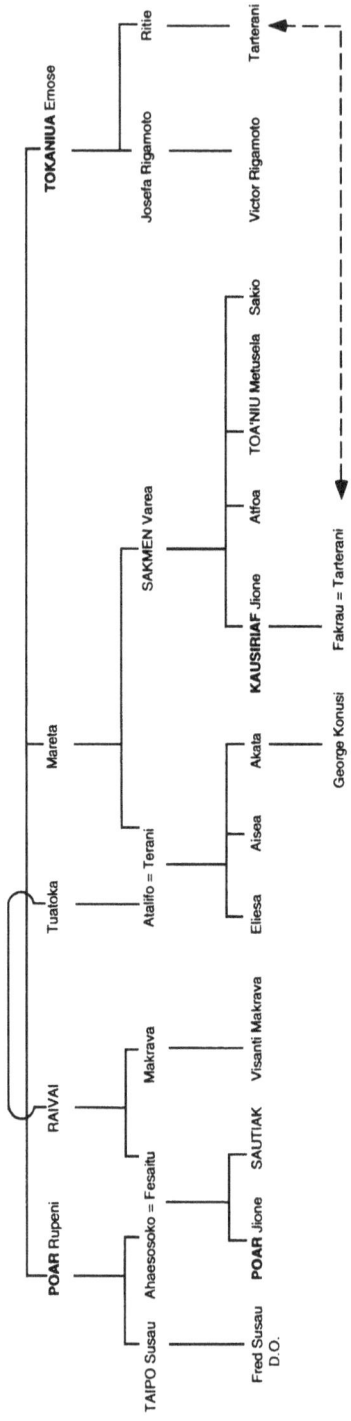

Abridged Oinafa Genealogy

Key: Names in Capital Letters indicate titles.
Names in Bold Capital Letters indicate Oinafa
district chiefs.

Note: This is a simplified genealogy insofar
as many of the individuals are related to one
another in multiple ways. We have diagrammed
here only the most direct relationships.

village events and kept to themselves, despite numerous attempts by friends, relatives, and neighbors to institute social repairs.

The Matter of Tourism

Around the time the flap over the generator was taking place, a more pervasive issue emerged, adding fuel to the fire. Up to the present, no tourist facilities exist on Rotuma. A few visitors come from time to time, but they must arrange accommodations with families. However, in 1986, Kausiriaf's brother, Atfoa, arranged to have the Australian tourist ship *Fairstar* stop at Rotuma. The plan was to have the ship disgorge its approximately 1,000 passengers for a day on the beach at Oinafa (one of the most picturesque on the island) where they could swim, sunbathe, be entertained by groups performing traditional dances, and buy Rotuman handicrafts. Rotuma was to be made a regular stop in the *Fairstar*'s South Pacific itinerary.

The plan to have such a large tourist vessel visit the island on a regular basis stirred a spirited debate within the Rotuman community, both on Rotuma and amongst Rotumans in Fiji. Those opposed, led by the Methodist clergy, argued that Rotuman morals would be threatened by tourists who could be expected to dress immodestly, drink and perhaps introduce illegal drugs, and seduce young women. They also felt that Rotumans would become greedy and money-grasping given this opportunity. Those supporting the idea pointed to economic benefits and argued that this form of tourism was preferable to hotel development.

The Rotuman Council debated the proposal and the chiefs, including Kausiriaf, voted against it. Despite the fact that his brother had formulated the plan, Kausiriaf spoke vigorously against it at district meetings and persuaded most of his people to oppose it. We were told that he was called to Fiji by his father, Sakmen, who admonished Kausiriaf for not supporting his brother Atfoa's plan. Allegedly Sakmen threatened Kausiriaf with eviction from the family homestead if he failed to comply. As a result, Kausiriaf returned to Rotuma and announced that he had changed his mind. He defied the council's ban on the *Fairstar*'s visit, thus angering the people of the two other villages in his district, Lopta and Paptea. Shortly thereafter, when a water pipeline was being laid in the district, the men from Lopta reportedly refused to work on the project beyond their village limits, citing the tourism issue as their reason for not cooperating.

The *Fairstar* visited Rotuma in 1986 without incident. Its $F4,000 docking fee went to Kausiriaf, with the understanding that he would pay expenses (including compensating the groups who entertained), with the remainder to be distributed among family groups (including his own) holding beachfront property. An estimated $F6,000 was earned in addition, through the sale of food and souvenirs. This money went directly to the sellers, who were invited from the general island populace to sell their wares. For the most part the *Fairstar*'s initial visit was considered a success, especially by those who benefited directly, but when we visited the island in 1987 feelings were still tender. Although we observed no direct expressions of open antagonism, Eliesa and some of his supporters remained aloof during communal activities.

The Healing Process

Over the following two years we witnessed a healing of the rifts within the district. In 1988 Eliesa formed a group, the Board for Enterprise Development, whose aim was to seek funds for entrepreneurial ventures on the island. He invited some of his key supporters and some men who had remained neutral to join the board. Meetings, which we were invited to attend, were held in his home. After a few meetings, when it looked like the project might succeed, several members of the group persuaded him that there would be advantages to having Kausiriaf as a member. Eliesa took the initiative and, without directly apologizing, told Kausiriaf he was prepared to forget the past. He invited the chief to the next meeting. On the urging of his wife and some neutral mediators, Kausiriaf agreed to attend.

Eliesa's invitation provided a basis for reconciliation and reintegrating discontents back into village life. He attended more and more village functions and began to assume increasing responsibility. Even the relationship between Eliesa and Sautiak, who had publicly insulted him, was healed to the point that they were seen sitting together, engaged in conversation.

The hard feelings that had erupted over the tourism issue also eased during the next year. Reconciliation took place in the form of a large-scale wedding between Sautiak's son and a young woman from Lopta. Significantly, the guardian of the bride had been one of the most outspoken critics of tourism, while Sautiak had been an active supporter. During the wedding, both sides gave a number of emotional speeches acknowledging past conflicts while glorifying the cooperation that had produced such a grand event.

Toward the end of 1989, district solidarity reached a zenith with the celebration of the 150th anniversary of Methodist missionization on Rotuma. Since Oinafa was the location of the first missionary landing, it was the center of celebration. In anticipation of a large number of visitors from Fiji and overseas, much effort went into planting vast quantities of food, sprucing up the villages, and making other preparations. Kausiriaf was in charge of these efforts and at this point enjoyed more general support than he had in years.

The Politics of Business

The stated goal of the Board for Enterprise Development was to acquire funds from abroad through grants and loans that would be allocated to worthwhile enterprises on the island. Among the projects discussed were cattle farming, a piggery, a garage for servicing and repairing motor vehicles, a handicraft industry, and a mat-weaving machine. More grandiose plans—for a set of fuel tanks near the beach that would be filled via a pipeline to visiting tankers, for a supermarket, and for an insurance brokerage—also were discussed.

The board was composed entirely of men from Oinafa village, although the potential benefits of including men with business experience from other districts were acknowledged. However, Kausiriaf argued against this on the grounds that it would make things more complicated, and his opinion was decisive. Eliesa had also sought the support of Oinafa expatriates in Fiji, most notably Josefa Rigamoto, Victor Rigamoto, Visanti Makrava, and George Konusi.

Josefa Rigamoto is the son of Tokaniua, the popular chief of Oinafa who preceded Kausiriaf. He had been the first Rotuman appointed district officer on Rotuma, shortly after serving with distinction in the Solomon Islands during World War II. Josefa enjoyed a long, distinguished career as a civil servant in the colonial and postcolonial administrations, retiring from the Fiji Land Board at age 80 in 1986. He is known to be well connected in Fiji and to have a thorough knowledge of bureaucratic procedures. Although untitled, the "Old Man" enjoys tremendous respect from Fijians, who honor him in chiefly fashion.[23]

Victor Rigamoto is Josefa's son. A graduate from an English university in the field of social work, he had risen rapidly in the Fiji governmental hierarchy, and held a position in the prime minister's office. Although young, he was thought of as someone who had a good deal of influence and could help see projects through the government maze. In 1989 Victor had been sent to Rotuma by the prime minister to help resolve a dispute over chiefly entitlement in the district of Itu'muta. Dissenters in the district had petitioned the prime minister to have their chief, Manav, removed from office. Kausiriaf and a number of other titled men rallied to Manav's defense. They expressed serious concern about allowing decisions concerning chieftainship to be decided by officials in Fiji. They were also concerned about the very possibility of deposing a chief, which they claimed was contrary to Rotuman custom. Titles are given for life, they argued, and cannot be taken away against the title holder's will; likewise, they contended, a chief cannot be deposed against his will. Other knowledgeable Rotumans, however, disputed this view, arguing that titles and chiefly positions belong to the *mosega* and can be recalled by the kin group. Victor attempted to mediate between Manav's supporters and the dissenters, but neither side would back down. Finally, during a return visit, he, in conjunction with the district officer, Fred Susau, persuaded Manav to agree to a vote of the whole district, and by a two-to-one margin Manav was voted out of office. While most of the district was jubilant, many Rotumans were disturbed by the precedent. They expressed concern that if a chief could be deposed simply because people did not like him, then the very foundations of chiefly authority would be undermined (for more details, see Howard 1990:283–85).

Following the coups in 1987, Visanti Makrava had been appointed general manager of the National Bank of Fiji (NBF). His family home was in Oinafa village, and he was seen as controlling vast resources that could be tapped by the Board for Enterprise Development. George Konusi worked as loan officer for the Fiji Development Bank.

A Note on Kinship Relations

All of the key individuals referred to—Kausiriaf, Toa'niu, Sakmen, Atfoa, Eliesa, Sautiak, Josefa and Victor Rigamoto, Visanti Makrava, George Konusi, and Fred Susau—are part of a closely knit kinship network (see figure), besides having roots in Oinafa village. At the senior level, Josefa Rigamoto and Sakmen are related as first cousins (FaSiSo/ MoBrSo). Their sons, Victor Rigamoto on the one hand, Kausiriaf, Toa'niu, and Atfoa on the other, are second cousins. Eliesa is second cousin to both sides of the younger generation through his mother. Sautiak is also related to Eliesa, Victor, and Sakmen's sons as second cousins through his mother. Fred Susau is first cousin to Sautiak, second cousin to Kausiriaf, Eliesa, and Victor. Visanti is first cousin to Sautiak, second cousin to Eliesa, and related affinally to Kausiriaf. George Konusi is Eliesa's sister's son. All of these men claim membership in the *mosega* that has the right to choose Oinafa's district chief. It should be noted, however, that none of the Fiji residents held titles (nor did the district officer), nor did they aspire to them, despite their prominence.

The Business of Politics

In October 1989 Visanti Makrava (the general manager of NBF) visited Rotuma and met with the Board for Enterprise Development. He suggested that the group move cautiously, concentrating on copra and fuel, rather than trying to do everything at once. He further proposed that the board should register as a holding company in Fiji, rather than as a cooperative. He pledged to help with financing and to play an active role in overseeing the venture. At the same time, Visanti suggested to the people involved in the Raho Cooperative that Raho be reorganized as a holding company. Eliesa assumed that his group, the Rotuma Enterprise Development Holding Company, would replace or take over Raho.

As pointed out above, the Raho Cooperative had suffered from serious problems, and under Toa'niu's management had not flourished. At one point Eliesa had been asked to join Raho, but did so only on the condition that he be made treasurer. Later he told us that he quit in frustration over Toa'niu's persistent misuse of funds. Toa'niu allegedly dipped into the cooperative's coffers to finance trips to Suva and to defray "campaign expenses" in his bid to be selected chairman of the Rotuma Council. Although only a subchief in his district (Juju), Toa'niu was a member of the council by virtue of his position as the district's elected representative. We were told by independent sources that Toa'niu gave monetary gifts to the chiefly members of the council in hopes of persuading them to choose him as chairman. He succeeded in his efforts. Meanwhile, however, Raho was suffering.

Raho's shops were closed, debts were mounting, and only the copra operations were still in business when Atfoa, who was seriously ill (he has since died), asked Visanti for help. Atfoa reportedly stipulated that neither of his brothers should be involved in Raho's management. In June 1989, Visanti arranged for loans from NBF to Sautiak and Aisea Atalifo, Eliesa's brother, who was Oinafa district representative to the Rotuma Council. These loans were for the purchase of two trucks, which Sautiak and Aisea used to transport copra for Raho. Aisea took over Raho's bookkeeping and managed the one Raho office in Oinafa. Under Visanti's supervision, Raho began paying back its debts from the copra receipts.

When we left Rotuma at the end of 1989, Eliesa's hopes were high that his project would succeed. He had formulated plans for requesting money from international agencies and had visions of several major projects, from fuel tanks to a service station to (ironically) tourist facilities. All that was needed was some $F200,000 to set things in motion. He anticipated that his nephew at the Fiji Development Bank would be able to help him get the loan for the fuel tanks to start the service station.

By the time we returned to Rotuma six months later, the entire scheme had collapsed. Eliesa related to us his tale of woe. He said that all the paperwork had been done and the company was registered. The only remaining step was for Visanti Makrava and Victor Rigamoto, as members of the board of directors, to sign the papers so that a loan could be obtained from the Fiji Development Bank. Eliesa said that he went with Josefa Rigamoto to Visanti's office, but that Visanti was reluctant to sign, so they decided to leave the papers with him. Later in the day, according to

Eliesa, Victor called and said that he and Visanti had decided not to sign, that they didn't want to be members of the board. When Eliesa asked why, Victor offered no explanation other than they didn't want to be on the board. Furthermore, Victor told him that they would have to reregister the company with a different set of directors (excluding him and Visanti).

Eliesa decided in disgust to give up on the whole venture. He expressed irritation over the fact that Visanti had offered encouragement from the very beginning, and had told them (the Oinafa residents on the board) to take advantage of his tenure as manager of the National Bank of Fiji. At home in Oinafa he openly criticized Visanti and Victor for failing to aid the Rotuman people.

The story we heard from the other side is revealing, however. It illustrates the gap in understanding between island residents and Rotumans occupying responsible positions in Fiji. Apparently the reason for Visanti and Victor's reluctance to sign as board members was over the matter of collateral. Eliesa had persuaded Josefa Rigamoto to put up his life savings as collateral for the proposed $F200,000 loan. Additionally, Visanti and Victor would have been liable, as board members, for unpaid debts. Given the history of past ventures on Rotuma, their reluctance to take on such a responsibility, and their desire to protect the "Old Man's" assets, were understandable. They reported that they had expressed their reservations to Eliesa earlier, not at the last minute. Visanti and Victor both related a whole series of previous occasions on which they had generously assisted Eliesa, and expressed disappointment at his ingratitude at this juncture.

Toa'niu was now chairman of the Rotuma Council. He was angry with his brother Atfoa for turning Raho over to Visanti, and since the district officer, Fred Susau, had assisted Visanti in various ways to revive Raho, he was angry with the district officer as well. This made it difficult for the council and the district officer to cooperate.

Toa'niu allegedly used his position as chairman of the Rotuma Council to get back at Visanti by instigating, over the district officer's objection, a $F100 per month rent for the space the NBF bank was using at the government station. Only after Visanti threatened to close down the Rotuma branch did Toa'niu and the council back off.

The Schoolbus Incident

One of the Rotuma Council's main priorities following Toa'niu's assumption of the chair in 1990 was to obtain two new buses. At the time the only buses on the island were two dilapidated vehicles that were continually breaking down, forcing children to walk considerable distances to school. Toa'niu convinced the council to let him go to Suva to negotiate a loan for the buses. When he arrived in Suva he telephoned Victor Rigamoto and asked his assistance. Victor obliged by contacting a colleague in Rural Development and arranged an appointment for Toa'niu, but explained that it would be inappropriate to accompany him. Victor also explained that since Toa'niu's request for a loan did not come from the council it could not be acted upon. Toa'niu was incensed that Victor would not take his word that the entire council was behind him. Victor responded that the loan request would have to go through official channels, and that a formal request from the council was required.

Toa'niu apparently took offense at this; instead of showing appreciation for Victor's efforts on his behalf, he later claimed to have been snubbed. Thereafter when the two met on social occasions Toa'niu turned a cold shoulder. Toa'niu also expressed irritation with Visanti and George Konusi, whom he accused of failing to show proper courtesies due the chairman of the Rotuma Council when he went to see them about the loan.

Toa'niu sent word back to Rotuma that he needed the rest of the council members' signatures immediately, so the district officer called an emergency meeting of the council and explained the problems of taking out a loan for the buses. Toa'niu was committed to buying one large bus (a sixty-six-passenger vehicle) in addition to a normal-sized vehicle. The district officer took the opportunity to outline an alternative, which was to buy outright a smaller bus using money from the Rotuman Development Fund. The larger bus proposed by Toa'niu would require a substantial loan and would end up costing nearly three times as much, including interest. The council members agreed with the district officer's proposal, but Toa'niu telephoned Kausiriaf and had him reconvene the council on a day when the district officer was unable to attend. Kausiriaf relayed a message from Toa'niu that he was confident he could obtain a grant to cover the loans. Based on his unwritten, secondhand assurance, the council again reversed itself.

The district officer, however, refused to sign the loan request and reported his opinion to his supervisor. He received a reply from Victor Rigamoto indicating that he had done his duty as district officer in advising the council not to go for the option they chose, but that he should not prevent them from pursuing it. The district officer then signed the request.

Things remained relatively quiet following Toa'niu's return until an article appeared in the *Fiji Times* on June 29, 1990. The article read:

The Rotuman Council of Chiefs has submitted a petition to the Prime Minister asking for the removal of two senior government officers for what they described as interference.

The chiefs have also expressed concern over the manner in which the two government officers, the Chief Assistant Secretary to the Prime Minister, Victor Rigamoto, and the District Officer on Rotuma, Fred Susau, settled a dispute which saw Gagaj Manav being deposed as the paramount chief of Itu'muta.

Mr. Rigamoto and Mr. Susau were the government representatives in the talks to settle the dispute.

According to a source, the two advised the Itu'muta district to meet to try to settle the dispute themselves.

The district clans then decided, after a meeting, to ask the chief to step down.

The Rotuman chiefs say, however, in their petition that Mr. Rigamoto and Mr. Susau had taken "the matter into their own hands" by motivating the people of the district to depose Gagaj Manav who had already been formally installed as paramount chief of Itu'muta.

"Because of this undesired ruling, we are of the opinion that the government is violating our sacred vows, and as it has been done to Gagaj Manav now, perhaps the same could apply to us later, if the District Officer Rotuma and Mr. Rigamoto so wish," the petition said.

As a result of a meeting of the seven chiefs on Rotuma, a number of resolutions were adopted.

Among other things, the chiefs expressed their sadness and concern over the removal of Gagaj Manav from his chiefly status.

The chiefs resolved that both Mr. Susau and Mr. Rigamoto should be removed from their posts.

The meeting also passed a resolution that the Rotuma Council be given the right to nominate the person to represent Rotuman interests in either the Prime Minister's office or in the office of the Minister for Fijian Affairs.

The chiefs also resolved that the Rotuma Council of Chiefs be granted more autonomy on Rotuman affairs.

The chiefs said that they were "shocked" at the lack of help and courtesy received from the Chief General Manager of the National Bank of Fiji, Mr. Visanti Makrava, and a Fiji Development Bank officer, George Konusi.

This came about when the chairman of the council, Gagaj Toa'niu, was unsuccessful in making an appointment with Mr. Makrava and received similar treatment from Mr. Konusi.

"We are very much disturbed and disappointed with the discourteous treatment Gagaj Toa'niu received from the men while in Suva."

The council was negotiating a possible loan to buy two school buses for Rotuma.

The petition was signed by five chief of the Oinafa, Itu'ti'u, Malhaha, Juju, and Itu'muta districts.

The assistant chief of Noa'tau also signed.

Publication of the petition caused a considerable stir on Rotuma. Most people from outside Oinafa saw it as an internal squabble; the real issue, they said, had to do with the running of Raho. The district officer agreed. He showed us a copy of the original petition with the signature page, which was appended. The petition was written on Rotuma Council stationery but it proclaimed three resolutions of a (nonexistent) body referred to as the Council of Rotuma's Seven Chiefs. Some of the signatories denied knowing what they were signing, and claimed to have been duped. They said Toaʻniu told the chiefs to sign a signature page that was needed to get a loan for the buses, but that they did not see the petition to which it was later attached. The chiefs of Malhaha and Ituʻmuta subsequently sent a letter to the prime minister disclaiming their involvement in the petition (*Fiji Times* [July 18, 1990]).

The Coup

In Oinafa, publication of the petition's contents generated a good deal of resentment. Sautiak and Aisea Atalifo, who had effectively taken over the management of Raho on Visanti's behalf, called a meeting of the chiefly *mosega* on July 4, 1990. They asked for an explanation from Kausiriaf, and demanded a formal apology. After all, they argued, the people he was attacking were from his district and were close kinsmen. *Mosega* members openly expressed their discontent, "saying that their opinions should have been sought on the matter of the petition because they were the ones who shouldered the burdens for the district's activities" (*Fiji Times* [July 18, 1990]). Kausiriaf told the assembled kin group that it was none of their business and walked out of the meeting. In his absence, a lively discussion took place among the sixteen people present. Eliesa argued that this was a tempest in a teapot and that people should calm down and forget about it. Aisea and Sautiak persisted, however, and called for a vote to oust Kausiriaf from office and install a new chief. Nine people voted for the motion, seven voted against it.

The district officer and Victor Rigamoto, both of whom are members of the *mosega*, were not present and decided not to interfere as long as Rotuman custom was followed. They took the stance that the position of district chief belongs to the *mosega*, which has the right to bestow it and to take it away. The district officer did, however, criticize Kausiriaf for signing the petition using his title since that implied he was acting on behalf of the *mosega*, which had given the title to him, and therefore he was wrong in not consulting them. He could have signed his personal name, Jione Varea, if he was just acting on his own behalf. The district officer also commented on the irony of Toaʻniu's calling on the chiefs (as distinct from a meeting of the Rotuma Council) to send the petition, since Toaʻniu himself was not a district chief and properly had no authority over them.

Those who argued in support of Kausiriaf claimed that once a chief is installed he can only be removed from office if he commits a legal offense and is sent to jail; otherwise he is chief for life unless he voluntarily resigns. They also argued that only a small portion of the whole *mosega* was present when Kausiriaf was ousted, and that the total *mosega* membership (including those abroad) should have been consulted. This argument was countered by claims that only *mosega* members resident in Oinafa had a stake in the position of chief and that they alone should decide.[24]

On July 14 Kausiriaf flew to Fiji to consult with his brothers, Atfoa and Sakio, and to hire a lawyer to contest his ouster.[25] Sakio was Permanent Secretary for Health in Fiji, but to this point had not been involved in business or politics on Rotuma. It should be pointed out that prior to this incident the Varea brothers were often openly antagonistic to one another. Indeed, Kausiriaf had reputedly led an earlier attempt to depose Toa'niu as chairman of the Rotuma Council; and as reported above, Atfoa had turned over the management of Raho to Visanti on condition that neither Toa'niu nor Kausiriaf be involved in its management. At the command of their father, Sakmen, however, the Vareas closed ranks and were united in their opposition to the dissident faction. They hired a lawyer to plead their case with the high court.

The man the *mosega* chose to replace Kausiriaf as chief was Jione Fesaitu, Sautiak's brother (see figure). He had spent most of his adult life in Fiji, where he was an agricultural officer. He had recently retired to a farm of his own, but Sautiak and Visanti persuaded him to take a title and assume the position of district chief in Oinafa.

Jione came to Rotuma by plane on the same day Kausiriaf left and was installed as chief four days later, on July 18. The ceremony was attended by the majority of subchiefs from Oinafa district, and Jione was officially given the name Poar, a title held by his grandfather, who had been district chief of Oinafa and an elder brother of Tokaniua (see figure). The chief of Malhaha district officially installed Poar and the ceremony was blessed by a local Methodist catechist.

On the following day, at a meeting of the Rotuma Council called by Toa'niu, Eliesa (whom Kausiriaf had appointed to fill in for him in his absence) described the situation in Oinafa as extremely serious, and urged the council not to recognize Poar as chief of Oinafa. He argued that there had been outside interference (presumably from Victor Rigamoto and Visanti Makrava) and that since the entire *mosega* was not present there was no legitimacy to Poar's title. The charges were answered by his brother Aisea, Oinafa's elected representative to the council and, along with Sautiak, one of the main perpetrators of the coup. Aisea denied outside intervention or influence, and reaffirmed that Kausiriaf was ousted because he was disrespectful to the *mosega*. If he had apologized instead of walking out of the meeting, the *mosega* would not have taken action against him.

Other members of the council (e.g., Gagaj Maraf, the district chief of Noa'tau) regarded the problem as an internal squabble within Oinafa and urged that the council not get involved in neighborhood brawls. No action was taken. Toa'niu himself, though castigating the dissidents, admitted that the animosities were caused by disputes involving the Raho Co-op.

These events split Oinafa village, and the entire district, into two hostile factions. Only a few families supported Kausiriaf, but they were militant in their actions. Led by Eliesa and Kausiriaf's son-in-law, Tarterani (Tokaniua's grandson; see figure), they went around the island mobilizing support. They warned that the coup leaders would suffer grave consequences, that they would be jailed. On the other side, people began openly to amplify gossip referring to Kausiriaf's corruption and meanness, listing instance after instance of his diversion of funds for his own use, his refusal to pay legitimate debts, his greed, and so forth. Typical was the story one woman told about the time her sister, one of the poorest people in Oinafa—a widow with no income, living with her daughter and son-in-law—had set her net in the bay near Kausiriaf's house to catch fish. When she went in the morning to check the net, there were no fish. But on the way back she ran into a neighbor, who told her that he had seen Kausiriaf go out in the middle of the night and take fish from her net. Information that had been suppressed in the interest of community harmony suddenly was brought to light in the form of malicious gossip.

The large majority of people in Oinafa supported Poar, although some sat on the fence, awaiting an outcome of the dispute. An indication of the relative levels of support for the two men is reflected in a *Fiji Times* article that appeared on September 26, 1990.

Two hundred and twenty people of Oinafa District in Rotuma have signed a petition objecting against Gagaj Kausiriaf being their district chief.

The district consists of three villages, Paptea, Lopta, and Oinafa, with more than 60 families residing in Oinafa District.

Of the 295 people living in the district, 63 [21 percent] are supporting Gagaj Kausiriaf, 220 [75 percent] the newly installed Gagaj Poar, and 12 [4 percent] are neutral.

The petition states: "We, the undersigned who live in Oinafa District, unanimously and whole-heartedly wish to voice our objection against Kausiriaf.

"We don't want Kausiriaf to be our district chief anymore.

"Therefore, we and our families have signed below to witness that we'll never again serve under Kausiriaf but we'll serve and live under our new leader, Gagaj Poar," says the petition.

The use of the news media to fight this case has put a new twist on political disputing in Rotuma. It is apparent that the chiefs who signed the original petition did not expect it to be made public. That it was publicized in the newspaper they saw as a deliberate leak meant to embarrass them. A subsequent story in the *Fiji Times* published on the day of Poar's installation, under the headline "Rotuma Clan Ousts Chief Over Petition," also was presumed by Kausiriaf and his supporters to be politically motivated. On July 24, 1990, six days after the article on his being ousted, Kausiriaf took out a paid advertisement in the *Fiji Times*.

Gagaj Kausiriaf Is Still the District Chief of Oinafa District

The report in your paper of 18/7/90 that "Rotuma clan ousts chief over petition" is sheer nonsense! The chiefly ceremony purported to have been carried out on Wednesday, 18/7/90 to install a new Chief was a complete farce.

The members of the Chiefly clan and the people of the district refused to attend the ceremony. My "MATANIVANUA" refused the invitation simply because I am still the District Chief of Oinafa. The TALATALA also refused to conduct the church service. The affair was confined mainly to family members of the two brothers [Sautiak and Emotama] (FESAITU) and Aisea Atalifo who confessed himself to another member of the chiefly clan that morning that he had realized that what was being prepared to be done was wrong and that, it was going to be an absolute farce. The ceremony could not be performed according to Rotuman chiefly custom.

The petition to the Prime Minister was made by the chiefs of Rotuma after the Chairman of the Council of Rotuma reported to them that there appeared that there was some kind of collusion by certain Rotumans in official positions to refuse to see him to discuss as to how best he could obtain financial assistance to buy two new buses to replace the two old buses on the island.

The arrogance and discourtesy shown by these Rotumans was most insulting to him as Chairman and also a high Chief of Rotuma, hence the petition. The Chairman had to turn to Mr. Paul Manueli who willingly gave the assistance he was seeking on behalf of the chiefs and the people on the island. From the information, I have so far gathered, I now believe to the best of my knowledge that the petition was leaked to the Press from the office of the Prime Minister.

The installation and/or dismissal of a District Chief is a very serious matter and, this is governed in Section 18 of the Rotuma Act, Cap. 122. District chiefs shall continue to the elected [sic] in accordance with Rotuman custom as heretofore. The Minister (the Prime Minister himself has replaced the Governor after independence in 1970) may in his discretion by notice in the Gazette remove from office any District Chief.

Who actually wrote this somewhat confusing ad was a matter of speculation on Rotuma. Since Kausiriaf speaks only a smattering of English it was assumed that one of his brothers drafted the document, but in any case it was seen as extremely provocative. Whereas traditional Rotuman dispute-resolution strategies involve denial of hurtful things said, the fact that Kausiriaf's accusations appeared in black and white was said to be permanent and unforgivable (it remains to be seen whether this will in fact be the case).

After a period of legal maneuvering the case was finally heard by the Fiji High Court on August 20, 1990. Justice Byrne ruled in Kausiriaf's favor. He interpreted the phrasing in the Rotuma Act of 1927 that dealt with the removal of chiefs as meaning there were no customary means of deposing an office holder.[26] Kausiriaf returned to Rotuma in triumph, but his victory was hollow since the majority of people in his district steadfastly refused to acknowledge him as their chief.

The Aftermath

Emboldened by their legal success, Kausiriaf and Toaʻniu decided to take up the case of Manav again, threatening to bring it to the High Court as well. Toaʻniu invited Manav to attend a meeting of the Rotuma Council in September 1990, saying he was still chief, rather than Osias, his replacement. This created quite a stir. The people in Ituʻmuta questioned Toaʻniu's authority over their district and agitated to have Toaʻniu replaced as chairman. When the council reconvened the next month, Osias demanded that Manav leave the meeting, and proposed a vote of no confidence in Toaʻniu. Kausiriaf and Toaʻniu apologized and Osias accepted their apology. Sensing a defeat, Toaʻniu begged to be allowed to stay on as chairman until the next election, at the end of the year (when he was replaced by Maraf, the chief of Noaʻtau).

Since the end of 1990, relationships in Oinafa have settled into a pattern of semi-stable avoidance between supporters of Kausiriaf and those of Poar. The latter, for his part, did nothing to protest Kausiriaf's right to sit on the Rotuma Council or to receive chiefly honors at ceremonies. He chose instead the role of a populist leader and has earned the trust of his followers,[27] who voluntarily built him an elegant Rotuman-style house and donated labor to prepare his yam plantation. The donation of labor is a tribute Rotumans paid to chiefs in an earlier era, but Kausiriaf had been denied the privilege because of the distrust he generated. By way of contrast, in 1989 Kausiriaf had to bring in a group of men from Ituʻmuta to help him with a yam garden. He paid them with kava.

Even within the village of Oinafa, where daily avoidance requires strenuous effort, the two factions conduct their affairs separately. Their refusal to cooperate with one another has cost them dearly in several ways, including financially. For example, the *Fairstar* was scheduled to visit Rotuma in March 1991 (arranged by Visanti) and again in June of that year (arranged by Atfoa). The first time Kausiriaf and his supporters wrote to the shipping company and complained, resulting in the cancellation of the visit; the second time Poar's group did the same. Poar said he suggested that the two groups get together and share the landing fees, but Kausiriaf refused. As a result the shipping company declared a moratorium on visits to Rotuma. The loss to the island's economy has been estimated at $F20,000 per visit.

So What's a Chief?!

The above narrative illustrates many of the dilemmas that confront modern Rotuman chieftainship. To begin with, it is clear that issues of chiefly authority cannot be disentangled from contemporary commerce. The key issue underlying the Oinafa dispute has deep roots in the struggle to control the Raho Cooperative. It has been exacerbated by problems related to the distribution of benefits from tourism, and suspicion of Kausiriaf's management of public funds.

Modern chiefs are jealous of their right to control district resources (and collectively, the island's resources), but they lack the skills to manage them efficiently. Under pressure to maintain their dignity through displays of generosity and occupation of impressive homes,[28] they are motivated to use a portion of funds under their control for personal use. This results in a loss of confidence and undermines the moral basis of their authority.[29]

The narrative also highlights problems of relationship between chiefs and educated Rotumans in Fiji who are in a position to assist Rotuma's development. People on the island, and particularly the chiefs, are determined to retain control of their destiny. The chiefs know they need the assistance of their educated kin, but expect unquestioned acquiescence to their wishes and formal courtesies in contexts where they are inappropriate. They are resentful when Rotuman businessmen and government officials do not quickly respond to their wants.

Complicating relations between chiefs and successful Rotumans in Fiji is that few of the latter have taken titles. From the chiefs' perspective, this suggests their own superior status, and generates an expectation of deference, if not obeisance. From the standpoint of Rotumans enmeshed in modern commercial establishments and government bureaucracies, Rotuman titles and chiefly positions are irrelevant off the island. In some cases they look upon the political infighting on Rotuma with bemusement. This was brought home to us during a conversation with Josefa Rigamoto following the Oinafa dispute. Arguably the most respected Rotuman alive, Josefa asked why his nephew Tarterani had so ferociously turned against his own relatives in his zealous support of Kausiriaf. We related a rumor that had been circulating, that Kausiriaf had promised Tarterani he would retire soon and appoint him as acting chief. This was the way Kausiriaf had become chief and presumably would keep the position in the immediate family (Tarterani is married to Kausiriaf's daughter, who is considered exceptionally ambitious). Upon hearing this explanation the old man threw up his hands, and with an expression bordering on disbelief exclaimed, "So what's a chief?!"

Whereas chiefs in many Pacific societies form a rallying point around which conservative cultural sentiment is mobilized in opposition to outside influences (a point made by Firth in 1969 and by numerous scholars since), the situation on Rotuma is much more ambiguous. On the one hand, chiefs represent a valued continuity with the past. The titles they assume were held by ancestors whose legacies encode the very essence of Rotuman history. Quite apart from the men who occupy them, titles represent the heart and soul of Rotuman culture. When Rotumans talk about past glories, about the supernaturally charged powers of their legendary ancestors, they almost invariably refer to former chiefs. By representing these titled ancestors in name, modern chiefs encode the dignity of tradition in the roles they play, whether or not their actions conform to expectations. Without chiefs, ceremonies of all kinds—births, marriages, welcomings, village and district fetes—would lose their significance, for it is the presence of chiefs that lends dignity and historical depth to such occasions. Virtually all formal ritual at ceremonies involves chiefs; without them nearly everything that is distinctly Rotuman would disappear.

For some Rotumans, chieftainship is central to their sense of selfhood. They consider themselves special because of their chiefly affiliations, either as descendants of prior chiefs, as close kinsmen of contemporary title holders, or as title holders themselves. For these individuals, chieftainship is hardly trivial. They see titles as embodying the Rotuman notion of ideal personhood, and feel themselves elevated as a result.

On the other hand, the chiefs are seen by many individuals as instruments of Fijian hegemony over Rotuma, as accepting Fijian dominance for what it gains them personally. The dissident Rotumans—those who favor independence and emphasize Rotuma's cultural uniqueness—focus their criticism on the chiefs. Central to most criticisms is the chiefs' alleged failure to consult the people they represent. But the issue of representation itself has become increasingly ambiguous as a result of the dispersion of the Rotuman community. In some respects—especially as symbolic embodiments of Rotuman tradition—chiefs represent all Rotumans, regardless of where they live. In other respects—as policymakers for the island of Rotuma—they represent all the people who live there. In still other ways, they represent the more limited interests of the people in their home district. And in an even more restricted sense, they represent their own kin group's interests within a district. It is therefore no longer quite so clear who should consult with whom, when.[30]

Furthermore, although they symbolically represent tradition, today's chiefs are not recognized as particularly learned in Rotuman custom, and despite occasional expressions of nostalgia for "the good old days" under colonial domination or before, the majority of Rotumans are more concerned with improving their standard of living and gaining increased autonomy over their lives than with glorifying the past. Many progressive Rotumans see the current chiefs, in their political and economic roles, as impediments to these goals.

Despite their criticisms of particular title holders, the *idea* of chieftainship is something few Rotumans on the island are prepared to abandon. While they freely complain about chiefs, singly and collectively, most people remain committed to the institution as a whole. A common suggestion is that chiefs be removed from positions of public administration, that the Council of Rotuma be reconstituted to exclude chiefs. That way, it is argued, the chiefs could concentrate on Rotuman custom and would be freed from involvement in secular politics and economic management. Such matters should be in the hands of Rotumans who have been educated and trained to deal with them, the argument goes. When chiefs take on such responsibilities, especially if they are inept, their moral authority is undermined, subverting the dignity of Rotuman custom.

Thus, while their symbolic ties to the past remain firmly embedded in Rotuman culture, the practical aspects of chiefly roles have become increasingly complicated and problematic. Whereas during the colonial era, chiefs were intermediaries between a resident commissioner or district officer and the people in their districts, today they are confronted with the much more difficult task of maneuvering between the central government in Suva and the people of Rotuma as a collectivity. Whether they like it or not, they are held responsible for fulfilling the material as well as the political aspirations of the Rotuman people—a task that requires skills beyond their current reach.

Understanding the dynamics of modern chieftainship on Rotuma, as elsewhere, requires an appreciation of the multilevel embeddedness of chiefly roles. As the inheritors of traditional titles, Rotuman chiefs are engaged in intra- and interfamilial politics with local histories of intrigue and contestation, sometimes going back for generations. They are also engaged in interdistrict competition with one another for prestige and dominance. Many aspects of the Oinafa case illustrate these complexities. As policymakers and administrators of development funds, along with elected representatives and the district officer, Rotuman chiefs are involved in the politics of business as well as the business of politics. In these roles they must engage institutions, such as banks and government bureaucracies at a national level, with or without the support of their more educated, Fiji-based, kin. Some, like Kausiriaf, have begun to use national-level institutions, like the press and the courts, to support their claims to legitimacy at home. Others have attempted to use their chiefly status to exploit opportunities in Fiji and abroad.

As the Rotuman case illustrates, the roles of traditional chiefs and modern administrators are often thoroughly interlaced, with the pressures and politics in the local arena influencing actions and interpretations of actions in the national arena, and vice versa. Only by coming to grips with the historically based interplay between these levels of social action will we come to appreciate the true significance of modern chiefs in the Pacific Islands.

Traditional Leaders Today in the Federated States of Micronesia

EVE C. PINSKER

THE CONTEMPORARY STATUS of "chiefs" in multicultural nations like the Federated States of Micronesia (F.S.M.) presents an interesting question: does it make sense, for the citizens of the nation or for us as analysts, to talk about "chiefs" who define their status within different traditional political systems as a group or category?[1] In other words, do chiefs interact with each other in ways made meaningful through chiefly status, and/ or do their subjects or constituents recognize some sort of status that is shared among chiefs from other islands as well as their own? The answer must involve the exploration of two different contexts: (1) historical— precolonial and colonial—precedents for interactions among chiefs between as well as within islands, and (2) the development of protocol and expectations for interactions between chiefs in the context of contemporary postcolonial national politics. Ideally, in examining the contemporary scene, we should investigate both discourse about chiefs and the practices engaging or engaged in by chiefs.[2]

The English term "chief" tends to obscure the differences between the statuses of different traditional positions between and within islands, and hence is often avoided in F.S.M. national political documents in favor of the term "traditional leader." I shall use the latter term here when speaking of the range of traditional statuses throughout the F.S.M.

If "chiefs" today find themselves "mediating local realities and the larger spheres of national and transnational interaction," as White and Lindstrom state in their introduction to this volume, then it becomes important to ask whether or how chiefs can transcend local rootedness, the local discourses that give them legitimacy and the possibility of their careers, in order to communicate with larger constituencies and function within a much wider community. Petersen's answer, later in this volume, is that an emphasis on the importance of local autonomy and a refusal to give to the state what should belong to the local community is itself a message sent to the nation-state and the international community questioning the requirement that people have to constitute their polities as nation-states in order to be taken seriously. I would add to that by positing that an emphasis on the local community does not have to mean a denial of the possible values of participating in larger communities. Individuals can belong to multiple communities, and leaders can learn to speak to multiple constituencies; and nation-states, perhaps, can leave room for heterogeneity and a measure of autonomy in localized political structures.

This chapter will describe some of the heterogeneity within the contemporary F.S.M., and briefly describe enough of its historical roots to indicate that leaders and their followers dealt with multiple levels of community prior to the establishment of the nation-state.[3] Traditional leaders continue to do so today, with the added complexity of defining themselves alongside government positions, sometimes in opposition to those positions, sometimes by conflating customary and elective/bureaucratic positions.

This leads to the complex task of understanding the evolving relationship between discourse about chiefs and the actions taken by and in regard to them: what options for action are comprehended as viable or legitimate, *by whom*, and how does this change over time? Change is real: in Yap, a century ago, a village chief could ask a chief from a village paired with his in the traditional alliance system to kill a young male troublemaker. Chiefs cannot do that now. In the late 1960s, a paramount chief from Pohnpei was a member of the Congress of Micronesia. The chances of a Pohnpeian paramount chief running for elective office in the Federated States of Micronesia Congress now are minimal, due to the increasingly different kinds of capital and different rhetorical strategies required for success in the two sorts of career. That could change in future generations, if a U.S. college–educated person becomes a paramount chief and perceptions of the split between traditional and elective leadership mutate again.[4]

The Federated States of Micronesia

The Federated States of Micronesia (F.S.M.) is a multi-island, multicultural nation of approximately 105,000 citizens (preliminary figures, 1994 census), living on 270 square miles worth of tiny islands, spread out over more than one million square miles of the western Pacific Ocean. From 1947 through 1986, these islands were administered by the United States as part of the UN Trust Territory of the Pacific Islands, which also included the islands of the Northern Marianas, Palau, and the Marshalls. The United States succeeded previous Spanish, German, and Japanese colonial administrations.

The F.S.M. was formed as a result of the process of negotiations with the United States over posttrusteeship status and financial assistance. In 1975, a constitutional convention of delegates from all the districts that then composed the Trust Territory successfully produced a draft constitution for a Federated States of Micronesia. In the referendum held in 1978, the citizens of the Marshalls and Palau rejected this constitution; the Marianas had already opted for separate commonwealth status. The districts that did vote to accept the constitution became the present four states of the F.S.M.: Kosrae, Pohnpei (formerly Ponape), Chuuk (formerly Truk), and Yap.

The F.S.M.'s constitutional government, with executive, judicial, and legislative branches, was implemented in 1979, still subject, however, to U.S. and UN authority. In 1986 the trusteeship relationship with the United States was replaced with a Compact of Free Association between the F.S.M. and the United States.[5] The F.S.M. was accepted into the United Nations as a sovereign nation in 1991.

Which former Trust Territory districts joined the F.S.M. and which did not had more to do with strategizing to achieve the best possible deal with the United States than it did with any nationalist sentiment or sense of shared traditions. Despite the low total population, the F.S.M.'s communities are amazingly heterogeneous, with recognized differences in language, custom, traditional political organization, and history, within as well as among the four states.

Kosrae is a single, high (meaning volcanically formed) island; the other states include a central high island or complex of high islands, and outlying low islands or coral atolls, referred to as outer islands. The inhabited atolls, rings of islets on a coral reef, are as small as half a square mile of total land area. The high islands are larger; Pohnpei Island, the largest, is about 129 square miles. The peoples of each island or atoll speak their own language or dialect, and there is some dialectal differentiation within the high islands as well. One might think that, with sometimes hundreds of miles between these small islands, one could describe cultural heterogeneity in Micronesia in terms of isolated, unified communities: each island with its own people. It is not, however, that simple. Even before the coming of European and American whaling and trading ships in the

1830s, very few of these islands were truly isolated. After all, the Micronesians that populated these islands 2,000 years before the Europeans did so by navigating in canoes over open ocean; that navigational knowledge survived on some of the low islands and linked island communities in alliances of trade and warfare. Warfare, migration due to typhoons, and intermarriage mixed island populations and histories. Conversely, on the larger, high islands, recognized differences in custom, language, and political allegiance between villages or sections of an island made identification with an islandwide community salient to people only in the limited context of contact with people from other islands. The contemporary picture is further complicated by the presence of people from the outer islands living on the high islands, some of whom still maintain ties and identify with their home outer-island community, even after several generations of more or less permanent residence on the high island.

The atoll lagoons in the western and central parts of the F.S.M. are generally larger than those east of Pohnpei, with more than one major inhabited islet. These islets, for some purposes, are regarded as distinct communities. The main island complex of Chuuk state, namely Chuuk lagoon, includes separate high islands, with recognized differences in dialect and customs, surrounded by a very large fringing reef.

Internally recognized divisions, however, do not stop there; most inhabited atoll islets and all the high islands, including those within Chuuk lagoon, are further divided into sections or districts. On the high islands of Yap and Pohnpei, these districts, corresponding to contemporary municipalities, are again divided up into distinct communities: villages (*binaw*) on Yap, "sections" (*kousapw*) on Pohnpei. The national constitution recognizes three levels of government: national, state, and local or municipal. Positions of political leadership exist at all three levels: elected governors, legislators, and councilmen; appointed judges; etc.

Leadership, Tradition, and Multiple Communities of Discourse

"Traditionally" defined leadership positions exist both below and alongside the governmentally defined positions. These leadership roles are not "traditional" in the sense of surviving unchanged from precontact times. Nor are they sanctioned by models consciously imported from outside and legitimized by outside audiences, such as the United States or the United Nations. Rather, they are sanctioned by contemporary understandings of custom developed over time through discussion within each community.

Previous experiences with outsiders' notions of leadership, however—for example, pressure from colonial administrators to designate a headman or high chief—have informed current understandings of what is traditional.

In speaking of discussions held within communities, I do not mean to imply that it is unproblematic to draw boundaries around communities, or that individuals belong primarily to only one community. Even outside the arena of imported government an individual can simultaneously belong to a household, a lineage, a clan, a village, a district, and an inter-island alliance, and have a different set of concerns shared with the other members of each of these sorts of community. It is not simply that communities provide arenas for discussion, but that discussions, based on and developing shared concerns and understandings, focused on situations that require practical action, can define communities.[6] Leaders shape their careers, not simply within territorial areas, but within what I shall call here "communities of discourse": ongoing discussions about what appropriate conduct for a leader is, who is a legitimate leader, who is a leader worth supporting, etc. "Communities of discourse" refers to the arenas in which discourse about a particular subject is seen as relevant and is developed, based on shared understandings that are continuously elaborated on and revised. Insofar as discussions of traditional leadership center on different issues from discussions of nontraditional leadership, they create separate spheres of action, separate possibilities for constructing careers of leaders and their followers, judged by separate standards. People can ask, as did the Rotuman leader quoted by Howard and Rensel elsewhere in this volume, "So what's a chief?!" However, concepts from other spheres, other discourses, can be brought in to answer or shape the questions, as in the case described by Adams (Chapter 14), when a Torajan official supported the act of making offerings to the traditionally defined *sokkong bayu* by referring to the Indonesian national rhetoric of Pancasila.

Communities of discourse and the practices the discourse refers to or indexes together form what Pierre Bourdieu has called a "field" (Bourdieu 1992: ch. 4). A field is a network of positions defined by the distribution of species of power, or capital (symbolic capital, economic capital, etc.). The sorts of capital that are relevant function in relation to a specific field: senior genealogical position, for instance, may constitute powerful capital in the field of a particular community's traditional leadership, but not in fields of elective leadership. Bourdieu compares a field to a game, but a game whose regularities are not codified or expressed in explicit rules. I would add, however, that a move to explicitly articulate the regularities of the field can be a way of reconstituting the field (following the logic of Bourdieu 1977:167–68): the question "So just what *is* a chief?" can certainly be a challenge.

The difficulty of determining the limits of a particular community of discourse relevant to a particular sort of leadership is paralleled in Bourdieu's discussion of fields: "The question of the limits of the field is a very difficult one, if only because it is *always at stake in the field itself* and therefore admits of no *a priori* answer" (Bourdieu 1992:61). The question of the limits of traditional leadership in Micronesian communities exemplifies this. In Yap state, for instance (see below), the chiefly Councils of Pilung and Tamol have the power to decide what decisions fall within the jurisdiction of tradition or custom, and have extended their jurisdiction to cover such matters as which municipalities can run buses. Surely this is a case of extending the limits of discourse about "tradition" and of broadening the chiefs' sphere of influence (or of refusing to have it narrowed by new technology or other legislative bodies).

Traditional Leadership in the Four States of the F.S.M.

I shall briefly summarize the traditional political statuses and their current functioning within each F.S.M. state before moving to a discussion of traditional leaders in the F.S.M. as a whole. (For a summary, see the table on page 156.) The states roughly correspond to precolonial networks of interisland alliance, trade, and conflict. High islands, in the past as now, provided needed resources and shelter in times of drought or typhoon to those living on the atolls' fragile ecosystems. Today, the current system of state centers, with the availability there of cash employment, jet travel, and educational advancement, has contributed to the creation of state societies: young people can think of their careers or life paths in terms of opportunities open to them within the state, not just their home island or municipal district. Traditional leaders, too, are increasingly defining their roles within a state context.

Yap and the Yap State Outer Islands

Precolonial Polity: Yap High Islands

I can only briefly touch on the complexities of the traditional Yap high islands polity and its relation to the outer island polities. (For fuller discussions of Yap and its outlying atolls, see Lingenfelter 1975 and Alkire 1989.) The authority of the chiefs on Yap proper comes not from control over all the land but from the rank of the piece of land, the estate or *tabinaw*, into which they were born. This estate is inherited patrilineally (but with residual oversight rights remaining in the matrilineal line, through

Summary of Information on Traditional Leadership in the Four States of the FSM

	Yap state	Chuuk state	Pohnpei state	Kosrae state
Precolonial polities	Yap proper: ranked estates within villages, ranked villages in ranked municipalities, joined in 2 alliances. Chiefs take rank from estate. Outer islands: islets, districts within islets with ranked matrilineages, head of senior matrilineage is chief.	Both in lagoon and outer islands: islets, districts within islands, with ranked matrilineages, head of senior matrilineage is chief. In lagoon: two competing alliances, with associated schools of *itang* lore.	Pohnpei proper: traditional ranked municipalities headed by 2 lines of chiefly titles (Nahnmwarki/ Nahnken lines). Outer islands: chiefly lineages, successions disrupted by Marshallese invasion, 1830s whalers/ traders.	Five traditional municipalities with chiefly titles: paramount chief and "prime minister" over whole island. Traditional leadership system completely disrupted by disease and depopulation in first half of 19th century.
Precolonial interisland relations	Outer islands/Yap joined through *sowai* tributary voyages, ties through leaders of districts in atolls and estates in Gagil, Yap.	Shifting alliances between districts in lagoon, clan allies between lagoon/ outer islands. *Itang* communication between islands.	No regular contact between all islands prior to European ships; Mwoakillese claim traditional relation with Madolenihmw in Pohnpei.	Kosrae state composed of only one (high) island.
Effects of colonial period	Pacification froze rank; increased importance of municipalities (relative to villages) in Yap.	Warfare no longer available as a means of gaining rank, territory for lineages.	Increased contact between outer islanders and Pohnpeians; freeze of traditional municipal boundaries and rank on Pohnpei.	Traditional title and leadership system replaced by church leadership positions after Christian conversion.
Current relation of traditional leaders to government	Councils of Pilung (Yap) and Tamol (Outer Islands) are fourth branch of state government.	Some municipal leaders claim both traditional chief and elected chief magistrate status. No body of traditional leaders in state government (draft constitution with such a body voted down).	Some Nahnmwarkis as chief magistrates in 1950s; ended in 1970s. No official body of traditional leaders in state government; group of Pohnpei chiefs meets. Outer islanders instituting titles parallel to Pohnpei's, outside elective government.	Church leadership not part of elective state government; church leaders sent as traditional leaders to national meetings.
Other comments	Outer islanders have low status on Yap.	Competition between outer islanders/lagoon, but little status distinction.	Outer islanders have low status on Pohnpei but can assimilate.	

the matrilineal clan). Each estate has a particular ranking within a section of a village; the sections within the village are also ranked, and the village as a whole is ranked in regard to other villages in the municipality. Several chiefly statuses are defined at the village level—the sitting chief (an advisorial, respected elder–type role), the executive chief (the chief most active in daily decision-making concerning the whole village), and the chief-of-young-men (who directs the young men as a work force and, formerly, as a military force). Sections within the village also have chiefly statuses associated with them.

Villages are situated within municipalities (*falak*). Although the ten existing municipalities and their boundaries are today spoken of as "traditional," the term *falak* itself is apparently of German origin (from the German *Flagge*, or flag; see Meller 1969:146), and there is evidence that the idea of municipalities as bounded units of continuous territory was instituted during the German colonial period prior to World War I (see Bashkow 1991). The older—and still existing—view of Yap as a polity is not one of a series of contiguous territorial units, but of a set of alliance relationships that bound villages and sections of villages together in a "nug" or net (Lingenfelter 1975). The municipalities today are ranked with respect to each other, with Tamil, Rull, and Gagil being considered the highest.

The system is further complicated by the two types of high-ranking villages: *bulce* and *ulun*. *Bulce* villages had a corresponding partner *ulun* village. The villages were joined into two competing Yap-wide alliances. There was a traditional network of communications, the *thaaq*, which went from one particular estate in a particular village to another estate in a higher ranking village and so on, joining in alliance the chiefs of villages in different municipalities.[7]

The *thaaq* network still functions today. When I was in Yap, in September 1986, I stayed in Choqol, a high-ranking village in Maap municipality. One of the chiefs from Bugol, a high-ranking village in Tamil, came to Choqol, the village traditionally joined to his estate by the *thaaq*, to campaign for the candidates for the legislature from Tamil (one of whom was his son).

Effects of Colonial Period: Yap High Islands

I will not describe here the traditional political system of Yap in any greater depth, but I want to emphasize that it is not a simple hierarchy in the sense of nested parts within wholes. The authority of the highest chief in Teb village in Tamil does not derive only from the rank of Tamil municipality or even from the ranking of Teb within Tamil, but from the particular *tabinaw* or estate that his father, and he himself, was born onto.

This means that the authority of chiefs in Yap proper was not as threatened by colonial policies favoring the issuance of individual land deeds as it was in other areas in Micronesia, where precolonial chiefly authority derived from residual rights over large tracts of land on which others were living. The legitimacy of Yapese chiefs came from connection with particular estates, over which they retained their control throughout the colonial administrations.

However, throughout Micronesia, colonial administrations stopped intraisland warfare, and this had important consequences for local politics. The rank of villages in Yap, previously subject to changes since war could result in gain or loss of rank, was frozen as it had been at the time of colonial contact. Following pacification, people in Yap were able to move more freely around the islands, between villages and municipalities, without fear of being killed, and that resulted in some lessening of the chiefs' power, since if people didn't like a particular chief they could move elsewhere. Also, of course, chiefs no longer had the power to mobilize young men for war. On Yap, the villages began to lose importance relative to the municipalities, since people no longer needed to fear for their lives when outside the boundaries of their own village. In precolonial Yap, intervillage rivalry had at times been very fierce; according to indigenous oral history, when a village member was thrown out of a village, he was almost certain to be killed if he could not find acceptance as a member of another village.

The Current Position of Yap High Islands Chiefs

In colonial Yap, in dealing with the outside administration, the chiefs of the highest village in each municipality became more important and acted for the whole municipality. Today, the village chiefs of a municipality choose from among their high-ranking chiefs the one who will represent them on the Council of Pilung, the group of chiefs from Yap proper that, together with the Council of Tamol or Outer Island Chiefs, constitutes the fourth branch of the Yap state government. The chief on the Council of Pilung acts as the chief magistrate for the municipality from which he comes. Sometimes more than one chief is angling for that position. The rivalries must be settled by traditional means—that is, exclusive of warfare—by exercising influence and gaining allies, by calling in favors and using kin ties, namely, the activities usually called "politicking." There are no elections for chief magistrate/member of the Council of Pilung, except in the municipality of Rull.[8] Rull has an elected chief magistrate, but the two men who have successively held that position have both been considered highest-ranking traditional chief as well and have served on the Council of Pilung.

Precolonial Polities and Interisland Relations

Prior to the colonial period, the inhabitants of the Yap Islands proper—
that is, the high islands of Yap: Gagil-Tamil, Maap', and Rumung, nestled
together within their fringing reef—maintained that they had political
dominance over the outlying atolls to the south and east: Ngulu, Ulithi,
Fais, Woleai, Eauripik, Sorol, Ifaluk, Faraulep, Lamotrek, Elato, Sata-
wal, Puluwat, Pulap, Namonuito, and Pulusuk (see fig. 19 in Lingenfelter
1975: 151). This dominance was rooted in particular relationships between estates (*tabinaw*) in the villages of Gacpar and Wonyan in Gagil and
particular islets or sections of islets in the outlying atolls. This relationship
is called *sowai* and can be glossed as either "trade" or "tribute": the outer
islanders were regularly required to send tribute to their *sowai* estates and
received gifts and protection from natural disasters in return. The Yapese
were thought to have the power to send or withhold typhoons and epidemics, and in any case, the high islands provided a possible place of ref-
uge from the more fragile environment of the atolls.[9]

The structure of the traditional polities, and the constitution of chiefly
status, in the outer islands of Yap state does not follow the same pattern
as the complex hierarchy of Yap proper. Rather, political organization in
these atolls shares the same general pattern found in Chuuk lagoon and in
the islands of Chuuk state north and south of the lagoon. Islets are divided
into districts (although sometimes an islet contains only one district). A
matrilineage claimed primary right to the land in a district, through first
settlement or through warfare, and became the highest-ranking matrilineage in that district. The senior male (in some cases in the Yap outer islands, a female) of the matrilineage acts as the chief of the district. The
chief of the district associated with the most senior matrilineage on the
islet acts as the chief of the islet, and sometimes the chief associated with
the most senior matrilineage and district in an entire atoll acts as the representative of the atoll. However, the authority of a chief was based on
his authority as matrilineage headman, and the support and strength of
the people in that matrilineage. The chiefs had very limited ability to act
without the support of the heads of the other matrilineages. An important part of the outer islands chiefs' role was (and is) to maintain alliance
and exchange relationships with other islands, including Yap proper. This
was formerly done through the *sowai* tributary voyages and is now done
through the Council of Tamol, the outer island chiefly council that meets
on Yap, and acts together with the chiefs of Yap proper in the Council of
Pilung as the fourth branch of the state government.

Note that the relationships between Yap proper and the outer islanders
were structured not as a relationship between "Yapese" as a group and

"outer islanders" as a group, but as particular relationships operating through holders of particular chiefly offices and pieces of land. This was also true from the point of view of the outer islanders. On their tributary voyages, the canoes traveled west to Yap, starting from the easternmost atolls, with the fleet assembling at Ulithi under the command of a Ulithi navigator prior to continuing on to Yap. Particular matrilineages on specific Ulithi islets, through their heads, sent tribute to their associated *sowai* estates in Gagil.

In turn, Ulithi matrilineages were the dominant partners in *sowai* relationships with specific islets in Woleai atoll and the other atolls further east in the chain. Those islands, whose canoes met at Woleai atoll before they sailed to Ulithi, were and are collectively referred to as "the Woleai" (although today Puluwat, Pulusuk, Pulap, and Namonuito are in Chuuk state, and I believe they are generally now not included when Yapese outer islanders speak of "the Woleai," certainly not when they are talking about political alliances within Yap state).

Colonial and Current Interisland Relations and the Chiefs

Japanese restrictions on long-distance canoe voyaging imposed after World War I stopped the tributary chain, although Lessa reported in 1950 that Ulithi had sent tribute to Yap only a few years before (Lessa 1950). He reports at that time, however, that Ulithians found their *sowai* relationships with Gagil increasingly onerous and one-sided. The Yapese considered their outer-island vassals to be like their "children," and although this implied an obligation to care for their needs, it also implied that the outer islands had to show the same sort of deference behavior shown by Yapese from low-ranking estates and villages ("low-caste" Yapese) to higher-caste Yapese, and also meant that the Yapese could demand that the outer islanders work for them. In terms of the Yap-proper ranking system, outer islanders were and are generally considered lower than low-caste Yapese proper. I heard complaints from outer islanders about Yapese behavior toward them in the 1980s.

Furthermore, outer islanders also perceive a split between Ulithi and "the Woleai," as well as differences between specific islands. My admittedly sketchy impression is that people from "the Woleai" sometimes see Ulithians as somewhat arrogant, like the Yapese and possibly because of their close traditional ties to the Yapese. Jockeying for control over political power and resources also goes on between the chiefs of Ulithi and "the Woleai."

The second president of the F.S.M. was from Euripik, hence from "the Woleai," a source of potential prestige to and a reflection of support from the eastern Yap state atolls, but this does not necessarily imply strong support from the Council of Tamol; the narrations I heard of his political career present a more complicated story. When he first won national political office, a seat in the Congress of Micronesia (the precursor to the F.S.M. Congress), he did so as a write-in candidate, without the support of the chiefly councils and against their official candidate. After he won, the chiefly councils supported him and fielded him as an official candidate in ensuing elections, but at times the Council of Pilung backed him more strongly than did the Tamol chiefs. This was attributed to lingering resentment of his independent initial accession to political office. In the F.S.M. capital in 1990 I heard rumors that Tamol support for the president had further eroded, because he had not given the council members sufficient respect and time during an official visit. In 1991 he lost the Senate seat from Yap that he was required to win in order to keep the presidency for a second term.

The Current Role of Yap State Traditional Leaders in Government

Yap state, more than any other state, has traditional leadership positions integrated into the constitutional government. Under the Yap constitution, the Councils of Pilung and Tamol have veto power over any legislation proposed in the Yap state legislature that they, the councils themselves, decide falls within their realm of authority over tradition. In practice this has been defined broadly, as when, in the mid-1980s, the Council of Pilung vetoed a proposal to run a bus to one municipality on the basis that it was not "traditional" to run a bus to one municipality and not to the other municipalities!

The members of the Council of Pilung received (as of 1987) US$1,000 a year for expenses. The members of the corresponding outer-islands chiefs' council—the Council of Tamol—receive monetary payment on a per diem basis for attending meetings that occur only once or twice a year; in practice, their total reimbursement has been less than that of the Pilung members. Neither Pilung nor Tamol members receive any salary for serving as executives within their municipalities.

It is widely held that it is the traditional chiefs in Yap who control who files for candidacy for elective office. Stories of potential candidates pressured to withdraw support this. Of the two chiefly councils, members of the Tamol usually seem to work in concert with and defer to the Pilung chiefs; their positions are not necessarily those that would be taken by a majority of the outer-island population, as is indicated by the earlier described outcome of the initial congressional campaign of the man who later became F.S.M. president.

Chuuk Lagoon and the Chuuk Outer Islands

Precolonial Polities and Interisland Relations

Chuuk state (formerly called Truk state) includes the high islands within Chuuk lagoon, and the outlying atolls of the Westerns (to the west of Chuuk lagoon); the Halls and Namonuito to the north; and the Mortlocks in the south. The traditional polities and chiefly statuses in the Greater Chuuk area roughly follow the model described above for the outer islands in Yap state, with islets divided into districts (*sopw*), with the head of the highest-ranking matrilineage in the district serving as district chief.

In precolonial Chuuk lagoon, there were two competing political alliances. Different districts within the same island could belong to opposing alliances. The alliances shifted over time, as the demands of war and diplomacy required. The outer islands were not formally part of these alliances, although they, or clans within them, apparently sometimes did participate as allies in lagoon conflicts. This pattern of shifting alliances continues into modern Chuukese state politics.

Each alliance had an associated school of *itang*: Chchun, centered on Fefen and Tonowas; and Sopwunupi, named after its leading clan and centered on Wone (the current state capital, also previously referred to as Moen). Uman was independent and had its own *itang* school. *Itang* is a body of lore, including knowledge of tactics of diplomacy, war, navigation, and rhetoric. The rhetoric of *itang* includes allusive proverbs and esoteric language that may be employed by knowledgeable and powerful people to warn or coerce, negotiate or resolve disputes. (Use of *itang* by someone not qualified to wield it is said to hurt the wielder.) A person can also be referred to as an *itang* if he is adept at the uses of *itang*. In the past, chiefs were not necessarily *itang*s; a chief could have an *itang* work for him. Today, some knowledge of *itang* is a powerful support for a claim of traditional chiefly status (as opposed to the elective/bureaucratic status of chief magistrate).

In Chuuk, throughout all of the remembered history of human settlement in these islands, there has been semiregular contact between the outlying atolls of the Westerns, the Halls, Namonuito, and the Mortlocks and the islands within Chuuk lagoon. The Westerns, even during the period when they participated in the tribute trade to Yap, also traded with Chuuk lagoon, without the implication of political subordination. Clan histories relate migrations of clans not only between islands in the lagoon, but between outer islands and the lagoon islands, in both directions. For instance, Gladwin and Sarason (1953:36) report that clans in the Halls,

Namonuito, and the Mortlocks trace their origins back to Chuuk lagoon, many specifically to Mechituw village on Wone. Mortlockese on Wone told me about clan and trading connections between the Mortlock Islands and Tol. Goodenough (1951:176) relates the history of a Romonum lineage that was started by a Pween clan brother and sister emigrating from Pulap. Clanmates on another island were supposed to provide hospitality for their traveling relatives, and thus clan dispersion made interisland exchange possible, through specific partners.

Although there are separate *itang* schools in the outer islands, *itang* wielders apparently could communicate with each other if they chose to, or at least that is the modern perception. A family from Oneiop, in the Mortlocks, told me about a pre-1914 incident in which an *itang* from their island and an *itang* from Wone (in Chuuk lagoon) were able to use their special knowledge and powers to communicate with each other using esoteric *itang* vocabulary: the Oneiop *itang*, then staying on Udot Island in Chuuk lagoon, paddled to Wone and warned the Wone *itang*, in allusive language, about a planned raid on Wone by warriors from Uman.

The close relationship between the Chuukic dialects spoken in Chuuk lagoon and the outlying atolls means that ordinary communication is not too difficult, although a person can understand and speak more easily with people from a nearby island than with those farther away. Precolonial contact among the outer islands and between those islands and Chuuk lagoon was mainly in the hands of the outer islanders: they controlled the knowledge of long-distance navigation. Thus the atoll people were the traffickers and carriers of influences (Goodenough, personal communication).

In summary, it does seem justifiable to speak of "greater Chuukese society" (Marshall 1981) in the precolonial period as well as in the colonial and F.S.M. eras. Trade, travel, and social ties existed between all the islands in the area, ties that were and are negotiated through matrilineages and their associated district chiefs. That does not mean that precolonial relations were always peaceful; quite the contrary: wars were important in forming and breaking interisland alliances and in forcing clan migrations. As elsewhere in Micronesia, pacification has had an important effect on the powers and limitations of chiefs.

Contemporary Interisland Relations

Unlike the situation in Yap or Pohnpei, in Chuuk the traditional political structures within the high islands of Chuuk lagoon are similar to those within the outlying atolls: islands divided into districts with associated senior matrilineages. The lagoon people are no more preoccupied with hierarchy or rank than are the outer islanders, and cannot view them as lesser beings on that account. On Wone itself, however, people are after other kinds of status—Western education and cash income–producing jobs. Early on in the American administration, immigrants from the Mortlocks took advantage of the educational opportunities offered and moved into government and teaching jobs. The cash incomes they received enabled them to buy land on Wone, thus engendering some resentment from lagoon Chuukese (and, according to Flinn [1992], other outer islanders).

In response to this, in the early 1970s the mayor of Wone, Petrus Mailo, widely respected for his leadership and his *itang* knowledge and considered to be both a chief magistrate and a traditional chief, made a memorable speech. (It must have been a memorable speech since it was described to me in 1987 by Wone Mortlockese.) He used the *itang* phrase "sefalin Wela" (my informant's spelling), or "go back and forth to Wone (Moen)." He elucidated, saying that a long time ago the people traveled back and forth, so a lot of people of the Mortlocks, the Halls, and the Westerns created part of Wone. So they are all part of Wone; and conversely, Sopwunupi clan is all over Chuuk. Petrus Mailo used this *itang* phrase to create solidarity between lagoon Chuukese and outer islanders, and to counter resentment of the Mortlockese.

The Current Position of the Chiefs and Their Relation to Government

In contemporary Chuuk state, many of the chief magistrates (the elected executive heads of municipalities) also claim traditional status as "chief," asserting that they are senior members of the highest-ranking clan in their municipality, clan rank being determined in terms of the history of the first settlement and/or the victors of precolonial wars. For most of the chief magistrates who claimed that status, however, I heard other Chuukese dispute it, either on the basis of living clan elders senior to the claimant, or on the basis of the claimant's clan or lineage not really being senior. One Chuukese man went so far as to say, "We don't have any chiefs any more—only chief magistrates," a position strongly denied both by chief magistrates who claim to be chiefs and by chiefs who claim to be chiefs but not chief magistrates. Some of the latter are former chief magistrates who subsequently lost an election.

In addition to clan seniority, if a man knows the higher levels of *itang*, that seems to count strongly with contemporary Chuukese in recognizing him as a traditional leader. Chiefs are judged on their ability to refer to *itang* in public speeches and to use it to shape public sentiment. People remember and retell usages of *itang* by chiefs now deceased, as in the above example of Petrus Mailo's speech. It is also acknowledged, however, that fewer people now know *itang* than formerly, and that much depth and complexity has been lost.

Chuuk state has no body of traditional leaders written into the present state constitution. An early draft constitution did include such a body; it passed the first Chuukese state constitutional convention, but that draft was voted down in the public referendum. A primary reason for its rejection, according to Chuukese I spoke with in 1990, was the unpopularity of the provision that a body of traditional chiefs be constituted as a branch of state government. The second draft constitution, which was accepted by the voters in 1989 and is now in effect, has only a provision parallel to the F.S.M. constitution's provision that nothing in the constitution shall be construed as negating the powers of traditional leaders. Chuuk municipalities, as I said above, have elected magistrates, but some are also considered traditional chiefs.

Today, chiefs form connections not only with other chiefs, or other chiefs/chief magistrates, but with congressmen and those in other elective statuses. One chief on Udot whom I visited (he lost his reelection as chief magistrate shortly after my visit, but is still considered a traditional chief) displayed the fiberglass motorboat he had received through his F.S.M. senator's public-projects bill. The chief told me that he was currently serving as the chairman of the *Muiich en Aramas*, "People's Party," a political party or alliance that supported the senator and his efforts to get greater political status and economic resources for the islands in his senate district (Faaychuuk, which includes roughly half of Chuuk lagoon).

Pohnpei and the Pohnpei State Outer Islands

Precolonial Polities on Pohnpei Island

Precolonial Pohnpei Island was divided into several paramount chiefdoms, or *wehi*, each headed by two lines of chiefs, roughly parallel to Polynesia's chief and talking chief: the Nahnmwarki and the Nahnken. (See Riesenberg 1968 and Petersen 1982 for comprehensive descriptions of the traditional polities on Pohnpei proper.) The *wehi* are ranked in respect to each other, with Madolenihmw the highest ranked. In each *wehi*, there is a high-ranked matrilineage (*keinek*) associated with the Nahnmwarki title-line and another matrilineage associated with the Nahnken title-line; ideally, the two matrilineages intermarried and kept control of the lines.

The Nahnmwarki of Madolenihmw had ritual precedence over the other Nahnmwarkis, but he had no authority over anyone outside of Madolenihmw and no ability to command the leaders of the other *wehi*. There was thus no paramount chief over Pohnpei as a whole, although, in Pohnpeian traditional history, in the period before the time of the

Nahnmwarkis, there was a line of paramount chiefs, titled *Saudelour*, who had authority over the whole island. Their rule, however, is regarded as tyrannical and less desirable than the more decentralized Nahnmwarki/ Nahnken system.

The Nahnmwarki and the Nahnken gave, and still give, titles to those below them in both lines. They also conferred, on the leaders of the sections within their *wehi*, the status of section head and his "cup-bearing chief," or *paliendahl*, the position corresponding to the Nahnken's role at the section level. These titles today are conferred only with the consent of the people of the section, and I believe that was also true, for the most part, in the past, as Pohnpeian sections or groups of sections always had the option to secede from the *wehi* and form an independent or semi-independent chiefdom. Several of the areas of contemporary Pohnpei, such as Awak in U municipality and Palikir in Sokehs municipality, have a history of being independent.

The Nahnmwarki, however, as long as he could enforce it, had control of all the land in his domain, except for parcels under the direct control of the Nahnken, and could theoretically assign it to whomever he wanted. This changed when the Germans began issuing individual titles to land in 1910—although the changes in land ownership had begun in the mid-1800s when the Nahnken of Kitti and his son had learned from the missionaries how to make a written deed, thus resulting today in their family, the Nanpei family, owning a quarter of all the land on Pohnpei.

The Colonial and Current Positions of Paramount Chiefs and Their Relation to Government

Contemporary Nahnmwarkis, though they do not have control over land, still have control over titles, and in return for titles people make a title feast, the *kapasmwar*, at which they give to the Nahnmwarki a pig, a big yam, and kava, at the minimum. Today they also give sacks of rice, canned goods, cloth, and cash, and there are cases of more expensive gifts such as beds or pickup trucks. This sort of feasting behavior is increasing rather than declining, as many writers on Pohnpei have noted (Fischer 1974; Petersen 1982).

The status titles in the Pohnpeian *wehi* have changed as a result of contact: the lists of ranked titles have become more uniform from one municipality to another. Up until about 1900 not all the *wehi* called their highest chief Nahnmwarki. Wasai Sokehs had been the highest title in Sokehs, and Lepen Nett the highest title in Nett. I hypothesize that this was due partly to the colonial administration calling all the paramount chiefs Nahnmwarki, and partly to the desire of the paramount chiefs from the lower-ranking municipalities to be more equal in status. There still are differences in the series of ranked titles in the different *wehi*, but probably less so than in the past. In colonial times, the ability of people to travel more safely around the island meant that it became easier to compare and systematize the title rankings.

Prestations to the Nahnmwarki in return for titles probably became more frequent as valor in war was closed off as a route to advancement. As many of the writers on Pohnpei have noted, there has been an increase in the number of *koanoat*, or honorary, *wehi* or municipal-level titles given by the Nahnmwarkis. In pre–World War II times, many people had section titles but not *wehi* titles. Today, anyone who wants a *wehi* title can have one if he gives enough to the Nahnmwarki over a long enough period of time.

Under the present state government (as defined in the 1984 Pohnpei state constitution) Pohnpei state is made up of eleven municipalities. Five of these municipalities are the precolonial *wehi* of Pohnpei Island: Madolenihmw, Kitti, U, Sokehs, and Nett. The sixth municipality on Pohnpei is Kolonia Town, the port town. (The F.S.M. capital and national government offices were formerly located in Kolonia Town, but are now located in Palikir, Sokehs.) The present Nahnmwarki and Nahnken of Nett blocked an attempt by a prominent leader and businessman of Kolonia Town in the early 1980s to constitute Kolonia Town as a traditional *wehi* and assume the title of Nahnmwarki. Kolonia Town was carved out of Nett, and the traditional leaders of Nett still consider it part of the *wehi* of Nett. (Some Nett people in Kolonia Town still bring first-fruits offerings to the Nahnmwarki and Nahnken of Nett.) However, Kolonia Town is not part of the territory covered by the elective/bureaucratic structure of Nett municipality.

All the municipalities of Pohnpei Island currently are functioning under municipal constitutions with elected chief executives, legislative councils, and municipal courts. These are salaried positions and function outside of the traditional leadership and title systems. In the 1950s, several of the elected chief magistrates were also the Nahnmwarkis, such as the Nahnmwarkis/chief magistrates of Kitti, Sokehs, and Nett. With the exception of Nahnmwarki Max Iriarte of Nett, who retained both positions until his death in the early 1970s (he also, in the mid-1960s, served in the Congress of Micronesia), the Nahnmwarkis moved out of elective government in the 1960s. Nahnmwarki Max Iriarte's son, the current Nahnken of Nett, attempted to follow in his father's footsteps in the early 1990s and ran for the office of district administrator of Nett municipality (the title given to the chief executive officer under the Nett municipal constitution). He was elected but was impeached before the end of his term. He retains his title of Nahnken and continues to function in that role, demonstrating the separation between traditional and elective leadership.

The municipalities of Pohnpei state, including the outer islands, have all had constitutional conventions since 1984. Most municipalities have followed the F.S.M. and state constitution models and have not formally written traditional leaders into the municipal constitution. Kitti municipality of Pohnpei Island, however, did provide for formal roles for both the group of high-titled men and the Nahnmwarki, who is designated the Kaun en Wehi or "head of state."

Pohnpei state's constitution, like Chuuk's, has no formal body for traditional leaders. The Nahnmwarki and Nahnken of the five *wehi* of Pohnpei Island meet monthly in the governor's offices to discuss issues of mutual concern, as a *Wiekupwur*, or traditional council. They have an elected chairman, preferring not to go by traditional rank and install the Nahnmwarki of the highest-ranking municipality, Madolenihmw, as chairman. The chairmen they have elected seem to be have been chosen on the basis of their extroversion, knowledge, and interest in Americanized government rather than on the basis of traditional rank or knowledge. The council does not include any outer-island leaders in its meetings.

Pohnpei State Outer Islands: Discontinuities in Traditional Leadership

Of the eleven municipalities of Pohnpei state, five are outer-island atolls: Mwoakilloa (formerly Mokil) and Pingelap to the east, Sapwuahfik (formerly Ngatik) and the Polynesian outliers of Nukuoro and Kapingamarangi to the south. There are several characteristics that distinguish Pohnpei state's atolls from those of Chuuk and Yap states. Some of the atolls in Chuuk and Yap states have large lagoons (ten to twelve miles across) with several habitable islets (large enough to have a taro patch and sustain permanent settlement). These islets function as separate communities or municipalities; in other words, there can be more than one municipality within an atoll. Pohnpei state's atolls are smaller and only have one large, permanently inhabited islet each (except for Kapingamarangi, which has two settled islets connected by a bridge).

In Chuuk and Yap states, the outer islands are considered, with some justification, to be conservative, largely isolated from extra-Micronesian outside influences (at least in comparison to the state centers), and to maintain a more traditional lifestyle, including continuity of traditional leadership. This is not the case with Pohnpei's atolls, which have experienced major disruptions in traditional leadership systems.

Marshallese war canoes visited several of the atolls in the eighteenth and nineteenth centuries. Mwoakilloa's system of succession to the paramount chiefship was disrupted because of Marshallese invasion and settlement, and Mwoakillese oral history relates that accession to the paramount chiefship for several generations prior to Christian conversion was through assassination. The most dramatic disruption came in Sapwuahfik: in the "Ngatikese Massacre" in 1837 (see Poyer 1993), American and British sailors and their Pohnpeian allies killed all the adult men on the island. After the massacre, Sapwuahfik people set up a title system parallel to Pohnpei's, with a Nahnmwarki and a Nahnken, superseding previous indigenous titles.

Both Mwoakilloa and Pingelap were stops for whaling ships in the 1830s, and were converted to Congregational Protestantism when the missionaries followed the whalers in the mid-1800s. Pingelap did continuously maintain a position of paramount chief, called Dokosa (cognate of the precolonial Kosraean paramount-chief title, Tokosra; however, currently he is also referred to as Nahnmwarki), and a traditional council with associated indigenous titles; however, like Pohnpei's titled *wehi* leaders, the traditional positions have declined in importance and economic power in relation to the new elective/bureaucratic municipal-government positions.

The municipal constitutional conventions provided occasions for Pohnpei state citizens to discuss the role of their traditional leaders; in the case of some of the atolls who had allowed their traditional chief position to lapse, this was a matter of considerable controversy. Mwoakilloa atoll, for instance, had not had a traditional chief for thirty years, with church organization and later elective government taking up leadership functions, until a man from the former chiefly family appointed himself Nahnmwarki of Mwoakilloa (using the Pohnpeian title; there was an earlier title that was Mwoakillese as distinct from Pohnpeian). Not everyone accepted him in this position; however, when state leadership meetings (including the Pohnpei state constitutional convention) called for a traditional leader as delegate, the Mwoakillese sent this man. When the Mwoakillese had their constitutional convention (in 1986–87), many of the Mwoakillese living on Pohnpei were actively against recognition of Mwoakillese traditional leaders in the municipal constitution. Some of them saw the Nahnmwarki's assumption of office as a move to gain power and recognition for himself, not an effort to embody values that were important to the community.

Similarly, the lapsed position of Nukuoro chief also caused controversy when the Nukuoro attempted to write a municipal constitution. The Nukuoro constitutional convention (in 1986) resulted in a draft constitution that was rejected by Nukuoro voters, as in Chuuk state, partly because of controversy over reinstitution of the traditional chiefship (the chairman of the convention was from the traditional chiefly family, and people said he had pushed through provisions validating the status of traditional chief).

Traditional Leaders and Interisland Relations

Unlike the situations in Yap and Chuuk states, there was no regular precolonial contact between all the islands in Pohnpei state. (Mwoakilloa history does, however, refer to ties between Mwoakilloa and Madolenihmw.[10]) Hence there are no precolonial precedents for relationships between Pohnpei chiefs and outer-island chiefs, compounded by the fact that, in several cases, there are no functioning outer-island chiefs. The Pohnpeian title and feasting system does provide a model for all outer islanders to use to incorporate themselves into the Pohnpeian traditional status system, but not all outer islanders want to do that.

Because the Pohnpeian title and feasting system can incorporate anyone who wishes to be a part of it, there is constant pressure for outer islanders (and foreigners) on Pohnpei to participate according to Pohnpeian expectations by contributing to feasts and observing deference behavior (including the use of high language) toward high-titled Pohnpeians. Many outer islanders do not like Pohnpeian markers of rank, however, especially the way food and other goods are distributed at Pohnpeian feasts, with high-titled people getting most of it and people with no titles (e.g., outer islanders) coming away with nothing, even though they were expected to bring something.

As I said above, Pohnpeian attitudes toward outer islanders are somewhat parallel to Yapese attitudes toward outer islanders—low islanders are low status. The difference is that on Pohnpei an outer islander can fairly easily assimilate into Pohnpeian society—if he or she is willing to do it on the Pohnpeians' terms. One outer-island response to this has been to create or rename chiefly positions in Pohnpeian terms—Nahnmwarki and Nahnken—thus elevating their islands to the status of Pohnpeian *wehi*. An alternative response to this has been to emphasize elective/bureaucratic offices and decrease the importance of traditional leadership positions. An example is on Pingelap atoll, where, with a population of approximately 1,000, there is a three-branch municipal government with a municipal court; an elected executive head with support staff; and eight elected council members serving in five council committees with five committee chairs, as well as the offices of speaker, vice-speaker, and floor leader.

One result of allocating delegate seats to traditional leaders at leadership meetings, constitutional conventions, etc., is that this puts pressure on all the islands to invent traditional leaders if they do not currently have them; otherwise the islands lose out in terms of representation. Because the position of Nukuoro chief had lapsed, there was some problem in seating the Nukuoro traditional-leader delegates to the 1983 Pohnpei state constitutional convention, as the Pohnpeians initially refused to recognize the Nukuoro claimants.

Kosrae

The Church and Disruption of Precolonial Traditional Leadership

The fourth state in the F.S.M. is composed of the high island of Kosrae. In precolonial, premissionary times, Kosrae had a paramount chief, the Tokosra, and a "prime minister" position analogous to the Pohnpeian Nahnken (see Schaefer 1977). The depopulation that ensued when the whalers and traders brought in smallpox and venereal disease in the 1830s (Kosrae was a stronghold of the pirate Bully Hayes) brought the population down from 3,000 to about 300—a major reason for the subsequent demise of the traditional chiefly system and the success of Christianity. After the missionaries left, subsequent generations of Kosraens modified the church and made it their own. The church provides an avenue for advancement in the community that replaced the extinct title system, with a series of deacon, pastor, and other leadership positions.

Kosraens no longer recognize traditional leaders, but instead consider their church leaders to be their functional equivalent. Whenever a national leadership meeting or constitutional convention requires a state to send delegates who are traditional leaders, the Kosraens send church leaders. "Kosraen custom," as Kosraens talk of it today, primarily involves the church and restrictions placed on the behavior of church members. These restrictions—no smoking, drinking, or fornication—must of course be observed by church leaders as well.

There is one remnant of pre-Christian ritual status that survives—the pounded taro that is used to make *fafa* (pounded taro balls covered with very sweet coconut syrup, which sit in one's stomach ten times heavier than the heaviest matzo balls) can only be pounded by members of certain families, who inherit the right to make this dish. They are said to be "cleaner" (i.e., ritually purer) than other families.

Family and Electoral Politics on Kosrae

Extended family has replaced clan in terms of prestige and political support. Though families no longer have acknowledged rank, as clans used to, some families are considered more important, more numerous, and more powerful, and most of the Kosraens elected to state and national office come from these families. Kosrae has elective municipal offices as well—there are five municipalities, all of which have municipal constitutions.

The restrictions placed on the behavior of Kosraen church members and leaders apparently do not apply to the behavior of Kosraen elective leaders chosen for national office, at least judging from their behavior off-island. The Kosraens are aware of the off-island behavior of some of their more flamboyant elective leaders and in several cases have reelected them anyway, although there are some limits. One longtime incumbent senator lost his seat in 1987 shortly before his death, the timing of which was undoubtedly hastened by his alcoholism.[11]

LOOKING BEYOND local communities to statewide society in the four contemporary states of the F.S.M., we see that there is some basis for asserting that there is mutual recognition and acknowledgment of traditional leadership positions among the islands *within* each of the four states, though that does not mean those leaders were, or are, recognized as equals. We can assert this more strongly for Chuuk and Yap states, because of contemporaneously recognized precolonial precedents for interisland relations, than we can for Pohnpei state. The case of Kosrae state is not particularly relevant, even if church leaders are considered traditional leaders, since it is composed of only one island.

Recognition of the Category "Traditional Leaders" in the F.S.M.

Chiefs as Actors in the National Field?

What about, however, meaningful interaction among traditional leaders across state lines? Talk about "traditional leaders" or "chiefs" as a category at the national level in the Federated States of Micronesia is an "invented tradition"—there is no precolonial precedent for mutual recognition of chiefly status among *all* the islands currently in the F.S.M. Some contemporary Micronesians, however, speak of a precolonial island empire (see Nakayama and Ramp 1974) encompassing most of the islands now in the four states of the F.S.M. Various versions of this legendary empire center it in Yap, Chuuk lagoon, or Kosrae. The historical evidence, however, points to consistent trading or alliance relations covering smaller areas, not the whole. Talk of island empires is itself, of course, part of attempts to "invent" or "imagine" (cf. Hobsbawm and Ranger 1983; Anderson 1983) the F.S.M. as a national polity with traditional legitimation. Acceptance of this discourse of legitimation has consequences for the current position of traditional leaders: it points to a way in which chiefly personages can be used to support the modern nation, although as tokens of a founding history, rather than as incumbents of offices with nationwide decision-making powers.

Using traditional leaders solely as tokens of a founding history takes place within a community of discourse *about* chiefs, rather than within a field including practices involving chiefs as active agents as well as discussions of those practices. The chiefs become props, as it were; references to them are used to set the scene, but even if they are physically present at a national government ceremony, there may be little consequence for their own careers or the fortunes of their local followers. Unlike precolonial intraisland tributary voyages or warfare, their rank and the rank of their local communities will not change—unless they become actors and not merely tokens. The Nahnmwarki of Kitti staged a reception, at his meetinghouse, for the national senators and the president and vice-president, after the latter two had come back from signing the compact in Washington, D.C. (in 1986). In this situation he *was* an active agent, and did stand to gain himself, if his hospitality was remembered kindly when the senators considered the Kitti public-projects bill. The Kitti public-projects bill subsequently passed by that Congress did include monies for a pickup truck for the Kitti Kaun en Wehi, "head of state," the office created for the Nahnmwarki in the Kitti municipal constitution. The Nahnmwarki's role as host was a rather different one from his appearances as a guest at government functions in the capital, where he was mainly a token.[12]

At his own party, the Nahnmwarki showed a lot of creativity in inventing rituals appropriate for a paramount chief hosting national officials: he presented each senator with a large steel fishhook, which he handed to them in the Pohnpeian style of crossing arms to show respect. Fishing, after all, is pan-Micronesian, but fishhooks are not commonly distributed at Pohnpeian feasts. So the event was clearly marked as being something other than a customary Pohnpeian, or Kitti, feast.

Indeed, traditional leaders are used in a legitimating role in the context of the periodical state/national leadership meetings held by the F.S.M. government—traditional leaders are part of the state delegations to these meetings, along with state legislators and elected municipal leaders—but in the leadership meetings that I observed or heard about, the traditional leaders did not play a very significant role in the decisions made,[13] although they were always addressed in the introductions to formal speeches. Significantly, when a national meeting was convened to discuss the very consequential question of the legislative procedure for accepting the amended

United States–Federated States of Micronesia Compact of Free Association in 1986, the traditional leaders were not officially included: the national leaders held a "national/state legislators' meeting" made up of state and national legislators, with some people defined only as traditional leaders present, but as observers, not delegates.

Similarly, although the 1990 F.S.M. constitutional convention adopted a proposed amendment adding a chamber of chiefs to the federal government (see Chapter 9), many of the delegates did not regard this as significant, expecting that it would not be approved in the subsequent public referendum, and indeed it was not. Overall, the traditional-leader delegates at the 1990 constitutional convention played a less significant role in the development and disposal of convention proposals than did the group of traditional leaders who were delegates at the original 1975 constitutional convention,[14] which is not to dispute Petersen's point that traditional leaders remain important and effective at the local level.

Levels of Community and Discourse About Chiefs

Turning from traditional leaders as actors on the national scene to a discussion of the discourse about chiefs: the discussion Petersen describes about chiefs at the 1990 constitutional convention is part of a developing national discourse about chiefs, which draws from and interpenetrates communities of discourse about chiefs at state and local levels. The complexities of what understandings about chiefs are shared and what are unshared mirror the complexities of drawing boundaries around "cultures" or "communities" in the contemporary F.S.M.[15]

Among the terms and titles used by contemporary Micronesians for their traditional leaders, there are some cognates: the Chuukese *samwoon* is cognate to the Central Carolinian *tamol*, and there is an archaic cognate in Pohnpeian, *samwohl* (seen in the title for the sacred eel kept at the politico-ritual center of Nan Madol prior to 1850, "Nahnsamwohl" or "He who is chief"; see Bernart 1977:135; Fischer et al. 1977:112; Hanlon 1988:14–15). However, while Chuukese and Central Carolinians, through histories of settlement, trade, and warfare, recognize shared origins and close similarities in their traditional political systems, when Pohnpeians discuss their current traditional chiefly statuses, they emphasize the ranked title-lines headed by the titles Nahnmwarki and Nahnken, and tend to classify Chuukese traditional political systems together with those of the Pohnpei state atolls as "low islander" (*mehn namwanamw*) systems, whose chiefs are not equivalent to the Pohnpeian paramount chiefs. Pohnpeians see their current traditional political system (created prior to European contact) as a result of an evolutionary or developmental process: the Nahnmwarki/Nahnken system was a reaction to an earlier, overly totalitarian system with a single islandwide paramount chief, which had come after an even earlier historical period with a less hierarchically oriented polity and fewer ranked statuses (see Bernart 1977). This is the lens through which many Pohnpeians view the chiefs of Chuuk lagoon and the atolls: they are representatives of less "developed" polities that do not have the same degree of *wahu* ("honor") inherent in the Pohnpeian title systems.

The etymology of the collective term for the chiefs on the high islands of Yap, *pilung*, from *lung*, or "voice"—the chiefs are the voice of the land, the ranked *tabinaw* or estate that is the source of their status—is totally opaque to Pohnpeians. There was probably no precolonial contact between Yap and Pohnpei; although some place names in the oral histories and legends of both areas can be interpreted as referring to the other, if there was any knowledge of each other it came through the atoll dwellers in the middle—those islanders who preserved the skills of long-distance navigation. Today, most Pohnpeians, outside of those who have been to school with Yapese (which does not necessarily increase their knowledge of Yapese society much) or are in government positions where they have worked with Yapese and traveled to Yap, still know very little about Yap and the outer islands in Yap state. In fact, in conversations with Pohnpeians living outside the port town of Kolonia, I found that many of them did not distinguish between Yap and the atolls outside of Yap, and hence did not recognize the distinction between *pilung* (the chiefs of Yap proper) and *tamol* (the chiefs of the atolls in Yap state). Despite the fact that, in regard to the islands within their own states, ethnic Yapese and Pohnpeians both make a high island/low island (atoll) distinction, with high-island chiefs having greater status or honor, this does not seem to carry over to according equal respect to the chiefs of the other high island.

The Yapese view of Pohnpei and its traditional leaders is influenced by the fact that the F.S.M. capital is located in Pohnpei, and hence there are a greater number of Yapese living in Pohnpei than Pohnpeians living in Yap. The Yapese have thus had a greater opportunity to see the Pohnpeian paramount chiefs drunk or behaving rudely.[16] The Yapese comment on what could be generally termed the anarchy of Pohnpeian society. Specific behaviors they remark on include what they see as the disorderly and rude way Pohnpeians walk. In Yap, public access to villages is through narrow, stone-paved paths. People walk on the paths in single file, and do not go off the paths onto someone else's land without permission unless allowed by their kinship relation with those living there. Yapese are shocked when they see people in Pohnpei walking three abreast on the road, expecting cars to go around them. They also comment on the way Pohnpeians walk through other people's property, and by the way Pohnpeians let their pigs run loose to forage; Yapese keep their pigs tied up. The conclusion is that Pohnpeian chiefs do not have the same kind of control that Yapese chiefs (at least in theory) do.[17]

The high island/low island distinction runs through the modern F.S.M. polity, but as the Yapese/Pohnpeian example shows, that does not mean that the distinction is loaded the same way for everyone, or interpreted the same way in reference to particular interisland relationships. While Yapese and Pohnpeians see themselves as more sophisticated than low islanders, and their own chiefs as more powerful, traditionally the people of the Central Caroline atolls in between have been more "cosmopolitan," in that, as I said above, they were the ones that traveled and traded, and consequently had the greater knowledge of the other Micronesian islands.[18]

F.S.M. Traditional Leaders and Communities of Discourse

The local, face-to-face community is still the strongest locus of talk and gossip about traditional leaders, and the arena in which the consequences of their behavior and their actions are most likely to be recognized and judged. However, people do function as members of larger, more encompassing communities as well—from the local community of village or section through the larger municipality, islandwide, state, national, and international communities. (If the latter category—international—seems somewhat remote from day-to-day life, it did not seem so to the Micronesians whose children signed up for the U.S. military and were sent to the Persian Gulf.)

The more shared communities of discourse are operant within a given level of community, the stronger the role that community is likely to play in a community member's life. If, within the same local community, people engage in discussions about traditional leadership, elective leadership, family gossip, and international news, that community is central in those people's lives. On the other hand, take the case of a Pohnpeian, say from Kitti, who works for the F.S.M. Congress. At work, she talks to the other employees about the congressmen and hears some discussions about their relationships to the communities they're from—whether their families are important, their relationship to the traditional leaders in their districts, etc. But when she goes home to Kitti, chances are, her family and the people in her local community will not be very interested in whether the Yapese congressmen snubbed the Yapese chiefs or not. They know little about the Yapese chiefs and feel that any actions the chiefs may take have little relevance for them.

They are likely to be interested, however, in what is happening with the

Kitti section of the Pohnpei state public-projects appropriations bill—for example, whether funding for new roads near their homes are likely to be included, or whether the Nahnmwarki of Kitti, as the Kitti Kaun en Wehi (head of state), is likely to have any more vehicles appropriated for him. Interactions between their own locally recognized traditional leaders and people from elsewhere in leadership positions are also subjects of interest and gossip: I heard Kitti people discussing the Nahnmwarki of Kitti, who, when he arrived in Kosrae for a leadership conference held in 1986, complained when he was not given a car to use; but one of the Yap state senators, understanding that chiefs should be treated with respect, turned over his car to the Nahnmwarki.

Discourse about traditional leadership is separable from discourse about elective/bureaucratic leadership in that different criteria are usually invoked for evaluation. For instance, in Pohnpei state in the last twenty years, several chief magistrates have been impeached or have had impeachment proceedings started against them because they were accused of using public funds for private purposes. However, in the case of Nahnmwarkis and Nahnkens, there is no such distinction made between private property and the property of the office. The pickup truck that the Nahnmwarki of Kitti got under the public-projects bill was his to do with as he liked. The insistence on the distinction between personal and public property in elective office was probably a major factor in the disappearance of Nahnmwarkis from the chief magistrate position (see Chapter 7, for parallel Rotuman disputes about distinguishing between personal and office property).

Modest and humble behavior is widely seen as desirable in both traditional and elected leaders; however, what is interpreted as modest behavior differs from community to community. "Speak softly but carry a big stick" behavior, which may be seen as modest in Faaychuuk, will not be seen as modest on Pohnpei or Yap, and behavior that is not seen as particularly immodest in Pohnpei—such as the example given above of walking three abreast on the street—may be seen as arrogant in Yap, and vice versa. In 1990, the Yapese sent the incumbent chief magistrate of Rull to the constitutional convention to occupy one of the two traditional-leader delegate seats allocated to Yap (a chief from the atoll of Ulithi held the other seat). I heard some of the Yapese complain about this man's behavior, saying he was not acting the way a chief should, because he was too boastful and arrogant (also he was drinking). In Yap, as in the rest of the F.S.M., ideal behavior for chiefs includes a publicly restrained, modest demeanor.

Pohnpeians, on the other hand, although they claim to value modest and humble behavior at all ranks, speak highly of younger people who have a modest demeanor while they are advancing up the title hierarchy, but seem to tolerate some rather flamboyant behavior in their highest chiefs. Since there is no one senior to them, there is really no one who can effectively criticize or control the chiefs' behavior. Sometimes a wife can, and Pohnpeians do talk as though the wife of a traditional leader plays a big role in how highly he is thought of. I did sometimes hear elderly people complain about particular Nahnmwarkis who frequently got drunk. Among Pohnpei Islanders, however, the most often heard comment evaluating Nahnmwarkis is how generous or stingy they are in redistribution of feast goods.

It does make sense to speak of a "community of discourse" about traditional leadership cutting across the F.S.M., but only at a very general level of shared understandings, and defining itself mainly in contrast to a community of discourse about elective leadership. The members of this community of discourse are those Micronesians whose social and political networks extend throughout the F.S.M., mainly the members of the national government and the state and municipal leaders, both traditional and elective/bureaucratic, who have attended national meetings. Some acknowledged shared criteria that constitute traditional leadership as a field across the F.S.M.: genealogy; a "modest" and humble demeanor as opposed to aggressiveness, coercive behavior, and arrogance; knowledge of custom and traditional history and assertions of their importance. The particulars of how traditional leaders participate in exchange and redistribution, what kind of rhetoric they are expected to master, what customs they are supposed to be knowledgeable about, and exactly how they demonstrate their modesty, however, vary from state to state and from island to island.

All these matters—both the general criteria of genealogy, modesty, and traditional knowledge and the particulars relevant in specific communities—are matters for disputation and discussion, as the term "discourse" suggests. For instance, genealogy, usually invoked as a key criterion (by both anthropologists and Micronesians) in differentiating a "traditional" as opposed to a modern elective/bureaucratic leader, is not as unambiguous as it may at first appear. Genealogical rules are subject to interpretation and manipulation (see Comaroff 1978 for an African case). Micronesians are well aware of this, and genealogy is one area of discourse where it becomes apparent that "discourse" means disagreement.

Sometimes Micronesians do not agree on who the incumbent or successor of a particular traditional leadership position is, even in cases where the successors to these positions are supposed to be determined by genealogical rules. In 1986 on Yap there were two men who claimed to be the highest-ranking *pilung* (that is, from the highest-ranking estate) in a particular municipality. Both came to the meetings of the Council of Pilung, to serve in a seat for which there was supposed to be only one incumbent. On Pohnpei in 1987 I heard different versions of the line of probable successors to the position of Nahnmwarki: the man who held the title second in the Nahnmwarki's line (the Wasai), and who later succeeded to the position of Nahnmwarki, was said to be of the wrong lineage (*keinek*) by the family of the then-Nahnmwarki. Other people said the Wasai's lineage was in fact the correct one, and the Nahnmwarki's lineage was not the one that should hold the paramount chieftainship. The Wasai and the Nahnmwarki were in different lineages, which is contrary to the stated rule that the Nahnmwarki and the high titles below him are all supposed to belong to one lineage. The younger man who had the Dauk title third in line, who was in the then-Nahnmwarki's *keinek* but not the Wasai's, was talked about by members of his family as the proper successor to the Nahnmwarki (despite his youth, which made him a somewhat inappropriate choice). When the Nahnmwarki died, the former Wasai, the more mature man, succeeded to the paramount chiefship. People outside of the late Nahnmwarki's family said that the new Nahnmwarki's lineage was in fact the correct one, and the late Nahnmwarki's lineage was not the one that should hold the paramount chieftainship. The point of disputation was apparently differing interpretations of the status of an adoption several generations back.

Traditional and Elective/Bureaucratic Leadership

Ambiguities about the proper person or the proper lineage to claim a leadership position are nothing new; they provided flexibility in the precolonial political systems to choose for chiefly status, from a pool of potential candidates, those who had the most skill at leadership and were best accepted by their community. As in political systems in other parts of the world, ascription/achievement is a dichotomy sharper in theory than it is in practice. This flexibility has a new application today, however, in the accommodation of traditional leadership statuses to elective/bureaucratic leadership statuses. For instance, the man who for more than forty years held the position of chairman of the Council of Pilung in Yap, the position supposed to be filled by a man from the highest-ranking estate in the highest-ranking municipality in Yap, was in fact not from that estate, but from what would technically be considered the second-highest-ranking estate. The man from the highest-ranking estate became Speaker of the Yap legislature, a position he filled very capably until he died. The Speaker and the chairman of the Council of Pilung, the chairman told me, had agreed between themselves to divide up the positions of power this way, in accordance with their own desires and aptitudes.

Elective leaders, particularly on the national level, tend to be judged and discussed in terms of standards and values different from those used to evaluate traditional leaders. Those elected and appointed to bureaucratic positions at the national level are fluent in English, have at least college-level American educations, and are cosmopolitan and used to dealing in Americanized contexts. Youth, outspokenness, the ability to speak in confrontational style, and even a certain amount of immodesty are apparently not seen as drawbacks. In most F.S.M. communities, these qualities are undesirable in incumbents in traditional leadership positions. The qualities seen as desirable in elective leaders have changed over time; the first generation of the Congress of Micronesia, in the late 1960s, included some senior traditional leaders, but by the time the Federated States of Micronesia Congress was established in 1979, these were replaced in favor of younger, college-educated Micronesians.

Many of these college-educated senators, while not occupying high traditional status positions themselves, do have family connections to high-ranking traditional status. The choices they would have had to have made early in their careers in order to eventually accede to traditional leader positions themselves, however, involving apprenticeship to elders knowledgeable in traditional lore and intense exchange relationships, are difficult to reconcile with going away to school.

Conversely, those most directly in line for traditional positions tend not to seek careers in elective office. I observed an exception at the state level in Yap, where a young man from a high-ranking estate who was being groomed by the chairman of the Council of Pilung as a possible successor chose to run for state legislator. This choice did not go uncriticized, however; one Yapese official said to me that he thought this was wrong, that one should either seek traditional office or elective office but not both. The young man did win a legislative seat, but unfortunately, he died soon afterward, so we will never know what his career would have been like.

Micronesians constantly talk about and criticize their traditional leaders. There is a Pohnpeian proverb that translates "Water under the cliffs—the chiefs"; one interpretation is that people always grumble about their chiefs. This grumbling is like the surf under the cliffs: it is constant and it makes noise, but the cliffs remain unchanged. Micronesians talk about their elective leaders, too, just as we do (although they apply different standards; Clinton's alleged girlfriend would not have lost him any points with Micronesians, as long as he was perceived to have been discreet about it). The ways that people judge the traditional versus the elective/bureaucratic leaders, the standards and values that are invoked, however, are different, constituting two contrasting but mutually defining discourses. Furthermore, the relationship between the two categories of leaders is itself a subject of discussion and controversy, at the national and state levels, as well as in local communities, and hence continues to change and evolve.

Micronesians—as aspirants for traditional leadership statuses, as candidates for elective office, and as chiefly subjects or constituents—make choices in the midst of all this discussion. They decide whom to vote for, which feasts to go to and what to bring to them, what traditional or elective leaders they will avoid and whom they will publicly support. Young people decide whether to go to school in the United States to get a degree in economics or political science or to stay home and apprentice themselves to a master of traditional history or navigation. Collectively, all these choices will shape the future of leadership in Micronesia. The only thing that is clear now is that there *are* choices, more choices and different choices than there were in the past. Each generation finds itself in a new context. As the generation of traditional leaders that came to maturity before World War II, before the American administration, becomes completely a part of the past, the practice of and the discourse about traditional leadership in the F.S.M. will inevitably change.

Returning to my original question, whether it makes sense in the contemporary F.S.M. to talk about traditional leaders as a category or a group: it does make sense to talk about "traditional leadership" as a category within the F.S.M., because there is a national community of discourse about the general characteristics of traditional leadership within the F.S.M., defined as a discourse largely by the opposition to elective/bureaucratic leadership. However, not all Micronesians participate equally in this national discourse. Those whose concerns lie primarily within their local communities participate more in local discourses that focus on matters not shared with other communities. The structure of discourses that are shared and not shared, however, is more complex than a simple national versus local opposition. Multiple and overlapping communities of discourse exist, as people move through contexts of interacting within their household, within their section or village, with their officemates if they have government jobs, with people from other islands if they go on church congregational exchanges, travel for work or school, or have family connections elsewhere. Those whose careers are more localized hear about state and national events and personages from people who do move in wider circles. There are practical reasons for talking about chiefs as well as elective/bureaucratic leaders: both bring resources to local communities or are seen as thwarting the flow of resources.

As far as whether it makes sense to talk about F.S.M. traditional leaders as a group, at the national level the answer, for the most part, is no, since they have not engaged in significant collective action. It is more justifiable to talk about emerging groups of traditional leaders on the state level, where traditional leaders from different islands do form alliances (in Yap and Chuuk more so than in Pohnpei). Another way of stating this is to put it in terms of Bourdieu's notion of field: while for those aspiring to elective/bureaucratic office there is a "field" of national politics within which one can define a career, thanks to the Micronesians who negotiated with the United States to establish that field, for traditional leaders there is not really a field of national action. Micronesian elective/bureaucratic national politics has its own collective forms of capital: a college education, parliamentary skills, personal ties across state lines, etc.

For traditional political leaders, capital is not so easily transferred across local or state lines. An *itang* proverb will not get one as far in Pohnpei or Yap as it would in Chuuk. The Nahnmwarki of Kitti managed to transmute some of his local legitimacy into a pickup truck, but not to gain much in the way of a stake in national leadership. As Petersen states in Chapter 9, many Micronesians prefer this state of affairs: it prevents a winner-take-all situation in which neither traditional leaders nor elective/bureaucratic ones dominate throughout local, state, and national levels. Even in Yap proper, where chiefs are said to rule behind the scenes, the college-trained politicians seem to be more active decision-makers when it comes to national contexts, paralleling the traditional balance between sitting chiefs and executive chiefs.

9

A Micronesian Chamber of Chiefs?

The 1990 Federated States of Micronesia Constitutional Convention

GLENN PETERSEN

MICRONESIANS continue to ponder the question of whether chiefs should hold an established place in their national governments. Within the nation-states carved out of the old United States Trust Territory of the Pacific Islands, various formats have been tried, and among the heterogeneous states of the Federated States of Micronesia (F.S.M.), different and still evolving solutions are being pursued. For the F.S.M. as a whole, the issue remains controversial: there are strong pressures both for and against creation of an F.S.M. Chamber of Chiefs. In this chapter I attempt to demonstrate that fairly strong support for the chamber has in fact created even stronger opposition to it, and that the overwhelming defeat of the proposed constitutional amendment establishing such a chamber during the Constitutional Ratifying Referendum of 1991 is evidence not of the Micronesian chiefs' declining importance but of their continuing relevance. Most Micronesians (i.e., the F.S.M.'s peoples), I believe, feel that their chiefs can more effectively serve them by remaining outside the national government.

I could not have conducted this research without the gracious cooperation of the entire constitutional convention. A grant from the City University of New York's Faculty Research Program underwrote my work there.

Throughout this chapter I use the term "Micronesian" to refer to the people of the Federated States of Micronesia. Though the term more generally applies to all the peoples of the various island groups that constitute the ethnological and geographical entity known as Micronesia, I am following what has become current international protocol: at the United Nations, it is the F.S.M. that is referred to as Micronesia.

In addition to exploring the history and meaning of the 1991 vote against the Micronesian Chamber of Chiefs, I also intend to raise a theoretical issue. I want to explore the proposition that it is precisely people's consciousness of the relationship between them and their chiefs that explains both the difference between the varieties of political organization anthropologists call chiefdoms and states and the existence of this strong opposition to formalizing the chiefs' relationship with the modern Micronesian state.

At the core of this chapter is a series of episodes from the 1990 F.S.M. constitutional convention (ConCon): the introduction and progress of an amendment establishing the Chamber of Chiefs; the initial defeat of the proposal; a dramatic ritual performed, apparently spontaneously, on the ConCon floor in the middle of a session; the struggle—eventually successful—to win approval for the measure; and the voters' ultimate defeat of the amendment. The data are drawn from my own, largely verbatim, notes of committee meetings, plenary sessions, and informal discussions among delegates. A general overview of the ConCon appears in Petersen 1994, and a lengthy analysis of ethnic and cultural issues at the ConCon appears in Petersen 1993.

The F.S.M. ConCon was held in July and August of 1990 at the national capital in Pohnpei's Palikir region. The thirty-one delegates (including eight "traditional leaders") from the F.S.M.'s four states introduced 104 proposed amendments, of which they approved twenty-four. Only four of these were then ratified by the F.S.M.'s voters in the referendum (though a change in forty-nine Kosraen votes would have meant approval for nearly all of the items—except the proposed Chamber of Chiefs).[1] In general, two salient aspects of the ConCon should be kept in mind. First, the delegates—and the people who elected them—were largely in agreement that a great deal of power and money should be transferred from the F.S.M. national government to the governments of the four states—that the F.S.M. should be decentralized. There is a widespread sense in the F.S.M. that Congress is far too powerful, particularly because it elects the president from among its number and thereby exercises enormous influence over the executive branch. During the period of American rule, district legislatures and the territorywide Congress of Micronesia—though established by American edicts—were almost entirely disenfranchised by the executive powers of the high commissioner and district administrators. A viable system of checks and balances never emerged during the colonial era, and despite indigenous Micronesian political systems' sophisticated means of constraining abuses of chiefly authority (Petersen forthcoming a), the contemporary F.S.M. national government inadequately distributes power.

Second, the ConCon failed to achieve any transfer of power away from the national government, primarily (although by no means entirely) because of basic structural tensions between Kosrae and Chuuk states. Kosrae, with a population of slightly more than 7,000, insisted that the equality of each state be recognized and preserved; its delegates continually emphasized "state sovereignty." Chuuk, with more than 55,000 people (constituting slightly more than 50 percent of the entire F.S.M. population), was equally insistent on population democracy. The classic big state/small state controversy, familiar to anyone who has studied American history or the problems inherent in any federal system, prevented the delegates from agreeing upon how they could best reorganize their national government, despite their basic agreement upon the need for some kind of change.

Differences among the island societies that make up the F.S.M. have developed over the course of at least 2,000 years, however, and opposition between Chuuk and Kosrae was cast as much in ethnic terms as it was in a structural framework. Indeed, most differences among the delegations were voiced in terms of custom and tradition, no matter what their origins. It is in this context that the attempt to establish a Chamber of Chiefs unfolded. The chamber was explicitly promoted by some delegates as a means of solving problems attributable to differences in customs and traditions, as well as a means of providing traditional or customary solutions to national problems ("custom," "tradition," and "chiefs" were terms used at the ConCon). On the other hand, delegates also opposed the chamber on grounds that these differences in custom and tradition would hinder—and perhaps even prevent—its operations.

A Role for Chiefs

At the original Micronesian constitutional convention in 1975, questions about the official status of traditional leaders—and a formal role in government for them—nearly brought the convention to a halt (Meller 1985: 261–86).[2] The debate's final outcome was a compromise in which Article 5, Section 3 specified that "the Congress may establish, when needed, a Chamber of Chiefs." The matter remained a sensitive one; in contrast with most other issues taken up by the 1990 ConCon, the delegations had given the Chamber of Chiefs issue a good deal of thought before they arrived. During the planning meetings that preceded the convention, Yap—having long maintained that its customs were not the province of the national government—proposed removing Article 5's Section 3 entirely from the constitution.[3] Kosrae strongly opposed any elevation of chieftainship to a formal status within the government. As the Kosraens pointed out insistently, they no longer had any "traditional leaders."

Pohnpei and Chuuk evidenced more ambivalence. Some Pohnpeian delegates maintained that voters had charged them with pushing for the establishment of a Chamber of Chiefs, while others pointed out that the delegation had ultimately decided not to submit such a proposal. Though traditional chieftainship provides a central organizing structure for the lives of most ethnic Pohnpeians, it holds somewhat less significance for Pohnpei state's outer-island societies; the role of Pohnpeian chiefs remains a thorny issue within Pohnpei state.[4]

Even more torn were the Chuukese. The proposal for a Chamber of Chiefs was introduced by eight of Chuuk's thirteen delegates. In itself, this was not unusual: although nearly all of the ConCon's business was transacted by state delegations acting as coherent units, and most amendments were proposed by state delegations, Chuuk's full delegation submitted only a handful of proposals. However, Chuuk voters had defeated the first draft of their state's constitution largely because it provided for a state chamber of chiefs. It had to be rewritten without this provision before it was approved. The character of traditional leadership in Chuuk is particularly ambiguous, and the relative ranking of these leaders is continually contested: many Chuukese, it appears, felt that formalizing the role of their leaders would result in some ossification of their relative ranking, whereas the continuous contesting of rank allows traditional political life to thrive in Chuuk.[5] Even though it was a group of Chuukese who introduced the national Chamber of Chiefs measure, much of the opposition to it came from Chuuk—and in this the delegates' ConCon behavior mirrored the character of political factionalism within their state.

In sum, Kosrae and Yap opposed the change, while Chuuk and Pohnpei were ambivalent. Given the degree of resistance to it, it is surprising that the proposal even reached the floor. That it did so is a good indicator of the chiefs' continued influence in the F.S.M. Few delegates were willing to speak frankly about denying the chiefs a formal role if that was what the chiefs wanted. Undoubtedly a key factor in the proposal's success was the presence of Pohnpei's highly articulate Nahnken of Nett (the "talking chief" of one of Pohnpei's five paramount chiefdoms), who served as vice-chairman of the Civil Liberties and Tradition Committee. The Nahnken's support for the measure in committee counterbalanced the Kosraen delegation's concerted opposition.

The proposal's progress was not smooth. When the plenary first took up the measure, unusually visible opposition to it surfaced immediately. This was relatively early in the course of the ConCon, and the committee's leaders, lacking experience with the larger group's internal dynamics, failed to have the proposal tabled until they could gather enough votes to ensure its passage. The measure was defeated on first reading. After sounding out the opposition, the committee arranged to have the proposal recalled and then offered amendments to it.[6] As it became clear that the proposal still lacked adequate support, it was deferred, taken up and deferred again, then reconsidered, amended, and finally passed by a 27–1 vote.

The Debate on Chieftainship

The delegates were not merely divided among themselves in their attitudes toward the proposed Chamber of Chiefs; many of them were personally ambivalent, at times pushing for the chamber, and at other points voicing doubts about its potential for serving the Micronesian people. This ambivalence was apparent from the outset. Repeatedly, delegates would raise some very fundamental questions: What would the Chamber of Chiefs do? How would it be organized? Would the chiefs be charged with making binding decisions, or would they function merely in an advisory capacity? Each time these questions were posed, one advocate or another would reply that its operations were better left undefined. Others would explain that its purpose would be to promote unity or peace, to resolve conflicts among the states, or to instruct the F.S.M. in "the significance of custom and tradition" (as one delegate phrased it). Then someone else would insist that the chamber's operations were solely for the chiefs to define.

Both the committee and the plenary grappled with questions about the very nature of chieftainship itself. Lying at the heart of the debate over the chamber was the matter of just how specific the amendment should be. Some argued that unless the ConCon spelled out exactly what the chamber was to do and how it was to be initially organized, Congress would implement the proposal in whatever fashion it chose, and that given Congress's tendencies, it would be sure to retain ultimate control over the chamber.

Again and again, a handful of delegates insisted that the only way the chamber could be entirely independent of Congress, and be beholden to Congress for neither its finances nor its structure, was for the ConCon to "spell out," in the constitution itself, just what it was that the chiefs would do in their chamber. Unless the ConCon did so, one delegate or another would insist, it would be up to Congress to define. Indeed, the head of the Public Finance and Taxation Committee argued that because Congress controlled all the F.S.M.'s finances, it would inevitably retain control over the chamber. Each time these sentiments were voiced, the response would be the same: "We cannot tell the chiefs what to do. It is up to them to decide what their role should be."

At a slightly deeper level, this observation was precisely the point on which the arguments about the Chamber of Chiefs turned. Delegates from every state, no matter what their position on the proposed amendment was, insisted that no one in Micronesia—neither the Congress, nor the ConCon, nor the people—could tell the chiefs what to do. The Pohnpeian Nahnken went so far as to acknowledge that he did not want to be told what to do. A Chuukese delegate explained that in Chuuk the chiefs tell the people what to do and the people tell the chiefs what to do. A Pohnpeian delegate, while acknowledging that his people are still "in awe" of their chiefs, insisted that even in matters of custom, Pohnpeian chiefs do not *tell* the people what to do, they *advise* them. In short, although these highly articulate Micronesian leaders were not entirely sure what the chiefs could or could not do, they unanimously agreed upon what Micronesians could not do with their chiefs.

There exist in contemporary Micronesia, despite the many significant cultural variations that distinguish one island society from another, certain notions about the essential underpinnings of chieftainship that are held in common. I have explored these shared characteristics elsewhere (Petersen forthcoming a and b). In brief, Micronesian chieftainship is rooted in principles of matrilineal descent, genealogical seniority within descent groups, and the relative seniority (determined in a variety of ways) of matrigroups. Even where chieftainship seems to be primarily territorial in nature, as it often does, it is the seniority of a particular group that confers legitimacy upon it. This said, it must be immediately noted that in reality few chiefs gain office on purely genealogical grounds; practical political success is accompanied and legitimized by reference to, and manipulation of, genealogical material.

As a consequence of this basic, shared notion of what constitutes chieftainship, the ConCon delegations voiced no doubts about who or what the chiefs were, or about what made them chiefs. Indeed, while the term "traditional leaders" was sometimes employed in certain technical contexts in deference to Kosrae (whose singularity I shall address presently), the term "chief" was routinely used by nearly all the delegates. As one of the Kosraen delegates observed, in discussing his state's problems with the issue, everyone else had "real chiefs," and it was in this same context that one of the ConCon's most influential leaders argued that within the chamber, the Kosraen members would be considered "chiefs."

This common understanding of chieftainship was also underscored by repeated references to those "born to rule." While this concept irritated some of the delegates, they did not deny its salience for most Micronesians. Pohnpei's Nahnken, who is in indigenous spiritual terms probably the highest-ranking person on the entire island, having been born after his father had already become paramount chief (*ipwen pohn warawar*—

"born above the ditch"), raised this matter of being born to rule, as well as making veiled references to other key spiritual aspects of his status.[7] But he was hardly alone, and even those who rather strongly opposed establishment of the chamber still acknowledged this difference in status: one delegate asked whether recognition of the chiefs' special standing would not violate constitutional guarantees of equal protection before the law. As Norman Meller (1985:261) notes, at the 1975 constitutional convention, Pohnpei's Heinrich Iriarte upset a number of his fellow delegates by observing, "Some of us are born to rule and some of us born to serve."[8] Iriarte, though an elected delegate, held a high-ranking traditional title and was younger brother of Nahnmwarki (paramount chief) Max Iriarte, one of the two Pohnpeian traditional leaders who had participated in the original convention. It was Nahnmwarki Max's son, Nahnken Salvador Iriarte, vice-chairman of the Civil Liberties and Tradition Committee, who in 1990 emphasized the status of those "born to rule."

The elevated status of chiefs, more than anything else, I think, lay behind Kosrae's steadfast opposition to the chamber. In keeping with their commitment to consensus, all but one of the Kosraen delegates ultimately voted for the proposal, but they nonetheless mounted the most concerted opposition to it, arguing both in committee and before the plenary that they had no traditional leaders or chiefs and that if they did choose leaders to represent them in the Chamber of Chiefs, they would be at a distinct disadvantage. Kosrae's last paramount chief long ago renounced the office, and the island has been without an effective chiefly system for more than a century. While recognizing the fundamental coherence of this argument, the others insisted that Kosrae did have leaders whose status derived largely from their positions in the church and that they were for all intents and purposes "traditional." Kosrae's delegates had argued at length that Kosrae's religion was its "custom" when they recognized that this tactic provided the most likely means of eliminating the constitutional prohibition against establishment of religion, and their colleagues were merely putting the same logic to work against them. The big question remained, however, and it troubled at least a few other delegates as well: could Kosraen members of the chamber in fact operate as equals among those "born to rule?"

"Will Kosraen members be able to speak freely in the presence of chiefs?" one Kosraen asked. Another wondered aloud, "How will real chiefs look at elected representatives?" The response to this quite reasonable concern was, in fact, rather disingenuous: within the chamber, it was suggested, all members would be equal. (Whether the delegates were prepared to acknowledge it or not, the basic principles of Micronesian chieftainship, organized around ranked seniority within and between matrigroups and territorial groupings, make it clear that there are very few equals in traditional Micronesian systems of rank.) Emblematic of the tenacity with which the Kosraens opposed the measure was their argument that if they were to send representatives to the Chamber of Chiefs in hopes of furthering unity within the F.S.M., these "traditional leaders"— lacking the inherent qualities and learned skills of chiefs—might not know how to properly comport themselves and could unintentionally give offense, thereby threatening unity and defeating the very goals the chamber was intended to promote.

In sum, opposition to the proposed Chamber of Chiefs had primarily to do with the chiefs' collective status. The key arguments were that relations between the chamber and Congress would be uneasy and that Kosraen representatives to the chamber would not know how to behave. But no one suggested that the chiefs would be ineffectual, or that they were irrelevant or anachronistic. To be sure, this may have been partly because no one wanted to give offense to the chiefs present as delegates. But the general lack of discussion about what constituted chieftainship, both in meetings and in casual conversations, along with repeated references to the inherent status of chiefs, make it clear that chieftainship itself was never at issue. Rather, the crucial problem was the place that the chiefly system itself should hold in the contemporary Micronesian political scene.

At least one additional concern was repeatedly voiced. A number of delegates, along with some of their advisors and individuals who testified at public hearings on the proposals, expressed apprehension about the consequences of reducing quintessentially fluid customary politics to intractable written codes. A range of doubt was expressed. The chief justice of Pohnpei state's Supreme Court spoke of a threat to the institution of chieftainship itself if chiefly roles were made subject to Western legal precepts. It was just this sort of legislation, he said, that took away the powers of European monarchs. A Chuukese delegate explained that his misgivings about codification of chieftainship were rooted in the likelihood that it would transfix the relative rankings of titles, lineages, and clans. Given that it is the very ambiguity of relative rankings that makes Micronesian political systems as successful as they are, his fear is quite understandable. As I noted earlier, the original draft of Chuuk state's constitution was rejected largely because it contained provisions for a chief's chamber, and voters feared that the body would serve mainly as an arena where competing groups struggled for rank, and thus would allow the short-term victors to fix these rankings as the law of the land.

Others worried that any advice rendered by the chief's chamber would be written down and treated as officially sanctioned "custom." It was in this context that one of the Chuuk delegates observed that in Chuuk, "The chiefs tell the people what to do and the people tell the chiefs what to do," and a Pohnpei delegate asserted, "The chiefs of Pohnpei *advise* me about my custom and tradition. The chiefs and the people *both* know about custom and tradition." A member of the F.S.M. Congress serving as a delegate (and one of the few delegates who had also been a member of the original constitutional convention in 1975) gave what was perhaps the most articulate expression to these shared apprehensions: "Anytime we try to reduce the function and role of traditional leaders to writing we put limits on their authority. We may unwittingly be putting limits on their authority. Words can be misconstrued."

Finally, there was also uneasiness about the possibility that the Chamber of Chiefs' operations might somehow be construed as implying that there was some sort of national, "Micronesian" custom. It would be better, suggested one delegate, for each of the states to have its own assembly of chiefs (as already exists in Yap). The states are the most appropriate place for this kind of activity, he said, because "no two states have the same customs or traditions—there are subtle differences among us." Another delegate, the chief justice of Chuuk state's Supreme Court, pointed out that it would be virtually impossible for chiefs to come to agreement over any genuinely customary issue, since "each state has a different custom in a given situation." If the chiefs were expected to advise the national government, "Who would choose which custom to follow?"

A Dramatic Interlude

The lengthy debate over the Chamber of Chiefs, which has prompted this rather detailed look into some of the Micronesians' feelings about chieftainship, was at least partially provoked by an incident that occurred just as the plenary began reconsidering the proposal after its initial defeat. A middle-aged Pohnpeian, stripped to the waist and bearing a stalk of sugarcane over his right shoulder, entered the convention's chamber and strode purposefully onto the ConCon floor.[9] ConCon president Resio Moses (who was at the time Pohnpei's governor and who is in line to become a paramount chief) called to the sergeant-at-arms to intercept him, but in seconds the man was crouching before the Pohnpei Nahnken's desk. The president quickly gaveled a recess as the man carefully placed the cane against his chief's upper torso and began speaking in a quiet voice.

A member of his family had died earlier that day and he was performing a *luhke*, the traditional request for his chief's presence at the funeral. In a few minutes he departed and another Pohnpeian delegate had the cane carried away. Later, there was disagreement among those present about

the extraordinary timing of the *luhke*, coming as it did just as the Nahnken
was about to speak. Some argued that it had been deliberately arranged,
while others said that this was hardly likely, given that the episode undoubtedly served to further alienate those already dubious about assign-
ing the chiefs a formal role in government. In either case it was probably
the ConCon's most dramatic moment. Following this interlude, the Nahnken rose to begin speaking on behalf of the Chamber of Chiefs proposal.[10]
He discussed the peace-keeping role chiefs traditionally play, emphasizing
that they could promote harmony and unity within the F.S.M., and that
they were ready to serve the nation night and day in these capacities. His
words were somewhat vague and contradictory: in the fashion of proper
Pohnpeian oratory, he sought to avoid any appearance of telling people
what to do.

Resolution

The episode served to reinforce the doubts of many delegates about formally empowering the chiefs, and the measure was deferred until more
satisfactory wording could be found. Eventually, three of the ConCon's
most influential delegates took charge of the proposal and worked skill-
fully to resolve resistance to it. This was the only occasion on which I saw
parliamentary skills deliberately brought to bear as a means of solving an
otherwise intractable problem—evidence of the proposal's significance.
These parliamentarians crafted phrasing that was at once vague enough
to assure that the chiefs themselves would be able to determine the chamber's official role, and specific enough to overcome fears that Congress
would exercise power over it. By combining a number of different amendments and drafts, they rewrote the constitution's Article 5, Section 3 so
that it would read, "a chamber of chiefs is hereby established." The chamber's primary role would be "to advise on matters of customs and traditions, to promote and protect customs and traditions, and to promote
peace and unity." The role of the national government—that is, the Congress—in establishing the chamber would be to "take every step necessary
and reasonable to provide" for the chamber's operations.

Lingering resistance to the proposal was ultimately overcome when a
Pohnpeian delegate, during debate in the Committee of the Whole, posed
the following question: "Ten years have passed [since the founding of the
F.S.M.] without establishing a Chamber of Chiefs—is this indicative that
there is no need for it? Has there been a problem in the past ten years?
The president has done nothing to establish it." The Committee of the
Whole's chairman asked Tosiwo Nakayama, head of the Chuuk delega-

tion and the F.S.M.'s first president (and president of the 1975 constitutional convention), to respond. "During my administration I felt the need for it. I put a request for funding in my budget, but Congress did not supply the money." The Micronesians' continuing respect for President Nakayama is enormous, and this simple affirmation of his support for the measure was sufficient to bring debate to a close.[11]

Aftermath

If the delegates were not prepared to gainsay the chiefs in the public arena of the ConCon, the Micronesian people were very much prepared to do so in the privacy of their ballots. The proposed change was defeated overwhelmingly in the 1991 constitutional referendum. It received fewer favorable votes than any other item in Kosrae and Pohnpei, placed second to last in Yap and Chuuk, and received the lowest number of affirmative votes overall. Ironically, only in Kosrae, seat of the most articulate opposition to it, did the proposal receive more than 50 percent approval (it got 55 percent). In Pohnpei 48 percent of the voters favored it, in Chuuk 39 percent, and in Yap 34 percent.

This massive opposition to the Chamber of Chiefs is evidence not of chieftainship's declining significance in Micronesia, but of just the opposite. The fact that in the traditional leaders' presence the ConCon delegates could not bring themselves to gainsay them testifies to the nature of the dilemma. The chiefs retain tremendous influence, of various types and springing from multiple sources. In general, Micronesian polities rely on the strengths of their chiefs to guarantee certain defensive functions—in relation to both the exterior and the supernatural worlds—and people are thus inclined to support them. At the same time, however, people strongly resist any attempts on the part of the chiefs to interfere too much in the everyday, domestic sphere of community life. Micronesians accomplish these dual, contradictory tasks with dual—or tripartite—political structures in which various leaders, factions, and communities ceaselessly compete with one another and thus serve to check overweening ambition and unwarranted attempts to exercise power.

As the entire thrust of the ConCon made clear, Micronesians have significant reservations about the power of their national government, generally perceiving the Congress as entirely too strong. Permitting the chiefs to take on a formal role in the national government not only would have enhanced their power, but also would have decreased the dual character of the present-day Micronesian scene, which now functions with Congress on the one hand and the traditional polities on the other. Keeping chiefs out of government seems to have been a deliberate means of preserving both their role as protectors of the people and the traditional structures of competing power blocs. For all that the F.S.M. constitution portrays itself as a guardian of Micronesian customs and traditions, the Micronesian people see their guarantees situated elsewhere, and aim to keep them there. It is solely from this perspective, I think, that we can understand why it was only in Kosrae, where there are no chiefs, that a majority actually voted in favor of the Chamber of Chiefs, while in Yap, which most observers would agree has the most viable traditional polity and the only state government with an official role for chiefs already in place, the chamber received its greatest opposition.

SINCE THE BEGINNING of colonial rule in Micronesia, outsiders have been attempting to reorganize local systems of chieftainship. To cite but one example, in the early years of this century, the German administration was trying to shore up the authority of Palauan and Chuukese leaders even as it was working to undermine Pohnpei's chiefs (Ballendorf 1989: 36). Though it is possible to offer certain generalizations about underlying similarities in Micronesian notions of chieftainship, it would be a mistake to overly generalize about the recent history of these political systems. During the past half-century of American rule, in particular, efforts at what is often called "political development" have swung back and forth between willingness to respect local cultures and attempts—sometimes vigorously prosecuted—to rectify the supposed inequalities of Micronesian polities, despite the early recognition by some anthropologists that political processes in the islands were generally more democratic than those in the United States; that is, individual members of communities were likely to have far more influence on the making of important decisions than most Americans do (Petersen forthcoming a).

Variations both in indigenous Micronesian political organization and in local colonial histories have meant that individual communities have been changing in quite distinct—if not unique—ways. Most Micronesians, of course, fully recognize these differences, and it is this awareness of variation, I think, that underlies much of the ConCon's—as well as the general populace's—ambivalence about the proposed Chamber of Chiefs. Micronesians are not keen on legislating for other communities: those who wanted the chamber knew full well that others did not; those who opposed the measure realized that it was of considerable importance to some of their neighbors. In the end, some delegates voted for the amendment against their better judgment, knowing that people at home were not likely to approve it in the referendum.

The history of Micronesian chieftainship and the Chamber of Chiefs, it would seem, bears out an observation Julian Steward made long ago. "It is not wholly revealing to record merely that a group had a chief," he said, for "the nature and extent of the authority delegated to the chief" is not "self-evident," while "novel conditions and concepts introduced by the white man often radically altered native groupings, bringing solidarity and chieftain's authority where it had not previously existed" (Steward 1937:628). It is equally the case that the meaning of the Chamber of Chiefs' ultimate defeat is not self-evident. The various delegations, and in some cases individuals within them, had differing reasons for taking the positions they did. Nonetheless, there was at no point any evidence that Micronesians have come to think of their chiefs as irrelevant anachronisms. Doubts about the proposal had to do with larger issues of what the chiefs' relationship to government would be, and the possible consequences of changes in the overall position of the chiefs, not with the nature of chieftainship itself. Most of the F.S.M.'s voters, I must conclude, consider the chiefs far too valuable in their current positions outside the government to see much value in the vague and perhaps ephemeral benefits attributed to a national Chamber of Chiefs.

If we step back from the particulars of this case, we confront a tendency among many observers lacking in firsthand familiarity with existing chiefdoms to view them as anachronisms, survivals from simpler times, destined to soon disappear. It is my contention that many peoples—in the Pacific, Africa, South America, Southeast Asia, North America, and perhaps elsewhere—are fully aware of the differences between chiefdoms and states and seek to preserve traditional forms. This is not because these people are particularly conservative, nor because they want simply to preserve traditions. It is because chieftainship (as a broad category, with many versions and local nuances) is designed to prevent the consolidation of power, while the ceaseless attempt to consolidate power defines the very nature of the state.

Chieftainship addresses a need many human communities find pressing. It is capable of simultaneously providing a measure of extremely visible organization that outsiders find forbidding, while promoting a high degree of individual autonomy within the community. The political character of the "state" has been generally triumphant because of its capacity to mobilize violence on its own behalf, but there are many peoples who are not prepared to deliberately impose this form upon themselves. Rather than wait for the state to wither away, they seek to prevent it from taking root in the first place.

Micronesians appreciate that as postcolonial peoples pursuing sovereignty in a world of nation-states, they, too, must possess a state capable of dealing with the existential absurdities of international law, which has proved itself capable of recognizing only a restricted range of political forms and structures. But that does not mean they have decided to inflict this entity inward upon their own communities. Micronesians seek not only to keep their national government and their chiefs in check, but also to preserve a political way of life that fully recognizes the tendency to abuse power and is therefore designed to prevent individuals and small groups from accruing it. In preserving chieftainship by keeping it outside the formal constraints of their nation-state, they are applying their own brilliant political theory.

Irooj Ro Ad

Measures of Chiefly Ideology and Practice
in the Marshall Islands

LAURENCE M. CARUCCI

THE DISCUSSION of chiefs, chiefly legitimacy, and authority in the Pacific has recently been transported into a new arena with the publication of Obeyesekere's *The Apotheosis of Captain Cook* (1992) and Sahlins's rebuttal of this work (1995). Obeyesekere contends that Sahlins miscontextualized and misconstrued documents that indicate that Cook was classified by eighteenth-century Hawaiians as a living god. For Obeyesekere:

the divinization of Cook is a structure of the long run in European thought, inasmuch as his chiefly deification is a Hawaiian example of the same phenomenon. . . . Sahlins's anthropological narrative of the life and death of Cook is not only a theoretical vindication of structural continuity and conjecture, as he claims, but it is also a continuation, albeit unwitting, of the European myth of the apotheosis of James Cook. Theoretical thought is often enshrined in nontheoretical traditions. (1992:177)

Sahlins believes that Obeyesekere's critique partakes of its own professed "orientalist" ethnocentricities that invert, rather than elucidate and ameliorate, the distinction between "the West" and "the Rest." Taken to its logical limit, Obeyesekere's approach deprives Hawaiians "of agency and culture, their culture is reduced to a classic meaninglessness: they lived and they suffered—and then they died" (Sahlins 1995:198). In classically ironic style, Sahlins notes of the historiographic principle underlying Obeyesekere's critical readings: "The European chroniclers are prisoners of their own myths, and however they may refer these myths to Hawaiians, the words are theirs" (ibid.:116). He goes on to say,

As Obeyesekere proceeds to explicate early Hawaiian concepts of White men by Sri Lankan beliefs and his own experience, he gets farther and farther from the Hawaiian and closer and closer to the native Western folklore of divine vs. Human, spiritual vs. material. This, again, because he dissolves the issue of whether men could be forms of god into whether the "natives" can discriminate between them. . . . This self-proclaimed defense of "preliterate people who cannot speak for themselves" is imperialist hegemony masquerading as subaltern resistance. (Ibid.: 196–97)

Readers of Obeyesekere and Sahlins will have to make their own judgments about the deification versus apotheosis debate based on close and contextualized readings of the eighteenth- and nineteenth-century Hawaiian accounts regarding processes used by Hawaiians and expatriate Europeans to interact with, discuss, and historicize selves and others. But, in spite of the unavoidable way in which "theoretical thought is ensconced in nontheoretical traditions," there is little doubt that Sahlins (1981, 1985b) has forced us to contemplate a widespread Pacific phenomenon: what Hocart referred to as "the divinity of chiefs" and, equally, of "the guest" (Hocart 1936, 1970).

Similar stories have been written many times over as European authors have attempted to portray Pacific views of chiefs and gods, charismatic leaders, and confrontations with outsiders. Our most detailed knowledge of these views is found in the substantial literature on cargo in which European representations of power are appropriated by Pacific peoples using a series of historically varied but ingeniously empowering mechanisms (Burridge 1960; Lawrence 1989; Worsley 1968; Guiart 1970; and Eliade 1970).[1] Confronted with representations of American force during and after World War II (including the nuclear-testing era), Marshall Islanders also developed histories to lay claim to their share of American displays of potency (Carucci 1989). These self-empowering constructions vested Americans with the ability to control sacred force as part of the Marshallese strategy to reappropriate some of that power for themselves. Thus, even if Sahlins has overly empowered Europeans' fleeting images of others in an attempt to resurrect the very roughly charted Hawaiian images of outsiders, his interpretation of Cook is far more than European self-apotheosis. He faithfully captures widely documented Pacific attempts to deify certain foreigners that are intended not to ennoble Europeans per se, but to represent the displays of power, quantify them, and bring those capacities within local control. In the Marshall Islands, and perhaps elsewhere, these symbolic transfers are, in part, innovative applications of the equation that associates living high chiefs and gods (Lessa 1979), that marks the "divinity" of outside visitors (Hocart 1970), that symbolically associates whiteness with purity, that sees physical size as a representation of rank, and that finds evidence of divine demeanor in magical and reproductive potency as well as in the demonstrated sharing of inexhaustible supplies of goods (particularly food). Further evidence of such potency is found in sophisticated firearms, aircraft, bombs, and nuclear armaments.

Answers to the Sahlins-Obeyesekere debate are not sequestered entirely in the past, for the logic that gives such encounters symbolic form and practical value is far more perduring than a single event. Indeed, in many senses, a logic analogous to that which led Hawaiians to incorporate Cook into their own history is reenacted with every Marshall Islander's discussion of the distinctiveness and potency of high chiefs. Contemporary local histories posit answers to questions of chiefly legitimacy and authority in order to refigure precisely how chiefs continue to have meaningful impact on, and value for, people in today's world. While today's chiefs are contested persons par excellence, the recurring focus of the discourses about chiefs and of the continued deference paid to them gives evidence of the potency of the idea of proper chiefly demeanor in the Marshall Islands today.

In the current-day Republic of the Marshall Islands, chiefs hold positions on the "Council of Irooj" as part of the new republic's governmental structure. Membership in this council, modeled after the House of Lords in the British system of governance, is based on a variety of claims and principles of chiefly right as well as on a set of newly constituted political compromises. More importantly, however, the rules that delineate who properly occupies a chiefly status are made evident in the ongoing flow of daily discourse. The basic conceptual categories have not changed over the twenty years that I have conducted research in the Marshalls, but the polemical nature of the arguments about chiefs have become more marked during this period. Talk about chiefs has always been of central concern, but today's discussions are more animated for a number of reasons. Since I have talked about the unique characteristics of Marshall Islands chiefs in several other locations (Carucci 1979, 1980, 1988, 1989, 1992), this chapter shall, for the most part, deal with the reasons for the increasingly animated discussion of chiefs in the Marshall Islands today.

Following Goldman (1970), Feinberg (1993) delineates a number of aristocratic principles that typify Polynesian chiefs. As Rynkiewich (1972: 61ff.) notes, a similar set of principles constitutes the taken-for-granted patterns that apply to Marshall Islands chiefs. Principles like lineage seniority, and the "double determination" of rank along "pathways" that lead through both the mother and father to construct the shortest roads to sacred sources, relate directly to the inherent sacredness of chiefs. This mythology legitimizes chiefly potency by establishing a fundamental difference between chiefs and commoners. It is in relation to this mythology that Sahlins has contributed the most to our general understandings of

Pacific chiefs. While Marshall Islanders describe chiefs in a variety of ways, the trope of initial divinity gives them a priori legitimacy. In the Marshall Islands, several critical prototypes are commonly used to talk about and interact with chiefs. These include:

1. The affinity between chiefs and gods (Carucci 1980), both of which in the Marshall Islands are termed *irooj*. Both are sacred, surrounded by tabu (*mo*), and held to exemplary standards not expected of ordinary humans.

2. The view of high chiefs as foreign deities, inherently unlike local people. Not only are chiefs welcome as long as their actions are honorable, their honor depends on a demonstrated "pristine" demeanor that distinguishes chiefs from commoners and represents a chief's credibility. Good chiefs must have the ability to bring the propriety and prelegitimized sanctity of the sacred to bear on affairs of the mundane world.[2]

3. The way in which local commoners attempt to engage both chiefs and deities in ongoing exchanges of mutual benefit to both parties. In its ideal formulation, the exchange *must* be continued by commoners in order to live productive lives (Carucci 1997). Since chiefs are neither local nor inherently landed (entities that bring themselves into being through working the land; cf. Schneider 1984 for a similar Yapese notion), they, too, must depend on commoners to welcome and coronate them in exchange for foods and other worldly goods that result from their own blessing of the lands that are "revealed" by commoners' labor. In this schema, continuity of the exchange is guaranteed since local people and chiefs are codependent. While chiefly coronation (*kairoojoj*) is no longer a common practice, people's recollections of the ceremonies provide them with evidence of chiefly dependence on commoners. This dependence is also noted by the saying: "The chief's strength is his/her *kajur* 'strength' [also meaning 'commoners']." While feudal understandings of chiefly rights to land were common among German ethnographers (e.g., Erdland 1912, 1914), Yanaihara believed that land was "the common property of the gens" (1940:170) and that "the chieftain was never the possessor of the land, nor was he regarded as a landowner" (ibid.:141). Minus the Morganian biases, Yanaihara's view of chiefs and chiefly rights is consistent with the principles of interdependence outlined above.

4. Principles of delayed reciprocity govern the exchange between chiefs and commoners (Carucci 1997). Anthropologists have often called this form of reciprocity "redistribution" since the commoners realize benefits that are not immediately tangible. In Sahlins's

terms, commoners often "eat the rank of their chiefs." Not uncommonly, commoners give gifts that are reciprocated by a chief's ability to bless a parcel of land and make it productive or bless a sea voyage and guarantee its success. In spite of the fact that chiefs are given large quantities of goods, not all of which must be redistributed, when common people are in need, the chief has the responsibility to impoverish himself/herself as part of "watching over" people. In the Marshallese metaphor Rynkiewich cites in note 2, the chief literally regurgitates goods stored in his/her stomach to care for commoners in times of need.

These prototypical characterizations of chiefs explain the special characteristics of chiefliness, the reasons chiefs are revered, and the aura of sacredness that, in the most marked instances, typifies a common person's demeanor when dealing with chiefs. Nevertheless, these characterizations fail to account for the multifarious contexts in which *today's* chiefs are deprecated, disowned, and even despised. To understand these situations requires a consideration of the many ways in which chiefs today differ from their mythologically and historically coronated ancestors.

Chiefs in the Marshall Islands today are fashioned out of the contradictions between a lengthy period of contact with four colonial powers and perduring proscriptions of indigenous design that cause them to honor the interests of local people—those who for centuries are said to have provided earthly sustenance for the objects of their power. The degree to which chiefly privilege has become marked by equivalent wealth is in precisely the same measure that chiefs have failed to endear themselves to the "workers" (*ri jerbal*: now used as the equivalent of *kajur*). Common complaints, or commoners' complaints, focus on the failure of today's chiefs to reciprocate since, by mythological precedent, it is a chief's prerogative to feed off of the labor of commoners but, concomitantly, to care for commoners in times of need.[3] Chiefs today, however, have become wealthy at the same time that the Marshallese masses have increased in number as well as in their level of impoverishment. Several paramount chiefs are said to be millionaires, but to get close to their fashionable and costly dwellings they must wallow through the same evidence of degradation as common Marshall Islanders. In essence, this is because their strength no longer comes from "the strength" (*kajur*: common people), but from their being properly positioned in a series of relationships with outsiders as a result of their privileged status to take advantage of new sources of economic wealth. With the entire system of local production in disarray, chiefs have become good politicians and businessmen at the same time that common people see them failing as chiefs.

Marshallese high chiefs are earthly gods who are separated from common people by generationally deep genealogies that, in the ideal instance, can be traced back to the primordial chiefs who are now represented by stars in the heavens (Carucci 1980). As sacred beings, a whole series of interdictions surround them that protect common people from harm by keeping them separate from that which is tabu (Radcliffe-Brown 1952). Here, however, chiefly practices under a set of exchange circumstances altered by colonial and postcolonial encounters have also changed the interpretations placed on them by other members of Marshallese society. This new set of representations and interpretations creates an equally new set of contradictions. If one element of chieftainship has been maintained, it is the inherently foreign nature of chiefs, for their newfound source of wealth has distanced the conditions of their lived existence from those of commoners. At the same time, simply by tampering in business and finance, chiefs have dirtied their hands in the world of the mundane, actions judged as inappropriate (*jekkar*) by other Marshall Islanders. As one island resident commented about a Majuro chief after the end of World War II: "Well the funny thing is, that chief started a store! A thing of amazement! A chief, and yet he was 'making business.' These two things are unsuited to one another (*jekkar*). Truly prohibited."[4]

Ideal types must always be compromised in practice, and island chiefs are no exception. As a long-standing practice, even the highest of chiefs must sacrifice the ultimate sanctity of sacred power in order to interact with others in the Marshall Islands. This is most evident in isolated and egalitarian locations like Āne-wetak and Wūjlañ, Pikinni (Bikini) and Kili, where relatively egalitarian exchanges between chiefs and commoners must be maintained by both parties since even the highest-ranking chiefs reside on the same small speck of land as those who provide them with a living. More closely spaced multiple atolls of the Ratak and Rālik chains allow chiefs to live at a distance from many of their subjects and to make the rounds of the atolls once or twice a year to collect their "share" of copra profits (*ekkan*). Nonetheless, in people's reminiscences, even these times of gathering (*kōmāātāt*) always involved chiefly distributions as well.

Colonization, and the arrival of copra and of the missionaries, transformed the chieftainship in many ways. As I have discussed elsewhere, Marshallese chiefs were unable to consolidate their rule over more than two or three atolls prior to the time of colonization. Around 1820, when Kotzebue visited the Ratak chain, for example, the high chief on Wotje could not maintain control over more than three atolls. Iron tools, given by Kotzebue to the chief of Wotje to encourage agriculture, were soon transformed into weapons and, within a short period of time, this "advanced technology" gave the chief the ability to extend his domain. In the latter half of the nineteenth century, more radical Western interventions increasingly empowered chiefs. The sailing vessels that Europeans gave Kabua on Jaluij in exchange for his cooperation in extending copra production throughout the Rālik chain, for example, enabled him to consolidate his rule of the southwestern Rālik chain and to extend his influence to the atolls to the north—places like Roñlap and Pikinni. Moreover, when homicide was discouraged by missionary teachers, then outlawed by German decree, primordial checks on autocratic abuse were eliminated. Commoners no longer had the communal ability to depose, and dispose of, despotic chiefs. In theory, despots could still be killed by magical means, since magic was legal (in the Westerners' eyes, magic could not work), but inasmuch as the strongest magic came from sacred sources controlled by chiefs, magic provided little recourse for commoners. Rather, the manipulation of magic further empowered chiefs, who could inflict magical deaths at the same time they were protected from the potential physical violence of ill-treated commoners. Contact with the West not only elevated high chiefs, it "fossilized" and extended their positions of power by eliminating the death sentence for evil leaders, by giving them Western-style "ownership" of the land,[5] and by placing them in intermediary positions in the developing copra trade (Carucci 1988, 1995).

In current-day reminiscences, Marshallese remember the colonially fashioned chiefs of the nineteenth century as being far preferable to those of the current day. Even during Japanese times, older residents recall that their whole lives focused on interactions with the chief. It was a source of inspiration to work for a chief because when the chief came to your district he would provide food, supplies, and often, a huge feast. Of course, the local producers would give him first fruits of every sort as well, but these gifts were reciprocated in kind. All of a worker's tools were provided by the chief and medical care was free—if someone was ill, the chief would pay for her passage to Jaluij, where she could see a doctor. Manutil Lokwot, for example, remembers chiefs from the nineteenth and twentieth centuries in the following terms:

You see, chiefs before had many people surrounding them—hundreds and hundreds of people. Today, it may be only one or two people with a chief. These people collected food and remained with the chief so that if some sort of damage appeared, they would stand up and fight in behalf of the chief. . . .

  [More recently] Jebdik, a chief from before, had a boat . . . and when he came to this islet . . . he would say, "Thursday, I will go to the head of the atoll." So then, all of the land heads met and talked things over. Onward and onward things would go until they were finished, then he [the land head] says, "We will now load the boat of the chief with, if it is baskets of taro, banana, breadfruit, fermented breadfruit—fill the boat." The boat next sails to the windward. Enemakij, the islet next to Kilok-en [next to the pass on Majuro], all of those places he knows he has lands to oversee, the boat lands in those spots to *take food off of the boat*. Sailing still to the windward, at each islet to the windward they again unload foods from the boat. The question while they are unloading food: "When is it that the boat will return?" "Saturday." So they unload food on each islet, onward, onward, onward, and, as they go, they ask again, "When will the boat return to Majuro?" It will proceed from there to seek out the windwardmost islet, as people finish preparing their provisions for the trip to Laura. Then they return to the [first] islet there and load the boat [with foods from the land destined for the chief]. Go to another islet there, load the boat; the reverse of the things he gave as food-class things for the people who live in those places, he now takes. Today, nothing [of this sort exists].

Chiefs also received a share of copra earnings in the Marshall Islands, but the share was considered a fair percentage, 3 *mil*: three one-thousandths of each pound produced. Like the fruits of the land, the chief's share of copra was imperative since the chief was given the ceremonially instantiated right to rule over the land by commoners who *were* the land. Commoners of the current day say that they ceded care of the land to deified chiefs through a series of rites of coronation. This was done in exchange for the chief's sacred blessings, rites that resulted in an abundance of natural products, both foods and copra. Even though these reciprocal arrangements between chiefs and commoners continued to have a very visible form until well after the war, many early colonizers overlooked them. And by overlooking the reciprocity, some colonizers came to the conclusion that high chiefs "owned" the land.

On Āne-wetak and Wūjlañ, the particulars of the reciprocity were somewhat different since chiefly "ownership" was not ossified in the same way by the colonial encounter. Here, lands that belonged to a chief—that is, the clan lands that were held at any one point by the currently living chief—were worked by commoners. The labor that went into harvesting the chief's copra was the chief's payment for leadership and blessing. The idea of a *"mil"* has no place on these atolls. Concomitantly, the lengthy isolation on these distant atolls required the intermarriage of chiefly and commoner clans, thereby diminishing the distinct character of sacred chiefly lines.

Today's chiefs, however, have different ways of making a living that engender an altered set of relationships with commoners and a renegotiated, if similar, tie to outsiders. The commonly accepted theory that chiefs in the Marshall Islands, and perhaps throughout Micronesia, are less powerful today than they were prior to World War II does not stand up to scrutiny. This line of reasoning contends that, under the Americans, chiefly rule was discouraged. Concomitantly, democratic institutions have replaced chiefly ones so that today's important leaders are democratically elected community representatives. To an outside observer, this theory may seem sound. Nonetheless, it fails to take account of local views of change, and only superficially accounts for extant realities.

Most Marshallese chiefs continue to hold positions of power in their local communities and in their emerging nation today. While many are elected to a public office, they have not won these elections in spite of their chiefliness. During Japanese days, chiefs always held appointed or elected government positions, and the tradition of electing "proscriptively endowed" leaders has continued. The high chief, Amata Kabua, is currently president of the Marshall Islands, and many other chiefs hold senatorial positions in the "Commons" governing body, Nitijelā. These practices of chiefly recognition occur despite the fact that the House of Irooj (after the British House of Lords) provides a governing body for chiefs. Their twice-coronated positions in the Nitijelā and other government offices continue to mark local confidence in the inherent potency of chiefly rank. Given the Marshallese belief that in the United States "anyone can become president," it is quite clear that the Marshallese have chosen a different pattern for themselves.[6] Marshall Islands chiefs are hardly disempowered, and they have far from disappeared.

Instead, chiefs under the Americans have become even stronger in a "bourgeoisified" sense, and, in a concomitantly requisite manner, they have become less sacred.[7] This is a pattern that began the moment chiefs became intermediaries in the capitalist ploys of copra traders and was intensified as chiefs further compromised their sacredness by claiming an identity with, and ownership of, land. Nonetheless, chiefs further compromised their sacredness during the American colonial era and have totally revamped their own sense of power since independence. The complaint of commoners and disempowered chiefs that today's chiefs do not properly care for *kajur* provides support for this thesis, since if chiefs were powerless, no one would complain. Their sense of dissatisfaction points to the radical transformation that has taken place in the relationship between chiefs and commoners, and it is the alteration of this relationship, not theories of chiefly disempowerment, that leads to an understanding of chieftainship today.

Indeed, some Marshall Islanders note that in the immediate post–World War II era, Americans were dissatisfied with the idea of Marshallese chiefs. Those Americans who worked with the Island Trading Corporation (ITC) are said to have told local people that they did not have to pay the "chiefly tax" on copra. At the same time, Americans, like the Germans and Japanese who had been colonizers before them, needed access to islanders as a source of labor and required intermediaries to communicate with local people. For this purpose, Americans relied on half-caste Marshallese born to German-era entrepreneurs, and on students of the American Board of Commissioners for Foreign Missions. This reinstated group of local power elites was limited in their power, though, without the support of the Marshallese chiefs, who, in the latter half of the nineteenth century, had expanded their own power through coalitions with foreigners, with foreign descendants of local women, and with foreign-sponsored institutions. Without the intermediaries, the Americans literally could not speak. Without the chiefs, the intermediaries' words lacked authority. The ability to profess, to convey sacred knowledge, rested with the chiefs. This is why they were sacred (*mo*), and why their words were invested with potency (*maroñ*). In spite of whatever ideological objections Americans may have had to the inherent powers of chiefs, they could not live without them.

Marshall Islanders, therefore, continued to have powerful chiefs not because Americans liked them, but because Americans needed them. During the era of the Japanese civilian administration, Marshall Islanders had become a colony of producers for the colonizing center and for other population centers in Micronesia. Under American governance, however, Marshall Islanders shifted to being a source of inexpensive labor on military bases that were detached from local people, distanced from their concerns, and largely uncommitted to locally sustainable lifestyles. An increasing population, coupled with dependence on outside foods and sizeable groups of people displaced due to nuclear testing, made many islanders totally dependent on Americans. From the first, the United States valued Micronesia for strategic military purposes. Some effort went into perpetuating copra, handicraft, and indigenous subsistence production, but not with any need to use these imports at home, nor with a serious attempt to provide markets for them elsewhere. Many residents who worked with the U.S. military after the war have humorous, yet perplexing, tales to tell about handicraft production:

So the ship would show up, an LCU, and they would load all of the handicraft on board. And they paid us well for all of the handicraft—fans, baskets, belts—all of the things that had become so popular with the soldiers after the battle. But to the Americans, these things were of no value. They were so powerful they had no need for them. So the ship would sail away, and then the Captain would say, "O.K., throw them away," and the sailors would dump all of the handicraft into the lagoon. (Carucci, 1991 field notes)

With a declining market, copra production also withered under the Americans, and the only substitute sources of income were labor positions on Kuwajleen and, particularly after independence, an expanding array of government-related positions on Majuro. While Americans have tried to repatriate Ebeye (Kuwajleen) residents to their home atolls, it should not be surprising that these efforts have failed dismally.[8] The only source of livelihood on the outer islands is subsistence production, by itself viable for small populations but totally unacceptable to islanders who have come to depend on a wide array of costly imported goods and foods during the past 130 years.

It is within this schema of change that today's chiefs have carved out a new niche. Chiefs, themselves foreigners, have always served as living intermediaries between ancient deified chiefs (to whom they are related) and earthly commoners. They have now found a new god. Elsewhere, I have discussed the way in which Americans are fashioned into chiefs of the highest rank by Marshallese (Carucci 1980, 1989), and indeed, the Marshallese chiefs fit into the new cosmological order as their local intermediaries. Two critical features of the old order have been altered, however, and it is these features that lead to an understanding of current-day contradictions commonly faced by chiefs and commoners. In the ancient cosmological order, the productivity of the land and sea was controlled by the deities and sought by commoners through their appeals to chiefs of an earthly and celestial order. Commoners benefited from continued productivity, and the first-fruits offerings were representations of the balance between subservience and guaranteed reciprocity in this ongoing exchange. At a more recent juncture, when copra was king, the *mil* or labor invested in the chief's copra served as an extension of the first-fruits logic.

In the new order, these relationships are again reshaped. Cash is controlled by foreign "deities," but, unlike fish and products of the land, it does not reach commoners first through processes of production. The logic of first fruits, and therefore of the *mil* levy on copra, does not operate. Instead, cash comes to Majuro, and it is the chiefs and the new elites who control its distribution. Of the millions of dollars that reached Majuro in 1991, US$2,000 per atoll for each outer atoll was designated to filter down beyond Majuro and Ebeye. As Poyer notes (1992:83), "Development efforts on the urban islands" of the Marshalls largely preclude the appropriation of funds for projects on the outer atolls.

Another source of income entering the Marshalls comes in the form of payments by the United States for nuclear damages and for lease agreements for military use of Kuwajleen atoll, an active military installation that serves as a missile-tracking location and "catcher's mitt" for rockets fired from missile ranges within the United States. Four Marshallese atolls receive nuclear damages payments: Pikinni and Āne-wetak (former nuclear testing sites), and Roñlap and Utrōk (whose residents were irradiated during the 1954 "Bravo" thermonuclear test). Āne-wetak, with its own chiefs, owes no share of its monies to Marshall Island chiefs. Nonetheless, the larger land claims of the atoll's chiefly lines would entitle the highest-ranked chiefs to greater amounts of money. The Āne-wetak people, however, have been unable to settle land disputes since returning to their home atoll in 1980. They have chosen to divide their payments on a head-by-head basis, creating an incredible incentive for increased population growth, rather than agree to relinquish control of outside monies to chiefs who lay claims to land that most residents consider undeserved.

Pikinnians are currently undecided about how they fit into the Marshallese chiefly order. Like the people of Āne-wetak, they have their own chiefs, but Marshall Islands paramount chiefs from the Rālik chain claim they have historically maintained control over the atoll. Recently, the Rālik chiefs, Kabua Kabua and Amata Kabua (joined by other members of the Lejōlañ/Mañiñi Kabua family), have contested which of them has certain rights in the central Rālik chain (particularly on Kuwajleen). Undoubtedly, this case will be followed by another to determine if either of these chiefs has rights over Pikinni or if Pikinnians, like Āne-wetak people, were governed solely by their own chiefs in ancient times. Whatever the outcome, the valorization of a single indigenous tradition is simply a current-day political act that replicates the same sort of stasis-generating colonial strategies that occurred in the Marshalls in the late nineteenth century and again after World War II.

Utrōk and Roñlap monies, like the $5 million yearly U.S. payment on Kuwajleen, are divided among chiefs (*irooj*), commoners (*kajur*), and land heads (*alab*). In the Ratak chain two chiefly levels are recognized in this division, whereas the western chain recognizes only high chiefs' rights to land. Thus, after lawyers' fees, Utrōk monies are divided into four parts, while Roñlap and Kuwajleen dollars are divided in thirds. On Kuwajleen, these are equal thirds. The disparity between this division and the "3 *mil*" levy on copra disturbs many commoners and disempowered chiefs. In 1990, a proposal supported by Amata Kabua would have eliminated the *alab* share, thereby increasing the chiefs' share to 50 percent and leaving 50 percent to be divided among *alab* and *kajur*.

From the commoners' perspective, the new relationships that empower chiefs leave *kajur* outside the networks of reciprocity and redistribution that ultimately determine their fate.[9] They no longer fill an integral niche in processes of production since outside monies come directly to chiefs and government elites from external sources. It is only the goodwill of chiefs or government leaders that compels them to distribute the goods they control. Stories about how chiefs should behave are the only way commoners can vocalize their dissatisfaction. Telling such tales in a public context is always risky, however, since it contradicts the "good words" one should have for one's chief. Many commoners fear supernatural sanction or the possibility of being expelled from their land. Disempowered chiefs, those who have sacred power but who were not recognized in the chiefly lines that were "fixed" in their rank during the colonial encounter, are better able to voice such objections without risk of sanction. Indeed, this group speaks most loudly, not only as a mark of their current disenfranchisement, but, equally, because they can counteract the magical sanction of currently empowered chiefs with their own potent magic. For example, one of the grandsons of the former high chief of the central Ratak chain frequently speaks with disdain about the actions of certain other Marshall Islands high chiefs. When I asked if he was not afraid of sanction, he responded:

Many commoners are afraid of the chiefs. They believe that they might be thrown off of the land or maybe even killed. But I have no fear. Their magic has little value because the magic from my grandfather is much stronger than that of the chiefs of this day. On account of this, they are the ones who are afraid to throw me off of the land or make any other sort of evil moves. (Carucci, 1989–95 field notes)

From the chiefs' perspective, as well, the situation has changed. Since the money they now control did not come to them from the commoners, they have no reason to "re-" distribute it. The ongoing exchange relationships that linked chiefs and commoners together are now radically different from what they once were. A colonially inspired set of exchange relationships with outsiders, now greatly expanded, currently governs chiefly dealings, and commoners are not a part of those exchanges.

Nevertheless, by becoming involved with worldly exchanges, chiefs are now accused of "making business." This is what I mean by "bourgeoisified" chiefs—chiefs who are powerful and distant from commoners as a result of differences in worldly wealth. Like the attained separation from worldly goods of the highest of India's Brahmins, however, Marshallese chiefs should maintain their acquired separation from commoners by distancing themselves from worldly affairs. To the degree that they engage in activities suited to commoners—claiming rights to land, running businesses, or dealing with money—they sacrifice their ritual purity and sacredness. In the eyes of purists, this downward move toward the middle also makes them increasingly common, or "bourgeois." Marshallese chiefs today, in other words, have sacrificed their rank to increase their power. This risky strategy allows current-day chiefs to maintain distance from commoners through radical disparities in wealth. At the same time, to the degree that chiefs deprecate the inherent characteristics of sacred status by trafficking in the pursuits of the mundane, chiefs risk a shift in the way their character is judged. In the ideal, a chief should mediate the actions of commoners by bringing the unquestionable purity of celestially inspired thought to bear on worldly problems. As chiefs increase their vested self-

interests in the worldly market, the sacred nature of their character becomes assailable. Indeed, chiefs who use wealth to distinguish themselves
from commoners bring themselves within the commoners' grasp, since,
unlike the unquestionable difference in identity guaranteed by a sacred
genealogy, wealth is attainable for commoners, even though its possession
in the current day seems unlikely to most Marshall Islanders, who just see
themselves becoming poorer.

11

Chiefs in Vanuatu Today

LAMONT LINDSTROM

ON MARCH 2, 1994, Jean-Marie Léyé was elected Vanuatu's third state president. Two months later, when he delivered his first official speech to Parliament, he had stretched his name to Jean-Marie Léyé Lenelgau—attaching a chiefly title, Lenelgau, to the previously frenchified Léyé. The president's decision to be addressed by a traditional chiefly title speaks to the continuing importance of the chief (or *jif* in Bislama) in Vanuatu. Since that country's independence from Britain and France in 1980, *jif*s have flourished. The state has at least partly encouraged the acquisition by *jif*s of increased legislative, judicial, and law-enforcement functions at both local and national levels. The capacities and reach of the recently independent state have also emerged and solidified within the same political process. If the state has to some extent defined what a *jif* can be, along with the proper compass of his powers and duties, men who call themselves *jif*s have influenced the expanse and effectiveness of state programs.[1]

Overlapping claims by national politicians and by *jif*s to each other's titles signal this jointly constitutive arrangement between state and *jif*. *Jif*s enumerate themselves along with politicians and ministers of religion among Vanuatu's national leadership; Jean-Marie Léyé Lenelgau and other political leaders, in turn, set about collecting chiefly titles and pose themselves as hybrid *jif*s/presidents, *jif*s/members of Parliament, or *jif*s/ministers of state.

There is considerable flexibility and creative potential within Vanuatu's local leadership systems—a flexibility that has underwritten the recent evolution of relations between chiefs and state. These local systems vary among Vanuatu's islands and cultural groups. In general, however, almost any ambitious and capable man, in some contexts, with a straight face, is able to call himself *jif*. *Jif* is an equivocal and commodious title. It subsumes a miscellany of characters who stake their leadership claims in both tradition (*kastom*) and modernity. These leadership claims trace inward, seeking roots in locally recognized systems of inequality, and outward, highlighting a chiefly ability to mediate with state organs and programs. The elastic expanse of the title serves ambitious individuals who scheme to claim it. It also serves the state, which, by recognizing and admitting *jif*s into government councils, puts to work able and ambitious local leaders within national political structures. But this accommodation between the *jif* and the state is not just the absorption and employment of enduring traditional leaders by modern institutions. The "traditional" *jif*, at least in his present form, has become known in Vanuatu within confines set by the colonialist and independent state.[2] He has grown up in the cracks and crannies that separate village from capital city, the country's numerous local polities from its overarching institutional state.

Kastom Jifs

Today's *kastom jif*s, although undoubtedly *kastom*, are not simply customary. The emergence and construction of the popular identity *jif*, from a plethora of local leadership positions, were shaped by the events and interests of postcontact, colonial society. Common use of the Bislama term *jif* itself may be relatively recent. Some New Hebrides condominium officials of the 1950s, for example, in their reports instead designated local leaders as "assessors" or "bigmen" (British District Agent 1950).

Vanuatu's indigenous leadership types varied considerably. Generally, the possession of a title legitimated a man's claims to authority, but there were several routes by which titles could be acquired. In the north of the country, men advanced through "grade societies," acquiring a new title at each stage in part by paying off titleholders above them in sacrificed pigs, mats, and food (Speiser [1923]1991:303; Deacon 1934:47; Guiart 1958: 166–67; Allen 1981; Patterson 1981; Blackwood 1981; Vienne 1984: 308). In the center of the archipelago, patrilineages possessed chiefly titles that were inheritable (Espirat et al. 1973:371–72; Facey 1981, 1988: 100; Philibert 1982:194; Haberkorn 1989:47). On Tanna, in the south, *every* male personal name was a landed title. In addition to these personal titles, local communities controlled one or more pairs of generic titles endowed with various ritual perquisites—*ierumanu*, "ruler" (i.e., sacred chief), and *ianinteta*, "spokesman of the canoe" (talking chief) (Guiart 1956:88–89; Bonnemaison 1987:121; Lindstrom 1990:55–56). In the far south, on Anatom, something closer to a Polynesian chiefly system may have existed, perhaps reflecting an intensified economic infrastructure of irrigated taro fields (Spriggs 1981:57–60).

Notably, this archipelago since the 1860s has experienced virulent epidemics, massive population decline, considerable labor migration overseas, and increased and better munitioned local conflict. "Traditional" political systems, as first ethnologically described in the 1910s and 1920s, must be read in a historical context of two generations of massive social conflict and disruption (see, for example, M. Rodman 1983). By the early years of this century, missionary and colonial institutional hierarchies had spread to overlay most of the archipelago, reorganizing whatever precontact systems once existed. The missions imported a sacerdotal hierarchy of Elder, Deacon, Pastor, *Mama* (Anglican priest), and also, in many places, promoted the claims of elect Christian leaders to be "paramount chiefs" of entire regions or islands (see Rubinstein 1981:143; Tonkinson 1981:245; Philibert 1982:195). The colonial government also identified its own proxy chiefs, inventing the title "Assessor," which it bestowed upon English- or French-speaking men in each region. Assessors advised European district agents, particularly within island court hearings (see W. L. Rodman 1982).

In some cases, missions and government no doubt located existing titled local leaders and promoted these to Elder or Assessor. The process clearly worked in reverse as well. Ambitious cultural mediators, nominated by Europeans to be an Assessor or Elder, parlayed this externally derived authority to advance claims to local chiefly titles (W. L. Rodman 1982:73). Some men discharged all three positions simultaneously: Elder, Assessor, and titled *jif*. For the 100 years before Vanuatu's independence, a reciprocal relationship obtained between local leaders, who came to call themselves *jif*s, and government/mission structures of authority. This authority extended its influence into the countryside by nominating Elders and Assessors who thereby came to possess at least *de jure* chiefly status. And local leaders or would-be title holders could amplify whatever authority they possessed in their home village and region by accepting and cultivating these new government titles.

The independent state of Vanuatu today has upheld this bargain with local leaders, although the popular term *jif* has now entirely supplanted the colonialist term Assessor and has also multiplied hierarchically and geographically. Vanuatu currently possesses village *jif*s, area *jif*s, island *jif*s, town *jif*s, and paramount *jif*s, among others. In independent Vanuatu, the official capacities of *jif*s—on paper, at least—are more powerful than those of yesterday's Assessor or Elder in the colonial New Hebrides. This, in large part, descends from the political dynamics and rhetoric of Vanuatu's independence movement of the 1970s. The Vanua'aku party, which led the colony into independence and ruled throughout the 1980s, although founded by young government officials, teachers, and Christian pastors, embraced and defended local *kastom* as useful, splendid, and honorable (Tonkinson 1982; Lindstrom 1982b). A political rhetoric that acclaimed the dignity and contemporary relevance of *kastom* unavoidably also raised the profile of *kastom* leaders. If *kastom* is politically conspicuous, legitimizing an independent Vanuatu, then so, too, must be traditional forms of leadership and inequality.

The National Council of Chiefs

A nationalist rhetoric of *kastom* has enfranchised the voice of *jifs* within the national political arena—but which *jifs*? Given the variety of traditional leadership positions, the widespread political significance of achievement over ascription, and the glut of claims to this Bislama title, Vanuatu has a lot of *jifs* to choose among. The creation of a National Council of Chiefs in 1977 provided one answer to Vanuatu's *jif* oversupply problem. An institutionalized chamber of chiefs permits the state to set parameters of chiefly identity and to police the number of authorized chiefly voices within state councils.

The National Council of Chiefs emerged from late colonial strategies to influence postindependence state structures.[3] Like the political identity *jif* itself, the National Council was rooted in both colonial and indigenous practices. The creation of a chiefs' council expressed local attempts to reproduce at the national level the sorts of joint conclaves and assemblies of elders and leaders that people regularly convene within their villages and regions. And the French, in particular, hoped that a chiefly council might serve as a conservative force within soon-to-be-independent Vanuatu. Continuing Anglo-French conflict throughout the 1970s was a fundamental motor, pushing the country's move toward independence (see Plant 1977; MacClancy 1980; Beasant 1984; Van Trease 1987). The French realized, belatedly, that most of the young, educated civil servants and professionals who were demanding independence were British-trained, largely hostile to French interests, and supporters of the National (Vanua'aku) party. In response, the French rapidly expanded their school system throughout the 1970s (Paitel 1985), and firmed up what political support they could among Catholic, Seventh-Day Adventist, "half-caste," and francophone communities. They also attempted to exploit divisions between educated young urban leaders calling for immediate independence and older, rural, *kastom* leaders back on home islands who would be more willing to live with the political status quo.

The colonial New Hebrides Advisory Council proposed that the country's first Representative Assembly—which would succeed the council— should include four "custom *jifs*," "to be elected by an Electoral College of Chiefs divided into four sections, each chief coming from one of the four administrative districts" (MacClancy 1980:126; see also Zorgbibe 1981:47). The four chiefs were to be selected in stages by fellow chiefs, rather than elected by popular suffrage: village chiefs within each island area would send representatives to an islandwide meeting that would select representatives to a districtwide meeting of chiefs that would vote for a single regional chiefly representative. Throughout this process, the exact character of this "Electoral College of Chiefs" and the specific qualifications of village, island, and district chiefs remained blurred and undefined; nor could they be easily codified from above, given Vanuatu's flexibility and variation in local leadership practices (MacClancy 1980:126). The self-identified pools of *jifs* involved in this process ultimately included anyone at the village level who was both willing publicly to assume the status label and able to confront anyone who might dispute his claims.

After some months of dispute about chiefly and other members of the Assembly, both sides agreed to a special sitting in June 1976, specifically to discuss the issue of chiefly membership (Plant 1977:85; MacClancy 1980:128). This meeting recommended the creation of a National Council of Chiefs "to act as an advisory body on matters of custom to the Assembly" (MacClancy 1980:128). The Representative Assembly charged the chiefs' council with advising

on all matters concerning New Hebridean custom. The Assembly must seek the views of the Council before taking any decision on these matters: the codification of custom; the judicial system, and legislation specifically affecting New Hebrideans; legislation concerning fishing and hunting; the organization of the registration of births, marriages and deaths; the determination of qualifications of Chiefs for election to the Assembly; land matters; any matter affecting the constitutional status of the New Hebrides. (Plant 1977:97)

The Representative Assembly met once again in November 1976—a year after it was elected. It was gridlocked, however; the National party (later renamed the Vanua'aku party) controlled twenty-one seats, as did its opponents. By mid-1977, the two colonial powers had decided to hold new elections the following November for a replacement Assembly. The Vanua'aku party boycotted these elections, and the Assembly remained ineffectual until all parties joined a Government of National Unity in 1978. The Vanua'aku party participated in, and won, a third round of elections in November 1978.

In the meanwhile, the National Council of Chiefs that the Representative Assembly had created met for the first time on February 8, 1977, elected Willie Bongmatur its chairman, and passed, 19 votes to 3, a motion calling for "internal self-government" by the end of the year (Plant 1977:115; MacClancy 1980:130). Bongmatur, from Ambrym Island, had been previously elected to the Assembly. He served as president of the National Council of Chiefs until he retired in 1993. In addition to Bongmatur, the original council included the three other chiefly members of the Representative Assembly and five additional chiefs from each of the colonial districts, chosen in November 1976 by the four loosely organized "electoral colleges of chiefs." Of these, fourteen *jifs* were associated with the Vanua'aku party, and ten with "moderate" parties that supported French interests (Plant 1977:95–96).

Following the establishment of a Government of National Unity, the colonial powers convened a committee of national leaders that met over several months in 1979 to tackle writing a national constitution. Bongmatur, as chairman of the National Council, was a member of this committee, along with three other official *jifs*. Bongmatur's concerns to codify chiefly authority within the constitution were seconded by party leaders from both sides (Zorgbibe 1981:62). The Vanua'aku party knew that it commanded the political support of a majority of council members; the "moderates" still believed that a Chiefs' council could protect minority rights along with island custom. Bongmatur recalled: "Since the National Council of Chiefs already existed, it would have been difficult to disestablish it. This facilitated its codification in the constitution. We were lucky that the National Unity government was led by a party that believed strongly in the *kastom* and culture of the country, and that chiefs should represent their own areas. This is how the Council of Chiefs made it into the constitution" (my translation, Bongmatur interview).

Actually, an initial French proposal presented to the Constitutional Committee by Charles Zorgbibe (appointed constitutional counselor to the New Hebrides in 1978) contemplated an even more powerful capacity for chiefs. In this draft, twenty chiefs would compose a Senate, an upper house of government (Zorgbibe 1981:82–83). This Senate—along with any official capacity for chiefs at all—vanished altogether in a second constitutional draft, presumably because of suspicions that chiefs in an upper house would undercut state (and party) powers to govern. Chiefs returned, however, in a third draft ultimately accepted by consensus. This institutionalized a national chiefly advisory body on custom that Parliament might choose to consult, rather than an influential upper house: "The National Council of Chiefs has a general competence to discuss all matters relating to custom and tradition and may make recommendations for the preservation and promotion of New Hebridean culture and languages. The Council may be consulted on any question, particularly any question relating to tradition and custom, in connection with any bill before Parliament" (Vanuatu Constitution, Chapter 5, Article 28[1–2]). Only on questions of land tenure does the constitution *require* Parliament to consult with the Council of Chiefs (Chapter 12, Article 74). The constitution also directs Parliament to "provide for the role of chiefs" in village or island courts (Chapter 8, Article 50). National Council chiefs, to be selected by their "peers," would meet at least once a year. The constitution finally directs Parliament "to provide for the organization of . . . the role of chiefs at the village, island and district level" (Chapter 5, Article 29).

Parliament thus in the end secured for itself powers to "provide for" and "organize" chiefs. Nonetheless, the National Council of Chiefs, which arose within the political struggles leading to Vanuatu's independence, survived this period of rapid institutional development and change leading up to the birth of an independent state.

Malvatumauri Operations

At its maiden meeting in February 1977, the National Council of Chiefs changed its name to the Malvatumauri (or, in alternative Bislama spellings, the Malfatumaori or Malfatumauri). This *kastom*ization of nomenclature followed, by two weeks, the National party's parallel metamorphosis into the Vanua'aku party. Bongmatur explained:

After I was elected chairman, we talked about the name. Since the Council stood for *kastom*, we felt it better to rechristen it with a *kastom* name. This is why we renamed it the Malvatumauri. *Mal* means *jif. Vatu* means stone, or island, since all land rests upon stone. *Mauri* is something that grows and expands in the light. When we agreed on the name, we placed a stone and *namele* [cycad] fronds in front of the government building where Parliament met. Then we killed a pig [on top of the stone] to christen the new name [Malvatumauri]. (My translation, Bongmatur interview)

Since 1980, the Malvatumauri has reorganized its membership several times. Until 1994, each of eleven island regions sent two chiefs to the council, with the exception of the smaller districts Epi and Paama, which sent one, and Tafea, the large southern province, which sent four. Regional (or island) councils of chiefs, as electoral colleges, select representatives to the Malvatumauri every four years. These councils may also subsume several area councils of chiefs, which, in turn, include village councils of chiefs.[4] Additional area councils continue to be established as components of regional councils. (For example, a Southwest Tanna Area Council was established in February 1993: *Vanuatu Weekly* 429 [Feb. 20]: 3.) In the elections of March 3, 1993, the eleven regional councils, serving as electoral colleges for the Malvatumauri, comprised the following numbers of state-approved chiefly electors (*Vanuatu Weekly* 430 [Feb. 27, 1993]: 1): Banks/Torres, 14 chiefs; Santo/Malo, 18 chiefs; Ambae/Maewo, 16 chiefs; Malekula, 10 chiefs; Pentecost, 9 chiefs; Ambrym, 6 chiefs; Paama, 4 chiefs; Epi, 8 chiefs; Shepherds, 16 chiefs; Efate, 18 chiefs; Tafea, 7 chiefs. In 1994, the government reduced the number of regions to six, although the number of chiefly representatives has remained the same. The regional councils are variously active. Membership is assorted and shifting, depending on an island's political unity and whether or not one or another political faction is boycotting a council, questioning the chiefly claims of its members (as has been the case in Tafea).

The government funds Malvatumauri operations, including travel grants to bring the twenty-two *jifs* to Port Vila for two meetings each year. The Malvatumauri's budget includes salaries for its president, a secretary, and one typist. In 1992, the Malvatumauri raised 10 million *vatu* (around US$90,000) to construct a large "national *nakamal* [men's meeting-house]" near Vanuatu's new Parliament House (*Vanuatu Weekly* 316 [Dec. 1, 1990]: 2). The chiefs christened the structure *Farea Saralana* (a North Efate language name that *Vanuatu Weekly* translated as "miting haus blong evri pipol"). This house, constructed partly of traditional materials, serves as a meeting hall for the assembled chiefs' biannual conferences and for other public events during the rest of the year.

The president of the Malvatumauri also serves as the chairman of the Cultural Center Oversight Committee; of Vanuatu Handikrafs (a traditional-arts sales cooperative); of the government's Social Concerns Committee; and of a committee to choose Sir Paul Reeves Scholarships (established by a former governor-general of New Zealand); and is a member of the Judiciary Service Commission. Former President Bongmatur at one time also chaired the Arts Festival committee that organized Vanuatu's participation in the South Pacific Arts Festivals.

Paramount *Jifs*

Beginning with structures left in play by the departed colonial authorities and the new state constitution, Malvatumauri *jifs* have engaged in a strategic process of elaborating and defining chiefly identity and prerogatives. National *jifs* claim a double authority founded in village tradition and state constitution and, tactically, may emphasize one or the other in different contexts. Mediating officially between village and state, *jifs* have attempted to expand their influence in both arenas. State politicians have been understandably supportive of increased chiefly powers in the village, but less sympathetic to magnified chiefly authority within the nation as a whole. But *jifs*, to date, have been more concerned to solidify their authority at home.

Given Vanuatu's boisterous local politics, it is no surprise that state-approved Malvatumauri *jif*s have faced challenges from other pretenders to traditional leadership. In the mid-1980s, francophone *jif*s, mostly from the small islands off northeast Malekula, established the United Council of Chiefs. This alternative chiefly conclave condemned the legitimacy of both the government of the day and the Malvatumauri (which the United Council of Chiefs president criticized as a bunch of upstarts who lacked true chiefly credentials or ancestry). As Brunton (1989) and many others have noted, local authority and political structures in Vanuatu are always under threat of challenge and erosion. State recognition of official island and paramount chiefs provides Malvatumauri *jif*s a significant external boost for their authority at home.

Malvatumauri *jif*s quickly took advantage of their official status to begin codifying *kastom* law. This codification of *kastom* appears necessary to many people to resolve irregularities within local customary practice and to lend force to chiefly decisions and decrees. In 1983, the Executive Committee of the Malvatumauri (consisting of eleven of the twenty-two chiefs) published a book of *kastom polisi*, organized into forty articles, and authorized by the "Paramount Chiefs—Malvatumauri" (Malvatumauri 1983; for an English translation, see Lindstrom and White 1994). Nearly all this policy aims at village-level delict and disorder, and much of it seems designed particularly to keep women and youth under closer control and to make chiefly supervision of village activities more muscular. For example, Article 1 gives *jif*s control over land-tenure disputes and decisions; Article 2 accords *jif*s the right to adjudicate village murders and arrange appropriate *kastom* compensation; Articles 4 and 5 allow *jif*s to control people's movement from village to village and from island to island; Article 6 gives *jif*s the right to command the free labor of villagers for public-works projects; Article 8 regulates marriages; Article 14 attempts to control unwed pregnancies (*pikinini blong rod*); Article 15 demands general village order; Article 17 attempts to forestall villagers from defecting to new religious denominations; Article 18 gives *jif*s authority over *kastom* law; Articles 22 and 23 regulate circumcisions and childbirth; Article 24 condemns adultery; Article 29 demands that children respect *jif*s and elders; Article 31 gives *jif*s control of village meetings; and Articles 33 and 34 give *jif*s the right to regulate spirit mediums and healers and the prices they may charge. Amendments to the Malvatumauri's original 1983 policy had been written, although not as yet published, as of 1992 (Bongmatur, interview). The regional councils of chiefs, too, have been charged with codifying island *kastom* policy. By 1992, Tanna (Tafea) had prepared and printed its code, and Ambrym and Malekula were in the process of writing policy.

Other Malvatumauri initiatives look out toward the state rather than back at the unruly village. Article 20.1 of Malvatumauri policy demands: "The work of chiefs in Vanuatu must be maintained and must develop significantly in the future" (my translation). One notable effort in this area was Bongmatur's invention of a National Conference of Chiefs. Whereas the Malvatumauri's codification of *kastom* policy has attempted to empower *jifs* at home by cuing their state-sponsored official paramountcy, initiatives such as the National Conference of Chiefs aspire to raise the volume of chiefly voices within national councils.

Unlike the Malvatumauri and its limited twenty-two chiefly slots, Bongmatur's National Conference of Chiefs is open, comprehensive, and meets every two years. Using the rule of thumb of one *jif* per village, Bongmatur estimated that Vanuatu boasts at least 2,200 *jifs*, all of whom he has invited into the conference (although these *jifs*, unlike Malvatumauri members, receive no government travel funds or other subsidies if they join). The Conference of Chiefs, in part, supplements and shields the reputation of the Malvatumauri, whose limited membership is open to attack as unrepresentative of the country's abundant company of *jifs*.

At the National Conference of Chiefs convened in September 1992 at Lolovenue, Ambae, the collected *jifs* passed seventeen resolutions. Many of these addressed issues on the national agenda (*Vanuatu Weekly* 410 [Oct. 10, 1992]: 4). Resolution 2, for example, demanded chiefly input into a scheme to construct a touristic "cultural and exhibition village" at Eratap, Efate; Resolution 5 attacked government plans to allow freehold land titles outside the towns; Resolution 7 condemned bank plans to foreclose on land used as loan collateral; Resolutions 8 and 9 recommended that *jifs* denounce any state police or court officer who appears corrupt or shows favoritism; and Resolution 15 directed that the Conference of Chiefs acquire an office in Port Vila.

The National Conference of Chiefs, more than the Malvatumauri, which by statute and budget comes under closer government scrutiny, is an independent body of self-nominated *jifs* who convene to influence national policy. Its self-appointed duties include criticizing state politicians and officials. Ad hoc *jifs* of this sort, and their lists of resolutions, potentially threaten the interests of state politicians and bureaucrats.

State *Jifs*

Miles has addressed "the search for appropriate models" (1993:31) for chiefly participation in the state administrations of Niger, Nigeria, and Vanuatu. The problem is for developing states to make useful work for chiefs. This must be the right sort of work—something that takes advantage of chiefs' traditional status and local authority but that will not disturb the sometimes unsteady authority of central governments. Miles locates five appropriate "modern functions" for traditional rulers within state apparati: (1) to broker incoming projects and deals for local economic development; (2) to boost the authority of state leaders by ennobling them on regular occasions with sundry traditional titles; (3) to police the hinterlands, overseeing "low-level" conflict resolution; (4) to serve as ombudsmen between their communities and the state bureaucracies; and (5) to rouse community solidarity and provide local social and administrative services in situations where central governments are ineffectual or even disintegrating. Chiefs, in sum, are to serve the state as its middlemen and brokers (see Rodman and Counts 1982). They extend the reach of the state into the remoter corners of the nation at the same time as they improve citizens' access to state bureaus and programs.

Many of Vanuatu's political leaders have embraced similar functionalist programs for chiefly employment, and they also recognize the dangers of an overly independent chieftaincy (see Jupp 1982). Although politicians themselves want to be *jifs*, they clearly would prefer *jifs* not to be politicians. Prime Minister Maxime Carlot (now Carlot Korman after accepting a chiefly title from Erakor village), echoing Vanuatu's first prime minister, Walter Lini (himself a courtesy-titled chief several times over), warned *jifs* to maintain *kastom*'s purity by keeping their noses out of crass politics: "*Jifs* must not mix the proper fashions of chiefly work with those of the white man. Mister Korman said that if a *jif* wanted to keep his job as a *kastom jif*, he must not act like an administrator or an official (*wan man we istap ranem wan Ofis*)" (my translation, *Vanuatu Weekly* 380 [March 14, 1992]: 7). Vincent Boulekone, onetime opposition leader but later allied with the former Vanua'aku party government, also spoke of the perplexing problem of conceding *jifs* just the right measure of power: "We are living in confusion because what is the kind of power the government can have with traditional authority? We don't really want to give full power to the chiefs because we would have some problems. But chiefly authority can be adapted with democracy" (Keith-Reid 1991:22; see Mangnall 1990:20).

Despite concerns to elevate *jifs* above the polluting waters of politics, the interests of government and of the political parties occasionally do impress themselves upon the Malvatumauri. When Bongmatur retired in 1993, for example, he was replaced by *Jif* Noël Mariasua of Emau, whose francophone skills and political background were more in tune with the government of the day, led by Prime Minister Maxime Carlot Korman. The dilemma for politicians is that the state must recognize and empower *jifs* in order that *jifs* may legitimate and serve the state. The dilemma for *jif*s is that they must at least appear to serve the state in order to promote their authority at home.

Vanuatu *jif*s, to date, have provided for the state two main services: a warrant of traditional legitimacy and, grossly, a mechanism of crowd control (most particularly a means by which to keep belligerent land disputants and wayward adolescents in line). These are the second and third political functions that Miles (1993) enumerates. Vanuatu's politicians since before independence have rhetorically deferred to *jif*s, who lend traditional legitimacy to state institutions, including the national constitution. Chiefly participation sanctifies government decisions and institutions, integrates local leaders within the national order, and accords with the general rhetorical importance of preserving and honoring Vanuatu *kastom*. Bongmatur recalled:

> When we had written the country's constitution, no one knew where to sign it since this was the sacred document of the country: The foundational law and life of the country. Now following *kastom*, they asked me, "*Jif*, do you agree we could sign the constitution on top of the stone on which you killed the pig?" I agreed and we signed the constitution on that stone. (My translation, Bongmatur interview)

In addition to lending *kastom*'s blessing to state endeavors such as lending its stone to constitutional signatories, the Malvatumauri performs minor bureaucratic housekeeping chores for government. At the state's request, the paramount chiefs have devised a "*kastom* marriage" certificate. Civil servants not married in church or by a judge can obtain one of these certificates at the Malvatumauri office in order to register their spouses and children for government benefits (Bongmatur interview).

The double role of chiefs as servants of the state yet guarantors of its legitimacy, and the difficult balance of powers between *jif* and state, have motivated ongoing debate within Vanuatu political circles. If chiefly powers are *too* constrained and of little consequence within the national arena, a *jif*'s capacity to legitimize state projects (and one prop of his authority over his village subjects) collapses. Yet, the constitution grants chiefs only meager powers to advise and be consulted. Bongmatur noted that Parliament only once since independence has actually followed Article 74 and consulted with the Malvatumauri about land law. Parliament notably neglected this duty before it passed a new land lease bill in 1992. Although the new national *nakamal* sits close to the new Parliament House, its location clearly does not symbolize, spatially, an equal partnership between chiefs and politicians. The *nakamal* is tucked away down a lane. Chiefs are close enough to be called on stage when required, but not constantly in Parliament's direct line of sight. The legitimizing auras of *jif*s are ambiguous—at least insofar as the identity *jif* is partly an artifact of the colonial and postcolonial state and, furthermore, is frequently locally contested. That sacred stone had been in place for less than three years, and its patina of hoary pig blood was shallow at best.

To celebrate and boost the state-affirmed powers of *jifs*, the government has proclaimed March 5 to be an annual "Custom Chiefs Day" national holiday. More substantially, in the late 1980s, leaders of the Vanua'aku party government began to talk up chiefs, and suggested that their official capacities should be expanded and strengthened. This was to occur by means of constitutional revisions, guided by a constitutional review committee. The Constitutional Review Committee traveled around the archipelago conducting hearings on the functions of custom chiefs and how their contributions to the nation could be enhanced, regularized, and codified. This review and its ambition of further empowering chiefs were clearly linked to an erosion of the government's influence that was in part due to factional infighting then under way within the Vanua'aku party. Once again, party leaders, seeking popular support, courted *jifs* and honored *kastom* by way of proposing a new constitutional deal that would devolve additional powers to local leaders.

This national debate about stronger chiefs began when Presbyterian pastor Fred Timakata (once the vice-chairman of the original Council of Chiefs) was elected Vanuatu's second president, replacing the ousted and temporarily jailed Ati George Sokomanu.[5] The new president proclaimed in his inaugural address that he planned "to revitalise the influence of the customary leaders . . . the real Melanesian Way does not involve party politics in decision-making" (Moale 1989:24; see also *Vanuatu Weekly* 380 [Mar. 14, 1992]: 7). *Vanuatu Weekly* took to describing Timakata as "Bigfala Jif blong evri nara Jif blong Vanuatu" (289 [May 25, 1990]: 5). This journalistic transformation of state president into paramount *jif* continued to blur, at least rhetorically, the lines between *kastom* and politics.

Similarly, the Constitutional Review Committee's hearings sought ways further to empower *jifs* by bringing *kastom* into political practice: "Custom should be invited in from the cold to provide the basis for democracy. One change is likely to be entrenching traditional chiefly powers in law" (Mangnall 1990:19). Grace Molisa, Prime Minister Lini's personal secretary at the time, explained:

Even before notions of Western democracy, Vanuatu always had individuals exercising authority over communities. "Government through elections requires so much training and certain learnt skills. . . . Our chiefs already have this in their upbringing and in their being." It would mean changes to the judiciary, giving more powers to village and island courts, while chiefs in Luganville and Port Vila would take charge of their own people living in town. (Ibid.)

The state newspaper, *Vanuatu Weekly*, publicizing the work of the Review Committee, offered a series of testimonies lamenting the lack of chiefly authority to settle definitively local land disputes and otherwise organize village life: "The *jifs* said that although they currently have a role to play in villages and island courts, they still face problems since the constitution does not give them enough power to straighten out all problems. . . . The *jifs* also recommended to the [Constitutional Review Committee] that only *jifs* should consider land disputes, not the magistrate or Supreme Courts as is the current practice" (my translation, *Vanuatu Weekly* 324 [Feb. 2, 1991]: 2, 6; see also 323 [Jan. 26, 1991]: 2, 4; 325 [Feb. 9, 1991]: 3; Keith-Reid 1991:22).

Continuing political feuding within the Vanua'aku party stalled the constitutional review process and led ultimately to the collapse of the Lini government. The rump Vanua'aku party, headed by Prime Minister Donald Kalpokas, lost in parliamentary elections held in November 1991. The francophone Union of Moderate Parties, led by new Prime Minister Maxime Carlot, formed a coalition government with the National Union party, established by Walter Lini after his expulsion from the Vanua'aku party leadership. The new government abandoned the constitutional review process and its plans for revising the constitutional functions of *jifs*.

Nonetheless, the Lini government had several practical motivations for advancing *jifs* beyond their symbolic capacity of epitomizing *kastom* legitimacy; and these are motivations that any government might share. An official chiefly hierarchy now exists that extends out from the Malvatumauri in Vila, down through the six regional/island councils, into various area councils, to terminate in many village councils of chiefs. This is a useful institutional device that links center to periphery. Any further codification designed to empower, regularize, or "organize" *jifs* will increase state control over the definition of chiefly identity and the scope of legally recognized, official chiefly functions. By bringing *jifs* more firmly into state bureaucracy—making civil servants out of them—the state obviates some of the possibility of an independent Malvatumauri voice.

Official *jifs* are functionaries within island courts and maintain a dispute-settlement apparatus that shadows the state judiciary system; and both *jifs* and state politicians argue the utility of regularizing and strengthening chiefly powers to police and judge (cf. Westermark 1991). Even police leaders recently suggested that chiefs establish unofficial village police forces:

Chiefs from the islands are being encouraged by Police to set up their own village police to help maintain law and order. . . . With the proposed system, the village chief council appoints the force which then reports to the chiefs of the village. The trouble makers then appear before the village court and are fined or sentenced to clean the village cemetery. Only serious crimes are handed over to the Central Police, Inspector Kalala said. (*Vanuatu Weekly* 497 [June 11, 1994]: 5)

Multiplying land disputes and pressures to clarify ownership in order to facilitate national and foreign investment and to assure collateral for development loans, increasing youth crime in town, and challenges to village stability from incoming Christian evangelical groups all were among the motivations behind the aborted constitutional review and its promise to reinforce chiefly powers. *Jifs* unhappy with their lack of powers to force people to come to village courts and to enforce court judgments, people who have unhappy experiences with land cases tried in state courts, and officers of these courts who are themselves uncomfortable with having to take such decisions, all called for giving *jifs* greater responsibility in land disputes (*Vanuatu Weekly* 325 [Feb. 9, 1991]: 3; Mangnall 1990:20).

People are first supposed to bring land problems and other disputes to a village, area, or island court staffed by volunteer local *jifs*. Practically, this is the only option anyway for many people who are distanced by geography or knowledge from the sittings of state magistrate courts. Village courts adjudicate disputes and *jifs*, sitting as judges, may impose communal service (e.g., clean the village cemetery) or "fines" of produce or money that disputants exchange between themselves, although the *jifs* do not always have effective means to enforce their decisions. These village courts, evolved from traditional dispute-settlement practices, however, mostly hear cases in which adversaries are ready to settle anyway, and thus they actually do resolve many local disputes, at least temporarily.

All levels of the official chiefly hierarchy are now involved in dispute settlement, up through the Malvatumauri. Bongmatur attempted to establish procedures for chiefly intervention into disputes, although these procedures appear to be variably applied. He explained:

When there is trouble that people don't know how to resolve, the *jifs* first work on this. We even have appointed *jif* representatives in the two towns, Vila and Santo, to work in these places. When trouble occurs, they all handle this first. When they are unable to resolve it, they bring the problem to my office for me to deal with. Even island councils of chiefs that are unable to resolve a problem sometimes ask for my intervention, especially in issues of land. (My translation, Bongmatur interview)

Jifs hear the case and assign "fines" of pigs, kava, mats (in the case of Northern Vanuatu disputants), and money. The Malvatumauri also has decreed that each side in a case must pay 2,000 *vatu* for chiefly judicial services. If disputants refuse a judgment or to pay a levied fine, Bongmatur noted that *jifs* can, at that point, summon the police and state courts to take charge:

When a person fails to pay his fine, I put him into the hands of the police, if the issue is criminal, and he goes to state court. When he goes to that court he will discover that he is sentenced to three or six months prison, sometimes a year if the trouble is serious and he is a real criminal. When he is in prison he will think back to the *jif*s: "Oh, if I had only exchanged the pig or mat that the *jif* demanded I would still be home caring for my children, with my family. Or perhaps I would have a job. Now I work [in prison] for nothing." So this [threat] makes people learn a lesson, when they experience the difference between the two systems of justice in the country: the work of *jif*s versus that of the national court system. (My translation, Bongmatur interview)

Bongmatur contrasted an inequitable and uncustomary Western system of justice that establishes winners and losers with traditional settlement practices, wherein *jif*s soothe strained relationships through ritual acts of exchange.

"Town chiefs" provide valuable policing as well as judiciary functions within Vanuatu's urban settlements. The Malvatumauri acknowledges the chiefly status of older men from outer-island communities resident in Vila and Santo. These town *jif*s assume oversight responsibility for their fellow islanders, particularly younger migrants, who are often unemployed. Town *jif*s also represent community members who come into conflict with residents from other islands. Bongmatur estimated that there were more than thirty such *jif*s active in Port Vila in 1992. Town *jif*s have one effective punitive sanction that they sometimes have been able to apply. Assisted by compatriots in the Port Vila police force, they exile back to home islands especially obnoxious and troublesome cases, typically young men and women. This practice is illegal, although many people accept its legitimacy if not its application in particular cases. One town *jif*, for example, criticized on the radio a second urban *jif* from North Tanna who had ordered his men to kidnap, beat up, and ship back to Tanna a woman who had become pregnant (I presume by a boyfriend from beyond North Tanna) (*Vanuatu Weekly* 324 [Feb. 2, 1991]: 2). The oversight of urban youth by town *jif*s no doubt contributes to the civility and order of Port Vila, at least compared with some other Pacific towns (Port Moresby, for example).

Chiefly powers in town, however, are not always entirely appreciated. The police and the judiciary have criticized chiefs for overstepping their authority, and stepping onto that of the state, in their attempts to resolve disputes intramurally by means of fine, exile, unofficial imprisonment, and other such punishment. In addition, women's organizations have occasionally condemned chiefly decisions that appear to privilege the rights and interests of men over those of women—as perhaps in the case above, where a posse of irregular police set upon a young woman and exiled her against her will. The sides are shifting, and the boundaries of authority blurred. *Jif*s serve the state, but threaten it as well, as when state police and judges see their authority usurped and sidetracked. *Jifs* serve the people, but also threaten them, or some of them, as when they evoke custom to maintain inequalities between men and women, the old and the young, and the urban and the rural.

JIF AND STATE share interests in shoring up chiefly political authority to regulate village affairs, keeping unemployed migrant youth, both male and female, under control, and resolving local disputes, particularly those occasioned by conflicting land claims. The *jif* here operates as a tamed, salaried civil servant who extends the reach and effectiveness of the state into rural and urban settlement areas. Because of vexatious land disputes and the disruptions of urban migration, and because of the legitimating, rhetorical significance of *kastom* within the national agenda, the state and *jifs* are now in bed with one another—one could even say firmly wedded. Official *jifs* perform valuable legitimating, policing, and judiciary functions. Despite its reproaches to *jifs* to stay clear of politics, the state maintains an opposite interest to sustain effective chiefly capacities that legitimate the national agenda and police and judge islanders and urban migrants. The challenge is to ensure that *kastom jifs* on the islands, town *jifs* in the settlements, and Malvatumauri paramount *jifs* hobnobbing in the national *nakamal* remain firmly committed state *jifs* as well.

But the *jif* presents potential dangers as well as services to the state. The balance within this relationship, despite the constitution's unequal distribution of powers and rights, is not entirely in the state's favor. Some future Malvatumauri paramount *jifs* might stand on their constitutional authority and denounce state leaders for failing to preserve and promote *kastom*. State politicians have been nervous about exactly how much independence and power to accord *jifs*, and how to ensure that chiefly action serves the state. *Jifs* and people share local interests that occasionally counter those of national politicians and state leaders. Insofar as state legitimacy and institutions require and enfranchise the role of *jifs*, state leaders are hard pressed to shut them up if they become unruly and difficult.

The Carlot Korman government, for example, has confronted *jifs* from Ifira Island who claim the lands upon which Port Vila has spread (*Vanuatu Weekly* 506 [Aug. 13, 1994]: 1). The state aims to condemn these lands and transfer clearer titles to the capital's inhabitants. Because the state has valorized a traditionalist rhetoric in which *jifs* control land, however, it has had to deal with Ifira chiefs. And these rejected out of hand the government's final compensation offer of 110,000,000 *vatu*. If state leaders move ahead with the threat to withdraw their offer, and to treat directly with individual Ifira families, they will find themselves in the unhappy position of diluting the "safer," official functions of *jif*s while intensifying their extramural hazards.

*Jif*s operate both inside and outside the state, and this double stance offers politically strategic possibilities. Both chiefs and state continue to work out the meanings of the increasingly popular and stylish title, the *kastom jif*. Aborted state plans to regulate and organize *jif*s by promising to increase their powers by means of a constitutional revision would have drawn *jif*s more firmly into state structures. And local leaders, on their side, continue to test their capacities and standing vis-à-vis the state. The Vanuatu *jif* today remains under active and ongoing construction.

12

The Discourse of Chiefs

Notes on a Melanesian Society

GEOFFREY M. WHITE

After ten years of independence, Mr. Boulekone said, it's about time to review the constitution . . . to see if the chiefs were where they were supposed to be and adjust their powers.　　—*Vanuatu Weekly*, June 8, 1990

To get the chiefs back to full spectrum of development of our nation, the following steps should be taken: i) Amend the Solomon Islands Constitution . . . to legislate the roles and functions of the chiefs.
—*Report of the Provincial Government Review Committee*, 1986–87,
Solomon Islands

Some people, mainly politicians, have used culture, custom, and custom chiefs for their own aims. Custom and culture must develop freely, and should not be encouraged or forced by any European system of legislation.
—Walter Lini, *Beyond Pandemonium: From the New Hebrides to Vanuatu*

A new breed of neo-politicians have [sic] emerged introducing chief-systems where there was none before . . . to confuse not only themselves but the people they claim to represent.
—Francis Bugotu, *Solomon Star*, July 1, 1988

ONCE REGARDED as relics of an earlier time destined for obsolescence, chiefs are more visible today than ever in the political life of Pacific Island states. As the governments of newly independent island nations de-

This chapter is based on a paper originally published in *The Contemporary Pacific* (4[1] [1992]:73–108). An earlier version of the paper was given at the 1990 annual meeting of the American Anthropological Association. I am indebted to David Akin for sharing historical materials, and to him, David Gegeo, Richard Feinberg, Bruce Knauft, Lamont Lindstrom, George Marcus, Cluny Macpherson, and Karen Watson-Gegeo for helpful comments and suggestions.

bate the course of development, "traditional chiefs" are a frequent topic
of discussion and legislative interest.[1] In the Polynesian states of Tonga
and Western Samoa, where political rights commonly are determined by
chiefly status, recent events reveal pressures for greater democratization
(see Chapters 2 and 3). Ironically, however, in Melanesia, where societies
often are said to have "bigmen" but no real chiefs, postcolonial political
development in Melanesia has been marked by regular efforts to empower
"traditional chiefs" by creating councils of chiefs and otherwise involving
them in the workings of government (see also Foster 1995).

What is this interest in chiefs all about? I take up this question by con-
sidering events in Santa Isabel, Solomon Islands, where people revived a
position of paramount chief in 1975 and have institutionalized a council of
chiefs as part of the apparatus of provincial government. On the one hand,
these developments may be seen as a response to developments in a postcolonial political arena where national leaders espouse policies of decolo-
nization and decentralization that include support for "traditional chiefs."
On the other hand, when seen in historical perspective, these activities
constitute but the latest manifestation of a continuing discourse of identity and power that has always occupied the borderland between local
and state polities. To foreshadow the conclusions to follow, I suggest that
a fuller understanding of this borderland requires an appreciation of
both local culture and local history; and that such an appreciation is the
best antidote to interpretations that variously romanticize or delegitimize
chiefs in contemporary Melanesian societies.

Historically, colonial governments throughout Melanesia sought out
local leaders they could recognize as their representatives for purposes of
"indirect rule"—a notion derived from African experience (Akin n.d.).
Even as colonial officers noted the absence of "hereditary rulers" in many
areas, they readily lent government recognition to leaders they called
"chiefs" wherever possible. Chiefs had some role in the colonial administrations of the British in Fiji (Jolly 1992a; Kaplan 1989; Chapter 6), in the
Solomon Islands (White 1991), and in Vanuatu (Allen 1984), and of the
French in New Caledonia and Vanuatu (Douglas 1982; Guiart 1956).
However, with the development of democratic institutions in these countries after World War II, chiefs became increasingly marginal to the course
of political and economic change. In counterpoint to these changes,
though, chiefs maintained and even increased their significance as symbols of custom and identity. At the time of independence, Fiji, the Solomon Islands, and Vanuatu recognized the status of chiefs through constitutional provisions specifying advisory roles for chiefs in government
(Powles and Pulea 1988; Ghai 1990). In Fiji, the 1970 constitution
granted the Great Council of Chiefs representation in the Senate and

dominion over customary affairs; in the Solomon Islands, reference was made to "traditional chiefs" advising local government; and in Vanuatu, the 1980 constitution created a National Council of Chiefs with powers to advise on land matters and certain appointments (see Chapter 11).

Whereas many people may have felt that these constitutional provisions were largely rhetorical in effect, subsequent events in all of these countries indicated that chiefs continued to be an important focus for postcolonial political reform. The renewed visibility of chiefs in national politics was most evident in Fiji, where the country's Council of Chiefs played a key part in legitimizing the two military coups of 1987 and in formulating a new constitution. In less dramatic form, both the Solomon Islands and Vanuatu undertook constitutional reviews that included attempts to broaden the role of chiefs in government. In Vanuatu, the Vanua'aku party's efforts in this direction were expressed recently in the construction of a ceremonial house or national *nakamal* for the National Council of Chiefs in the capital, Vila. In the Solomon Islands, the Parliament passed an amendment in 1985 to the Local Courts Act that expanded the powers of chiefs to act as magistrates in land disputes. The government there also undertook reviews of the constitution and of provincial government that recommended including "chiefs and traditional leaders" in new legislative positions (Ghai 1990:325; Solomon Islands 1987: ch. 5).[2]

Even though the specific political issues are framed somewhat differently in each country, chiefs today are everywhere potent symbols—symbols of the indigenous and the traditional in contrast with the foreign and the modern. To talk of chiefs is to talk of "custom." In island communities where moral and political debates often revolve around oppositions of local/foreign, indigenous/Western, and inside/outside, chiefs stand for the local-indigenous-inside dimension of these polarities. Whatever their status or meaning in the pre-European past, chiefs in the contemporary Pacific are today icons of "custom"—personifications of larger ideologies of cultural identity. Inevitably, then, the rhetoric of the old and the customary applied to the new evokes questions about the meaning and authenticity of modern-day chiefs, particularly when they become the subject of official interest from national and provincial politicians. The critical comments of two prominent Melanesians quoted at the outset of this chapter, Walter Lini and Francis Bugotu, reflect worries that legislating custom may reify the fluid, personal, and often ambiguous power of traditional leaders (see below). Similarly, for political theorists examining the emergence of class and labor relations in the Pacific, talk of chiefs constitutes a rhetoric used to reproduce power and privilege (M. Howard 1983; Young 1990). In short, contemporary discourses of chiefs have raised what Jolly (1992b) has called the "specter of inauthenticity." As a result, talk of chiefs provides an opportunity to explore the construction of tradition as it occurs in settings ranging from village meetings to parliamentary debates—and in anthropological writings.

For anthropology, the discipline that formulated the distinction between Melanesian "bigmen" and Polynesian "chiefs" (Sahlins 1963; Lindstrom 1982a; Marcus 1989),[3] new Melanesian discourses of chiefs are likely to be seen as a process of inventing or constructing tradition. For example, the ironic title of Roger Keesing's 1969 article, "Chiefs in a Chiefless Society," presumes two kinds of chief—the first ideological and historical, created by the Kwaio of Malaita for specific purposes at a particular historical moment, and the second a more timeless variety as defined by comparative ethnology (a type lacking among the Kwaio). Keesing (1969, 1982c) located the introduction of Kwaio chiefs within the context of the postwar Maasina Rule movement. In that historical moment, the rhetoric of custom worked to legitimate the voice of local leaders challenging British rule:

To establish the legitimacy of kastom required legitimation of its spokesmen. Hence the scheme of chiefs had to be validated as customary. . . . (Pre-war experiments in indirect rule probably conveyed to Malaita leaders the message that the authority of local leaders would be bolstered if it was depicted as traditional, validated by custom and accepted by the community.) (Keesing 1982c: 361)

In this interpretation, Kwaio chiefs, like Melanesian ideologies of custom in general, originated in the experience of colonial invasion (Keesing 1982c; Babadzan 1988). This is a particular case of the more general hypothesis that self-conscious constructions of tradition emerge under conditions of colonization, as a kind of counterdiscourse to the dominating forces of Western intrusion. Extending the hypothesis further, local conceptions of tradition may even be seen to derive from colonial categories and institutions (Hanson 1989; Keesing 1989). Recent commentaries on the "invention of tradition," however, have questioned the validity of any rigid separation between self-conscious, constructed custom and the rest of unspoken, tacit culture (see Jolly 1992b; Linnekin 1991). By implication, "real" tradition tends to be seen as static and ahistorical rather than as an adaptive and changing process.

In this discussion of chiefs I suggest that even though these arguments provide a more sophisticated concept of culture as always creatively reconstructed (cf. Wagner 1975), the focus on cultural invention draws attention away from the substantial cultural and historical continuities that give so-called invented forms much of their emotional and political power. Interpreting concepts of "custom" and "custom chiefs" as responses to

colonization tends to overlook the force of indigenous models that contribute to cultural continuity. Furthermore, seeing all culture as created or
invented obscures the fact that local distinctions of the traditional and the
modern may be crucial to debates about truth, power, and legitimacy.
Much more careful ethnography is required to understand the operative
force of local conceptions of tradition. In this chapter I examine a case of
ongoing cultural "invention" that nonetheless draws upon cultural models and historical precedents that have shaped ideas about chiefs over the
course of 100 years of colonial history and probably longer. Even brief
consideration of local discussions of chiefs reveals complex and competing
views of the role of perceived custom in constituting the status of "traditional chiefs."

Historicizing Custom:
Santa Isabel Chiefs Through Time

The efforts on Santa Isabel to create a council of chiefs (or, as it is sometimes phrased by leaders of these efforts, to "revive" a "system of chiefs")
certainly reflect the influence of Western forms. Chiefs are to be empowered by creating a bureaucratic apparatus modeled on that of a "council"
composed of members from "districts" who receive allowances, and so
forth. The concepts and terms of Western-style government are appropriated to make something new using the rhetoric of the old. But the new is
not so new. A close look shows that attempts to create new roles for chiefs
in government and church were pursued from the earliest moments of
culture contact. Furthermore, these efforts built upon cultural models of
leadership in which chiefs have historically been regarded as mediators
of knowledge, power, and identity. In this mediating position, ideas about
chiefs are inherently a source of innovation and incorporation.

Chiefs have been objects of political talk and debate on Santa Isabel for
more than a century. Chiefs not only are discussed locally, as one would
expect, but also historically received considerable attention from missionaries and government officials, who frequently voiced interest in preserving the status and vitality of "traditional chiefs." Foreigners and Santa
Isabel people alike talk about chiefs in oppositional terms, counterposing
traditional or chiefly leadership with modern Western forms. But the
meanings of these oppositions have not been static through time. The
significance of chiefs has shifted with changing social and political circumstances. Nineteenth-century Anglican missionaries sought to convert
"chiefs" as primary conduits for the work of missionization. They regarded strong Christian chiefs as important allies in promoting and main-

taining the new Christian society in the absence of government. But once colonial government was introduced in the twentieth century, chiefs on Santa Isabel came to be regarded by missionaries and others as a kind of antidote for, or complement to, government institutions—institutions regarded as exploitative and/or mismatched with local custom. More recently these historical meanings of "traditional chiefs" are further transformed by national discourses of "development" concerned to gain access to land and natural resources for large-scale economic projects. In this context, the rationalization of the traditional chief provides a vehicle for managing relations between rural localities and the new nation-state (which in turn functions as an intermediary with multinational corporate interests).

One way of describing the political history of Santa Isabel is as a series of episodes or movements that have attempted to redefine or readjust relations between local polities (often identified with one or more chiefs) and encapsulating systems of power. Beginning with wholesale conversion to Christianity, followed by efforts to resist the establishment of a colonial office on the island in 1918, the tumultuous events of World War II and a major postwar movement for political autonomy, and, most recently, national independence in 1978, each juncture was marked by organized attempts at revising the political order. In each epoch the symbolism of chiefs focused and condensed sociopolitical issues of the day. I have discussed Santa Isabel's episodic cultural history in more detail elsewhere (White 1991), and here give a brief accounting, highlighted by examples of talk about chiefs that marked each epoch.

First, however, a few remarks are in order about the nature of indigenous leadership in Santa Isabel. Although my interpretations pertain primarily to one of the island's four major language groups (Cheke Holo) (see White et al. 1988), there are enough similarities across the island to refer here to "Santa Isabel chiefs." It should be noted, however, that generalizing in this way glosses over important differences that require more careful study. This point is relevant to the revival of an islandwide "paramount chief" based on an emergent islandwide "Santa Isabel" identity.

Among Cheke Holo speakers, leaders in general and chiefs in particular are referred to as *funei* (from *funu*, "start," "begin," reflecting the chiefs' role in initiating collective activities such as feast-exchanges, raids and peacemaking, and religious ceremonies). Even allowing for the romanticized views of Europeans, whose descriptions of Isabel chiefs were often modeled on Western notions of kingship (e.g., Fleurieu 1791), and the larger-than-life quality of many local histories (e.g., Naramana 1987), there is abundant evidence that the most powerful *funei* of the Isabel past exercised considerable political and religious authority, like that commonly associated with Polynesian chieftainship (Marcus 1989).

Chiefly status was marked by the control and display of wealth such as a large house, numerous pigs, and especially the shell valuables that could be worn on important occasions and exchanged with other chiefs. Interactions with chiefs were supposed to be circumscribed with numerous distinctive forms of etiquette. And, while there were no strict rules pertaining to the inheritance of chiefly status, chiefship was nonetheless commonly regarded as transmissable.

Although the English word "chief" appears less frequently in anthropological writings about Melanesia than the more favored "bigman," the term has a long history in the region and may be heard (along with its Pijin counterpart, *sif* or *sifi*) throughout Melanesia today (e.g., Alasia 1989). Beginning with the very first encounter between the indigenous population of Santa Isabel and Europeans, prominent leaders termed "chiefs" were the object of interest and comment by Westerners. When Alvaro de Mendaña first landed in the Solomons in 1568 at Estrella Bay in Santa Isabel, he entered into a series of alliances (and conflicts) with local leaders referred to as "chiefs" in the English translation of his narrative (Amherst and Thomson 1901). Mendaña himself appears to have been granted some kind of chiefly status by one leader, who, adorned with shell decorations, enacted a brief ritual of recognition by hanging a clamshell pendant around Mendaña's neck and placing shell armlets on his arms (ibid.: 126). As Mendaña wrote of this: "I understood that he was making me a great present, and that they thought a great deal of it, for these things are worn only by chiefs. When he saw fit to speak, he told me that . . . he wished to be my friend, and his Indians should be my naclonis ['people'], and he and I would be chiefs of that country" (ibid.).

Throughout colonial history in the Pacific, the prominence and prestige of chiefs were read as indices of the health of indigenous traditions. As the colonizing forces of mission and government were seen to erode or supplant the roles of chiefs, their diminished authority and influence personified larger narratives of cultural decline. For example, the missionary Alfred Penny, who was involved with the first wave of Anglican conversions in the nineteenth century, wrote that "with the Tindalos [ancestor spirits] the power of the chiefs has greatly declined. This was inevitable: a chief was powerful because he possessed a powerful Tindalo. I do not speak of this as a benefit. Were it not that in Christian unity at least an equivalent can be found, I should consider it a loss" (Penny 1888: 216–17).

Similarly, in the western Solomons, the cessation of headhunting and the expansion of the Methodist mission were bemoaned by many through expressions of regret about the loss of prestige among well-known chiefs (Hocart 1922). But the narrative of colonization ran somewhat differently in Santa Isabel. Because the island suffered through several decades of victimization at the hands of raiding headhunters from islands to the west (Jackson 1975; White 1991), relations with mission and government originated in alliances that saw new forms of expanded chiefship emerge, including that of the first "paramount chief" (see Naramana 1987 and Zeva 1983 for comments on the origins of the paramount chief by local authors).

In 1899, the resident missionary Henry Welchman was concerned about the maintenance of civil order and urged local leaders "to settle among themselves who should be the leader and the sole judge for Bugotu" (Wilson 1935:57). When those present selected someone as paramount chief, Welchman commented, "The next step will be to have the election confirmed by the Resident Commissioner, and then I hope we may look for a return to . . . more law-abiding days" (Melanesian Mission 1895–1946, 1901:142). This somewhat remarkable convergence of church and state support for an Isabel paramount chief follows from the island's unique history of conversion by a single church. Seventy-seven years later, in 1975, this same unique configuration would enable the ritual installation of a new paramount chief sanctioned by a newly self-governing nation.

With the arrival of a European district officer and the initiation of plans to collect taxes in 1921, the colonial administration based at Tulagi in neighboring Nggela became an increasingly intrusive force in local affairs. Not surprisingly, perhaps, these developments were received with some consternation by the Christian chiefs and chiefly catechists who already were well established as the dominant religious-political authorities in the island's newly formed Christian villages. They attempted bravely to submit protests through the offices of the Anglican bishop, beseeching the resident commissioner:

If it be possible that this White Officer leave us and go away, we do not wish any other white man to take his place for we have already made trial of the White man dwelling among us and all Government laws seem unfair to us. But we wish that our own chiefs should rule us. . . . We recognize Our Governor of the British Solomon Islands him alone who lives at Tulagi [the resident commissioner]. (Western Pacific High Commission, Jan. 3, WPHC 426/1921)

During the early 1930s, and subsequently when the missionary Richard Fallowes led an interisland movement in 1938 to establish an indigenous "parliament," talk of "traditional chiefs" became a recurrent trope in political discourse seeking greater local power and autonomy. As Keesing's statement quoted earlier makes clear, these meanings of the "chief" as a symbol of local autonomy emerged with particular force and clarity in the ideology of the postwar Maasina Rule movement that challenged colonial rule in the Solomons after World War II (Laracy 1983). Interpreters of Maasina Rule have noted the importance of "chiefs" for the movement's organization. The spread of Maasina Rule ideology across Malaita and beyond was marked by the enactment of ceremonies installing movement leaders in positions of chiefly office.

Throughout Santa Isabel's colonial history, the chief remained a central figure as the field of power and meaning in village life was differentiated increasingly by processes of colonization and Christianization. In their former roles as feast-givers, alliance-makers, and warriors, chiefs embodied the vitality and integrity of their regions. It was perhaps inevitable, then, that they would become the focus for efforts at managing relations with external forces of change. By approaching recent attempts to institute a council of chiefs as an activity with significant cultural and historical antecedents, I hope to avoid the twin risks of interpreting talk of "traditional chiefs" as either a reification of tradition or a modern invention reflecting the political rhetoric of the moment.

Creating a Council of Chiefs

In 1975, the year of Solomon Islands self-government and three years before independence, talk of "custom chiefs" and "paramount chiefs" circulated in both Santa Isabel and the national center, Honiara. Local leaders from throughout the archipelago elected to the protectorate's governing council discussed the development of national political institutions, and one of the themes in their discussions was the importance of custom and chiefs for the postcolonial political setup. For example: "That in the proposed review of government a function should be found for chiefs in local government bodies; consideration should be given to according chiefs some form of recognition; consideration should be given to holding an annual conference of Elders" (Solomon Islands 1972).

The governing council also discussed giving recognition to paramount chiefs (meaning simply chiefs who stood above village-level chiefs and represented a whole region or language group). No other Melanesian islands in the Solomons had traditions of islandwide paramount chieftainship, and Santa Isabel's tradition was an avowedly invented one. Given Santa Isabel's unique history of creating a church-supported paramount chief for the entire island, government support for chiefs resonated well with local interests. The impetus for this latest episode, similar to previous instances of paramount chiefs on Santa Isabel, came from a convergence of local and national forces. The voiced support of national leaders for chiefs coincided with the presence of a unique candidate for the Santa Isabel

paramount chief—the man who was then bishop of the island, Dudley
Tuti—to make things happen. Tuti's position as bishop, together with his
personal reputation and genealogy (Tuti was also the maternal nephew of
two men regarded as previous paramount chiefs), crystallized the forces
that ultimately produced a major ceremonial installation of him as paramount chief in 1975. This event marked the beginning of efforts to "revive
the system of chiefs" that continue to the present.

Many Santa Isabel people are not aware of the history of the paramount chief. And those who are may disagree about how many paramount chiefs there have been, or who they have been. Despite this thicket
of disagreement, nearly all agree on the first (Monilaws Soga) and the last
(Dudley Tuti). It is important to keep in mind that the recognition of Tuti
as paramount chief was not a simple matter of succession, of finding a
person to fill a vacant office. When Dudley Tuti was made paramount
chief, he did as much to make the status as the status did to make him
"paramount."

One of the prime movers in the preindependence discussions on reviving a "system of chiefs" was a man who would become one of the island's
first parliamentarians, Willie Betu. Betu wrote a paper sketching a plan
for chiefs, headed by a paramount chief, to have formal position in Santa
Isabel government. Betu acknowledged that the Santa Isabel paramount
chief originated in the conversion era. In his words, "There were many
chiefs, but no paramount chief until Christianity came." Betu's paper
outlined a plan in which three "great chiefs," each of whom would represent one of the three major clans on the island, would be selected (by consensus?). These chiefs would then select a paramount chief from among
themselves. Betu went on in his paper to list eleven recommendations for
implementing such a system, including having the three chiefs sit on the
Santa Isabel council with the paramount chief as cochairman. Although
the idea of three clan chiefs never took hold, other recommendations, such
as including chiefs in council meetings, were eventually instituted after
independence. In particular, Betu's recommendation that "the paramount
chief's elevation ceremony . . . take place . . . next year" turned out to be
true to the mark.

During the first half of 1975, plans were made for a major feast
and ceremony that simultaneously would mark the independence of the
Church of Melanesia and install a new paramount chief. And, since nearly
the entire population belonged to the Church of Melanesia, the occasion
conveniently could combine two islandwide events and make practical an
event recognizing a paramount chief for the whole island. Because Dudley
Tuti was uniquely suited to the position of paramount chief at the time,
little effort was expended to determine who should be paramount chief.

As bishop, Tuti traveled around the island speaking at meetings where plans for installing a paramount chief were discussed. At one meeting that I attended, Tuti spoke to a group of representatives assembled from several villages about the purpose of the upcoming ceremony. He did not emphasize the connection with the church (particularly through him, the bishop), but referred to the initiatives toward supporting chiefs at the national level by the governing council in Honiara. Speaking somewhat coyly (in Pijin), he talked as if no one had yet been finally designated to be the paramount chief (my translation):

The governing council [in Honiara] have thought about this for a long time. . . . They want to include some chiefs in the government for governing the country. . . . And every island will choose one or two or three, according to their custom. . . . That's our idea for holding [the ceremony] at Sepi. Although we [you and I] have not found who will be the paramount chief, this might be the work of the Church and all the people in the council; and especially all the people are for finding out who will be the paramount chief. In our system according to our custom, we do not have an election . . . for finding out who will be the paramount chief, we should follow our own way, follow our custom. (Tape-recording from author's files)

Here Tuti assumed the voice that would be expected of him as a representative of Santa Isabel knowledgeable of events and issues in the wider national arena. He located the origins of the idea in that larger context by ascribing it to an initiative of the governing council. The Santa Isabel event was thus part of a mandate to put up paramount chief(s) on every island "according to their custom." Although Tuti referred to the national mandate, he emphasized that implementing the idea ultimately derived from "our custom." This invocation of both national events and "custom" was more than expedient rhetoric. It reflected the syncretic character of the paramount chief (and of chiefship in general). "Our custom" referred to the things Santa Isabel people ordinarily did, independent of government procedures and such peculiar exercises as elections.

In July 1975 Tuti was installed as paramount chief in a large islandwide ceremony. When I talked with Willie Betu the day before the installation ceremony, he indicated that he could foresee the possibility of the paramount chief setting a precedent for new forms of provincial government that might emerge after independence. In his view, the position could be a prototype for a kind of provincial governor. Tuti had voiced a similar view before the Sepi ceremony. He envisioned the paramount chief as part of an islandwide body of chiefs representing each "district." He also speculated about the possibility of these chiefs, with the paramount chief, forming a future government council.

Once Tuti was installed as paramount chief, he began thinking more specifically about how to implement his vision. For example, he said that he wanted to convene a meeting of chiefs from each "district," possibly seven in number, who would meet to discuss matters of "custom" and "development." When Tuti announced in 1980 that he would retire as bishop in two years' time, one of his reasons was that he wished to devote more of his time to the work of the paramount chief. Events since then have seen these visions gradually take shape, although the gap between the activities of chiefs and the formal institutions of government remains a continuing source of difficulty.

Just at the time that Tuti retired as bishop of Santa Isabel, he began a collaboration that proved important in enabling the formal involvement of chiefs in island governance. In each manifestation of the paramount chief, alliance between the aspiring chief and one or more persons who occupied positions of influence in the Church or government was an important factor in linking the position with wider institutions. In this case, in the postindependence Solomon Islands, that person was Dennis Lulei, an influential leader (and one of the first Santa Isabel men to receive a university degree) who was also one of the island's two members of Parliament between 1980 and 1988. According to Tuti, after Lulei first was elected, he sought out Tuti in order to jointly formulate plans for developing a council of chiefs under the aegis of the paramount chief.

During the 1980s, Tuti as paramount chief and Lulei as secretary to the emerging council of chiefs led efforts to create a chiefs' council—a quasi-bureaucratic structure for involving chiefs in the management of island affairs. These efforts consisted mainly of large meetings of chiefs held to discuss all manner of issues connected with "development," including lengthy debate about just how the council of chiefs should constitute itself. Much of this interest in formalizing political roles for "traditional chiefs" was connected with the formidable problems and conflicts surrounding land ownership. With new possibilities for commercial development in the form of mining, forestry, and fisheries fueling divisive disputes about land, local political leaders sought ways of resolving land conflicts. Since the chief was above all else a spokesman for land-owning descent groups, talk of somehow formalizing the chief's status in government aimed at legitimizing chiefly pronouncements in the context of national legal discourse. This was precisely the intent of the amendment to the Local Courts Act passed by the national Parliament in 1985 to ensure that "chiefs" heard land cases before they were taken into the court system.

Space does not allow a detailed review of the process by which the idea of a council of chiefs has become a political reality in Santa Isabel, but a brief sketch will indicate the level of interest in and activity toward one that has been sustained for more than fifteen years. The picture that emerges is one of an evolving discussion about how to go about instituting a new political entity. Even now, years after a 1984 meeting billed as the "first meeting of the Council of Chiefs," details of its composition and responsibilities remain in flux. Indeed, this persistent fluidity (resisting bureaucratic fixity) is one of the puzzles posed by the discourse of chiefs in Santa Isabel—a puzzle considered briefly in the next section of this chapter.

A large "meeting of chiefs" attended by the premier of the Provincial Assembly and the new bishop of Santa Isabel (among others) convened near Tuti's house adjacent to the provincial government center in April 1983. That meeting discussed a plan to form a council of chiefs by having each of five areas or "districts" select a representative chief. The first meeting of the proposed council of chiefs was held at the same location in March 1984, less than one year later. As an indication of the growing legitimacy of these moves to incorporate chiefs in government, this meeting also was attended by the provincial premier and secretary. At this meeting, the number of districts was expanded to six, and the selection of members was left up to the paramount chief.

In that same year, before the March Council of Chiefs meeting, the Santa Isabel Provincial Assembly, made up of fifteen elected members, passed a resolution allowing for the Council of Chiefs to select six persons, one from each of six districts, to participate in assembly meetings as "appointed members." And indeed, six such members participated in the next assembly meeting in June 1984, just a few months after the first Council of Chiefs meeting. The assembly meeting passed a "Council of Chiefs" resolution that began, "BE IT RESOLVED that the Isabel Provincial Assembly recognizes the existence and traditional role of the Council of Chiefs, their powers with respect to matters of tradition and custom." This document went on to enumerate areas where chiefs exercised power in local life, focusing mainly on land and genealogy. Beyond that, the document spelled out the role of the Council of Chiefs as essentially "promoting traditions and customs" and "making recommendations" on such matters to the various bodies of local government.

Although the provincial premier and others indicated at an early stage that a portion of the provincial budget was earmarked for support of travel by the chiefs, financial support did not materialize through government channels. At one point the district of Bughotu formed its own council of chiefs, and the government area council approved its request for support in the amount of $1,200 (at that time about US$700), only to have the request denied by the provincial executive office. The extent to which new powers and resources may in fact devolve to chiefs through such a process remains uncertain. But to examine this resurgent rhetoric of chiefs and custom only in the context of bureaucratic institutions would miss the more fundamental point that the process of meeting, discussing, planning, and creating does itself constitute a discourse or set of truths of the type envisioned by those who talk of a role for chiefs in island affairs (cf. Brison 1989).

Once plans for a council of chiefs were laid with the provincial government in 1984, Tuti and Lulei traveled to every district to convene meetings for the selection of "district chiefs" who would constitute district-level councils analogous to the provincial government's "area councils." And, analogous to the manner in which "church chiefs" were instituted in the 1930s by Richard Fallowes, these selections were then ritually validated in a church service in which Tuti, the retired bishop, would bless the chiefs and give them certificates signed by him as paramount chief. But these meetings did more than select chiefs. They also provided a new set of contexts for local-level discussions of politics, economic projects, and cultural change—discussions that have always taken place in village meetings, but were now cast in the global rhetoric of modernization and economic development. By defining these meetings as congregations of "chiefs" or a district's "house of chiefs," these "conferences" or "seminars," as they were called, worked to reframe political discussion as organized in terms of local polities, and not the more arbitrary definitions of a national bureaucracy. Roger Keesing stated this succinctly in referring to similar activities among the Kwara'ae of Malaita: "The rise of the new 'paramount chiefs' and 'tribal chiefs' represents an attempt to keep Kwara'ae Kwara'ae" (1982c:370).

Meetings and festivities organized under the aegis of the Council of Chiefs make cultural sense by framing their purpose in terms of localized definitions rather than the decentered discourse of a modern nation-state. But the hybrid form of these meetings, incorporating elements from national institutions and the idiom of modern development, may also evoke questions and puzzlement. When I participated in one such meeting held in 1987 to bless chiefs from one of the districts and at the same time to conduct a "development seminar," one of the participants grumbled to me that he and some others were confused by the presentations on this occasion, many of which were from experts invited from various government ministries to speak on development issues.

During recent years, the topic of chiefs and their role in island life has become a common theme in ceremonial occasions attended by national and foreign dignitaries. For example, the day chosen to mark the provincial government's anniversary is now also designated as "Chiefs' Day." And in March 1987, the prime minister of the Solomon Islands, Ezekiel Alebua, was invited along with other national dignitaries to the "annual convention of chiefs" held at the Bughotu village of Nagolau. On this occasion and others like it, the idiom of custom provided a language of shared values and identity that symbolically linked national and local institutions.

Tuti's installation as paramount chief and the subsequent effort to form a council of chiefs must be seen in the context of regional efforts to find "paramount chiefs" in many of the islands that make up the newly independent Solomon Islands. During the year following the Sepi ceremony, parallel events were unfolding in the Kwara'ae area of neighboring Malaita. Three paramount chiefs were selected in West Kwara'ae (David Gegeo, personal communication), and numerous others in the eastern district. These activities led to a major meeting in 1978 at Auki on Malaita at which some 180 men were designated as "chiefs" to act as upholders of custom (Burt 1982:393–94; Gegeo and Watson-Gegeo 1996). These activities continue today in other areas where attempts are being made to reconstruct positions of chiefly leadership. In June 1988 about 4,000 people from Guadalcanal attended a ceremony to install the outgoing governor-general of Solomon Islands, Sir Baddeley Devesi, as paramount chief of the Tasimboko area of that island. And in that same year, local leaders on Nggela, seeking to model their efforts on the experience of Santa Isabel, invited Paramount Chief Dudley Tuti to speak to them at a meeting devoted to discussing plans for "chiefs" and "paramount chiefs" in their society. Extending the scope of regional influences even further, Tuti and Member of Parliament Lulei were planning a trip to Fiji to learn about the Fijian Council of Chiefs when the 1987 military coup in Fiji, backed by the Council of Chiefs there, led them to abort their plans.

As previously noted, these various regional efforts to revitalize "traditional chiefs" were given impetus by national political developments that had produced periodic statements affirming their importance for local government. Beginning with the governing council before independence, and recorded in a constitutional provision acknowledging "the role of traditional chiefs" (Section 114.2), the topic of chiefly leadership recently was given further attention by a national committee established to review the structure of provincial government. This committee devoted a chapter of its report to "the desire to involve Chiefs and Traditional Leaders more fully in the process of Government at both Provincial and rural levels of Solomon Islands Community" (Solomon Islands 1987:63–67). The fact that the thrust of this report was closely in line with the direction of events on Santa Isabel reflects the fact that the committee was chaired by Dennis Lulei, at that time a member of Parliament and secretary to the Santa Isabel Council of Chiefs.

This report recommended that national and provincial governments encourage chiefly involvement in government in a variety of ways, including the establishment of chiefly councils in all provinces, and national support for overseas educational tours by chiefs and annual conventions of chiefs. In addition, the report recommended that the Solomon Islands constitution be amended to require provincial assemblies to "legislate the roles and functions of chiefs" (ibid.: 66). For Santa Isabel, this action had already been taken in 1984, with the Provincial Assembly's Council of Chiefs Resolution.

The irony in this is that the report reproduced the dominance of government as the source of legislative initiative and funding. Although intended to enhance the visibility and legitimacy of chiefs, the report's own recommendations bracketed the role of chiefs within specified structures of the state apparatus. The report asked whether chiefs should be appointed into the national Parliament or the provincial assemblies, and concluded that "the rightful place for chiefs is at the Area Council level" (ibid.: 66). In other words, the plan for empowering chiefs was to fit them within a specified niche in the government's bureaucratic apparatus—specifically, the area council, the most local of local government, composed of village representatives reporting to the provincial assembly.

To what extent are current attempts to create paramount chiefs and chief councils, such as that under way in Santa Isabel, evoked and shaped by the categories and institutions of centralized government? How much influence does colonial discourse exert over local meanings? Since many of the Provincial Review Committee's recommendations already have been implemented or are under way on Santa Isabel, events there reveal the cultural dynamics of the seemingly ironic enterprise of strengthening chiefs through government.

As already pointed out, one of Santa Isabel's first national politicians, Willie Betu, was a catalyst for the installation of Dudley Tuti as paramount chief (actually scripting a program for the event). And, as shown above, Dudley Tuti himself discussed the rationale for the installation ceremony in terms of the national agenda of promoting traditional chiefs in government. And yet, from the perspective of many local participants, the installation of Tuti as paramount chief and the attempts to empower "traditional chiefs" manifested cultural understandings of person and history that were strongly rooted in local experience.

Custom Chiefs, Contested Culture

Now that it has been several years since the Isabel Provincial Assembly passed its Council of Chiefs Resolution in 1984, and since Dudley Tuti retired as bishop to concentrate on his role as paramount chief, what developments have taken place with regard to the status of custom chiefs? The answer was given best by Dudley Tuti himself in his speech before a meeting billed as the eighth meeting of the Isabel Council of Chiefs on May 16, 1990. In that speech he commented that the role of chiefs with regard to the Council of Chiefs was not well understood and that there was a need for wider recognition:

[It has been] eight years now since the Council of Chiefs came into existence and yet many people wish to know the roles of the chiefs and I would dare to say that the roles of the chiefs are not new from the ones that have been exercised by our forefathers of the past. . . . There is not a village in Isabel without a chief and it is in the interest of our people to encourage, recognize and maintain the chieftain system, and because of its important concept it still prevails in our own society. But it needs wider recognition. It needs to be accorded some recognized status and functions by both Provincial and National government. (Tuti 1990, slightly edited)

Having said this, Tuti went on to outline some of the roles and functions of chiefs, much as they were specified in the Provincial Assembly's 1984 resolution, including "promoting unity," "taking care of land and custom," "organizing feasts and celebrations," and "promoting the work of church and government" (ibid.). Fifteen years earlier, when Tuti first was installed as paramount chief, he had framed the purpose of and the need for reviving chiefly leadership in Santa Isabel in very much the same language. When addressing a large Christmas feast in 1975 (in English, with translation), he spoke about the meaning of the paramount chief position as follows:

People ask me, "What is your job as a paramount chief?" But my answer is this. [The] paramount chief is not yet completed. There are other people in every area, in every village who are chiefs in their right. People look up to them. . . . So those [chiefs] got to be recognized first. They are still here, but we are misled by the new election of members in the Council, head people in the districts. But you know them. In the village you know them. In the district you know them. So those people got to be brought back. (Dudley Tuti, Dec. 24, 1975; tape-recording from the author's files)

Comparing these statements across the fifteen-year interval, which has seen extensive discussions of the role of chiefs in government, these questions arise: Why has there been so little change in the institutional position of chiefs? And why is the agenda for empowering chiefs more or less the same today as it was in 1975 (cf. Akin 1985)? One could point to the difficulties of enacting national legislation on these matters in a country that grapples with such a wide spectrum of regional and cultural diversity.[4] And yet there have been significant national initiatives during these intervening years to promote roles for chiefs in government, such as the 1985 amendment to the Local Courts Act, and the Provincial Government

Review Committee of 1986–87. Why, then, do chiefs remain symbolically potent but politically marginal?

One approach to this question would be to use the anthropological distinction of chiefs and bigmen to question the authenticity of government-sponsored "chiefs" in societies characterized by fluid, personalistic forms of leadership. We might speculate that the problems of institutionalizing "chief systems" stem from attempting to graft invented chiefs onto actual bigman systems. While appealing in some respects, this explanation draws upon definitional differences between chiefs and bigmen, and between "invented" and "authentic" culture, that obscure the cultural and historical processes that have sustained local discourses of chiefs for most of colonial history.

Without presuming a categorical distinction between bigmen and chiefs, we might consider the different premises that underlie talk about chiefs in government circles as opposed to the everyday contexts of village life. The latest round of discussion and debate (which is but the latest phase of a much longer history of debate) is essentially a kind of translation exercise, an attempt to legitimize or empower chiefly status by translating it into the systematic forms of Western government. Ultimately, however, efforts to conjoin these realms are constrained by differences in their assumptions and purposes.

Talk of chiefs from national politicians and government committees tends to objectify its subject matter as a static reality that simply requires a concerted attempt at codification to bring leaders called "chiefs" into active participation in government. As an example, consider the report of the Provincial Government Review Committee. That report acknowledged regional variation in leadership types in the Solomon Islands, but it overlooked (1) the syncretic quality of chiefs capable of becoming "church chiefs" and the like, and (2) the inherent ambiguity and variability in "chief" statuses in any given area.

On the first point, when the report spelled out possible ways that government might support or formalize the position of chiefs, it presumed a concept of "chiefs" and "chieftain system" that was separate from the forces of modernization:

The impositions of modern bureaucracy, the dominance of religious leaders and the withering away of chiefs' powers and influences by political and administrative machineries have had a cumulative effect on our traditional leaders. Whilst it is true that chiefs are generally respected and their services are still called on by politicians and the government, the traditional leaders have been stripped of their once political and social authority. Even their legitimacy and existence have been questioned. (Solomon Islands 1987:65)

By using a language of objectification, the report implied that there was an identifiable set of "traditional leaders" separate from leaders in church and government. For Santa Isabel this presumption glossed over the long history of adaptation that had produced syncretic or combined forms of leadership of all sorts. From the early years of Christianization and colonization, chiefs were extensively involved in the institutions of both church and government. All the powerful district headmen during the colonial period were also among the most prominent chiefs on the island. Two of these are commonly cited as previous paramount chiefs. Other well-known chiefs were catechists and priests in the Anglican church. And, of course, the present paramount chief was also the island's first bishop. Even one of the principal authors of the report cited above, Dennis Lulei, expressed a more open-ended view of chiefs as any important leader with local legitimacy. While speaking in Parliament in favor of an amendment that would empower chiefs to decide land cases, Lulei observed that the members of Parliament themselves must be chiefs: "All of us here or most of us in our traditional way where we come from; we are Chiefs in our own way, when you go back home you are regarded as somebody in a Society [sic] a very big man you are a Chief" (Solomon Islands 1985a: 578).[5]

Seen in the perspective of this history of evolving creolisms, chiefship is better regarded as an adaptable model and set of practices than as an objective position with a fixed set of rights and duties. For example, the position of paramount chief in Santa Isabel is overtly a syncretic status, combining elements of Christianity and custom that give it much of its cultural and emotional power. When Tuti was installed as paramount chief, the ceremony was conducted as a communion church service in which the Anglican archbishop "anointed" Tuti as paramount chief at the event's climax. Indeed, Christian terms and concepts were regularly appropriated through history to reconstitute and reinvigorate chiefly leadership, as in Welchman's association with Soga and Richard Fallowes's installation of "church chiefs." These historical appropriations are also reflected in understandings of custom as something that consists of both "good" and "bad" elements that may be selectively applied and transformed. For example, in one of his speeches just after being installed as paramount chief in July 1975, Tuti described his new job as

finding out about our tradition, our custom, our culture. . . . Because if we only base our thinking, our progress in our own culture, we will go forward. But not what our grandfathers used to do. . . . Maybe in all our chiefs before there were different kinds of paramount chief. Maybe there was hatred in them. And there were people who grab people's property. . . . And now we are in Christianity . . . probably one of the jobs of the paramount chief [is] to unite the people. (Tape-recording from the author's files)

Tuti here expresses a widely shared view of the Santa Isabel paramount chief as a vehicle for integrating desirable aspects of both custom and Christianity. In some instances, innovations may also be questioned or contested by invoking local ideas about the strictly traditional. Such challenges are often available. For example, when the relatives of one aspiring chief said that he might be "ordained" (*taofi*) at an upcoming feast, others pointed out that such a rite should be reserved for priests. Similar arguments also occur elsewhere in Christian Melanesia, as in a recent controversy reported for Emae Island in Vanuatu, where people argued about the legitimacy of "ordaining" a paramount chief for that island (*Vanuatu Weekly*, June 8, 1990).

In addition to difficulties in discussing chiefs as a discrete, isolable status, attempts to institutionalize the involvement of "traditional leaders" in government grapple with the problem of how to formalize modes of leadership that tend to be both personal and variable. In Santa Isabel, as in most Melanesian societies that lack formalized titles, the extent of chiefly powers is usually implicit and open to contention. The authority of powerful chiefs extends across a gradient of influence from village-level leadership to entire regions and even islands. Hence, efforts to formalize the multiple, overlapping, and ambiguous claims of chiefs in the form of bureaucratic categories and structures inevitably evoke disagreements and debate.

Even though Dudley Tuti as bishop and paramount chief has achieved a degree of power and prominence unique in the large Melanesian islands of the Solomon Islands, even the process of installing him as paramount chief was not without voices of discontent. When Willie Betu put forward his plan for reviving the paramount chiefship to be discussed further around the island, the island's main government body—the Isabel District Council, composed mostly of young elected members—decided to discuss the paramount chief status among their various constituencies. As the primary body of local government administration for the island, the council discussed the idea of instituting a paramount chief as part of district government and eventually decided to reject it. As already seen, despite the fact that the council reached this determination in two meetings in 1974, and again in January 1975, most of the island's population enthusiastically supported the large celebration and ceremony that installed Tuti as paramount chief in July 1975.

At least one local ethnographer writing about cultural traditions and chiefship in his area of Santa Isabel made a point of qualifying the extent of influence of the paramount chief. He explicitly denied that Soga, the man known as the first paramount chief, was ever the chief of the whole island. In doing so he noted that Soga achieved his influence by virtue of his involvement with the mission's work of conversion.

As for Soga, he was one of the chiefs of his own tribe not the chief of Ysabel, as mentioned in some history books. It was only through the influence of christianity [sic] which he helped exert over other chiefs that made him famous. Had he not been the first converted chief, people would never believe that Soga was chief. (Naramana 1987:45)

In asserting that Soga's chiefly power was actually circumscribed by the limits of his "tribal" domain, the author (from a neighboring language group) argued a point that is in fact generally accepted: Soga the paramount chief was a product of the mission era. However, the fact that Naramana makes this assertion reflects the worries about the limits of chiefly power that frequently surround prominent chiefs. Chiefly status in Santa Isabel is always open to expansion or contraction. The extent of any one individual's influence usually remains implicit and subject to multiple interpretations. As the boundaries of influence become the object of overt discussion, as in deliberations about how many chiefs should make up the Council of Chiefs, how they should be selected, and what powers they should wield, disagreements are bound to emerge that are more likely to produce long debates about custom and politics than decisive changes in institutional arrangements.

Even though there has been little change in the legal status of chiefs, it would be a mistake to measure the significance of the movement to reinvigorate chiefly leadership with the legalistic yardstick of legislation passed or government bodies created. In between Tuti's two speeches quoted above, villagers all over the island repeatedly organized feasts, celebrations, and meetings defined as occasions for deliberations of chiefs dealing not only with the parameters of their own involvement in island affairs, but also with all kinds of contemporary social and economic issues. Although these efforts might appear to the instrumentally minded outsider to have produced little practical result, they in fact went a long way toward creating the reality of a political discourse centered upon local "chiefs." And the discourse is given further credibility by virtue of government statements regarding the desirability of strengthening "traditional chiefs," even if the institutional arrangements for doing so are slow to emerge. Some people may contest the authenticity or legitimacy of district chiefs and councils, but these phenomena are to a large extent just what they say they are. And the "say" is important here, because talk in most Pacific societies, especially political talk, often constitutes the reality it seeks to represent (Brenneis and Myers 1984; Brison 1989; Watson-Gegeo and White 1990). The fact that "chiefs" are discussed, and discussed often, in major political and ritual events is a constant reminder that, in the postcolonial era, "chiefs" constitute a strong focus for cultural value and aspiration rather than a shrinking remnant of a past way of life.

Chiefs, and the paramount chief in particular, are integrative symbols that have acquired particular significance for the people of Santa Isabel in light of the historical circumstances of Christianization and colonization. Furthermore, as stated at the outset, models of chiefs relate to broader concepts of moral and social conduct. With the advent of new types of leadership through church and government, the prototypic chief is conceived of as an exemplar of the indigenous, of local modes of thought and action that contrast with Western (especially government) ways. The chief personifies aspects of cultural value and identity that are seen increasingly as threatened by the incursion of Western-type individualism or materialism. Viewed in this light, talk of chiefs and efforts to incorporate them in government become at once a mode of resistance and an attempt at revitalization.

Certain of the themes expressed in bold relief through the more visible activities of the paramount chief are also evident in quieter forms of talk about chiefs as a focus for customary practice. In one village meeting I recorded in 1975, two cousins argued about an incident that landed them in court. The argument focused on the way the incident was handled: the police were called in before there was an attempt to resolve the problem through talk and the mediation of village chiefs. Although the two men disagreed about the role of the police, the court, and chiefs in this particular incident, they both expressed a view of chiefs as agents of tradition and community-based practices, in contrast to the institutions of modern government such as the police and the courts. As one cousin stated,

When these things happen we should first work them out among ourselves. We handle it ourselves before concluding, "This business is bad, it's suitable for that place [the district court]." That could have happened with this business. . . . Chiefs are supposed to do this, are supposed to decide about these things with us. . . . Modern ways are alive now. The way previously would have been to be sympathetic with a person before going that way [to court].

In this fragment of conversation, the speaker recreates local understandings about the opposition of custom and modernity in his talk about working things out "among ourselves"—with chiefs—rather than resorting to coercive forces centered outside the community.[6] In this context, talk of chiefs constitutes a kind of counterdiscourse based on ideas about desired forms of social conduct and interpersonal relations. Such perceptions of the progressive encroachment of government on the power of chiefs reflect larger narratives of historical accommodation (see White 1991). The argument I have been making here is that these ongoing processes of historical transformation are constituted in and through local understandings of persons and chiefs.

. . .

HAVING DESCRIBED some of the contemporary talk about chiefs in Santa Isabel, what may be said about the issues of cultural invention raised at the outset of this chapter? Inevitably, the mixing of a rhetoric of the old with the politics of the new raises questions of cultural authenticity. On the one hand, attempts to "revive" chiefly leadership by creating new roles for chiefs in government are giving chiefship new significance. At the same time, these efforts also draw upon cultural models and historical antecedents that have considerable depth—a tradition, as it were.

Whereas recent discussions of the issue of authenticity have questioned static or reified concepts of tradition by noting that culture and tradition are always (re)constructed in the present (Jolly 1992b; Linnekin 1991), the case of Santa Isabel chiefs illustrates a process of "invention" that enjoys a substantial tradition, dating to the earliest moments of contact with the West and probably earlier. Colonial history in Santa Isabel, as in many parts of the Solomons, is marked by periodic attempts to remake or revitalize local leadership through the installation of new kinds of chiefs. In Santa Isabel this episodic history is expressed most vividly in the occasional installation of "paramount chiefs" who have emerged at critical historical moments to aspire to positions of islandwide influence made possible through association with the Church (cf. Naramana 1987; Zeva 1983).

For Santa Isabel people who reflect about such things, the concept of "paramount chief," like the related categories of "Christian chief" or "church chief," is avowedly a creation of mission society. At the same time, however, these ideas include self-conscious conceptions of "custom"—of practices regarded as old, local, and indigenous as opposed to the new, foreign, and introduced. Whatever the antiquity of these externalizations of custom, they incorporate understandings about persons and power that are basic to local experience and modes of leadership.

As in previous episodes of attempted revitalization, the latest round emerges in the conjunction of local processes and political developments centered outside the island (cf. Sahlins 1985b). The impetus for a council of chiefs originates in the politics of a postcolonial Melanesian state. At the same time, however, its local significance is formed by long-standing ideas about the nature of persons, politics, and community (as well as about colonial experience). It would be a mistake to assign conceptual priority to either the indigenous or the exogenous in the transactions that cross these spheres. Chiefs are symbolic mediators, constituting objects of reflection in which ideas about identity and change contend for a hearing, whether in parliamentary debate or in village meetings. In the process, both indigenous and Western categories are susceptible to transformation.

The fact that this latest round of chiefly revitalization has yet to formalize positions of chiefship within government suggests that local discourses are not readily assimilated to bureaucratized schemes of state-sponsored chiefs. Whereas local models center upon contingent personal qualities and social practices, official discourse would inscribe power in formalized chiefly offices. It is here that the anthropological distinction between "bigmen" and "chiefs"—as problematic as that may be as a comparative typology—is useful in pointing to the kinds of ambiguity and ambivalence associated with the person-centered forms of leadership found in many Melanesian societies. Not only do national initiatives run up against the problem of regional diversity (in a country of more than sixty language groups), but within any one area, leadership practices depend upon a degree of fluidity and ambiguity that resists legal codification. Any one individual's status as chief is likely to overlap with that of others. Furthermore, claims to chiefly status emerge through time as individual careers combine multiple identities and activities. Parliamentary debate on the subject of traditional chiefs suggests that national politicians are themselves aware of many of these ambiguities, such that legislation is written in ways that accommodate a range of definitions.

Returning, then, to the initial question, "What is this resurgent talk of chiefs all about?"—it is apparent that there is more to it than an attempt to create new government positions. Given that, in Santa Isabel, discussions about new roles for chiefs in government have gone on for nearly twenty years, and that these discussions have produced very little institutional change, one might be pardoned for concluding that the process has no real political consequence; or that it is mainly an exercise in rhetoric. Such a conclusion, however, would miss the power of talk to create and legitimize (as well as to mystify) local realities. The last few decades in Santa Isabel have seen sustained discussions and ritual activities focusing on chiefs as symbols of local identity and power. These activities reconstitute meanings and interests that extend throughout the island's colonial history. Although "traditional chiefs" have yet to be empowered in any substantial way, the continuing talk of chiefs establishes and maintains a discursive space that might otherwise be crowded out by global modernizing forces, especially the institutions of church and state, which have fundamentally transformed Santa Isabel society. Perhaps one of the reasons that the short postcolonial history of new Melanesian states has produced so many surprises for outside observers is the failure to anticipate the potential force of local models put to use in redefining political futures.

Tuesday's Chiefs Revisited

ROGER M. KEESING

IN A PAPER published more than a quarter-century ago (Keesing 1969), I described the curious and paradoxical nature of the Kwaio (Malaita, Solomon Islands) political system as I had encountered it in 1963–64 fieldwork. The pagans with whom I was working had a highly fragmented social structure, with tiny descent-based local groups whose secular leaders—if any—were mainly very small men in comparison to the Big ones by then stereotypic in the literature. Many local groups had no clear-cut entrepreneurial leaders; and all adult men, and some women, were feast-givers in their own right. An almost anarchic spirit of individualism and antihierarchy prevailed in quotidian political relations. Yet every Tuesday, in the meeting area next to my house, a "Sub-District Committee"[1] gathered to discuss and "straighten out" *kastomu*.[2] In that setting, the Kwaio distinguished between *sifi* (chiefs)[3] and *koomani fiifuru* (common people), deferred to the chiefs of their "lines" in questions of custom, and spoke and acted in terms of chiefly hierarchy. In that early paper, I reflected on the significance of a society that had chiefs only on Tuesdays.

In the intervening years, Solomon Islands has become independent (1978) and has been organized into provinces to which more and more powers have devolved. With the devolution of powers, the importance of custom and "traditional chiefs" recognized in general terms in the constitution has been reinforced. "Traditional chiefs," and in particular "paramount chiefs," have received formal recognition, and have been assigned responsibilities for upholding, adjudicating, and preserving "custom." Through this period, the Kwaio, too, have put forward a "paramount chief," who has figured prominently in the recent phases of their historical struggle to preserve ancestral ways against the incursions of Christianity and an alien legal system.

Here, I reexamine the paradoxes surrounding Kwaio "chiefs," in this changed political context, and against the background of the "paramount chiefs" who have arisen and been given recognition around the Solomons in the postcolonial period, many in places that had no such leaders in precolonial times.

Although many of the contemporary "paramount chiefs" may have had no counterparts in precolonial political systems, it would be misleading to sustain, for the Solomons, the old stereotype of a precolonial Melanesia populated with bigmen (and not chiefs). Many parts of the Solomons seem to have had leaders whose title was hereditarily established, and who commanded by virtue of right, not of power and entrepreneurship. Early European intrusion and then invasion disrupted the relations of trade and warfare that sustained chiefly powers; and the coastal, lagoon, and strand zones where chiefly power seems to have been most pronounced were the ones most directly exposed to and transformed by European interventions. Much more ethnohistorical research is needed to establish what indigenous political systems were like, though that becomes increasingly difficult with the overlay of new ideologies about "traditional" leadership and *kastom*.

Tuesday Chiefs in the Kwaio Mountains

A central element in the ideology of Maasina Rule, the anticolonial political movement that arose at the end of the Guadalcanal campaign among Malaita workers in the Solomon Islands Labour Corps, was that an indigenous hierarchy of "chiefs" must be put forward both to organize matters of custom and community and to confront the colonial hierarchy of headmen and district officers, in demanding political rights and the application of customary law (Fifi'i 1989; Laracy 1983; Keesing 1978, 1992a). The principal ideologues of the movement, Nori and Aliki Nono'oohimae, were from 'Are'are, in southeastern Malaita. The model of chiefly authority as an indigenous element of *kastom*, the *araha*, was drawn from the hereditary leaders of southeastern 'Are'are and Small Malaita. The idea of a leader who would have a higher authority spanning the chiefly heads of lineages was put forward by Nori and his colleagues in negotiations with the British colonial administration, using the Small Malaita term *araha 'ou'ou* (Keesing 1978).[4]

Around Malaita,[5] hierarchies of *sifi* were put forward: line chiefs, full chiefs, and head chiefs, representing subdistricts (which, on Malaita, roughly corresponded to language groups). For the Kwaio, at least, the political counterorganization was based squarely on the administrative system that had been created by the colonial administration in the 1920s, for the collection of taxes and the local maintenance of law and order through headmen. Fragmented local descent groups had been agglomerated into "lines" (for purposes of tax collection and administration); and it was these "lines" for whom Maasina Rule *sifi* were chosen. Tax collection was organized according to the old "passages" of the labor trade, each of which had a village constable, and later a headman. It was these passages for which full chiefs were put forward, as a kind of oppositional political structure.

At the end of 1962, when I arrived to begin fieldwork, Maasina Rule had been outwardly smashed by heavy repression, yet particularly in the more conservative inland areas, anticolonial political activity still smoldered. The 'Are'are leader Waiparo from Takataka on the east coast had mobilized a strong movement to codify *kastom*, and thereby demand its recognition and legitimation by the colonial state.[6] Waiparo and his followers sought to incorporate Kwaio descent groups further up the coast into the movement; but though many were drawn in, these groups chafed under the hegemonic place being assigned to 'Are'are *kastom*, rather than their own. Kwaio leaders from Sinalagu, many of whom had been active in Maasina Rule, summoned Jonathan Fifi'i, who had been their head chief until he was imprisoned by the government, to join in a counter-movement that would codify and legitimize *their* customary law and ancestral tabus. It was in this political climate that I, as an American who had come "to write down your customs," entered the Kwaio Mountains.[7] Scant wonder that I was incorporated into their historical project, and that I inadvertently acted as a catalyst renewing political energies. It was at Ngarinaasuru, a thousand feet up the precipitous mountain above Sinalagu Harbor, where my house had been built, that a meeting place for work on *kastomu* was established.[8] There, through the period of my first fieldwork, crowds of people from the pagan communities inland from Sinalagu, and often delegations from Uru and 'Oloburi,[9] gathered to "straighten out the custom." It was in this setting, on Tuesdays, that the division into "chiefs" and "common people" that had so struck me was enacted.

The *sifi* of the *koumitii* (committee) gathered in the large building constructed for this purpose[10] to discuss and sometimes adjudicate matters of customary law, and worked with me in recording genealogies and compilations of lands, shrines, and ancestrally imposed tabus. While talk of *kastomu* was going on, women, children, young men, and others cast as *koomani fiifuru* stayed outside, cutting grass, gathering firewood, cooking, playing, or exchanging talk. Although the gatherings were impressive mobilizations of people and energy, senior men lamented the lack of commitment and spoke enthusiastically of the Golden Age of Maasina Rule when commitment was unflagging, solidarity unbroken, and energies sustained.

Through the 1960s and most of the 1970s, energies and commitment did indeed waver, waxing and waning as *bungu 'ifi*, meeting places for discussion of *kastomu*, were constructed in the interior, then abandoned to the advancing jungle. Ngarinaasuru remained a potential meeting place, but when already dilapidated buildings were further damaged by torrential cyclone rains in 1970, they were not rebuilt. My own base was moved to the nearby settlement of my longtime neighbor Folofo'u, well known as a diviner,[11] but otherwise a man of limited means, whose ritual role and position in traditional contexts of feast-giving were marginal. Although his proximity to Ngarinaasuru and fiery rhetoric had made him something of a presence in *koumitii* activities, he had alienated many leaders from the interior and some of his kin and neighbors with his penchant for theatrical curses and ancestral injunctions.

Independence and the Rise of Kwaio Fadanga

By 1977, independence was in the air. Most of the old leaders of *koumitii* were dead; the few who survived had built *bungu 'ifi* in the interior to stay clear of Folofo'u and his curses. Something of a political vacuum had been created around Ngarinaasuru, just at the time when the last colonial administrators were seeking to renegotiate the old head tax and issues of local government. Fifi'i was Kwaio member for Parliament, and as a member of a 1977 constitutional delegation to London he alarmed British counterparts by introducing claims for compensation for the depredations of a 1927 punitive expedition after Kwaio warriors had killed a district officer and massacred his entourage (Keesing and Corris 1980). The question of whether the Solomons would retain or reject the queen as sovereign was genuinely at issue; and this and discussions about what "independence" meant invited extremist interpretation among diehard pagans in the mountains who had for decades fought against the colonial imposition of alien law and rule. Independence, they argued, should mean freedom from alien laws—the right to follow ancestral customs on ancestral lands. Foremost among the extremists were Folofo'u, who increasingly arrogated a role as spokesman for *kastomu* vis-à-vis the administration, and Laefiwane, whose father had initiated the 1927 massacre and killed the district officer.

In 1978 and 1979, matters came to a head, as an alliance of pagans and Christians from the coastal villages joined to boycott payment of taxes, and then collected their own tax and kept it. Folofoʻu refused to allow the police to take two Kwaio who had attempted murder and gravely wounded their victims, and demanded that matters be resolved by exchange of compensation, according to custom.

In 1979, a Kwaio Cultural Center was built at Ngarinaasuru, with David Akin and Kate Gillogly as Peace Corps volunteers to teach literacy in the vernacular and establish a craft cooperative. At the formal opening, Kwaio defiance to the government, led by Folofoʻu, was close to the surface.

In the next several years,[12] it surfaced with a vengeance. Folofoʻu was elevated, with the support of Christian scribes and schemers, to the government-created position of paramount chief and was dealt with by the government as the legitimate customary leader of the Kwaio people. He and his scribes, leading sometimes reluctant *sifi* from the interior (a mainly new, young cast of characters), assumed a collective identity as Kwaio Fadanga (or Council) in defying the provincial and central governments. A demand for several hundred billion dollars in compensation for the devastation wrought by the 1927 punitive expedition was presented (see Keesing 1990); the claim was fiercely pressed by the fire-breathing Folofoʻu, a charismatic orator and messianic figure. Rumors swept the area that Folofoʻu was arranging for the Americans to bring "development." In the name of Kwaio Fadanga, he demanded the compensation—and later, millions of dollars for "development," to be entrusted personally to his hands;[13] and he threatened to withdraw from the Solomons and proclaim independence on his ancestral soil. In dramatic confrontations, he boycotted parliamentary elections, threatened violence (leading to evacuation of the Atoifi Adventist Hospital on the coast at Uru), and led pagan warriors to armed confrontation and the very brink of war—all the while flinging ancestral curses and injunctions, and demanding massive compensation in the name of custom if the injunctions were transgressed.

I have documented these political events elsewhere (especially in Keesing 1992a; see also Fifiʻi 1989). What interests me here is the *symbolic process*, the drama in which Folofoʻu, a bogus chief if there ever was one, a man whose title and power were created by the postcolonial state, *became* a chief—a traditional one, at that—in the discourses of custom and confrontation. In style, the Tikopian chiefs of Firth's day—Pa Fenuatara and the rest (Firth 1969)—pale into insignificance in comparison with a tall and haughty Folofoʻu, surrounded by his bodyguards and retainers and symbols of "office," in dramatic confrontation with the prime minister: each a sovereign in his kingdom. It is this dialectical process, through which political myths become political realities, and through which hegemonic structures generate their counterhegemonic mirror images,[14] that

fascinates me. The government recognized and legitimized Folofoʻu's customary status as paramount chief of "the Kwaio people"—indeed, they
had created and conferred it.[15] The "Kwaio people" joined in this discourse as well. I was surprised to hear a press statement issued by a young
Kwaio Christian that the government had to pay Folofoʻu massive compensation for violating his injunction against the election. In Kwaio custom, he announced, if a chief issues an injunction, no one can perform
the prohibited act without having to pay major compensation.[16] Tikopia
(a Polynesian chieftainship) has indeed been relocated in the mountains of
central Malaita.

Meanwhile, the pagans go on in their day-to-day regimens of gardening, feasting, sacrificing to the ancestors, performing magic, and stealing
one another's pigs. When I was there in 1990, I heard little talk of *sifi*, although there is renewed talk of the compensation claim, reframed and
more realistically cast; and still talk, especially after Fifiʻi's death, about
the old project of "writing down *kastomu*," now conceived of as *baelo* (by-
laws) or *konusitusan* (constitution). Although leadership is fragmented,
the old political goals are still there, the old projects still unrealized. There
is talk of *bungu ʻifi* being rebuilt yet again. Tuesday's chiefs are still there—
a new set, from the generation of the children of those with whom I worked
in the 1960s, some now armed with the power of literacy. Folofoʻu died in
November 1991. His oldest son, Kwaʻilamo, a man in his late thirties, was
designated his successor as "paramount chief": Tikopia in the mountains
again, hereditary succession and all. He is a solid but by nature lazy young
man who certainly lacks his father's charisma; but perhaps his "office" will
sustain his power to lead. I have no clear evidence yet of what stance the
younger generation of pagan leaders from the bush will take toward this
new incarnation of Kwaio Fadanga. But Kwaʻilamo is intent on rebuilding
Ngarinaasuru, as the base of Kwaio *kastom* politics, center for negotiations with provincial and central governments, and reestablished site for a
cultural center and school.[17] Two of the moderate younger Kwaio leaders
have written to ask for my endorsement for use of their development funds
for this project,[18] so this seems to be a period of fence-mending.

Around Malaita and other parts of the Solomons, many of Folofoʻu's
fellow "paramount chiefs" are alive and well. It is to them I turn.

Paramount Chiefs in the Contemporary Solomons

I shall not attempt a regional tour of the Solomons to sketch the place of
paramount chiefs in each island's political landscape. For most of the
Solomons, I have little or no information. Work on contemporary chiefs
on Santa Isabel by Geoffrey White (1991), and on Kwaraʻae chiefs by

David Gegeo and Karen Watson-Gegeo (1996), reveals two variations on the theme of paramount chieftaincy useful for my purposes. (I will touch shortly on contemporary Polynesian chiefs in the Solomons, for whom Bill Donner [1993] and Rick Feinberg [1993] have given us useful recent information.) In the Isabel case, the elevation of Bishop Dudley Tuti, one of the first two Melanesian bishops in the Solomons, to the position of paramount chief in 1975 will serve to underline the close intertwining of Anglican religious hierarchy and recreated custom. Coastal Isabel and large parts of the interior were devastated and almost emptied by head-hunting raids in the late nineteenth century; Kia, Bishop Dudley's stronghold, serves as a kind of cosmological center and symbol of the cultural synthesis created by the refugees out of indigenous and European Christian elements; and Tuti himself, installed as paramount chief as well as bishop, served as symbol of that synthesis. As White (1992) argues, the Isabel case is a particular one in that something of a precedent existed in the person of Monilaws Soga, early in the century, and in that the elevation as paramount chief occurred before independence. It also seems likely that, at least in some parts of precolonial Santa Isabel, hereditary chiefs had considerable, if local, power (see White 1991, 1992). I will touch briefly on this question later.

In the case of the Kwara'ae, the Malaita people immediately to the northwest of the Kwaio, the emergence of paramount chiefs has been closely entwined with the proliferation of a syncretic and mythical cultural tradition reconciling Kwara'ae origins with biblical accounts, by bringing wandering Israelites to the Solomons (Burt 1982). Again, *kastom* is celebrated and proclaimed; but it is a custom forged out of evangelican Christian as well as indigenous elements. The paramount chiefs of contemporary Kwara'ae exercise an authority that seems to my eye almost as bogus in terms of the sociopolitical organization of nineteenth- and twentieth-century communities[19] as that of Folofo'u. Yet not only have they, too, gained recognition and a goodly measure of power from the postcolonial state, but also a new generation of educated Kwara'ae unquestioningly assume that they represent the ways of the ancestral past, and that their status is sustained by and sustaining of cultural tradition.[20]

A further variant on the theme of paramount chiefs in the postcolonial Solomons, touched on by White (1992), is the installation of the outgoing governor-general of the Solomons, Sir Baddeley Devesi, as paramount chief of the Tasimboko district of Guadalcanal in 1988. Here, the accumulated power, wealth, and prestige of a prominent politician (who returned to a position as parliamentary member and minister after his period as governor-general) made Devesi an appropriate paramount chief symbolically and politically, however Westernized he may be.[21]

A final illustration of the post-independence installation and empowerment of paramount chiefs comes from 'Are'are. What is interesting for our purposes about the installation of Aliki Nono'oohimae is that, although his traditional status as an *araha* gave him cultural credentials much more impressive than those of Folofo'u's, it was more politically important that he was the senior surviving leader and architect of Maasina Rule. There is a direct line, in the political thinking of Malaita cultural conservatives, between Maasina Rule as a defense of embattled ancestral custom and local sovereignty and the paramount chiefs of the postcolonial epoque, symbolically mobilized in defense of tradition against the engulfing forces of Westernization and modernity.

It is precisely here that the paramount chiefs and their empowerment (largely symbolic though it may be, in most cases) serve the interests of the neocolonial elite who run the country. Westernized Solomon Islanders learned overseas that "natives" ought to have "chiefs"; and they have made of the invented chiefs useful foils of postcolonial state politics. As I have noted in recent papers about *kastom* (Keesing 1989, 1991), for Melanesian elites to proclaim a commitment to ancestral cultures and local traditions (and hence "chiefs") serves as an effective ideological denial and disguise of the progressive pauperization and environmental devastation of hinterlands regions; of the marginality and powerlessness of tiny states, dominated by foreign investment, resource extraction, and tourism, within the world system; and of the pursuit by these very elites of Western lifestyles and development strategies squarely at odds with the interests of village people, and in reality highly destructive of whatever cultural traditions remain. Totems may be good to think with. Ironically, paramount chiefs are good to Westernize with.

It is idle to ask whether all the paramount chiefs around the contemporary Solomons are bogus. That would rekindle the by now tiresome arguments about the "invention of tradition" in the Pacific and the postmodernist counterarguments relativizing all constructions of the past. It would also, I think, be to misunderstand the nature of the political process, the dynamic in which leaders and leadership roles emerge (whether in the Pacific or in Pennsylvania or Poland) to fill spaces created by contingent historical circumstances.[22] In the contemporary Solomons, the arenas for political action, the resources at stake, the rewards of power, and the idioms and symbols of status have all changed so dramatically that it is hard to know what a culturally legitimate chief would look like and do[23]— except perhaps on Tikopia or Anuta, where they have been there all along, and where connections to the rest of the country and the world system are so tenuous and sporadic. It is perhaps significant that it is precisely from these isolated Polynesian outliers, with their strict indigenous regimens of right, authority, and hierarchy, that the most coherent challenges to the hegemony of the postcolonial state have emerged. The challenge from the Kwaio hillbillies was louder and more dramatic, but in the end deeply subverted by the real anarchy that underlies fake hierarchy.

Precolonial Sociopolitical Systems

All this should not be taken as an endorsement of the traditional anthropological stereotypes of Melanesians with bigman systems and Polynesians with chiefs, à la Sahlins (1963). The ethnohistorical research done in the Solomons in the past twenty years by such scholars as Judy Bennett (1974, 1987), Kim Jackson (1972, 1975, 1978), Peter Corris (1970), Shelley Sayes (1976), and John McKinnon (1975) points to drastic transformations in political structures in the early contact period, especially along the coasts. The early ethnographies by such scholars as Ivens (1927) and Somerville (1897) suggest that in coastal and lagoon areas of the precolonial Solomons, at least, hereditary chiefs of considerable power and status were widespread. Several parts of the New Georgia group, parts of Makira, the Shortlands, and Small Malaita apparently had systems of strong, hereditary chiefly authority. For many areas, we simply have no reliable information.

It would seem that, at least in the eighteenth and nineteenth centuries, the maintenance of strong chiefly hierarchy was associated with coastal and maritime orientations. Doubtless, the reasons were not strictly material; but among the factors that would seem to have sustained chiefly hierarchy were control over large, composite, seagoing canoes and large marine nets (which required major mobilizations of labor to construct, use, and maintain), and the consequent control over interisland and interdistrict trade by sea (and subsequent monopoly access both to political alliances and to symbolically valued objects and scarce resources). Further, coastal orientations enabled warfare and predatory raiding on a larger geographical scale and with larger and more mobile deployments of warriors than was possible in the steep and broken mountain zones. However, all of these sources of power were easily overturned by European interventions (as well as potentially enhanced by them in the short run, as illustrated by New Georgia headhunting and the great power of the Malaita passagemasters).[24] Trading and exchange monopolies, access to symbolically valued objects, and warfare depended on freedom from outside intervention, although the new objects and technologies that reached coastal zones and their leaders before they were available in interior areas initially gave short-term new sources of power. Pacification, in itself, diverted leadership efforts from fighting to feasting: as one avenue to prestige closed, another widened (Keesing 1985). In some ways, then, the Melanesian bigman (so much drawn initially from Oliver's [1955] Siuai *mumi* and Hogbin's [1939] To'abaita *ngwane inoto*) was a creation of the early historic period.[25]

If we step back and look at the longer archaeological picture, there are some grounds for arguing that hereditary chiefs and regional sociopolitical structures were more pervasively present in what we now class as Melanesia[26] as of, say, 1,500 years ago than they were 500 years ago. Pawley (1982) persuasively suggests that bigman systems are a result not simply of European invasion of southwestern Pacific waters, but of a much earlier breakdown of systems of trade and regional political order, with attendant political devolution and involution. Exchange, he suggests, may represent a kind of imploded and devolved trade. Parallel arguments have recently been made by several prehistorians.

Does that mean that there were once chiefs in Kwara'ae or Santa Isabel? (And would this be relevant to the "legitimacy" of paramount chiefs in any case, if we are talking about a gulf of several centuries?) Let me first consider the Kwara'ae case. I am less persuaded than David Gegeo and Karen Watson-Gegeo (1996) that in the past there were strong, hereditary secular leaders who might be called "chiefs" in Kwara'ae.[27] As I have argued (Keesing 1985), there is throughout Malaita[28] a *conception* of a hereditarily entitled secular leader (northern Malaita *ngwane inito'o / ngwane inoto*); but I have seen no convincing evidence that in interior areas, such men ever had a strong position. My inference is that at least in the last several centuries—and for earlier periods we have no evidence other than the *'ai'imae* oral epics, which are very equivocal in this regard—strong hereditary secular leaders have been a kind of nostalgic fantasy or imaginary ideal, only occasionally partly realized, in interior areas; and a role often concretized, but perhaps only cyclically in labile and impermanent structures and through the temporary outcome of local battles and feuds, in coastal zones.

Santa Isabel is a more intriguing case because we have remarkably substantial accounts of indigenous political leadership in the sixteenth-century records of Mendaña's expedition. I find quite compelling the accounts of what sound like chiefs, in a kind of Polynesian style, around "Estrella Bay." I see no reason to doubt their accuracy, even though these leaders were obviously interpreted through Spanish eyes of the period. Despite the enormous disruptions and depopulation that characterized late nineteenth-century Isabel (see Jackson 1972), there were still at least echoes of strong local leadership and specially marked statuses.

All this, I think, constitutes an argument for much more ethnohistorical research in the Solomons. Even in areas long Christianized, where outwardly traditional customs seem to have been whittled away almost to nothing, rich oral tradition and much submerged cultural stuff remains, as Edvard Hviding's remarkable research in Adventist and other long-Christianized communities in the Marovo lagoon of New Georgia attests (Hviding 1993, 1996). While we watch with wonderment the dramas of paramount chiefs invented and empowered by Westernized Solomon Island leaders, some of us might work harder at exploring local oral traditions, and work harder to inspire young Solomon Islanders (as well as historians) to join us in a search for useful evidence on the political structures and processes of the precolonial past.

14

Constructing and Contesting
Chiefly Authority in Contemporary
Tana Toraja, Indonesia

KATHLEEN M. ADAMS

THIS CHAPTER explores the construction and contestation of chiefly authority in the Toraja highlands of Sulawesi, Indonesia. Examining such
dynamics in the Austronesian societies of Eastern Indonesia is critical to
our understanding of chiefs in the contemporary Pacific. As Scaglion has
recently observed, hierarchy and chiefly orientations are primarily Austronesian characteristics (Scaglion 1996; see also Douglas 1979:12). Given
that it is precisely in Eastern Indonesia where hierarchy in its most ex-
treme precontact Austronesian form is seen, and where it resides adjacent
to nonhierarchical Papuan forms of social organization, an exploration of
the ideology and practices pertaining to authority in this "fringe" region
of the Pacific offers a useful basis of comparison. Moreover, attending to
the case of Indonesia promises unique insights into the ways in which
some contemporary Austronesians strive to articulate their "traditional"
hierarchical orientations in dialogue with a postcolonial nation that prop-
agates a rhetoric that is, albeit superficially, relatively egalitarian.

In Indonesia, as in other postcolonial nations of the Pacific, political
independence has ushered in a host of new ideas regarding the structure
of sociopolitical relations in society. Through the rhetoric of "Guided Democracy," the adoption of a national language (relatively free from the
honorifics characteristic of many indigenous Indonesian languages), and
the expansion of Christian churches in the outer islands, new notions of
egalitarianism are, for some Indonesians, supplanting old hierarchical
ideologies.

A number of years ago, Benedict Anderson ([1966] 1990) explored the salience of the "new Indonesian" language in shaping younger Indonesians' national consciousness. As he observed, the almost statusless character of Indonesian (previously the Malay trade language) offered an escape from the hierarchical modes of indigenous linguistic intercourse (ibid.: 139). In short, for a number of Indonesians, the new language carried the possibility not only of national unity but also of an egalitarian lifestyle.

With the new language of independence came a new rhetoric of nationalism. The values and ideals for all social relations in the new state were first enunciated by President Sukarno in June 1945 as the Pancasila (the Five Principles of Indonesian Government). The five principles are belief in one God, humanitarianism, national unity, democracy based on consensus and representation, and social justice (in the form of political and economic equality). Although crafted to resonate with indigenous conceptions of social order (cf. Drake 1989), for some citizens the philosophy of Pancasila promises a new egalitarian nation.[1] In 1978, President Suharto's New Order government began to "operationalize" Pancasila by launching an intensive program of Pancasila education. All Indonesian citizens became legally required (Statute no. II/MPR/1978) to take courses in the comprehension and practice of Pancasila (Weatherbee 1985). By the time of my initial fieldwork (1984–85), the slogans of Pancasila had become ubiquitous. Taught in schools throughout the archipelago, aired every half hour on television, emblazoned on village signposts, and recited at all government events, these nationalist ideologies, which some saw as imbued with egalitarianism, were having reverberations in even the more remote villages of Indonesia.

For many of the Toraja people of upland Sulawesi, the ideals of guided democracy, combined with recently embraced Christian notions of equality before God, are prompting a rethinking of the traditional hierarchical institutions of local leadership. Almost twenty years ago, Eric Crystal (1974) addressed the persistence of traditional Torajan leadership orientations within the context of a rapidly changing political structure. In his classic study, Crystal detailed how a Torajan aristocrat, Puang Kapala, maneuvered traditional loyalties and allegiances for contemporary political ends, winning himself an elected position in the regency's government. In this chapter I wish to reexamine this interplay between indigenous patterns of authority and national political rhetoric. Today's Torajan chiefs may no longer bank on traditional loyalties: they are faced with ever-increasing internal and external challenges to their authority. In the following pages I will illustrate how contemporary Torajan aristocratic leaders attempt to maintain their eroding power bases not only by invoking *adat* (custom) but also by hailing those very national Indonesian institutions and symbols that have threatened their social preeminence.[2]

Though many who have written on contemporary chiefs in the Pacific have explored the ways in which locally meaningful categories of leadership are used in opposition to the national level, this chapter investigates how local Torajan chiefs draw on the authority of the new nation to bolster their eroding standing in their own communities. Following a discussion of the Torajan social hierarchy and the "ingredients" of chiefliness, I shall turn to focus on a recent event that threw the issue of chiefly legitimacy and authority into relief. The case involves an uproar that erupted at a funeral ritual for a low-ranking Torajan when the sponsors decided to dispense with the customary tokens of esteem for the local aristocratic chief.

The Ethnographic Setting

The Sa'dan Toraja people reside in Tana Toraja regency in upland Sulawesi (formerly known as the Celebes), Indonesia. Torajans speak Tae' Toraja, an Austronesian language closely related to other South Sulawesi languages (Mills 1975) and in the same language family as all of Polynesia and Micronesia. Moreover, as citizens of Indonesia, most Torajans are also fluent in Bahasa Indonesia.

In a nation of 185 million people, the Toraja are a minority group, numbering approximately 350,000. Their closest neighbors are the Islamicized Buginese and Makassarese peoples, the dominant ethnic groups of the region. Despite the fact that these neighboring groups boasted highly developed and extensive kingdoms, the Toraja never formed a centralized political unit. Traditionally, they lived in scattered mountaintop settlements, maintaining social ties through an elaborate system of ritual exchanges (see Nooy-Palm 1979, 1986; Koubi 1982). For this reason, some writers favor the term "big men" to describe local leaders.[3]

Toraja, however, was (and continues to be) a stratified society. Toraja society is hierarchically organized on the basis of descent, wealth, age, and occupation. In precolonial times, there were essentially three social strata: the aristocracy (*puang* or *to parengnge'*), commoners (*to buda, to sama*), and slaves (*kaunan*). Status was determined by birth, although financial success or failure allowed some individuals to permeate the barriers of rank. Although slavery is illegal in modern Indonesia, many elite Torajans still euphemistically refer to those of low birth as their "grandchildren" or "people from behind,"[4] an allusion to the fact that slaves traditionally lived behind the nobles.

Today, as in the past, the Toraja are primarily wet-rice agriculturalists. Since the 1960s, land shortages and limited local economic opportunities have prompted many Torajans to seek wage labor away from the homeland (Volkman 1985). Although some nobles have moved away to urban centers in Indonesia, the large majority of Torajan migrants are upwardly mobile commoners and descendants of slaves. As most of these expatriate Torajans remit portions of their wages to family members back home, a number of nonaristocratic Torajans have enjoyed a rise in their standards of living and, in some cases, have begun to adopt the traditional power markers of the elite (e.g., elaborate funeral rituals).

Although they reside in a predominantly Muslim country, the majority of Torajans have embraced Christianity rather than Islam as their faith. Missionaries from the Protestant Dutch Reformed Church first arrived in the Sulawesi highlands in 1913, shortly after the colonial administration was in place. By the 1960s most Torajans had converted to Christianity. Today only about 11 percent continue to practice the traditional "Ways of the Ancestors" (*Aluk to Dolo*), which involve the veneration of spirits, gods, and ancestors. In short, Christianity is an important aspect of Torajan identity.

Since the 1970s, Tana Toraja has become a popular tourist destination. The elaborately carved kindred houses (*tongkonan*) and mortuary effigies of the Torajan aristocracy combined with the region's spectacular scenery have helped fuel Torajans' touristic celebrity. Moreover, each year droves of Indonesian and international tourists are lured to the region by the prospect of witnessing Torajan funeral rituals, featuring spectacular pageantry and dances, as well as dramatic water-buffalo sacrifices. To sum up, contemporary Torajans are hardly an isolated people. In 1989 alone, just over 200,000 tourists visited the area. Tana Toraja's booming popularity not only has provided an alternative source of income for poorer commoners and descendants of slaves, but also has prompted a number of Torajans to rethink their identity and their relationships to other Indonesians (Adams 1984, 1988; Volkman 1984, 1990).

Indigenous Patterns of Leadership

Anthropologists have selected a variety of glosses for Torajan leaders. Whereas Eric Crystal (1970, 1974), who worked in the southern areas of Tana Toraja regency, writes of "ruling princes," Toby Volkman (1990), working in the north, uses the term "big men," and Hetty Nooy-Palm (1979) refers to leaders in the central valleys as "chiefs" or "heads." Nooy-Palm (1986:320) suggests that this contrast between the southern and northern regions of Tana Toraja is the result of historical settlement patterns. In her view, the earliest groups of people arriving from the south quickly settled in the expansive southern regions and fertile river valleys. These groups brought with them a hierarchical structure reminiscent of the Buginese kingdoms in the southern coastal regions of Sulawesi. Later arrivals (and possibly the "have-nots" who fled the southern settlements of Toraja) tried their luck farther north in the less-accessible hills. One might add that the limited plots of land in these rugged northern highlands did not facilitate the development of the same degree of hierarchical structure as existed in the fertile southern valleys.[5] Moreover, due to their more remote situation, these northern villagers were less likely to have been directly influenced by the more hierarchical Buginese and Makassarese peoples. My focus in this chapter is on the central region of Tana Toraja, known as Kesu, where I conducted two years of field research.

In the Kesu area, traditional political authority is organized around two concepts, one geographical and one genealogical. The first arena of authority is the *tondok*, which carries with it the notion of a locality, but also includes individuals linked to the locality by marriage and ritual interaction. Each *tondok* selects a headman, *to parengnge'*, who plays key roles in both ritual and political affairs.

The *tongkonan*, or kindred house, is the second traditional arena of political organization. As Torajan kinship is bilateral, a given *tongkonan* belongs to all male and female descendants of its founding ancestor. In short, it is the visual symbol of a descent group. Not all *tongkonan* are equal: there are greater and lesser *tongkonans*. Fully carved older *tongkonans* that have undergone a series of ritual consecrations are the most prestigious and are associated with the nobility. (Commoners are restricted to carving only certain sections of their *tongkonan* and slaves were strictly forbidden to embellish their *tongkonan*.) More recently established *tongkonans* that have splintered off from these older "parent" *tongkonans* are less prestigious. Each celebrated *tongkonan* has its own titled leader, or *to parengnge'*.

As in other areas, when Dutch colonial officials took over the region, they adopted *to parengnge'* to serve as representatives of each of the twenty-nine districts they had mapped. It appears the Dutch also invented a title, *Ampoe Lembang*, for their *to parengnge'* representatives (Wilcox 1949:272). Today, in postcolonial times, key political positions in the Sulawesi highlands still tend to be dominated by *to parengnge'*. Perhaps because of this legacy, there is currently some confusion around the concept of *to parengnge'*. Whereas some of my informants assert that *parengnge'* constitutes a social rank, others describe it as a specific title. Nooy-Palm (1979:49–50) reports similarly conflicting accounts from her informants.

As she observes, whether *to parengnge'* is a specific office or a high social rank, it is clear that the title entails certain charges and is the prerogative of those of high rank.

The designation *to parengnge'*, rooted in the word *rengnge'*, refers to bearing a burden on one's back (Tammu and van der Veen 1972:477). As Nooy-Palm (1979:49) notes, this is a metaphorical reference to the responsibilities these leaders bore for orchestrating the rituals of a titled ancestral house (*tongkonan*) or *tondok*. As an elite group, the *to parengnge'* enjoy special privileges. Traditionally, it was only the *to parengnge'* who could dress in the color yellow, adorn themselves with shimmering golden jewelry, or wear ornately woven hats. At rituals these noble *to parengnge'* have the privileged seats on the elevated rice barns, while those of lower status squat on the ground or are charged with running errands and cooking. Even today, the fine wooden and ceramic eating bowls of the *to parengnge'* are carefully segregated from the tin utensils used by commoners and descendants of slaves.

In the Kesu region a special appellation is reserved for the highest title-holder in the area: *sokkong bayu*. The term literally translates as "collar of the jacket," possibly alluding to the individual's position at the top. As Nooy-Palm describes, the *sokkong bayu* is "the spiritual as well as the worldly leader of his cognatic descent group" (1979:54). The *sokkong bayu* not only plays a key role in rituals but also officiates at village meetings and is sought out to resolve disputes. This chiefly status is not simply an ascribed status; rather, it is awarded to the individual who best combines several qualities. As my Torajan friends stressed, beyond having aristocratic rank, a *sokkong bayu* must exhibit charisma, knowledge of *adat* (traditions) and civil affairs, wealth, and bravery.[6] In short, if we subscribe to the classic anthropological distinctions between Melanesian "big men" and Polynesian "chiefs," the indigenous Torajan model of leadership appears to combine the features of both (cf. Oliver 1955; Sahlins 1963; Lindstrom 1982a; Godelier 1986:163–64; Marcus 1989).

In Toraja, hereditary claims to authority and wealth are certainly critical, but without charisma and skill one will never achieve a position of leadership. To illustrate, consider the case of Lolok,[7] an extremely prosperous aristocrat who aspired to become the leader of his much-celebrated *tongkonan*. Unfortunately, Lolok was notoriously short on charisma. Locally, he had a reputation for having a terrifying temper: there were ample (and probably much-embroidered) tales of him chasing acquaintances through the streets of Rantepao[8] for imagined slights, brandishing his knife and bellowing thunderously. As a result of Lolok's fabled outbursts, in concert with his often arrogant manner, no one took Lolok's leadership aspirations seriously. Instead, attention was turned toward other aristocratic men who were perceived as better natured and potentially charismatic. Though not much has been written on this topic, there seems to be general consensus that Torajan leaders should exhibit humility and possibly a self-deprecating sense of humor. One popular *to parengnge'* I knew was celebrated for his jokes about being no more than a poor, simple little farmer (the Toraja equivalent of a "country bumpkin"). Though everyone knew he was tremendously wealthy, his constant self-deprecation appeared to have general appeal.

Today's aristocratic Torajans recognize that *to parengnge'* or even *sokkong bayu* status alone is not enough to guarantee a family power and authority. The abolishment of slavery, cash received from tourists and migrant workers, combined with the ideological shifts brought by Christianization and nationalism, have led to eroding rank distinctions in the Toraja highlands (Adams 1988). Many of my noble informants confided their strategies to maintain their traditional positions of authority in these changing times. Generally these strategies involved seeking titles in both the indigenous system and the national political system. As one Torajan elder put it, "I had one son get a government position, another I instructed to pursue a military career and the last two I have been grooming to become traditional *tongkonan* leaders. . . . This way, if there is ever a conflict between internal *tongkonan* policy and government policy, we can prevail." Another younger Torajan man, currently being eyed as a potential traditional leader, conveyed his family's strategy quite graphically using three matches. Placing one match on the mat in front of us to represent his family's ultimate goal of solidifying local esteem and authority, he then carefully laid down two matches side-by-side just below the first match. Each of these two matches, he explained, represented different "lanes" toward achieving the family goals. The first match represented achievement of power in the traditional way, as a *sokkong bayu*, and the second match represented the new lane of the government official. As he concluded, today it is only by following both of these "lanes" that the authority of the family can be assured. In the following section I examine a controversy, which erupted at a 1984 funeral ritual, that illustrates the complexity of invoking national Indonesian offices and symbols of power to bolster (or challenge) the indigenous order of authority.

The Funeral "Revolt"

Early on in my fieldwork I accompanied my aristocratic Torajan hosts to what was to become one of the most controversial funerals in years. As we traversed the rice fields to the funeral site, my Torajan family told me that this would be a very simple funeral, as it was for an elderly woman of low birth. Traditionally, descendants of slaves were prohibited from staging grand, pageantry-filled funerals. Their mortuary ceremonies were generally short in duration and entailed neither the large-scale sacrifice of water buffalo nor the all-night *ma'badong* chants for the deceased that are typical of elite funerals. Upon entering the funeral arena, my aristocratic Torajan "mother" expressed audible shock at hearing *ma'badong* chants being played on a cassette over the loudspeaker system. As she whispered to me, "This should not have been allowed at a funeral for someone of such low birth." I was struck by the use of tape-deck technology to manipulate and escape the tabus traditionally associated with low rank. In this case, as there were not any human *ma'badong* performers present, the tabu was technically unbroken. Nevertheless, elite guests at the funeral were soon remarking that this "disregard for tradition" did not bode well for what was to come.

The following is an extract from my field notes on this funeral.

We were greeted by the hosts and ushered to our seats on the sitting platform of one of the rice barns. As people conversed softly and pigs squealed in the background, we were served syrupy coffee and sweet rice cakes. . . . When darkness fell, the Protestant preacher gave a sermon over the loudspeaker. He spent some time talking about the importance of the Indonesian government and Pancasila. Emphatically, he stated that "we are not Bonoran village people, we are not Torajans, but Indonesian!" From here he turned to religion, stating that we all had to obey not only Pancasila, but the Lord's laws. . . . Following the meat auction, the emcee announced that the *ma'badong* dancers were to begin shortly. I overheard someone off to the side comment, "That's a tabu!" and shortly thereafter my family began gathering up their bags and sandals to head home for the night.

Given the subsequent series of challenges to the prerogatives of the elite, the preacher's speech was noteworthy. Though it is typical for government officials to make speeches about national loyalty and policies at funeral rituals in Tana Toraja, religious figures do so much less frequently. The preacher's speech met with the nodding approval of the funeral hosts, who had invited him to officiate. A few noble funeral guests, however, later spoke of this speech as undermining their authority by stressing the subservience of Torajan identity to Indonesian identity, and Torajan regulations to the Lord's rules.

We returned to the funeral the next morning. Again, my account of what transpired is drawn from my field notes.

We arrived around 10:30 and things were already well under way. Speeches were being made over the loudspeaker and there was quite a throng of people, with more arriving all the time. Four water buffalo had been slaughtered earlier in the morning and the meat was being divided up. A few palm leafs had been planted in the ground to shield the meat from the bright sunlight. There were many flies, much blood and buffalo excrement—the air was heavy with these earthy smells. . . .

I began to focus on the increasingly animated speeches, realizing that they all concerned the division of the meat. Apparently, just before our arrival, the sponsors of this funeral had announced their intention to defy the tradition of giving select cuts of meat to the local aristocratic leaders (*to parengnge'* and *sokkong bayu*). Instead, they planned to distribute all of the meat amongst themselves. This declaration had been met with shock and a volley of speeches by noble title-holders, government officials (most of whom were from elite families), and the funeral sponsors. . . .

When we arrived, an elite government official (the head of the Development Office) was speaking into the loudspeaker urging the hosts not to break with tradition. He spoke of how "giving meat to the local leaders was not just a feudal gesture of respect, but a symbol of the unity of all Torajans and their traditions. Like Pancasila, meat to the *sokkong bayu* is a tradition we must guard." . . . Following an impassioned speech by a respected traditional leader and cousin of the local *sokkong bayu*, another elite government official (the district head) said, "As Indonesian citizens there are regulations and responsibilities we must adhere to, like paying taxes. . . ." He continued, drawing a parallel between national regulations and the traditional regulation of giving meat to the *sokkong bayu*, as nobles on the sidelines nodded with approval. The hosts, however, declared that "regulations can be changed, and that is what we are doing here!" [For the next five hours the debate continued, as tempers on both sides mounted.] . . . Finally, when it was clear that the *to parengnge'* were not to be offered the customary portion of meat, my elite host family quickly grabbed up their *sarong*s and bags and, along with other noble guests, made an indignant departure. The action was so sudden and abrupt that I was caught somewhat unawares—my Torajan "sister" tugged frantically at my sleeve, urging me to hurry, as I snatched up my notebook, pens, and camera and hunted under the mat for my mud-caked thongs. Although I wanted to stay and continue recording the events, it was clear that I was expected to leave with my hosts.

Later, back at the house, a steady stream of nobles stopped by to discuss the controversy with my host family. Most of these aristocratic Torajans chose to ignore the fact that the low-ranking funeral sponsors had originally couched their rejection of a custom that reinforced the traditional status hierarchy in terms of the "egalitarian" rhetoric of Pancasila and the Church. Instead, the group of leaders gathered at the house proposed an alternative exegesis of the "funeral rebellion" that constructed a contrast between their own traditionally based allegiance to Pancasila and the questionable loyalties of these former slaves. As the *sokkong bayu* framed it for me,

Back in 1958 the Communist party was active and we're seeing the remnants of it here. Too few people want to repair tradition, which is what we want to do—and this could ruin it all. . . . [In their refusal to give the traditional offering of the water buffalo head to us] the sponsors of this funeral are attempting to destroy tradition. It's a Communist tactic to destroy tradition, end religion, then build Communism. No identity is left if those two things are destroyed. That's clearly what they're trying to do here, and we can't let it happen.

Others nodded in assent that this was the work of political agitators. One young woman likened the funeral "rebellion" to a violent Islamic rebellion that had occurred in Tanjung Priok (a Jakarta district) the week before. It should be said that others present were quick to point out that they were not quite the same, as "the Tanjung Priok riot was an Islamic rebellion and this was a Communist one." According to newspaper accounts and political analysts (Awanohara 1984; Weatherbee 1985), the bloody Tanjung Priok riot erupted because strict Muslims perceived the aggressive propagation of the state ideology of Pancasila as threatening the role of religion. In the sense that both these protests were fueled by the propagation of Pancasila, there was actually a degree of accuracy in the young Torajan woman's claims.

There was much concern amongst the nobles that this publicly witnessed rejection of their traditional authority would prompt others to follow suit. Conferring with each other as to their course of action, they devised a strategy. Couching the ex-slaves' symbolic rejection of the traditional indigenous order of authority in terms of Communist agitation, the local nobles summoned the military to suppress this "rebellion." Reportedly, that evening the general himself picked up the most outspoken sponsor of the ritual and took him back to the base for intensive questioning. Later that night the funeral sponsors sent a teenaged grandchild to the homes of the local *to parengnge'* with a belated offering of the meat that had been denied them earlier in the day. Recognizing their victory, all of the aristocratic leaders proudly refused the meat, proclaiming it could no longer be received as a heartfelt gift of respect.

A few weeks later the *to parengnge'* were less sure of their triumph, when they learned that the "instigator" of the funeral rebellion had not been punished by the government (after being detained by the military for approximately ten days, he was released, and he promptly fled to a large coastal Buginese city, where he remained for six months).[9] Two older aristocrats summed up their sense of discouragement for me. As his voice rose with emotion, the first elder explained,

A while back we had a *tongkonan* meeting to decide what to do [about challenges to the tradition of giving a water buffalo head to the *sokkong bayu*]. We agreed that at each funeral one water buffalo must be given to the church and one or two should go to the *tongkonan* [*sokkong bayu*]. What he did at the funeral went against what we had all decided at that meeting. He wanted to ruin tradition.

The second elder chimed in,

Yes, and feelings were so heated at that ritual—things stopped just short of actual fist-fighting! In situations like that, when the *tongkonan* leaders [*to parengnge'*] can't resolve the problems, the government has to step in.

At this point his friend interrupted,

But what did they do?! Even he [the funeral sponsor] knew he was wrong—he fled. He was caught and he admitted he was wrong—but he wasn't sanctioned. So why did the government pick him up if they weren't going to punish him? Since *adat* [traditional] law doesn't operate anymore, it's the government's responsibility to punish him. Even though he admits he was wrong, he did a lot of damage. A lot of *those* people [ex-slaves in the region] were influenced by him.

For these noblemen, the national Indonesian government was supposed to act as their ally. Moreover, national Indonesian law was conceptualized as a roughly analogous replacement for traditional law, expected to reinforce the local order. Hence their sense of dismay and disappointment when agents of the Indonesian government did not see fit to punish an offender of the local order.

In subsequent conversations about this funeral, a number of elite leaders further elaborated on what they saw as the source of the disorder. Many agreed that newfound wealth and the rhetoric of Indonesian independence were creating a good deal of confusion. Noting that there had recently been a number of instances where low-ranking funeral sponsors refused to offer the traditional buffalo head to local aristocratic leaders, several older noblemen noted that Pancasila was prompting ex-slaves to think in new ways and reject the indigenous hierarchy. As a local nobleman and teacher explained,

The problem is, according to Pancasila, "all people are the same." But don't misapply that principle [as the ex-slaves are doing]. This idea in Pancasila is a moral idea. Our system of social stratification in Tana Toraja guarantees good morals. And that's what Pancasila wants—good morals. Indeed, any traditions that aren't in accordance with Pancasila should be thrown out. But the goal of our traditional system of social stratification is in accordance with Pancasila—*both* want to protect morals. So I think we should uphold tradition. The problem is that maybe the authority of the *to parengnge'* is slipping. If that's the case, *adat* [tradition], too, will slip, and then morals will slip.

In the eyes of another older noblewoman, it was not so much the misapplication of Pancasila that was at the root of the problem; rather, it was lower-ranking Torajans' misunderstanding of the semantics of Indonesian independence. As she explained to me,

Although we can't use the word "slave" anymore, this doesn't change their birth. The descendants of slaves at that funeral think "freedom" with Indonesian independence means "freedom for slaves," but in fact it only means "freedom from the Dutch." They aren't free because they were bought by our ancestors. If they want to be free, they must stage a *ma'talla'* ritual [a traditional ritual in which slaves earns their freedom by presenting their noble with 100 of each object of importance to Torajans: 100 water buffalo, 100 pigs, 100 chickens, and so forth].

While this woman was perhaps unusually forthcoming and devoted to traditional hierarchical orientations, in her comments we see once again how both traditional leaders and those struggling to challenge their authority draw on (and interpret to their own ends) the same nationalist rhetoric of freedom.

ALTHOUGH this "funeral rebellion" (as it has come to be known) occurred several years ago now, it is still a frequent topic of conversation amongst Torajan nobles. For them, the "rebellion" embodies an array of anxieties about alternative sources of authority in the new world: the national government, Christianity, and migrant money, to name a few. Savvy leaders have devised an array of strategies to appropriate these new sources of authority. As we have seen, some send their children to pursue titles in each of these competing arenas (government, church, and indigenous systems). Others, rather than wait for their children to achieve in these new arenas of power, try their hands at ideological manipulation. The more successful of these traditional leaders attempt to appropriate the rhetoric of the very systems that undermine their local power and authority, as illustrated by the case of the funeral. Elite Torajan leaders today couch their claims to authority not only in "tradition" but also in the rhetoric of devotion to democracy, anticommunism, and Pancasila.

If anthropologists are to contribute to scholarly understandings of authority and political power in postcolonial states, we need to investigate the ways in which new nationalist political rhetoric figures in concrete local rituals where authority is constructed and challenged. In this chapter I have attempted to illustrate the ironies and complexities of this evolving discourse between the local and the national.

15

Conclusions

Chiefs and States Today

PETER LARMOUR

CENTRALIZED bureaucratic states have become the preeminent form of political organization in the world today. Their numbers have proliferated with the breakup of colonial empires and the Soviet Union. New states have been formed in the South Pacific, and the chapters in this volume show how their rule has been enhanced and challenged by the persistence and revival of traditional forms of authority.

These conclusions use some ideas from political science, rather than anthropology, to review the relationships between chiefs and states identified in the previous chapters, and put them into a comparative context. The first part considers the equivalence of chiefs and states; the second analyzes the relationship in terms of different types of power; the third extends the relationship between chiefs and states to include commoners and antichief movements.

Chiefdoms and States

In comparing states and chiefs, are we comparing like with like? Are states and chiefs the same kind of thing? In most of the chapters here, chiefs appear as persons, or types of person. Sometimes they are contrasted with other types of person—elective leaders, in Pinsker's chapter on the Federated States of Micronesia (Chapter 8), or town officers, in James's chapter on Tonga (Chapter 3). As such, they can occupy the three positions iden-

I am very grateful for the comments of a reviewer, but I remain responsible for the final content.

tified by editors in their introduction: within the state, as marginal agents of the state, or leading the opposition to its rule.

"The state," by contrast, is a larger, more shadowy but pervasive entity, defined in part by its claims to impersonality. To bring states and chiefs into closer equivalence, the chapters suggest two strategies. First, we could, like Macpherson (Chapter 2), talk about the institution of chieftaincy, or about chiefdoms, rather than about chiefs. Second, we could notice that states, too, are constituted by persons, and talk about state officials as the equivalent to chiefs.

Talking about chiefdoms draws attention to differences in territorial scope and centralization discussed in several chapters. Although states in the South Pacific are small by comparison with the original European states, they are generally much larger than the chiefdoms they now include. Marshall Islands chiefs, for example, were "unable to consolidate their rule over more than two or three atolls prior to the time of colonization" (Carucci, Chapter 10). Lawson argues that "there was no sense in which Fiji had comprised a single political unit or entity before colonization" (Chapter 6). The territorial unit of chiefly power in the east was the much smaller *matanitu*. But Fiji is also the exceptional larger traditional system. The precolonial political links between Fiji, Tonga, and Samoa constituted a looser, more extensive political system than the four separate states that succeeded it.

A wider territorial scope gives states some obvious relative advantages: access to greater resources (to the extent that these vary with land area), and the ability to divide and rule multiple chiefly challengers. Boyd's account of the Mau movement in Western Samoa, quoted by Macpherson (Chapter 2), gives a glimpse of the heroic organizing work required to confront a territorially extensive colonial state: "Loosely knit village communities of *matai* grouped around a large nuclear working committee of up to sixty or seventy high-ranking title-holders, in almost daily contact with [the leader of the Mau movement]" (Boyd 1969:156–57). As a result of this territorial mismatching, chiefs and states have often engaged at the local rather than the central government level. Central chiefly institutions have been correspondingly weak, and chiefs have had a particular interest in secession or federalism, which has exacerbated central government suspicions of them.

Centralization is a persistent theme in chief–state relations, partly a consequence of their territorial mismatching. Several chapters ask if colonial rule interrupted longer endogenous cycles of political centralization and decentralization in (at least) Polynesia and, as Keesing suggests (Chapter 13), Melanesia. Franco (Chapter 4) describes Samoa as centralized around the twelfth century, after the expulsion of the Tongans, and Tonga itself beginning to break up in the early nineteenth century. Tupou is described as wanting to "reunite" it, not for the first time.

There have been many attempts to reconstitute chiefly authority around monarchies on the same scale as colonial states (successfully in Tonga, and Hawai'i for a while; more controversially and with less success in Western Samoa, Fiji, and New Zealand). The Solomon Islands' Maasina Rule movement, described by Keesing (Chapter 13), got halfway: successfully achieving a new level of islandwide integration, which survived colonial repression to become officially recognized as the Malaita Council.

European intervention had centralizing and decentralizing consequences for chiefly political systems. One the one hand, Europeans brought their own "state traditions" with them. They tended to look for a political center, and to try and create one if they could not find it. Macpherson (Chapter 2) cites Gilson's brisk summary of the reasons Europeans desired "the Hawaiian solution" in Samoa: "Because it was familiar to European settlers; on the basis of its "success" in Hawaii; it was supposed to be natural to Polynesians and because it was a form of governance through which Europeans could hope to gain and exert influence on developments in Samoa" (Gilson 1970:188). But there were contrary tendencies: Europeans were divided into competing imperial teams, while colonial purposes might be frustrated as well as facilitated by local unity.

State Officials and Chiefs

The second strategy to bring states and chiefs into closer equivalence is to emphasize the personal quality of states, which are, after all, constituted by the routine actions of low-level officials, high-level leaders, and international diplomats and soldiers, who act as if states exist "out there," independent of people. At this microlevel, the state is its officials, claiming resources and compliance in its name, sometimes against counterclaims by "chiefs." Thus James describes (in Chapter 3) how the Tongan nobility began to be pushed aside by town and district local government officers. Local officers were called upon to protect the environment by cleaning villages and surroundings and to help with other development projects (including channeling foreign aid to build pig fences). In one case the town officer set an example by working regularly on strips he had cleared from land owned but not used by a noble.

Particular persons may be both chiefs and state officials. At the time of this writing, for example, Ratu Joni Madraiwiwi, the Fiji government's permanent arbitrator in industrial disputes, had just been installed as the Roko Tui of Bau (*Fiji Times*, Nov. 13, 1995). Sometimes the line between "chiefly" and "stately" activities is hard to draw. The same activity that is "corrupt" for a state official is acceptable in a chief. Pinsker (Chapter 8) notices the way that the distinction between public and private property is invoked against "corrupt" state officials who use government trucks, but not against chiefs in the F.S.M. Though Pohnpeian magistrates were impeached for use of public funds, a pickup truck that a chief received under a public-projects bill was "his to do with as he liked." Similarly, Pinsker describes (without comment) a Udot chief in Chuuk with the motorboat received through his F.S.M. senator's public-projects bill. In Pohnpei several magistrates have been impeached for using public funds for private purposes, but "no such distinction" was made for chiefs, and Pinsker concludes, "The insistence on the distinction between personal and public property in elective office was probably a major factor in the disappearance of Nahnmwarkis from the chief magistrate position." On Rotuma, Howard and Rensel (Chapter 7) found that chiefs were "strongly tempted to use public funds to pay for personal privileges and to support a more elegant lifestyle," but that such use "undermines the moral basis of their authority." Chief Kausiriaf's apology for embezzling the Rotuma Co-op was rejected by committee as appropriate for personal offenses but not for a business where money was involved. "The state" here amounts to a legitimating rhetoric, on a par with "tradition," both of which may be applied to the same act, with different consequences.

The Moral Dimension of Stateness

These examples draw attention to the moral dimension of "stateness." In the Western European tradition, for example, "the state" refers both to a set of organizations (departments, ministries, etc.) and to the idea that these organizations should act coherently and impartially. Dyson (1982) argues that the idea of the state as an absolute, impersonal authority acting in the public interest does not travel well outside Western Europe. Liberal societies like Britain and America, with political traditions suspicious of government interference and even-handedness, are to that extent "stateless." In the South Pacific and Indonesia, colonial officials may have seen themselves as absolute, impersonal rulers acting in the public interest, but their colonial subjects were probably less convinced.

Petersen's explanation of the vote against a council of chiefs in the F.S.M. (Chapter 9) brings together two kinds of antistate tradition: the experiences of indigenous people in "the Pacific, Africa, South America, Southeast Asia, and North America" at the hands of states, and a United States federalist emphasis on checks and balances. The wide discussion of constitutional options that continues to take place in many South Pacific countries (as in the F.S.M. constitutional convention described by Petersen) has provided the opportunity to express, reconsider, and perhaps reconstruct state traditions. In this sense, "talk about the state" partly constitutes "the state" as a moral order, in much the same way as the endless "talk about chiefs" identified by Pinsker (Chapter 8) and Carucci (Chapter 10).

To recognize the state as a moral (or immoral) order also draws attention to the relationship betweens chiefs and missionaries, considered particularly by Macpherson (Chapter 2). The Christian missions in Polynesia are often said to have tried to separate the religious and political strands of chieftaincy, but the new paramount chieftaincy on Santa Isabel in Solomon Islands was promoted by the Anglican church, and the first incumbent was a bishop (White, Chapter 12). Lindstrom describes how there was little criticism of chiefs who were also pastors, or National party officials, in Vanuatu.

The issue of morality is also related to violence. Weber's famous definition of the state as "a human community that (successfully) claims the monopoly of the legitimate use of physical force within a territory" (1983: 111) draws attention to the contingency of state activity, and to its basis in violence. The stately monopoly is precarious. The Papua New Guinea state, for example, is famously unable to achieve it against, on the one hand, continual so-called tribal fighting, and on the other, "raskolism" (Dinnen 1994). And Macpherson describes (Chapter 2) how Samoa's Village Fono Act concedes powers of punishment to chiefs.

The chapters here show that if the state could achieve that monopoly, it affected the power of chiefs in opposite ways. On the one hand, by ending warfare, travel became freer in what is now the Federated States of Micronesia: people could vote with their feet against chiefs they did not like. On the other hand, chiefs became protected from commoner violence against them, and thus "primordial checks on autocratic abuse were eliminated."

Chiefs, States, and Power

To look for equivalences between chiefs and states may be to miss the extent to which one may dominate but not displace the other. "States" and "chiefs" both express, and draw upon, wider forms of social power. Carucci (Chapter 10) suggests a common currency of power, with different degrees of consolidation. He describes chieftainship as a broad category with many versions and local nuances, designed to prevent the consolidation of power. Lawson (Chapter 6) and Keesing (Chapter 13) also locate chiefs and states in a wider context of social power and inequality. Lawson finds that in Fiji, "Though membership in the political elite is not restricted exclusively to bearers of chiefly status, the patronage of the chiefly establishment has been a crucial factor to date." For Keesing, the empowerment of paramount chiefs serves the interests of the neocolonial elite who run the Solomon Islands. The promotion of custom "serves as an effective ideological denial and disguise of the . . . pursuit by these very elites of Western lifestyles and development strategies squarely at odds with the interests of village people."

The power relationship between states, chiefs, and third parties can be understood in several ways: along three "dimensions" of power; as between "infrastructural" and "despotic" power; and as between "sovereign" and "disciplinary" power. The role, and extent, of what Keesing calls ideological denial and disguise becomes particularly important when we go on to consider the relationship between chiefs, states, and commoners.

Three Dimensions of Power

In an influential set of arguments, Lukes (1974) distinguished three "dimensions" of power as it had hitherto been analyzed in political science. The first, commonsense, definition had to do with A's ability to get B to do things he or she would not otherwise want to do. Chiefs, for example, may resist the development plans of states, or states may resist chiefly demands to be paid allowances.

The chapters here show that land tenure is an important issue in power struggles between chiefs and states in the first dimensional sense. Policies to individualize land tenure typically threatened chiefs (Migdal 1988: 57–66). In parts of Micronesia, the chiefs' precolonial authority derived from residual rights over land on which others were living. Chiefs in Pohnpei had granted land titles, until Germans began issuing individual titles in 1910. James (Chapter 3) quotes a young noble: "The land was our power base and we used to have the respect of the people because we owned the land."

Tonga's nineteenth-century constitutional settlement granted male taxpayers an entitlement to land, but (from 1915) they required "permission of the noble before registering" the customary allotment. Some nobles delayed "in order to retain access to the goods and services of the people living on their land." In this case, chiefs are forcing commoners to do things they would rather not do (provide presents).

Lukes's second dimension of power was less visible. This was the power to set the agenda, and to ensure that challenging or uncomfortable issues were not even raised. Chiefs might be the subjects or objects of power in this second dimension. As subjects, their control of the agenda in institutions like village *fono* serves to keep awkward issues off the agenda: accusations of "disrespect" are second-dimensional exercises of power. As objects, chiefs may be ignored, sidelined, or "get the run-around" from state officials, who nevertheless would lose an open trial of strength. In an earlier version of their chapter for this volume, Howard and Rensel (Chapter 7) refer to a second-dimensional exercise of power in their description of Rotuman chiefs "befuddled by the bureaucratic complexities to which their projects and requests of developmental assistance are subjected in Suva."

Victims of power in the second sense know they are being beaten, but cannot do much about it. Lukes's third-dimensional use of power, however, disguised itself from its victims. It was the ideological power to change values and preferences, exercised through education and advertising. Chiefs might be beneficiaries as well as victims of the third-dimensional exercise of power. They are beneficiaries in Lawson's critique of traditional justifications of chieftaincy (Chapter 6), which rests on a third-dimensional idea of power exercised through concealment and mystification. They are victims when schools, the media, and churches undermine respect for traditional authority. I shall return to this question of ideology in the last section of this chapter, which considers antichief movements.

Infrastructural Versus Despotic Power

Power may also be a positive, enabling force. Writing about the development of European states, Mann distinguished between "infrastructural" power and "despotic" power. The former was the ability to get things done—a characteristic of the relatively high levels of resource mobilization and coordination achievable by centralized bureaucratic states—"the capacity of the state actually to penetrate civil society, and to implement logistically political decisions throughout the realm" (Mann 1986:113). Despotic power, however, referred to "the range of actions which the elite is empowered to undertake without routine, institutionalised negotiation with civil society groups" (ibid.). Mann's example was Lewis Carroll's fictional chief, the Red Queen, who could (despotically) shout, "Off with her head!" but could (infrastructurally) only execute people within close reach.

Historically, chiefly power seems to have changed along both of Mann's dimensions. Precontact chiefs in the Federated States of Micronesia had considerable despotic power. Pinsker (Chapter 8) describes how "a century ago, a village chief could ask a chief from another village . . . to kill a young troublemaker. Chiefs can't do that now." Macpherson (Chapter 2) describes how chiefs in Western Samoa wielded infrastructural power when they "commanded the physical, capital, and organizational resources necessary to create capital assets for the extension of missionary activity." Pinsker also describes how the end of warfare in the Federated States of Micronesia reduced the need for one kind of chiefly infrastructural power: the power to mobilize young men for war.

Carucci (Chapter 10) describes Marshall Islanders' nostalgia for colonial chieftaincy in infrastructural terms: chiefs then provided feasts, tools, and medical care (funded from a tithe on copra earnings). The current revival of interest in chiefs may thus have less to do with nostalgia for tradition, and more to do with nostalgia for the ability to "get things done."

By contrast, the long-running dispute over the power of village *fono* in Western Samoa is, in part, a matter of despotic rather than infrastructural power. As described by Macpherson (Chapter 2), chiefly claims to the right to banish offenders from villages and to control commerce were coming under constitutional challenge. The 1990 Village Fono Act confirmed that chiefs had "despotic" powers to impose fines and forced labor, and limited the right of appeal against their decisions. But the reach of these powers remained limited to the particular village, while a government funded by foreign aid probably had more effective infrastructural power.

Disciplinary Versus Sovereign Power

In Foucault's famous (1984) distinction, "sovereign" power is absolute, externalized, devolving from the monarch, but uncertain in its implementation at the limits. It is cruel, and exemplary, but not widely effective. "Disciplinary" power, however, is more dispersed via "capillaries" (in Foucault's phrase) and internalized. It is exercised by professionals in "normalizing" institutions like prisons, asylums, and schools. Unlike "sovereign" power, it is kind but unavoidable. This new form of power emerged in Europe without completely displacing its "sovereign" predecessor. Mitchell (1988) has used the idea of "disciplinary" power to understand British colonialism in Egypt, particularly through its characteristic institutions of town planning, military training, and boarding schools. Colonial power in parts of the Pacific can be understood in a similar way (Thomas 1994: 105–42; Kaplan 1995: 206–7).

In a related but more functionalist vein, Carucci (Chapter 10) identifies "valorization of a single indigenous tradition" as "a stasis-generating co-lonial strategy." Lawson (Chapter 6) makes the same point about Fiji, whose Great Council of Chiefs, native administration, and land-tenure system are "colonial artifacts that served the essential purpose of imposing uniformity on the otherwise diverse and heterogeneous people who occu-pied the Fiji islands at the time of colonization."

Early colonial rule in parts of Melanesia was typically "sovereign" in Foucault's sense: violent, cruel, exemplary, but ineffective at the margin. It was avoidable, and not internalized by its subjects. Chiefs opposed it, when they did so, with counterclaims to sovereignty. Both sides were ar-guing about the same thing.

Chiefs made, and to some extent are still making, counterclaims to sov-ereignty, but colonial rule also introduced new forms of "disciplinary" power to which chiefs had no obvious counter. The power embodied in missions, schools, prisons, and (later) universities was kinder, more pro-fessional, and more internalized. Nevertheless, James (Chapter 3) notes how chieftaincy might normalize itself. In Tonga, Queen Sālote "encour-aged the education of members of the noble families so that there would be a 'unity of rank and fitness to lead.'" Boys went to Tupou College, and girls to Queen Sālote College, as sovereign power became the matron of disciplinary power.

Once we have seen the various forms power may take, it is hard to conclude that states are generally or always more powerful than chiefs, either in relation to each other or in relation to third parties. Both exercise power in each of Lukes's three dimensions: getting others to do what they otherwise would not want to do; keeping issues off the agenda; and bene-fiting from ideology. Chiefs used to have infrastructural and despotic power. South Pacific states today derive infrastructural power from exter-nal sources, such as aid donors, but they often seem unable to deliver it to rural areas. Neither chiefs nor states exercise as much despotic power as they used to (though the Papua New Guinea government's restoration of the death penalty suggests a nostalgia for it). The shift from sovereign to disciplinary power undermines both states and chiefs, even as both contest for the emptying prize of sovereignty.

States, Chiefs, Commoners, and Antichief Movements

Finally, to make full sense of the chief–state relationship, we need to look at the third corner of the triangle. Who occupies this corner? In Tonga, chiefs are contrasted with "commoners"; in Vanuatu, according to Lind-strom (Chapter 11), "commoners do not exist": "Almost any ambitious and capable man, in some contexts, with a straight face, is able to call himself *jif*."

The distance between chiefs and commoners varies. Franco (Chapter 4) suggests there may be "kingly" and "populist" forms of chieftaincy, typified in turn by Tonga and Samoa. Yet he also cites Marcus, who found two sides of chieftaincy within Tonga itself: an affected disdain for formal titles, yet liking to have one's chiefliness known about (all the stronger because it is not shouted about).

Petersen (Chapter 9) has Micronesians voting strategically to maintain the triangular relationship between state, chief, and commoner. By voting against incorporating chiefs into the state, he argues, they ensured that chiefs would continue to protect them against it. They need a state to deal with other states; "but that does not mean they have decided to inflict this entity inward upon their own communities." (I wonder: people also need chiefs to deal with other chiefs, and chiefs are finally as "existentially absurd," in Petersen's phrase, as states). Petersen quotes a Chuukese account of codependency between chiefs and commoners: "The chiefs tell the people what to do, and the people tell the chiefs what to do." Such a codependency had a material basis. Chiefs often depended on commoners for subsistence, and were vulnerable to challenge from competitors, or assassination by commoners, if they overstepped the mark. Carucci (Chapter 10) notes how this social contract has broken down in Marshall Islands. Chiefs no longer need commoners. Resources now come from outside, and "it is only the goodwill of chiefs or government leaders that compels them to distribute the goods they control." The chief–commoner relationship has its counterpart in the contrast with states: ordinary people appear to states as subjects or, more democratically, as citizens.

So whom are chiefs against and who is against them? Lindstrom (Chapter 11) notes that Vanuatu's 1983 *kastom polisi* was "designed . . . to keep women and youth under closer control." Van Meijl's account of devolution to chieftaincies in New Zealand (Chapter 5) suggests that the opposition was between chiefs on the one hand and pantribal, urban Maori movements on the other.

In the "funeral rebellion" described by Adams (Chapter 14), ordinary people refused to distribute "select cuts of meat" to the local chiefs. They justified their rebellion in the egalitarian language of Pancasila, the state ideology, and Christianity. The chiefs naturally saw it as "a Communist tactic to destroy tradition, end religion, then build Communism." Similarly, James (Chapter 3) describes Tongan tenants refusing to bring pigs and foodstuffs, and berating their chief in front of guests. Or they "listened silently, then simply [would] not [carry] out the orders given to them."

The similarity of these Indonesian and Tongan occasions suggests we are dealing with a regular feature of rural life, whatever its cultural clothing or regional location. It is often described in historical or developmental terms, as a breakdown or falling away from an earlier period in which chiefs behaved as they should, and ordinary people "knew their place." Certainly, as Lawson suggests (Chapter 6), it is now easier for people to imagine alternatives to chiefly rule, though I suspect Fijian commoners may have always harbored utopian fantasies of a "world turned upside down" (as in the mixed feelings about the events of 1987, which were both for and against the chiefs). Political and economic changes have allowed chiefs to turn their backs on villagers.

Nevertheless, the contrast between the "true" chief and actual chiefs we meet every day seems to involve more than a statement about social change. Chiefs were probably always failing to live up to the high standards of their predecessors. Franco (Chapter 4) notes a sort of good chief/bad chief routine in Tonga, with the recently ennobled *nōpele* unfavorably contrasted with the preconstitutional *'eiki*, described by Marcus (1989: 20) as the "submerged aristocracy . . . in the shadows of the official chiefly establishment." What James (Chapter 3) calls the "estrangement between nobles and people" may have been always thus. And when a noble concedes that "antinoble sentiment" might be "due in part to some nobles abusing their authority and being dishonest to their people," he is making a general statement about rural power relationships, rather than a specifically modern statement about urbanization, or class conflict.

In this sense, "traditionalist" ideology can be critical as well as, in Lawson's argument (Chapter 6), conservative. It can justify the assassination of a chief for failing to live up to our expectations of chieftaincy. Or, as James notes (Chapter 3, quoting from the radical paper *Kele'a*), Tongan radicals can argue that impeaching a noble is a way of "maintaining the integrity of His Majesty's government and of promoting the confidence of the people in the system." James Scott's (1990) account of rural resistance and rebellion helps explain this critical quality of tradition. He argues that the historical record often only shows the "official transcript"—in our terms, the familiar rhetoric of reciprocal rights and obligations, caring and sharing, and respect for chiefs. But neither side really believes it. The powerful are always on guard against subversion. The powerless share a "hidden transcript" of secret languages, jokes, and dumb insolence that criticizes the powerful.

Scott goes on to argue against the idea of a dominant or hegemonic ideology, through which the powerful persuade the powerless that their rule is right and good. Instead, the picture is more complicated: on the one hand, neither the powerful nor the powerless believes completely in the ideology. On the other hand, the powerless criticize the powerful within their own terms: chiefs are criticized for being unchiefly; liberals for being illiberal; Marxists for being un-Marxist; bureaucrats for not following the rules. These internal critiques may be just as compelling as the construction of alternative ideologies, such as democratic critiques of chieftaincy, or anarchist critiques of the state. Chiefly and stately ideologies may well coexist today, and each contains the basis of its own critique.

REFERENCE MATTER

Notes

1. Although we use male pronouns to refer to chiefs in this chapter, it should be recognized that this is only a kind of default value, and that many significant instances of female chiefs exist throughout the Pacific. The gendering of local leadership categories is a topic that merits further exploration.

2. One could argue that the importance of traditional chiefs within the colonial state, particularly those in which rule was "indirect," might be explained by the colonialists' deficit of political legitimacy, by the absence of an educated elite to man the bureaucracies, by people's lack of familiarity with local democratic governance, and so forth. National independence, if all this were indeed the case, would soon see out the chiefs. Indigenous and legitimate central authority would now take the place of the retiring European colonials; educational systems would produce manpower for state bureaus; and the organs of democracy would metathesize throughout the countryside. Village mayors, community councils, and provincial parliaments would replace the antique chieftaincy. But this has not occurred. Rather, independent Pacific states have continued to find value and utility in chiefs, and the chiefs themselves have refused to surrender their traditional authority to modern politicians and bureaucrats.

3. This is not to invalidate the importance of efforts at systematic comparison and classification. Two papers presented at the symposium that gave rise to this volume indicate that important issues have yet to be resolved with regard to regional similarities and differences in indigenous forms of leadership. Richard Scaglion (1996) argues that in Papua New Guinea, forms of political hierarchy appropriately labeled as "chiefs" are generally found among Austronesian-speaking peoples (cf. Jolly and Mosko 1994). Similarly, Richard Feinberg (Feinberg and Watson-Gegeo 1996) finds a hierarchy continuum made up of diverse types of leadership characterized by different permutations of a limited set of cultural characteristics.

4. The preeminent among such labels has been "bigman," a word that Margaret Mead was among the first to use academically in a 1935 book, *Sex and Temperament in Three Primitive Societies* (see Lindstrom 1982a). This label, "big-

man," is particularly appealing in that it is a translation of indigenous terms for "leader" in numerous island vernaculars. The bigman has matriculated into a key figure in Melanesian ethnography. He stands at the center of a complex of economic and political structures found generally across the region, although the prototypic bigman inhabits Papua New Guinea, the Solomon Islands, and, to a lesser extent, Vanuatu.

Recently, anthropologists have bifurcated the bigman to locate yet another category of Pacific leader—the "great man" (see Godelier and Strathern 1991). Great men exist in societies whose exchange practices are constituted differently from those where bigmen operate. Great men flourish where public life turns on male initiation rather than ceremonial exchange, on the direct exchange of women in marriage, and on warfare pursued as homicide for homicide (ibid.: 1). Exchange in this sort of society requires a manifest balance—pig for pig, marital partner for marital partner, and homicide for homicide. This equivalence disallows the sorts of clever investment and exchange schemes that bigmen elsewhere use to turn economic obligation into political power. Great men instead deal in knowledge and services whose exchange is less constrained by demands for equivalence.

5. A central question has concerned the means by which bigmen acquire and hold power without the traditional authority that chiefly status accords, and without other institutionalized mechanisms of social control. A bigman who underperforms or overdemands may be elbowed aside by his competitors and/or abandoned by his community. Bigmen must rely on skills of oratory and persuasion, leading by example or by cajolery in hopes—not always fulfilled—that others will follow. Many bigmen acquire their influence through economic production and exchange. Other bigmen are such because of their specialized knowledge of genealogy, myth and history, curing, and magic; and the influence of some leaders once depended on physical strength and on strategic abilities in war as well.

CHAPTER 2

1. References within this chapter are to Western Samoa, not American Samoa. No attempt is made here to outline or explain the significant differences between the two.

2. As Gilson noted of the Me, "The missionary gave way to the Samoans . . . for the objects of the meeting—to generate enthusiasm for the *lotu* and to collect gifts from the congregations—were best served by letting the Samoan genius for ceremonial take its own course" (1970:100).

3. It is a moot point to consider what might have happened in other circumstances. Williams makes it clear that the chiefs enjoyed considerable power, and in any confrontation the missionaries would have been the likely losers.

4. Just how difficult this might have been became apparent to the priests of the Society of Mary, who found villages placing total bans, or *sa*, on the performance of Catholic religious services in villages and on their members' participation in any such services (Franco 1976:9).

5. To this day, pastors' activities are constrained by their dependence on their congregation for support. Congregations have been known to "discipline" pastors

by sudden, conspicuous withdrawal of financial support. When the value of the *alofa* or offertory declines by a significant amount, it generally indicates the congregation's reservations about a pastor's performance.

6. In view of the impact of commerce on other Pacific Island societies, notably Hawai'i and Tahiti, this concern was a valid one. The missionaries' concern was shared by the Samoans, who were also aware of the consequences of uncontrolled commerce.

7. One who chose sides, W. Pritchard, was treated later as a member of the *Vaivai*. Chiefs from the *Malo* petitioned the consuls for his removal on the grounds that this was the way the defeated were treated in Samoan custom.

8. Though Europeans could not control the chieftaincy and prevent war, they were able to exploit war to obtain land by exchanging weapons for land from both sides.

9. At the head of this government was the administrator, who, aided by various executive offices, was primarily responsible for the initiation and administration of policy. Below the administrator was the "native administration," an advisory body consisting of two high advisors (*fautua*); 31–33 deputies (*faipule*); 27–29 native judges (*fa 'amasino*), who acted as district executives and judicial officials; 14 native land commission advisors (*komisi*); 16 or 17 plantations inspectors (*pulefa 'atoaga*); 28–31 native clerks (*failautusi*); 56 policeman-messengers (*leoleo*); and between 142 and 150 mayors or managers (*pulenu 'u*), who acted as the government agents in the villages (F. M. Keesing 1934:145).

10. While in practical terms the power of the head of state is proscribed by Parliament (Articles 19, 20, 21, 23, 24, and 26), its symbolic significance should not be underestimated in status-conscious Western Samoa.

11. In this case, the Electoral Act of 1963 (Sections 16[a] and [b]).

12. Not all did so. In *Olomalu and Others v. the Attorney General* (1982), five untitled citizens alleged on various grounds that the Electoral Act had disenfranchised them and denied them equality before the law, which they were guaranteed in the constitution. Aeau S Epati persuaded Chief Justice St. John to state that "nothing short of universal suffrage for all citizens male and female who have attained the age of 21 years will suffice to satisfy the constitutional strictures as they now stand" (Powles 1986:210). The significance of this judgment forced the government to appeal, and the Court of Appeals in *The Attorney General v. Olomalu and Others* (1982) found that the electoral provisions were discriminatory, but accepted that "it was never intended that Article 15 of the Constitution should apply to electoral arrangements" (Powles 1986:211).

13. Amongst these were such titles as Apa Kerosini (Kerosene Can) and Apa Masi (Biscuit Barrel).

14. The legal grounds for this legislation were that under Section 16(b) of the Electoral Act of 1963, electors' names had to appear on the Register of *Matai* established and kept pursuant to the [Samoan] Lands and Titles Protection Ordinance (1934). These newly created "titles" did not in most cases qualify. In addition, the new titles were not held in accordance with Samoan custom and usage, and with law relating to Samoan custom and usage as required in Section 100 of the constitution.

15. The Electoral Amendment Act was passed in November 1990 and was the first amendment to the earlier act.

16. The Law Society's submission noted possible conflicts between an individual's rights guaranteed by the Western Samoan constitution and those rights assigned to *Fono*. Their reservations were not considered sufficiently pressing to lead to significant revision, and the Act was passed without substantial amendment.

17. The court in this case is the Lands and Titles Court and not a civil court (Section 11.8)

18. The Council of Europe's aid, for instance, is connected with recognition by recipients of rights set out in its *Strasbourg Consensus* of 1983 (Davidson 1993).

CHAPTER 3

1. The 1862 "Emancipation Edict" is quoted in Chapter 4.

2. Some town officers who are not high-ranking men in their villages by traditional criteria have managed to manipulate new sources of power and wealth to build up their own reputations in ways that the Falahola officer has never attempted. For example, when hurricane relief funds flowed into Tonga after Cyclone Isaac occurred in 1982, town officers were given the dual responsibilities of recording the extent of damage to individual households for the purpose of compensation, and immediately allocating the tents, food, tools, and other equipment that had been rapidly flown in by overseas aid agencies. The more cunning officers tried to imbue their carrying out of government orders with nuances of a gift (*me'a 'ofa*), which traditionally accompanies the largesse of the great to the small, to impose upon recipients of the foreign aid a sense of personal obligation to the town officers involved. Clearly, the power lay with the "givers," and villagers had to appease in some degree the agents of so much wealth and authority. But they inwardly sneered at "the little men who have suddenly become big." The mixture of outward deference to form, but inward jealousy and opportunism, typically accompanies attempts to control new sources of power in this highly competitive society.

3. Remarks made by H.R.H. Princess Pilolevu Tuita, patroness of the Tongan History Association, at its May 1992 meeting held at Brigham Young University, Laie, Hawai'i.

CHAPTER 5

1. For a historical reconstruction of the model of Maori tribal organizations presented in this section, see Van Meijl (1995a).

2. Since it is unlikely that the *waka* or "canoes" accomplished political functions in precolonial Maori society, it is also improbable that leadership at this level was distinguished.

3. Elsewhere I have developed this argument in more detail (Van Meijl 1994). In this article I also develop a critique of Dumont's assumption of ideology as a coherent and consistent system of beliefs.

4. It is beyond the scope of this chapter to explore the transformation of Maori

sociopolitical organization in the period extending from the beginning of colonial settlement in New Zealand until the implementation of the devolution policy in the 1980s. For a brief analysis of the changes in the sociopolitical organization of one tribal confederation, that of the Tainui people, see Van Meijl 1994.

5. The main argument of this chapter on chiefly interests in the policy of devolution of the Department of Maori Affairs is ethnographically illustrated with examples of the Tainui confederation of tribes, among which I conducted fieldwork for a period of twenty-five months altogether in 1982–83 and again in 1987–88.

6. In the Maori version of the Treaty of Waitangi, the term "sovereignty" was translated with *kawanatanga*, a hitherto unknown transliteration of "governship." It is often argued that if the British concept of sovereign power and authority had been translated more correctly with the term *mana*, the Maori chiefs would have been reluctant to sign the treaty (cf. Orange 1987:40–41).

7. Traditionally a *marae* was the courtyard in front of an ancestral meetinghouse used for community assembly. Recently this narrow meaning of *marae* has been distinguished as *marae aatea* or "*marae* proper." Nowadays the strict meaning of *marae* is frequently broadened to include the complex around the plaza, such as the meetinghouse, a dininghall, an ablution block, and sometimes various dwellings (Metge 1976:227–45; Salmond 1975:31–90). Colloquially, however, the term *marae* is often also used in reference to the community that owns the *marae* complex and that, occasionally, resides in its vicinity.

8. This compensation agreement has meanwhile been superseded by a new comprehensive settlement of the confiscations signed by the British Crown and the Maori queen in 1995. The most recent settlement includes a formal apology from the Crown, acknowledging it acted unjustly in dealing with the King Movement in 1863, and it provides for the return of 15,790 *ha*, or approximately 39,000 acres, of Crown land, which is about 2% of the lands originally confiscated, over a period of five years, in most cases excluding all buildings. The value of the lands recently returned is estimated at approximately NZ$170 million, while the proceeds from the rents and leases of the lands could amount to between NZ$7 and 14 million a year.

9. In the past, aristocrats of chiefly descent were categorically distinguished from commoners of lower rank as *rangatira* on the one hand, and *ware* or *tuutuuaa* on the other (cf. Winiata 1956:229). In contemporary circumstances, however, these labels are completely outdated, in spite of the continuing significance of the chiefly or nonchiefly nature of genealogies.

10. Although "devolution" dominated the political debate on "Maori Affairs" in the late 1980s, publications on the issue are still extremely limited. I know of only one article dealing specifically with "devolution" (see Fleras 1991; see also Fleras and Elliott 1992:172–218); it discusses the political development of devolution from 1988 and its impact on the relation between Maori tribes and the New Zealand government. It does not address the sociocultural implications of the policy of devolution, which are the object of the discussion here.

11. A synopsis of submissions to the government about the paper on its devolution policy was published in July 1988 (Maori Affairs Department 1988b).

12. These views were quoted in the Maori language in an article by Piripi Whaanga and Tawini Rangihau published in the *New Zealand Listener* (1988).

13. Maaka (1994) and Levine and Henare (1994) also question the use of tribal organizations as the primary vehicles for Maori development.

14. Maaka (1994:329) has made the important point that a policy making immigrant Maori groups in cities dependent on the "hospitality" of local Maori tribes would simply involve a diversion from dependence on a European-dominated state system to dependence on a system controlled by bureaucratic organizations of tribes to which they were not affiliated.

15. Lawson (Chapter 6 in this volume) discusses in more detail the conflicts between democratic discourses and chiefly authority in Fiji.

16. The National party of New Zealand was reelected to the office of government in November 1993.

CHAPTER 6

1. See especially Section 156 of the *Constitution of the Sovereign Democratic Republic of Fiji* (Fiji 1990), which sets out the biological requirements for claiming status as a "Fijian," a "Rotuman," or an "Indian." Here the father's biological/ethnic status is decisive, while the mother's may only be used where the father is unknown (or unacknowledged). This section also makes provision for persons to be recognized as Fijians "by virtue of custom, tradition and practice," making it possible under some circumstances for persons without the requisite biological credentials to acquire "Fijiness." This, however, is subject to confirmation or determination by the Native Lands Commission. Nonetheless, it has enabled one prominent businessman, Jim Ah Koy (of undisputed Chinese paternity, but with close links to the Fijian political elite) to acquire legal status as a Fijian. See "So Who Really Is a Fijian?" (*Islands Business Pacific* [Feb. 1992]: 19, 20, 23.

2. For an account of the 1994 elections, see Lal 1995.

3. Lal's 1995 study incorporates some interesting aspects of local Fijian politics, as does his earlier study (Lal 1992). A discussion of historic regional factors and their significance in Fijian politics may also be found in Lawson 1990.

4. Again, Lal's (1992 and 1995) studies provide some analysis of this. Also very useful is an analysis, written in the wake of the coup, by J. D. Kelly (1988).

5. Economic considerations played a part, too; thus Governor Gordon summarized the advantages of indirect rule through a chiefly system as the means by which the colony could be "most peaceably, cheaply and easily governed" (see Great Britain 1887, no. 11:34).

6. For a historical account of the descending thesis of government in Europe, see Ullman 1975: esp. 13, 18, 33–34.

7. For further discussion of "Occidentalist" discourses, see also Lawson 1993, 1996a; and Carrier 1995.

8. More extensive treatments of these and other relevant aspects of the early colonial history of Fiji can be found in France 1969; Lawson 1991; and Lal 1992.

9. In the period immediately before colonization, Cakobau had assumed the title of Tu'i Viti, or "King" of Fiji, largely as a result of political machinations and

conflicts involving Europeans. The latter were keen to attach such a title to a leading chief so as to try and establish some kind of supreme central authority in the islands, thus making dealings more convenient.

10. It should be noted, however, that by the time of formal colonization, contact with missionaries and traders had already wrought changes in political relations within Fijian polities.

11. Gordon's determination to protect the "Fijian way of life" was also a major factor in the decision to import Indian indentured labor to work the colony's plantations (on which the colony's hopes for economic viability depended) rather than disrupt Fijian village life by using indigenous labour.

12. This follows the general framework set out in Sahlins's seminal article (1963:285–303) and applied to Fiji by various writers including Norton (1977: 54). The accuracy of the labels "Melanesian" and "Polynesian" in the Fijian context has been challenged by Thomas (1989:33), but defended as conceptually and analytically useful in Lawson 1990:801–3.

13. Since Ganilau's death, Mara has moved on to the presidency.

14. Even with this, it should be noted that the elements now comprising the eastern chiefly establishment were themselves quite diverse in the precolonial era, and their subsequent consolidation as a political entity clearly took place as a result of the exigencies of colonial administration.

15. For a brief survey of this debate, see Jolly and Thomas 1992:241–48.

16. This is an excerpt from a statement issued by the governor-general's post-coup Council of Advisors, reported in the *Sydney Morning Herald* (June 25, 1987:13).

CHAPTER 7

1. See Marcus 1989 for a discussion of these two aspects of Polynesian chieftainship.

2. For more on the importance of reciprocity in Rotuman social organization, see Rensel 1994.

3. In 1951 H. S. Evans identified 121 titled men in a population of 2,780; he estimated that 17% of adult males held a title (Evans 1951). Today it is much more difficult to determine how many title holders there are or what their ratio is to adult males since the major portion of Rotumans resides off island in Fiji. Many title holders leave the island, either for extended periods or permanently. Others make regular sojourns abroad, resulting in significant variations in number of resident title-holders from month to month.

4. The Rotuman term *gagaj(a)*, as a noun, translates as "chief," "lord," "sir," "gentleman," "lady." It is also used as a respectful collective reference to the people of a designated locality or district. As an adjective it not only designates chiefly rank, it can also be used as a complimentary adjunct, as in *'ou han gagaja*, "your good wife." As a verb it means "to treat as a chief," "to respect," "to look up to" (Churchward 1940:209).

Although previously Rotuman chiefs were known simply by their individual titles, following independence from British colonial rule they decided to append the term "Gagaj," e.g., Gagaj Maraf, Gagaj Kausiriaf. They explicitly rejected using "Chief" on the grounds that the term is used in English to designate common occupations such as "chief cook" or "chief engineer." Nevertheless, when speaking in English, almost all Rotumans refer to titled individuals as "chiefs."

5. The term *ho'aga* is the noun form of the word *ho'a*, "to carry," the prototypical form of productive labor.

6. Although in fact all known title holders have been male in recorded history, it is not inconceivable for a woman to hold a title and assume a chiefly role. A few years ago, a highly regarded retired female schoolteacher was seriously considered for the position of district chief. Presumably she would have taken a title if installed.

7. Recorded in a dispatch from H. Romilly to Western Pacific High Commissioner, Sept. 28, 1880 (Outward Letters).

8. Ibid.

9. Dispatch from C. Mitchell to Governor of Fiji, Oct. 12, 1881 (Outward Letters).

10. For examples, see Minutes of the Rotuma Council of Chiefs, Sept. 1, 1910, and dispatch from A. E. Cornish to Colonial Secretary, Jan. 30, 1939 (Outward Letters).

11. Dispatch from W. Carew to Colonial Secretary, Feb. 5, 1931 (Outward Letters).

12. Previously each district sent a representative—but that representative was chosen by the chief, and acted more or less as the chief's assistant.

13. As pointed out earlier, the Rotuman chiefs who ceded Rotuma to Great Britain expected to be granted the same prerogatives as Fijian chiefs, only to be thwarted by the colonial administration. The postindependence government, however, is based in Fijian chieftainship and appears to support chiefly privilege in Rotuma based on the Fijian model. Although we have no way of verifying it, the backing of the prime minister for the chiefs may well have been inspired by an intensification of the politics of indigenous tradition following independence.

14. Parliamentary Debates (Dec. 11, 1984); district officer of Rotuma, personal communication, Mar. 1992.

15. Letter from the dissident leaders to the president of the Republic of Fiji, dated Apr. 27, 1988.

16. *Fiji Times* (June 10, 1988): 12, 13, 41. For a broader discussion of the independence movement, see Howard 1992.

17. In testimony to the Constitutional Review Committee, a representative of the dissident group specifically objected to proposals to classify Rotumans as *taukei*, demanding "the right to be called, FAMOR ROTUMA [Rotuman People] or KAINAG ROTUMA [ethnic Rotumans] and not Taukei Rotuman."

18. See Rensel 1993 for more on the socioeconomic impacts of Rotuma's connection with Fiji.

19. Between the start of the loan program in 1988 and June 1990, more than 130 personal loans were given out by the Rotuma branch of the National Bank of Fiji. At least two-thirds of the individuals who took out loans were employed. The average loan was $F3,300. Most were used to make housing improvements or to

purchase vehicles or appliances. Only two of the seven district chiefs were loan recipients, one for $F1,500, the other for $F520. It was bank policy to favor wage earners since they were regarded as better risks.

20. Some caveats are in order concerning the nature of the information we have used to construct our account. Although we were witness to some of the events described, we have relied to a great extent on verbal accounts related to us by Rotuman friends and acquaintances, including the main actors in the drama. The narrative should therefore not be regarded as an authoritative account of what actually occurred, but rather as a distillation of Rotuman conceptions of events and their social significance. Biases—ours and those of our informants—no doubt color the account. Although we did our best to remain neutral vis-à-vis the disputes that occurred, attitudes were attributed to us by Rotuman participants, and this affected what they told us.

In many respects our account is superficial. Disputes on Rotuma are usually multilayered, sometimes going back several generations. They are complicated by multistranded networks of shifting social relationships. It is therefore impossible to fully fathom motivations for actions taken, even for intimates. Nevertheless, we believe this narrative, at a minimum, accurately reflects the issues with which Rotumans are currently grappling as they strive to adapt chieftainship to modern conditions.

We also wish to acknowledge that Oinafa district should not be taken as representative of all Rotuma. One of two chiefly districts (the other being Noa'tau), Oinafa is particularly noted for taking chieftainship and chiefly protocol extremely seriously. Also, a disproportionate number of successful Rotumans abroad are from Oinafa, possibly reflecting its chiefly heritage. In addition, the district is notorious for its pattern of interbreeding, reflected in the close kin relations among its elite. However, we should point out that the problems brought out by the account have definite resonances in other districts. For example, in October 1995, upon the death of the district chief of Itu'ti'u, two factions formed, each installing its own chief. The dispute continued until October 1996, when it was resolved via the government-sanctioned intervention of Paul Manueli, Minister for Home Affairs. Parts of the district, dissatisfied with the decision, have threatened to leave the district.

21. See Howard 1994 for a biography of Wilson Inia and a more comprehensive history of the Rotuma Cooperative Association.

22. Kausiriaf's apology is a good example of an attempt to adapt chiefly practice to contemporary circumstances. The fact that it did not work provides further evidence of the erosion of traditional mechanisms available to chiefs.

23. Fijians evidently found it hard to accept that as eldest son of a Rotuman chief, Rigamoto was not also a chief. Furthermore, his leadership qualities and general demeanor apparently fit their notions of chiefliness. For their part, Rotumans also recognize behavior that is *fakgagaja*, "in a chiefly manner," quite apart from holding a title (see Howard 1986:21).

24. The *mosega* seems to have become increasingly problematic with regards to the selection of a chief since it has become so large, spread out, and amorphous. It is difficult to determine who belongs and who does not, and to assemble a rep-

resentative group. The question of whether *mosega* members in Fiji and abroad should have a say is ambiguous and subject to debate. This is one of several factors operating to undermine the legitimation of chiefly authority.

25. It was also rumored that he was planning to see the president of Fiji, Ratu Ganilau, who is presumably a distant relative of Kausiriaf's wife.

26. Justice Byrne based his ruling on Section 18.2 of the Rotuma Act, which says that the prime minister of Fiji can remove a Rotuman district chief from his position. He interpreted this to mean that *only* the prime minister could do so.

27. Poar told us that he was content to lead and organize the people and let Kausiriaf have the title and fill the ceremonial role. In fact, he said, when he first came from Fiji, his intention was to propose that Kausiriaf apologize to the *mosega* and that he would help lead the district. But when he arrived Kausiriaf was in Suva. Then when Kausiriaf published the ad in the paper (after Poar had been installed), it was too late to make amends.

28. For a discussion of the importance of houses in the Rotuman value system, see Rensel 1991.

29. See Howard 1996 for an extended discussion of moral authority on Rotuma.

30. The effects of this ambiguity have been compounded by radical changes in media availability. Rotumans in Fiji have access to radio (and more recently to television) time, they post letters to the editors and write stories for Fiji's newspapers, and they produce pamphlets and booklets for special occasions. Expressions of opinion in these media reach a much larger audience than those reached by the (largely ceremonial) speeches of chiefs. In a very important sense, therefore, chiefs have been marginalized from communication networks that inform Rotuman opinion. As our case study illustrates, however, some of them have recognized the power of mass media and have made efforts to use it in the service of personal politics.

CHAPTER 8

1. This begs the further question: what sort of group or category? I shall return to this question after discussing the F.S.M. data; but of course the answers for other contemporary Pacific multicultural nations may be different from the answer for the F.S.M.

2. Of course, discourse itself can be analyzed as practice, and both indigenes and outside analysts can engage in meta-discourse, or talk about talk, e.g., discussions of chiefly oratory or discussions of the appropriateness of the etymology of a status title. However, I think it is important to emphasize that social action extends beyond discourse. We are in danger of losing our connections to the worlds of social actors if we use discourse as a metaphor or methodological tool that encompasses everything. Social actions (including, but not limited to, talk) have consequences that go beyond discourse—people engage in behavior that can harm or kill themselves or others, make or break exchange relationships and end up changing their options for whom they can marry or foster, make or break political careers with potential ramifications for the larger social order.

3. This chapter can be read as background to Petersen's Chapter 9 on the discussion in the 1990 F.S.M. constitutional convention on the proposal for a Chamber of Chiefs, demonstrating the complexity obscured by talk about "chiefs" in the F.S.M. as a single category. My own interpretation of what happened with that proposal at the constitutional convention itself is somewhat different from the one Petersen gives here. The discussions about the proper role of the chiefs were certainly a part of the story, but what was more crucial in gaining support for the proposal at the convention was the role that the Chamber of Chiefs could potentially play in checking the power of the F.S.M. Congress and supporting the executive branch. That was why former F.S.M. president Nakayama supported the proposal. As Petersen says, the importance of checks on power seems to be a common element in indigenous Micronesian political theory. No other viable alternative for correcting the imbalance between the Congress and the president—arguably a mistake made at the 1975 constitutional convention—had emerged during the 1990 convention.

4. Cf. Meller (1969:126) on the withdrawal of the Pohnpei paramount chiefs from the Ponape Island Congress in the 1950s.

5. The compact between the United States and the F.S.M., which holds for a fifteen-year period terminating in 2001, retains U.S. control over Micronesia only in regard to matters of defense and military denial of the area to other powers. In return, the F.S.M. receives over $1.4 billion in aid from the United States over the fifteen years.

6. Benedict Anderson's (1983) notion of a nation as an "imagined community" is relevant here: he cites particular sorts of discourse, e.g., newspapers and novels, as being critical in the formation of nationhood. I would argue, however, that his notion of imagination is somewhat too passive and literary. In regard to leadership, discourse about leadership develops in relation to practical action, as is exemplified by many of the cases described in this volume. These actions, and reactions to them, shape communities in ways that are not only imagined, but also embodied in the routines of everyday life.

7. The "q" in *thaaq*, following the new Yapese orthography instituted by the Yapese Orthography Committee in 1972, stands for a glottal stop (Jensen 1977). I have not here modified the spelling of Yapese words frequently used in the previous anthropological literature on Yap (*tabinaw, sowai*) to reflect the new orthography.

8. Elections were formerly held for chief magistrate, under the Trust Territory administration, but they are no longer held. The 1974 Yap District Code includes a provision for the election of chief magistrates, but it was later repealed by the legislature. Lingenfelter examined the data from chief magistrate elections (1952–68) and showed that the results of the elections closely followed traditional ranking: "In all recorded elections since 1952, a majority of the magistrates have been selected from the traditional hereditary elite of the highest ranking village in the municipalities" (Lingenfelter 1975:221).

9. Lingenfelter describes the tributary relationships and the associated estates as follows:

> [In Gacpar the estate] Ethow . . . holds a *sowai* "trade" relationship with Fasulus, Mogmog, the Yap-defined residence of the paramount

chief of Ulithi. The estate Pebinaw . . . is second in Gacpar to Ethow
with regard to the outer islands and maintains a trade relationship with
the house at Falaglow, Mogmog. In Wonyan, the chief of Riyeleb estate
(who is also sitting-chief of Wonyan) is high chief over trade from the
outer islands and second in rank to Ethow [another estate]. The chief of
Riyeleb is the chief of the atolls east of Ulithi and has direct trade relationships with the chiefs of Fais, Woleai, (Wotagay and Fananus sections, respectively), and Ifalik [Ifaluk] (Lugalop section). The chief of
the estate Low, who is also village chief of Wonyan . . . , is second to the
chief of Riyeleb, and maintains trade relationships in Fais and Woleai.
Other titled estates in Wonyan and Gacpar have trade relationships
with particular islands or sections of islands in each atoll. (Lingenfelter
1975:150)

10. In this connection, it is interesting to note that when the Nahnmwarki of
Madolenihmw died in 1990, there were two funerals held for him on Pohnpei:
one, following Mwoakillese custom, in an area of Mwoakillese settlement in Kolonia; the other, following Pohnpeian custom, and with some of the Pohnpei
Nahnmwarkis and other high-titled people as guests, held in the Pohnpei state
nahs (a meetinghouse recently built for state functions, in traditional style, located
behind the state office buildings). Some Mwoakillese consider themselves closer to
Pohnpeians than the other outer islanders, somewhat analogous to the position of
Ulithi within Yap state. Feasting and funeral customs are major markers of ethnic
boundaries between Pohnpeians and outer islanders.

11. He had been involved in a notorious incident in 1983, while on Pohnpei
for a session of Congress. He had been caught with a Chuukese man's wife. The
man waited for him outside the Congress chambers with a machete for three
weeks. Finally, one of the Chuukese congressmen interceded and pacified the man,
and the Kosraen senator was able to return to work. He was subsequently reelected; his family was large and powerful, and people also said that he was very
generous. In 1987, when his health was failing, a challenger defeated him. The
longtime congressman's older brother is a respected pastor—he has represented
Kosrae at national meetings as a traditional leader delegate. He leads a very different lifestyle, to which he attributes his better health.

12. Perhaps as a way of commenting on the absurdities of his role-shifting from
prop to agent, although I do not think he consciously thought of it that way, this
Nahnmwarki had two costumes in which he appeared at large public gatherings.
One, which he wore at the feast at his meetinghouse, was a "grass" skirt made out
of a burlap rice-sack, an updated version of the precolonial Pohnpei men's fiber
skirt. The other, which he usually wore at government functions, was a three-piece
suit, complete with vest (this, in a very humid tropical climate).

13. Micronesians sometimes comment that the Yap traditional leaders run the
Yapese delegation from behind the scenes, but my information—from my own observations and from interviews—leads me to conclude that the traditional leaders
defer to the expertise of college-educated Yapese holding elective/bureaucratic office in matters relating to national legislation, international relations, and most
things that belong in the world outside of Yap. These traditional leaders, however,

do play an important role in deciding who among the bright, younger Yapese has the chance at higher education and political office, so most of the Yapese now in elective/bureaucratic office were their protégés.

14. See Meller 1985 and Pinsker 1981 on the 1975 Micronesian constitutional convention.

15. For a discussion of reworking the concept of culture to adequately reflect the complexities of the differential distribution of knowledge in contemporary communities, see Hannerz 1992.

16. There was one incident in 1985 that was much discussed among the Yapese, when the Nahnken of Nett accosted the lieutenant governor of Yap in a bar, reportedly grabbing him by his shirt collar. The lieutenant governor managed to get out of the Nahnken's grasp and walk out, but then one of a group of Pohnpeian boys who had come in with the Nahnken hit a Yapese outer-island boy on the head, and a brawl ensued. Some Pohnpeians apparently suggested that the Yapese bring the Nahnken to court, but they declined, not wanting to offend Pohnpeians, especially because a traditional leader was involved.

17. When I was in Yap, living in the north in Maap, people there said the Yapese chiefs in the south could not control the young men in their villages. They also commented on the general problem of finding enough older people to fill chiefly statuses; there are few older people and many younger people, because of previous depopulation followed by a recent rise in the birth rate. Since the traditional Yapese polity was more or less a gerontocracy, that has created problems for social control.

18. In contemporary F.S.M., many atoll people have left the limited space of the atolls, and come to the state centers in the high islands (Yap, Wone in Chuuk lagoon, Pohnpei, Kosrae), which are centers of governments and business-related employment. Low islanders have a limited ability to gain status within the traditional systems of the high islands (although, over time, marriage and other forms of alliance and exchange can create opportunities to gain, at least for the next generations, traditional status within the high-island society). This has resulted in many low islanders taking advantage of the opportunities for advancement offered by Western education and the colonial and postcolonial government. Hence many of the positions in the Chuuk and Pohnpei state governments and the national government have been taken by people whose families are from the atolls in the southern Chuuk state and eastern Pohnpei state. Several Yapese outer islanders have achieved high positions in the national government (the second president of the F.S.M. was outer-island Yapese), but their opportunities within the executive branch of the Yap state government have been more limited than for outer islanders in Chuuk or Pohnpei.

CHAPTER 9

1. One item on the referendum ballot would have changed the requirement for approval from a three-quarters majority in three states to a simple majority in three states. Had forty-nine more voters in Kosrae voted in favor of this item, a majority of the proposed amendments would have been approved.

2. The 1975 Micronesian constitutional convention included representatives from the Marshalls, Palau, and Marianas districts, each of which went on to negotiate separate political status agreements with the United States. One of the reasons the F.S.M. called the 1990 ConCon was the widely shared sense that the constitution should be shriven of these non-F.S.M. influences.

3. In this matter, the Yapese position was similar to Pohnpei's: the national government in Micronesia is not a traditional category and thus does not represent traditional values or practices. In being "Micronesian" it is neither Yapese, Chuukese, Pohnpeian, nor Kosraen.

4. Pohnpei state, like Chuuk and Yap, is composed of a large high island with a *relatively* homogenous society, and a number of outlying coral atolls inhabited by peoples with cultures more or less distinct from that of the high island.

5. Although Yap's and Pohnpei's chiefly systems also entail ceaseless status competition, it is usually possible to find *some* agreement on which titles are currently ascendant. This is one of the marked differences between Chuuk on the one hand and Yap and Pohnpei on the other.

6. A request to recall a defeated proposal had to come from someone who had voted against it.

7. A major aspect of rank on Pohnpei is *wahu*, which generally means "honor." Pohnpeians explain that the term is a metaphor, referring to the "valley" (*wahu*) that separates those of high rank from the rest of the populace. Being "born above the ditch" refers to the great gulf that distinguishes a paramount chief from all others. A child born to a paramount chief, in Pohnpeian political theory, is indeed born to rule, or at least to reign.

8. For the most part, delegates to the 1990 ConCon turned a blind eye to the original constitutional convention. In the case of the Chamber of Chiefs proposal, however, the delegates made continual reference to the attempts in 1975 to grapple with issues of custom and tradition, and much of their debate can only be understood in the context of questions left open by the ambiguous outcome of the 1975 convention—i.e., the clause that allowed for but did not require establishment of a Chamber of Chiefs.

9. While the ConCon was in session, access to the chamber floor was strictly limited to delegates and official staff. This episode was the only occasion on which I saw anyone else enter onto the floor.

10. This was the only delegate speech made from a podium. Acting in his capacity as "talking chief," the Nahnken was assuming the normal chiefly position: raised up above everyone else present.

11. It is worth noting that this expression of President Nakayama's support for the proposal came in response to a direct request, from the chair, for his views. His comportment in this instance illustrates exactly the restraint that is so highly valued in Micronesian leaders.

CHAPTER 10

1. As Lindstrom points out, each of these authors constructs a view of cargo that elaborates upon a certain interpretational frame or genre and relies on recurrent

tropes (Lindstrom 1993). But knowing that the interpretations vary does not imply that all are of equal value. Indeed, the richness of any particular interpretation can be assessed by a close consideration of its relation to local discourse and practice.

2. Rynkiewich notes:

> Aristocratic women are to be very demure and circumspect in their behavior. Aristocratic men must refrain from speaking loudly and staring lest the intensity of their presence destroy both people and houses. Paramount chiefs are expected to be fair and generous. "The paramount chief has three stomachs: one for food, one for storing people's gossip, and one as a storehouse of goods for the people." The paramount chief is said to be in a position to manipulate people and land rights for the good of the community because only he has an overview of the whole. (1972:65)

3. One tale that legitimizes this relationship and subtly criticizes today's chiefs is as follows:

> Do you see those fellows who are my agemates, in their stories [on the radio] they say that all of us should look upward and watch the approach of a bird which is the highest of all in the Marshalls, the frigate (*ak*). This is the chief of all of the birds of the sky. Well, all of the birds should look upward and observe the bird that is highest up. . . . Now the bird will stay up there on high and watch all of the other birds gather together below, feeding on the sea and making food for themselves. So it goes, onward, until they are full and fly upward to the middle part of the sky and, then, [the frigate] flies downward to scream out "AAK!" And all of the birds vomit, and now [the frigate] eats [these regurgitated morsels] solely from the air. Now, this is true if one is a chief nowadays. Nonetheless, the frigate must watch over the "strength" [commoners], and the common birds must also care for the frigate. The chiefs also watch their commoners and the commoners must watch out for their chief. But if the chief does not still care for the commoners, well, that is in error. Now, these days, when we look at how things are, it is not very good the way the chiefs watch over us. (Carucci, 1990 field notes)

4. In this chapter, I avoid attributing quotes to their authors in order to protect them from sanction. From an analytic perspective, this is a bad choice, since the ability to understand the genesis and form of utterances and social actions derives from the way in which they can be contextualized in relation to components of social identity, both general and specific. Nevertheless, in today's Marshall Islands the risks to consultants outweigh all analytic advantages.

5. Yanaihara agrees with this assessment, noting that "the German government gave proprietorship to the first and second chieftains" (1940:142).

6. Few Marshallese are aware of the contradictions between American ideology and practice. Nonetheless, the way in which American practice, not ideology, has imposed itself on the Marshallese situation to create a new set of contradictions is most apparent to those who live in this newly negotiated order.

7. The degree to which class can be used to describe emerging Pacific social

orders is a topic of current concern. While I do not believe it to be a very useful category in the analysis of the Marshall Islands, there is little doubt that the difference between rich and poor has increased dramatically in the past thirty years. I use "bourgeois" in regard to chiefs, to refer to the new conflation between rank and monetary well-being, and to the contradiction between this new arrangement and the previous status quo, where chiefs who meddled in earthly affairs placed their sacred rank at risk.

8. Kuwajleen and Majuro atolls combined today contain well over three-quarters of the total population of the Republic of the Marshall Islands.

9. A common strategy used by Marshall Islanders to voice their dissatisfaction with current chiefs is to valorize the relationships between ancient chiefs and commoners and to see current-day relationships as being less sufficient than in the past. Rynkiewich makes note of this same strategy on Arno in the early 1970s (1972: 81), and it was frequently used on Wūjlañ in the late 1970s. This strategy safely distances the speaker from the implication that any particular one of today's chiefs is to blame. It also reinforces a widely accepted theory of degeneration in which current-day activities and beings are but meager representations of their ancient counterparts (Carucci 1997).

CHAPTER II

1. Following Larmour (1992:102), I define the state as "a permanent, largely bureaucratic apparatus" that is staffed by a government of "politicians and senior officials who try, with more or less success, to give state activity coherence and direction." Definition of "chiefs" is discussed in the text. As far as I am aware, all Vanuatu *jifs* are male.

2. Vanuatu's traditional "chieftaincy," it seems to me, was less solidly established an institution than Miles (1993) sometimes implies.

3. I draw here on discussions with Jif Willie Bongmatur, who served as the Malvatumauri's first president until his retirement in 1993 (see Aaron 1981). He was succeeded by Jif Noël Mariasua of Emau.

4. See W. L. Rodman (1985:617–19) for an acccount of the founding of the Ambae Island Council of Chiefs.

5. Sokomanu got in trouble when he supported Barak Sope's challenge to Walter Lini's leadership of the Vanua'aku party.

CHAPTER I2

1. I use quotation marks here and elsewhere in this chapter to indicate that I am referring to English-language phrasings commonly used in the Solomon Islands.

2. Many other examples could be cited of legislative interest in "traditional chiefs" elsewhere in the Pacific. For example, in Bougainville—another society troubled by deep national divisions and military confrontation—district chief councils sought to represent local interests in national and international discussions. In the French colonial territory of New Caledonia, the high commissioner met for the first time with the territory's Council of Traditional Chiefs in 1991 and

is reported to have said that the council "had a voice in most major questions in the territory" (Radio Australia, Feb. 9, 1991). In the Federated States of Micronesia, one of the amendments produced by a recent constitutional convention concerned the creation of a "chamber of traditional chiefs" that would "advise on and promote custom and tradition as well as promote peace and unity in the F.S.M." (JK Report on Micronesia 4[10] [Apr. 1991]:4; see Petersen, ch.9).

3. The now-classic distinction between the personalistic, achieved legitimacy of the Melanesian "bigman" and the inherited, titled position of the Polynesian "chief" (Sahlins 1963) has been increasingly challenged as a basis for interpreting the many varieties of Melanesian leadership, especially those of eastern Melanesia in the Solomons, Vanuatu, and New Caledonia (Douglas 1979; Allen 1984; Lilley 1985). Ironically, these challenges come at a time when the term "bigman" has become almost standard usage in writings about the Pacific, including those by Melanesian authors (e.g., Alasia 1989).

4. An example here would be the comments of some of the members of the national Parliament during debate on the 1985 amendment to the Local Courts Act, which empowered chiefs to hear land cases before entering the formal court system. During that debate, the member from northeast Guadalcanal commented: "My contention really is that I find that in my own area we do not really have chiefs as such, land matters are dealt with by people who know about land matters [but] they do not necessarily have to be chiefs. They could either be tribal leaders or heads of families and so forth" (Solomon Islands 1985a:594).

5. The legislation produced from these discussions sidestepped the definitional problems associated with such open-ended conceptions by defining "chief" in terms of itself: "'Chiefs' means chiefs or other traditional leaders residing within the locality of the land in dispute who are recognised as such by both parties in the dispute" (Solomon Islands 1985b:4).

6. The cousins' contrast between local, chiefly styles of dealing with conflict and modern legalistic methods reflects the comments by Andrew Nori, member of Parliament, during the parliamentary debates about the Local Courts Act amendment. Nori, principal sponsor of the act, described its purpose in terms of the ideals of Melanesian consensus and reciprocity (as opposed to Western confrontational practices):

> In Solomon Islands Mr. Speaker whenever there is a dispite [sic] whether it be over land ownership . . . or an infringement of customary norms, the basic aims [sic] of those persons entrusted with the responsibility of resolving the dispute is not winning or losing, their aim is to bring about happiness, friendship, peace and harmony in the community, in the end . . . there may be a feast which will reduce tension and human relationship normalised. (Solomon Islands 1985a:571)

CHAPTER 13

1. The "Sub-District Committee" was historically derivative of the postwar Maasina Rule anticolonial movement. See Keesing 1978, 1980, 1981, 1982c, 1992a; Fifi'i 1989; and Laracy 1983.

2. I use *kastomu*, the local rendering, to indicate that I am referring to the specifically Kwaio usage of this term; when I refer to other language groups or to the general regional ideology hypostasizing an idealized cultural tradition, I use *kastom*.

3. Or alternatively, *alafa*, an indigenous term but one relatively empty of salience in Kwaio; its cognate *araha* designates chiefly statuses in the languages of the more hierarchically ordered peoples to the southeast, speakers of 'Are'are and Malamasike ("Sa'a").

4. The substantial regional hereditary authority of Small Malaita chiefs (such as Doraweewee of Sa'a) is hinted at by Ivens (1927).

5. And in parts of Guadalcanal, Makira, Santa Isabel, and other islands where Maasina Rule was supported.

6. See de Coppet and Zemp 1978 for information and photographs on 'Are'are custom politics and the funeral of Waiparo.

7. Ironically, I had originally intended to do fieldwork in Takataka, and had changed my plan at the last minute because I had learned that Daniel de Coppet was also intending to study 'Are'are. The Kwaio *kastom* leaders, hearing that an American was coming to 'Are'are to work on custom, had prayed and sacrificed to their ancestors to divert him to come to Sinalagu instead. I arrived, fortuitously or not (there have been great benefits, but costs as well), in answer to their prayers, and in fulfillment of prophecies. See Fifi'i 1989 for an account of these events.

8. The Maasina Rule term *bungu 'ifi*, "conch-shell village," was used for this and other political meeting places for discussion of *kastomu*.

9. Uru and 'Oloburi are the other east-coast Kwaio "passages."

10. Keesing 1992a: photographs 8 and 9.

11. See Keesing 1982b: 112–16.

12. For which my data are secondhand, since I was forbidden by the government to visit Malaita for almost ten years, between 1979 and 1989, because of suspicion that I must be advising and assisting Folofo'u and Kwaio Fadanga.

13. See Fifi'i 1989 and Keesing 1992a.

14. See Keesing 1992a: ch. 24.

15. The present Kwaio parliamentary representative, a Christian from the very edge of Kwaio-speaking country, continues to insist on Folofo'u's legitimacy in terms of custom.

16. The young Christian, now a political figure and successful businessman in the South Sea Evangelical Church village on the harbor below Ngarinaasuru, grew up as a pagan in Folofo'u's clearing.

17. The original Cultural Center complex was largely destroyed by Cyclone Namu in 1986; and by then it had in any case lost much of its bush constituency because of Folofo'u's curses and ritual injunctions.

18. This refers to funds from royalties on my Kwaio publications, all of which have gone, since 1977, to the Kwaio people. The request for my blessing is unnecessary, since I have abstained from decisions regarding use of these funds, most of which remain in savings accounts.

19. At least of the communities of the interior. The coastal strip and small offshore islands of Kwara'ae were probably rather different in sociopolitical organi-

zation from the bush communities, as was the case in Kwaio—where they were rather different culturally and linguistically as well.

20. I discovered the strength of this assumption when I talked to secondary-school students at Selwyn College and touched on this issue. I was arguing that students could probe local oral traditions in their home communities to explore and clarify the nature of precolonial political systems. In doing so, I spoke of the contemporary installation of paramount chiefs in places where there had been none, using Kwara'ae and Kwaio as cases in point. The reaction of Kwara'ae students was stunned disbelief. I will touch later on the question of whether there is an older Kwara'ae political system that was more hierarchical than the bigman systems of the earliest contact period.

21. My friends among the Solomons elite all refer to him as "Davis": Devesi is as Oceanic a name as Salote.

22. See Keesing 1992b for a development of this argument with regard to the nineteenth-century northern Malaita strongman Kwaisulia and his son, who became a headman in the colonial state partly through his father's ("bogus") chiefly position.

23. Although Africa and the Polynesian states offer some semiotically intriguing examples of chiefly status as cultural collage. The chief is the one with the biggest Mercedes and the stereo videocassette recorder.

24. Such as Kwaisulia. See Corris 1970 and Keesing 1992b.

25. Oliver 1955; Hogbin 1939.

26. "Melanesia" is a category I heartily dislike, on archaeological, linguistic, and cultural grounds.

27. In any case, for them and for Ben Burt (1993), working in historically South Sea Evangelical Church communities on the east coast of Kwara'ae, these questions are so entangled with contemporary ideologies of *kastom* as to be impossible, ethnographically and politically, to investigate in a skeptical spirit.

28. And more strongly to both the north and the south of the Kwaio.

CHAPTER 14

1. It should be noted that not all Indonesians see Pancasila as resonating with egalitarian values. For some Indonesians it is more paternalistic than egalitarian.

2. Though this chapter does not address tourism as such a force, for an exploration of this topic, see Adams 1990, 1995.

3. It was not until Dutch colonial forces arrived in 1906 that the Toraja were united under a single political authority.

4. More precisely, the Tae' Toraja expressions *ampo* and *to boko'* are the euphemisms used.

5. A similar argument has been advanced by Engerman (1973), who demonstrates that free land in certain political conditions can enhance individual autonomy. In his classic work on highland Burma, Leach ([1954] 1965) has also linked land base with social hierarchy.

6. *To parengnge'* are also expected to exhibit these features.

7. Pseudonyms have been used throughout this chapter.

8. This town is the local regional center.

9. When he finally returned to Tana Toraja toward the end of my stay, I had the opportunity to interview him. As part of my interview schedule, I routinely asked who merited the most respect in Tana Toraja today, government officials, local nobles (*to parengnge'*), teachers, or church officials. Clearly shaken by his recent experiences, he wasted no time in answering "local nobles."

Bibliography

Aaron, Daniel B. 1981. "Chief Willie Bongmatur." In B. Macdonald-Milne, ed., *Yumi Stanap: Some People of Vanuatu*, pp. 94–99. Suva: Institute of Pacific Studies, University of the South Pacific.

Aborisade, Oladimeji, ed. 1985. *Local Government and the Traditional Rulers in Nigeria*. Ile-Ife: University of Ife Press.

Adams, Kathleen M. 1984. *Come to Tana Toraja, "Land of the Heavenly Kings": Travel Agents as Brokers in Ethnicity*. In C. F. Keyes and Pierre van den Berghe, eds., *Tourism and Ethnicity, Annals of Tourism Research* (special issue) 11(3): 469–85.

———. 1988. "Carving a New Identity: Ethnic and Artistic Change in Tana Toraja." Ph.D. dissertation, University of Washington.

———. 1990. "Cultural Commoditization in Tana Toraja." *Cultural Survival* 14: 31–34.

———. 1995. "Making Up the Toraja? The Appropriation of Tourism, Anthropology, and Museums for Politics in Upland Sulawesi, Indonesia." *Ethnology* 34(2):143–53.

Adriani, N., and Albert C. Kruyt. 1914. *De Bare'e-sprekende Toradja's van Midden-Celebes*. Vol. 3. Batavia: Landsdrukkerij.

Akin, David W. 1985. "Codifying 'Kastom' Law in East Kwaio, Malaita, Solomon Islands." Paper presented at the meetings of the Association for Social Anthropology in Oceania, Salem, Mass., March 6–10.

———. N.d. "History II—Post-Bell to Maasina Rule." Unpublished manuscript.

Alasia, Sam. 1989. "Politics." In H. Laracy, ed., *Ples Blong Iumi: Solomon Islands, The Past Four Thousand Years*. Suva: Institute of Pacific Studies, University of the South Pacific.

Alkire, William H. 1977. *An Introduction to the Peoples and Cultures of Micronesia*. 2d ed. Menlo Park, Calif.: Cummings.

———. 1989. *Lamotrek Atoll and Interisland Socioeconomic Ties*. Rev. ed. Prospect Heights, Ill.: Waveland.

Allen, Michael. 1981. "Innovation, Inversion and Revolution as Political Tactics in West Aoba." In M. Allen, ed., *Vanuatu: Politics, Economics and Ritual in Island Melanesia*, pp. 105–34. Sydney: Academic Press.

———. 1984. "Elders, Chiefs, and Big Men: Authority Legitimation and Political Evolution in Melanesia." *American Ethnologist* 11:20–41.

Amherst, Lord (of Hackney), and B. Thomson, eds. 1901. *The Discovery of the Solomon Islands*. London: Hakluyt Society.

Anderson, Benedict. [1966] 1990. "The Language of Indonesian Politics." In *Language and Power: Exploring Political Cultures in Indonesia*, pp. 123–51. Ithaca, N.Y.: Cornell University Press.

———. 1983. *Imagined Communities: Reflections on the Origin and Spread of Nationalism*. London and New York: Verso.

Awanohara, Susuma. 1984. "A Matter of Principles." *Far Eastern Economic Review* (Oct. 25):16–17.

Ayeni, Victor. 1985. "Traditional Rulers as Ombudsmen: In Search of a Role for Natural Rules in Contemporary Nigeria." *Indian Journal of Public Administration* 31:1318–30.

Babadzan, Alain. 1988. "*Kastom* and Nation-Building in the South Pacific." In Remo Guidieri, Francesco Pellizi, and Stanley J. Tambiah, eds., *Ethnicities and Nations: Processes of Interethnic Relations in Latin America, Southeast Asia, and the Pacific*, pp. 199–228. Houston, Tx.: Rothko Chapel and University of Texas Press.

Ballendorf, Dirk. 1989. "Perplexity and a Propensity for Perseverance: German Administration in the Eastern Carolines, 1900–1910." *Pacifica* 1(2):33–45.

Bashkow, Ira. 1991. "The Dynamics of Rapport in a Colonial Situation: David Schneider's Fieldwork on the Islands of Yap." In George Stocking, Jr., ed., *Colonial Situations: Essays on the Contextualization of Ethnographic Knowledge*, pp. 170–242. *History of Anthropology*, vol. 7. Madison: University of Wisconsin Press.

Beasant, John. 1984. *The Santo Rebellion: An Imperial Reckoning*. Honolulu: University of Hawai'i Press.

Bennett, J. 1974. "Cross-Cultural Influences on Village Relocation on the Weather Coast of Guadalcanal, Solomon Islands, c. 1870–1953." M.A. thesis, University of Hawai'i.

———. 1987. *Wealth of the Solomons: A History of a Pacific Archipelago, 1800–1978*. Pacific Islands Monograph Series no. 3. Honolulu: University of Hawai'i Press.

Bergendorff, Steen. 1993. "The Reproduction of the Mekeo Chieftainship: The Complexity of Cultural Contact." *Folk* 35:37–64.

Bernart, Luelen. 1977. *The Book of Luelen*. Trans. and ed. John L. Fischer, Saul H. Riesenberg, and Marjorie G. Whiting. Canberra: Australian National University Press.

Besnier, Niko. 1993. "The Demise of the Man Who Would Be King: Sorcery and Ambition on Nukulaelae Atoll." *Journal of Anthropological Research* 49:185–215.

Betu, Willie. 1974. Discussion Paper for Ysabel Council and Ysabel Regional Diocese. (Files of G. White.)

Bigalke, Terance. 1981. "A Social History of 'Tana Toraja,' 1870–1965." Doctoral dissertation, University of Wisconsin-Madison.

Blackwood, Peter. 1981. "Rank, Exchange and Leadership in Four Vanuatu Societies." In M. Allen, ed., *Vanuatu: Politics, Economics, and Ritual in Island Melanesia*, pp. 35–84. Sydney: Academic Press.

Boggs, Stephen, and David Gegeo. 1996. "Leadership and Solomon Islanders' Resistance to Plantation-Based Political Economy: Roles and Circumstances." In Feinberg and Watson-Gegeo 1996:272–97.

Bonnemaison, Joël. 1987. *Tanna: Les Hommes Lieux*. Paris: Éditions de l'ORSTOM.

Bott, Elizabeth. 1981. "Power and Rank in the Kingdom of Tonga." *Journal of the Polynesian Society* 90:7–81.

Bourdieu, Pierre. 1977. *Outline of A Theory of Practice*. Cambridge: Cambridge University Press.

———. 1992. *An Invitation to Reflexive Sociology*. Ed. Loic J. D. Waquant. Chicago: University of Chicago Press.

Boyd, M. 1969. "The Record in Western Samoa to 1945." In A. Ross, ed., *New Zealand's Record in the Pacific Islands in the Twentieth Century*. Auckland: Longman Paul for the NZIIA.

Brenneis, Donald L., and Fred Myers, eds. 1984. *Dangerous Words: Language and Politics in the Pacific*. New York: New York University Press.

Brison, Karen J. 1989. "All Talk and No Action? How 'Saying Is Doing' in Kwanga Meetings." *Ethnology* 28:97–115.

British District Agent, Southern District. 1950. "Kava Control. (Your Circular Memo 26 of Jan. 19, 1950)." Letter to British Resident Commissioner, Port Vila, Mar. 21, 1950.

Brunton, Ron. 1989. *The Abandoned Narcotic: Kava and Cultural Instability in Melanesia*. Cambridge: Cambridge University Press.

Buck, Sir Peter (Te Rangi Hiroa). 1949. *The Coming of the Maori*. Wellington: Maori Purposes Fund Board.

Bugotu, Francis. 1988. "Solomons: A Classless Society No Longer." *Solomon Star* (July 1, 1988):10–11.

Burridge, Kenelm. 1960. *Mambu*. London: Methuen.

Burt, Ben. 1982. "Kastom, Christianity and the First Ancestor of the Kwara'ae of Malaita." In R. M. Keesing and R. Tonkinson, eds., *Reinventing Traditional Culture: The Politics of Kastom in Island Melanesia, Mankind* (special issue) 13.

———. 1993. *Tradition and Christianity: The Colonial Transformation of a Solomon Islands Society*. Chur, Switzerland: Harwood Academic Publishers.

Campbell, Ian. 1990. "The Alleged Imperialism of George Tupou I." *Journal of Pacific History* 25(2):159–75.

———. 1992. *Island Kingdom*. Christchurch: University of Canterbury.

Carrier, James, ed. 1995. *Occidentalism: Images of the West*. Oxford: Clarendon.

Carucci, Laurence Marshall. 1979. "The Enewetak Conception of Chiefs and Foreigners." Paper presented at the 1980 meetings of the Association for Social Anthropology of Oceania, Galveston, Texas.

———. 1980. "The Renewal of Life: A Ritual Encounter in the Marshall Islands." Ph.D. dissertation, Department of Anthropology, University of Chicago.

————. 1988. "Small Fish in a Big Sea: Geographical Dispersion and Sociopolitical Centralisation in the Marshall Islands." In J. Gledhill and B. Bender, eds.,
*State and Society: Emergence and Development of Social Hierarchy and Politi-
cal Centralisation*, pp. 33–42. Oxford: Oxbow.

————. 1989. "The Source of the Force in Marshallese Cosmology." In G. White
and M. Lindstrom, eds., *The Pacific Theater: Island Representations of World
War II*, pp. 73–96. Honolulu: University of Hawai'i Press.

————. 1992. "We Planted Mama on Jeptan: Constructing Continuities and Situ-
ating Identities on Enewetak Atoll." In D. H. Rubinstein, ed., *Pacific History*,
pp. 191–99. Mangilao: University of Guam and Micronesian Area Research
Center Publication.

————. 1996. *In Anxious Anticipation of the Uneven Fruits of Kwajalein Atoll.*
Huntsville, Ala.: United States Army Space and Strategic Defense Command.

————. 1997. *Nuclear Nativity: Rituals of Renewal and Empowerment in the
Marshall Islands.* DeKalb: Northern Illinois University Press.

Churchward, C. Maxwell. 1940. *Rotuman Grammar and Dictionary.* Sydney:
Australasian Medical Publishing Company Limited for the Methodist Church
of Australasia, Department of Overseas Missions.

Clark, Paul. 1975. *"Hauhau": The Pai Marire Search for Maori Identity.* Auckland: Auckland University Press.

Clifford, James. 1988. *The Predicament of Culture.* Cambridge, Mass.: Harvard
University Press.

Codrington, R. H. 1891. *The Melanesians: Studies in their Anthropology and
Folk-Lore.* Oxford: Clarendon.

Colson, Elizabeth. 1975. *Tradition and Contract: The Problem of Order.* London:
Heinemann.

Comaroff, John L. 1978. "Rules and Rulers: Political Processes in a Tswana Chiefdom." *Man*, n.s. 13:1–20.

Coppet, D. de, and H. Zemp. 1978. *'Are'are: Un peuple Melanesien et sa musique.*
Paris: Seuil.

Corris, P. 1970. "Kwaisulia of Ada Gege: A Strongman in the Solomon Islands."
In J. Davidson and D. Scarr, eds., *Pacific Islands Portraits*, pp. 253–65. Canberra: Australian National University Press.

Crocombe, Ron, Uentabo Neemia, Asesela Ravuvu, and Werner Vom Busch, eds.
1992. *Culture and Democracy in the South Pacific.* Suva: Institute of Pacific
Studies, University of the South Pacific.

Crystal, Eric. 1970. "Toraja Town." Ph.D. dissertation, University of California,
Berkeley.

————. 1974. "Cooking Pot Politics: A Toraja Village Study." *Indonesia* 18:
118–51.

Davidson, A. 1993. "European Democracy and the Pacific Way: Strategies for
Reconciliation." Paper presented to the Pacific Islands Political Studies Association, Cook Islands, December.

Davidson, J. W. 1967. *Samoa mo Samoa: The Emergence of the Independent State
of Western Samoa.* Melbourne: Oxford University Press.

Davies, A. E. 1990. "The Fluctuating Fortunes of Traditional Rulers in Nigeria."
Plural Societies 19:133–44.

Deacon, A. Bernard. 1934. *Malekula: A Vanishing People in the New Hebrides.* London: George Routledge & Sons.

Dinnen, Sinclair. 1994. "Public Order in Papua New Guinea—Problems and Prospects." In Alan Thompson, ed., *Papua New Guinea: Issues for Australian Security Planners*, pp. 99–116. Canberra: Australian Defence Force Academy.

Donner, William. 1993. "Rich Man, Poor Man, Big Man, But Not Chief: Resistance to Centralized Authority in a Polynesian Society." Paper presented at a meeting of the Association for Social Anthropology in Oceania, Kona, Hawai'i.

Douglas, Bronwen. 1979. "Rank, Power, Authority: A Reassessment of Traditional Leadership in South Pacific Societies." *Journal of Pacific History* 14(1): 2–27.

———. 1982. "'Written on the Ground': Spatial Symbolism, Cultural Categories and Historical Process in New Caledonia." *Journal of the Polynesian Society* 91:383–415.

Drake, Christine. 1989. *National Integration in Indonesia.* Honolulu: University of Hawai'i Press.

Dyson, Kenneth. 1982. *The State Tradition in Western Europe: A Study of an Idea and an Institution.* Oxford: Martin Robertson.

Eliade, Mircea. 1970. "Cargo Cults and Cosmic Regeneration." In S. L. Thrupp, ed., *Millennial Dreams in Action*, pp. 139–44. New York: Schocken.

Engerman, S. L. 1973. "Some Considerations Relating to Property Rights in Man." *Journal of Economic History* 33:43–65.

Erdland, P. August. 1912. "The Natives of the Marshall Islands in Traffic with Their Iroij." *Anthropos*: 559–64.

———. 1914. *Die Marshall-Insulaner, Leben und Sitte, Sinn und Religion eines Südsee-Volkes.* Internationale Sammlung Ethnologischer Monographien, vol. 2, no. 1. Munster: Anthropos.

Espirat, Jean-Jacques, Jean Guiart, Marie S. Lagrange, and Monique Renaud. 1973. *Systèm de titres, électifs ou héréditaires dans les Nouvelles-Hébrides Centrales, d'Efate aux Iles Shepherd.* Paris: Musée de l'Homme.

Evans, Humphrey S. 1951. "Notes on Rotuma." Typed manuscript. Central Archives of Fiji, Suva.

Facey, Ellen E. 1981. "Hereditary Chiefship in Nguna." In M. Allen, ed., *Vanuatu: Politics, Economics and Ritual in Island Melanesia*, pp. 295–314. Sydney: Academic Press.

———. 1988. *Nguna Voices: Text and Culture from Central Vanuatu.* Calgary: University of Calgary Press.

Farrar, Tarikhu. 1992. "When African Kings Became 'Chiefs': Some Transformations in European Perceptions of West African Civilization, c. 1450–1800." *Journal of Black Studies* 23:258–78.

Feinberg, Richard. 1993. "Elements of Leadership in Oceania." Paper presented at a meeting of the Association for Social Anthropology in Oceania, Kona, Hawai'i.

Feinberg, Richard, and Karen Ann Watson-Gegeo, eds. 1996. *Leadership and Change in the Western Pacific: Essays Presented to Sir Raymond Firth on the Occasion of His 90th Birthday.* London School of Economics Monographs on Social Anthropology, no. 66. London: Athlone.

Field, M. J. 1984. *MAU: Samoa's Struggle Against New Zealand Oppression.* Wellington: A. H. and A. W. Reed Ltd.

Fifi'i, J. 1989. *From Pig-Theft to Parliament: My Life Between Two Worlds.* Ed. and trans. by R. M. Keesing. Honiara: University of the South Pacific and Solomon Islands College of Higher Education.

Fiji. 1883. *Regulations of the Native Regulation Board, 1877–1882.* London.

———. 1989. *Report of the Fiji Constitutional Inquiry and Advisory Committee.* Suva.

———. 1990. *Constitution of the Sovereign Democratic Republic of Fiji.* Suva.

Finau, Patelisio. 1993. "How Migration Affects the Home Country." In G. McCall and J. Connell, eds., *A World Perspective on Pacific Islander Migration,* pp. 307–10. Sydney: Center for South Pacific Studies, University of New South Wales.

Firth, Raymond. [1929] 1959. *Economics of the New Zealand Maori.* Wellington: Government Printer.

———. 1969. "Extraterritoriality and the Tikopia Chiefs." *Man* 4:354–78.

Fischer, John L. 1974. "The Role of the Traditional Chiefs on Ponape in the American Period." In Hughes and Lingenfelter 1974:166–77.

Fischer, John L., Saul H. Riesenberg, and Marjorie G. Whiting. 1977. *Annotations to the Book of Luelen.* Honolulu: University of Hawai'i Press.

Fleras, Augie. 1991. "'Tuku Rangatiratanga': Devolution in Iwi-Government Relations." In Paul Spoonley, David Pearson, and Cluny Macpherson, eds., *Nga Take: Ethnic Relations and Racism in Aotearoa/New Zealand,* pp. 171–93. Palmerson North: Dunmore.

Fleras, Augie, and Jean Leonard Elliott. 1992. *The "Nations Within": Aboriginal-State Relations in Canada, the United States, and New Zealand.* Toronto: Oxford University Press.

Fleurieu, M. L. C. de. 1791. *Discoveries of the French in 1768 and 1769 to the Southeast of New Guinea.* London: Printed for John Stockdale.

Flinn, Julianna. 1992. *Diplomas and Thatch Houses: Asserting Tradition in a Changing Micronesia.* Ann Arbor: University of Michigan Press.

Fonua, Pesi. 1991. "Soldiers of Fortune." *Matangi Tonga* (July–Aug.): 7.

———. 1992a. "Debating the Future of the Tongan Monarchy." *Matangi Tonga* (Sept.–Nov.): 8.

———. 1992b. "The Nobles: A Leadership Crisis in the Villages." *Matangi Tonga* (July–Aug.): 14–15.

———. 1993. "The Pro Democracy Movement: 'Akilisi Wants to Be the Opposition." *Matangi Tonga* (July–Sept.): 17.

Fonua, S., ed. 1975. *Land and Migration.* Nuku'alofa: Tonga Council of Churches.

Foster, Robert J. 1991. "Making National Cultures in the Global Ecumene." *Annual Review of Anthropology* 20:235–60.

———, ed. 1995. *Nation-Making: Emergent Identities in Postcolonial Melanesia.* Ann Arbor: University of Michigan Press.

Foucault, Michel. 1984. "Right of Death and Power over Life." In Paul Rabinow, ed., *The Foucault Reader,* pp. 258–72. New York: Pantheon.

France, Peter. 1969. *The Charter of the Land.* Melbourne: Oxford University Press.

Franco, Robert W. 1976. "The History, Role and Function of the Contemporary Catholic Church in Western Samoa." M.A. thesis, Department of Anthropology, California State University, Chico.

———. 1987. *Demographic Assessment of the Samoan Population in Hawai'i.* Honolulu: East-West Center Population Institute.

———. 1991. *Samoan Perceptions of Work: Moving Up and Moving Around.* New York: AMS.

———. 1993. "Samoan and Micronesian Migration: 'Relative Economies.'" In G. McCall and J. Connell, eds., *A World Perspective on Pacific Islander Migration*, pp. 161–70. Sydney: Center for South Pacific Studies, University of New South Wales.

Friedrich, Carl J. 1972. *Tradition and Authority.* New York: Praeger.

Geddes, William R. 1959. "Fijian Social Structure in a Period of Transition." In J. D. Freeman and W. R. Geddes, eds., *Anthropology in the South Seas*, pp. 201–20. New Plymouth, New Zealand: Thomas Avery & Sons.

Gegeo, David Welchman, and Karen Ann Watson-Gegeo. 1996. "Priest and Prince: Integrating Kastom, Christianity, and Modernization in Kwara'ae Leadership." In Feinberg and Watson-Gegeo 1996:298–342.

Geschiere, Peter. 1993. "Chiefs and Colonial Rule in Cameroon: Inventing Chieftaincy, French and British Style." *Africa* 63:151–75.

Ghai, Yash. 1990. "Constitutional Reviews in Papua New Guinea and Solomon Islands." *The Contemporary Pacific* 2:313–33.

Gilson, R. P. 1970. *Samoa, 1830–1900: The Politics of a Multi-Cultural Community.* Melbourne: Oxford University Press.

Gladwin, Thomas, and Seymour B. Sarason. 1953. *Truk: Man in Paradise.* Viking Fund Publications in Anthropology no. 20. New York: Wenner-Gren Foundation for Anthropological Research.

Godelier, Maurice. 1986. *The Making of Great Men: Male Domination and Power Among the New Guinea Baruya.* Cambridge: Cambridge University Press.

Godelier, Maurice, and Marilyn Strathern, eds. 1991. *Big Men and Great Men: Personifications of Power in Melanesia.* Cambridge: Cambridge University Press.

Goheen, Mitzi. 1992. "Chiefs, Sub-chiefs and Local Control: Negotiations over Land, Struggles over Meaning." *Africa* 62:389–412.

Goldman, Irving. 1970. *Ancient Polynesian Society.* Chicago: University of Chicago Press.

Goodenough, Ward H. 1951. *Property, Kin, and Community on Truk.* Yale University Publications in Anthropology, no. 46. New Haven, Conn.: Yale University Press.

Gordon, Sir Arthur. 1878–79. "Native Taxation in Fiji." *Proceedings of the Royal Colonial Institute* 10:175–95.

Great Britain, Colonial Office. 1887. *Correspondence Relating to the Native Population of Fiji.* London: HMSO.

Guiart, Jean. 1956. *Un Siècle et demi de contacts culturels à Tanna, Nouvelles-Hébrides.* Paris: Musée de l'Homme.

———. 1958. *Espiritu Santo (Nouvelles Hébrides).* Paris: Librarie Plon.

————. 1970. "The Millenarian Aspect of Conversion to Christianity in the South Pacific." In S. L. Thrupp, ed., *Millennial Dreams in Action*, pp. 122–38. New York: Schocken.

————. 1982. "A Polynesian Myth and the Invention of Melanesia." *Journal of the Polynesian Society* 91:139–44.

Guidieri, Remo, Francesco Pellizi, and Stanley J. Tambiah, eds. 1988. *Ethnicities and Nations: Processes of Interethnic Relations in Latin America, Southeast Asia, and the Pacific*. Austin: University of Texas Press.

Gunson, Niel. 1978. *Messengers of Grace: Evangelical Missionaries in the South Seas, 1797–1860*. Melbourne: Oxford University Press.

————. 1987. "Sacred Women Chiefs and Female 'Headmen' in Polynesian History." *Journal of Pacific History* 22:139–72.

————. 1990. "The Tonga-Samoa Connection, 1777–1845." *Journal of Pacific History* 25(2):176–87.

Haberkorn, Gerald. 1989. *Port Vila: Transit Station or Final Stop?* Canberra: National Centre for Development Studies, Australian National University.

Hanlon, David. 1988. *Upon a Stone Altar*. Honolulu: University of Hawai'i Press.

Hannerz, Ulf. 1992. *Cultural Complexity: Studies in the Social Organization of Meaning*. New York: Columbia University Press.

Hanson, Alan. 1989. "The Making of the Maori: Culture Invention and Its Logic." *American Anthropologist* 91:890–902.

Harrison, Simon. 1993. "The Commerce of Cultures in Melanesia." *Man* 28:139–58.

Hau'ofa, Epeli. 1987. "The New South Pacific Society: Integration and Independence." In A. Hooper, Steve Britton, Ron Crocombe, Judith Huntsman, and Cluny Macpherson, eds., *Class and Culture in the South Pacific*, pp. 1–12. Auckland: Centre for Pacific Studies, University of Auckland; and Suva: Institute of Pacific Studies, University of the South Pacific.

————. 1992. "Hereditary Titles 'Unfortunate'." *Matangi Tonga* (Sept.–Nov.): 12.

Hawke, Gary Richard. 1988. *Report of the Working Group on Post Compulsory Education and Training in New Zealand*. Unpublished report prepared for the Cabinet Social Equity Committee. Hamilton, N.Z.: University of Waikato Library.

Helu, Futa. 1991a. "Tonga and the Chosen Ones." In *Pacific Islands Monthly* (Feb.) 5.

————. 1991b. "Diaspora of Pacific Islanders." In *Pacific Islands Monthly* (June): 7.

Helu-Thaman, Konai. 1974. *You, the Choice of My Parents*. Suva: Mana.

Hempenstall, P. J. 1978. *Pacific Islanders Under German Rule: A Study in the Meaning of Colonial Resistance*. Canberra: Australian National University Press.

Hereniko, Vilsoni. 1994. "Clowning as Political Commentary: Polynesia, Then and Now." *The Contemporary Pacific* 6:1–28.

————. 1995. *Woven Gods: Female Power and Ritual Clowning in Rotuma*. Honolulu: University of Hawai'i Press.

Hilliard, David. 1974. "Colonialism and Christianity: The Melanesian Mission in the Solomon Islands." *Journal of Pacific History* 9:93–116.

Hobsbawm, E. J., and Terence Ranger, eds. 1983. *The Invention of Tradition.* Cambridge: Cambridge University Press.

Hocart, A. M. 1922. "Cult of the Dead on Eddystone." *Journal of the Royal Anthropological Institute* 61:301–24.

———. 1936. *Kings and Councillors.* Cairo: Paul Barbey.

———. 1970. "The Divinity of the Guest." In *The Life-Giving Myth*, pp. 78–86. Reprint. London: Tavistock.

Hogbin, H. I. 1939. *Experiments in Civilization: The Effects of European Culture on a Native Community of the Solomon Islands.* London: George Routledge.

Honderich, Ted. 1991. *Conservatism.* London: Penguin.

Howard, Alan. 1966. "The Rotuman District Chief: A Study in Changing Patterns of Authority." *Journal of Pacific History* 1:63–78.

———. 1986. "Cannibal Chiefs and the Charter for Rebellion in Rotuman Myth." *Pacific Studies* 10:1–27.

———. 1989. "The Resurgence of Rivalry: Politics in Post-Colonial Rotuma." *Dialectical Anthropology* 14:145–58.

———. 1990. "Dispute Management in Rotuma." *Journal of Anthropological Research* 46:263–92.

———. 1992. "Symbols of Power and the Politics of Impotence: The Mölmahao Rebellion on Rotuma." *Pacific Studies* 15(4):83–116.

———. 1994. *Hef Ran Ta (The Morning Star): A Biography of Wilson Inia.* Suva: Institute for Pacific Studies, University of the South Pacific.

———. 1996. "Money, Sovereignty and Moral Authority on Rotuma." In Feinberg and Watson-Gegeo 1996:205–38.

Howard, Alan, and Jan Rensel. 1994. "Rotuma in the 1990s: From Hinterland to Neighbourhood." *Journal of the Polynesian Society* 103:227–54.

Howard, Michael. 1983. "Vanuatu: The Myth of Melanesian Socialism." *Labour, Capital and Society* 16(2):176–203.

Hughes, Daniel, and Sherwood Lingenfelter, eds. 1974. *Political Development in Micronesia.* Columbus: Ohio State University Press.

Hviding, E. 1988. "Sharing Paths and Keeping Sides: Managing the Seas in Marovo Lagoon, Solomon Islands." Thesis, University of Bergen, Norway.

———. 1993. "Guardians of Marovo Lagoon: The Sea as Cultural and Relational Focus in New Georgia, Solomon Islands." Ph.D. thesis, University of Bergen, Norway.

———. 1996. *Guardians of Marovo Lagoon: Practice, Place, and Politics in Maritime Melanesia.* Honolulu: University of Hawai'i Press.

Institute for Pacific Studies. 1988. *Pacific Constitutions.* Vol. 1, *Polynesia.* Suva: University of the South Pacific.

Ivens, W. G. 1927. *Melanesians of the South-East Solomon Islands.* London: Kegan, Paul, Trench, Trubner.

Jackson, K. B. 1972. "Head-hunting and Santa Isabel, Solomon Islands, 1568–1901." B.A. honors thesis, Department of History, Australian National University.

———. 1975. "Head-hunting and the Christianization of Bugotu, 1861–1900." *Journal of Pacific History* 10:65–78.

———. 1978. "Tie Hokara, Tie Vaka: Black Man, White Man, a Study of the New Georgia Group to 1925." Ph.D. thesis, Australian National University.

James, K. E. 1983. "Gender Relations in Tonga, 1780 to 1984." *Journal of the Polynesian Society* 96:233–43.

———. 1992. "Tongan Rank Revisited: Religious Hierarchy, Social Stratification, and Gender in the Ancient Tongan Polity." *Social Analysis* 31:79–102.

———. 1993. "Political Review: The Kingdom of Tonga, 1991–92." *The Contemporary Pacific* 5(1):163–66.

———. 1994. "Political Review: The Kingdom of Tonga, 1992–93." *The Contemporary Pacific* 6(1):192–95.

———. 1995a. "Political Review: The Kingdom of Tonga, 1993–94." *The Contemporary Pacific* 7(1):164–67.

———. 1995b. "Right and Privilege in Tongan Land Tenure." In R. G. Ward and E. Kingdon, eds., *Land, Custom and Practice in the South Pacific*, pp.157–97. Cambridge: Cambridge University Press.

———. 1996. "Political Review: The Kingdom of Tonga, 1994–95." *The Contemporary Pacific* 8:202–6.

Jensen, John Thayer. 1977. *Yapese-English Dictionary*. Honolulu: University of Hawai'i Press.

Jolly, Margaret. 1992a. "Custom and the Way of the Land: Past and Present in Vanuatu and Fiji." In M. Jolly and N. Thomas, eds., *The Politics of Tradition in the Pacific*. *Oceania* (special issue) 62:330–54.

———. 1992b. "Specters of Inauthenticity." *The Contemporary Pacific* 4:49–72.

Jolly, Margaret, and Mark Mosko, eds. 1994. *Transformations of Hierarchy: Structure, History and Horizon in the Austronesian World. History and Anthropology* (special issue) 7(1–4).

Jolly, Margaret, and Nicholas Thomas. 1992. "Introduction: The Politics of Tradition in the South Pacific." *Oceania* (special issue) 62:241–48.

Jupp, James. 1982. "Custom, Tradition and Reform in Vanuatu Politics." In *Evolving Political Cultures in the Pacific Islands*, Proceedings of the 1982 Politics Conference, pp. 143–58. Laie: Institute for Polynesian Studies, Brigham Young University, Hawai'i.

Kaeppler, A. L. 1978. "Exchange Patterns in Goods and Spouses: Fiji, Tonga, and Samoa." *Mankind* 11:246–52.

Kaplan, Martha. 1989. "Luve Ni Wai as the British Saw It: Constructions of Custom and Disorder in Colonial Fiji." *Ethnohistory* 36:349–71.

———. 1995. *Neither Cargo nor Cult: Ritual Politics and the Colonial Imagination in Fiji*. Durham, N.C. and London: Duke University Press.

Keesing, F. M. 1934. *Modern Samoa: Its Government and Changing Life*. London: George Allen and Unwin.

Keesing, R. M. 1967a. "Statistical Models and Decision Models of Social Structure: A Kwaio Case." *Ethnology* 6(1):1–16.

———. 1967b. "Christians and Pagans in Kwaio, Malaita." *Journal of the Polynesian Society* 76:82–100.

————. 1969. "Chiefs in a Chiefless Society: The Ideology of Modern Kwaio Politics." *Oceania* 38:276–80.

————. 1970a. "Shrines, Ancestors and Cognatic Descent: The Kwaio and Tallensi." *American Anthropologist* 72:755–75.

————. 1971. "Descent, Residence and Cultural Codes." In L. Hiatt and J. Jayawardena, eds., *Anthropology in Oceania*, pp. 46–65. Sydney: Angus and Robertson.

————. 1978. "Politico-Religious Movements and Anti-Colonialism on Malaita: Maasina Rule in Historical Perspective." *Oceania* 48:241–61; 49:46–73.

————. 1980. "Further Notes on Maasina Rule." *Journal of Pacific History* 13: 102–7.

————. 1981. "Still Further Notes on Maasina Rule." *Journal of the Anthropological Society of Oxford* 12:130–33.

————. 1982a. "Kastom in Melanesia: An Overview." In Keesing and Tonkinson 1982:297–301.

————. 1982b. *Kwaio Religion: The Living and the Dead in a Solomon Island Society*. New York: Columbia University Press.

————. 1982c. "Kastom and Anticolonialism on Malaita: Culture as Political Symbol." In Keesing and Tonkinson 1982:357–73.

————. 1983. *Elota's Story: The Life and Times of a Solomon Islands Big Man*. New York: Holt, Rinehart and Winston.

————. 1985. "Killers, Big Men and Priests on Malaita: Reflections on a Melanesian Troika System." *Ethnology* 24:237–52.

————. 1989. "Creating the Past: Custom and Identity in the Contemporary Pacific." *The Contemporary Pacific* 1(1, 2):16–35.

————. 1990. "Colonial History as Contested Ground: The Bell Massacre in the Solomons." *History and Anthropology* 4:279–301.

————. 1991. "Class, Culture, Custom." Paper presented to Workshop on the Global Anthropology of Oceania, University of Lund, Sweden, October 1991.

————. 1992a. *Custom and Confrontation: The Kwaio Struggle for Cultural Autonomy*. Chicago: University of Chicago Press.

————. 1992b. "Kwaisulia as Culture Hero." In J. Carrier, ed., *History and Tradition in Melanesian Anthropology*. Berkeley: University of California Press.

Keesing, R. M., and P. Corris. 1980. *Lightning Meets the West Wind: The Malaita Massacre*. Melbourne: Oxford University Press.

Keesing, Roger M., and Robert Tonkinson, eds. 1982. *Reinventing Traditional Culture: The Politics of Kastom in Island Melanesia*. *Mankind* (special issue) 13(4).

Keith-Reid, Robert. 1991. "Can They Win? Can They Stay? Vincent Boulekone on Vanuatu's Election Questions." *Islands Business Pacific* 17(5) (May):21–22.

Kelly, Celsus. 1964. *La Austrialia del Espiritu Santo*. Cambridge: Cambridge University Press for the Hakluyt Society.

Kelly, John Dunham. 1988. "Fiji Indians and Political Discourse in Fiji: From the Pacific Romance to the Coups." *Journal of Historical Sociology* 1:399–422.

Koubi, Jeannine. 1982. *Rambu Solo', "La Fumee Descend": Le Culte des morts chez les Toradja du Sud*. Paris: Éditions du Centre National de la Recherche Scientifique.

Lal, Bril V. 1992. *Broken Waves: A History of the Fiji Islands in the Twentieth Century.* Honolulu: University of Hawai'i Press.

———. 1995. "Rabuka's Republic: The Fiji Snap Elections of 1994." *Pacific Studies* 18:47–77.

Laracy, Hugh. 1983. *Pacific Protest: The Maasina Rule Movement, Solomon Islands, 1944–1952.* Suva: Institute of Pacific Studies, University of the South Pacific.

Larmour, Peter. 1992. "States and Societies in the Pacific Islands." *Pacific Studies* 15:99–121.

Lātūkefu, Sione. 1974. *Church and State in Tonga.* Honolulu: University Press of Hawai'i.

Lawrence, Peter. 1989. *Road Belong Cargo.* Reprint. Prospect Heights, Ill.: Waveland Press.

Lawson, Stephanie. 1990. "The Myth of Cultural Homogeneity and Its Implications for Chiefly Power and Politics in Fiji." *Comparative Studies in Society and History* 32:795–821.

———. 1991. *The Failure of Democratic Politics in Fiji.* Oxford: Clarendon.

———. 1993. "The Politics of Tradition: Problems for Legitimacy and Democracy in the South Pacific." *Pacific Studies* 16:1–29.

———. 1995. "The Authentic State: History and Tradition in the Ideology of Ethnonationalism." In Joseph A. Camilleri, Anthony P. Jarvis, and Albert J. Paolini, eds., *The State in Transition: Reimagining the Local, National and International,* pp. 77–90. Boulder, Colo.: Lynne Reiner.

———. 1996a. *Tradition Versus Democracy in the South Pacific: Fiji, Tonga and Western Samoa.* Cambridge: Cambridge University Press.

———. 1996b. "Culture, Relativism and Democracy: Political Myths About 'Asia' and the 'West'." In Richard Robison, ed., *Looking North: Reassessing the Framework and Unravelling the Myths,* pp. 108–28. St. Leonard's: Allen & Unwin.

Leach, E. R. [1954] 1965. *Political Systems of Highland Burma.* Boston: Beacon.

Lessa, William A. 1950. "Ulithi and the Outer Native World." *American Anthropologist* 52:27–52.

———. 1979. "The Apotheosis of Marespa." In W. A. Lessa and E. Z. Vogt, eds., *Reader in Comparative Religion,* pp. 169–73. New York: Harper Collins.

Le Tagaloa, A. F. 1992. "The Samoan Culture and Government." In Crocombe, et al. 1992:117–38.

Levine, Hal, and Manuka Henare. 1994. "Mana Maori Motuhake: Maori Self-Determination." *Pacific Viewpoint* 35(2):193–210.

Lian, Kwen Fee. 1987. "Interpreting Maori History: A Case for a Historical Sociology." *Journal of the Polynesian Society* 96(4):445–71.

Liki, Asenati. 1994. "E Tele A'a o le Tagata: Career Choices of Samoan Professionals Within and Beyond Their Nu'u Moni." M.A. thesis in Development Studies, University of the South Pacific, Suva.

Lilley, Ian. 1985. "Chiefs Without Chiefdoms? Comments on Prehistoric Sociopolitical Organization in Western Melanesia." *Archeology in Oceania* 20:60–65.

Lilomaiava-Niko, Saili. 1993. "An Analysis of Approaches to Migration: The Western Samoan Case." M.A. thesis, University of Hawai'i.

Lindstrom, Lamont. 1982a. "Big-Man: A Short Terminological History." *American Anthropologist* 83:900–905.

———. 1982b. "*Leftemap Kastom*: The Political History of Tradition on Tanna (Vanuatu)." *Mankind* 13:316–29.

———. 1990. *Knowledge and Power in a South Pacific Society.* Washington, D.C.: Smithsonian Institution Press.

———. 1993. *Cargo Cult: Strange Stories of Desire from Melanesia and Beyond.* Honolulu: University of Hawai'i Press.

Lindstrom, Lamont, and Geoffrey M. White, eds. 1994. *Culture, Kastom, Tradition: Developing Cultural Policy in Melanesia.* Suva: Institute of Pacific Studies, University of the South Pacific.

Lingenfelter, Sherwood G. 1975. *Yap: Political Leadership and Culture Change in an Island Society.* Honolulu: University of Hawai'i Press.

Lini, Walter. 1980. *Beyond Pandemonium: From the New Hebrides to Vanuatu.* Wellington: Asia Pacific Books; Suva: University of the South Pacific.

Linnekin, Jocelyn. 1990. "The Politics of Culture in the Pacific." In J. Linnekin and L. Poyer, eds., *Cultural Identity and Ethnicity in the Pacific*, pp. 149–73. Honolulu: University of Hawai'i Press.

———. 1991. "Cultural Invention and the Dilemma of Authenticity." *American Anthropologist* 93:446–49.

———. 1992. "On the Theory and Politics of Cultural Construction in the Pacific." *Oceania* 62:249–63.

Lukes, Stephen. 1974. *Power: A Radical View.* London: Macmillan.

Lutkehaus, Nancy C. 1996. "'Identity Crisis': Changing Images of Chieftainship in Manam Society." In Feinberg and Watson-Gegeo 1996:343–75.

Maaka, Roger C. A. 1994. "The New Tribe: Conflicts and Continuities in the Social Organization of Urban Maaori." *The Contemporary Pacific* 6(2): 311–36.

MacClancy, Jeremy. 1980. *To Kill a Bird with Two Stones: A Short History of Vanuatu.* Port Vila: Vanuatu Culture Centre.

McKinnon, J. M. 1975. "Tomahawks, Turtles and Traders: A Reconstruction of the Circular Causation of Warfare in the Oceania Group." *Oceania* 45(4): 290–307.

Macnaught, Tim. 1982. *The Fijian Colonial Experience: A Study of the Neo-traditional Order Under British Colonial Rule Prior to World War II.* Canberra: Australian National University Press.

Macpherson, C. 1985. "Public and Private Views of Home: Will Western Samoans Return?" *Pacific Viewpoint* 26(1):242–62.

Mahuta, Robert, and Kenneth Egan. 1983. *The Tainui Report: A Survey of Human and Natural Resources.* Occasional Paper no. 19. Hamilton: Centre for Maaori Studies and Research.

Malvatumauri, Paramount Chiefs. 1983. *Kastom Polisi blong Malvatumauri, National Kaonsel blong Kastom Chiefs long Republic blong Vanuatu.* Port Vila: Malvatumauri.

Mangnall, Karen. 1990. "A New Direction: Vanuatu Changes Courses a Decade Later." *Pacific Islands Monthly* 60(9) (Sept.): 18–21.

Mann, Michael. 1986. "The Autonomous Power of the State: Its Origins, Mechanisms and Results." In John Hall, ed., *States in History*, pp. 109–36. Oxford: Blackwell.

Maori Affairs Department. 1988a. *He Tirohanga Rangapu, He Whakawhitiwhiti Whakaaro; Partnership Perspectives, A Discussion Paper.* Wellington: Department of Maori Affairs.

———. 1988b. *Synopsis of Submissions on "He Tirohanga Rangapu."* Report to the Minister of Maori Affairs, July.

———. 1988c. *Partnership Response, Policy Statement; Te Urupare Rangapuu, Te Raarangi Kaupapa.* Wellington: Department of Maori Affairs.

Marcus, G. E. 1977. "Contemporary Tonga—The Background of Social and Cultural Change." In N. Rutherford, ed., *Friendly Islands: A History of Tonga*, pp. 210–27. Melbourne: Oxford University Press.

———. 1989. "Chieftainship." In Alan Howard and Robert Borofsky, eds., *Developments in Polynesian Ethnology*, pp. 175–209. Honolulu: University of Hawai'i Press.

Marshall, Mac. 1981. "Sibling Sets as Building Blocks in Greater Trukese Society." In Mac Marshall, ed., *Siblingship in Oceania*, pp. 201–24. ASAO Monograph no. 8. Ann Arbor: University of Michigan Press.

Martin, J. 1827. *An Account of the Natives of the Tonga Islands: From the Extensive Communications of Mr. William Mariner.* 2 vols. Edinburgh; originally published London 1817.

Maude, A. 1965. "Population, Land and Livelihood in Tonga." Ph.D. thesis, Australian National University, Canberra.

Mead, Margaret. 1935. *Sex and Temperament in Three Primitive Societies.* New York: W. Morrow and Co.

Meijl, Toon van. 1990. "Political Paradoxes and Timeless Traditions: Ideology and Development Among the Tainui Maori, New Zealand." Ph.D. thesis, Department of Prehistory and Anthropology, Australian National University, Canberra.

———. 1993. "The Maori King Movement: Unity and Diversity in Past and Present." *Bijdragen tot de taal-, land- en volkenkunde* (special issue on "Politics, Tradition and Change in the Pacific," ed. Paul van der Grijp and Toon van Meijl) 149(4): 673–89.

———. 1994. "Maori Hierarchy Transformed: The Secularization of Tainui Patterns of Leadership." In Jolly and Mosko 1994: 279–305.

———. 1995a. "Maori Socio-Political Organization in Pre- and Proto-History: On the Evolution of Post-Colonial Constructs." *Oceania* 65(4): 304–22.

———. 1995b. "Community Development Among the New Zealand Maori: The Tainui Case." In Peter Blunt and D. Michael Warren, eds., *Indigenous Organizations and Development*, pp. 191–211. London: Intermediate Technology Publications.

Melanesian Mission. 1895–1946. "The Southern Cross Log." *Monthly Journal of the Melanesian Mission.* Auckland. Australia and New Zealand edition.

Meleisea, Malama. 1987. *The Making of Modern Samoa*. Suva: Institute of Pacific Studies, University of the South Pacific.

———. 1991. "Migrants and Remittances: The Samoan Concept of Tautua." Macmillan Brown Centre for Pacific Studies, University of Canterbury. Paper presented at the Pacific Science Congress, Honolulu, Hawai'i.

———. 1992. *Change and Adaptations in Western Samoa*. Christchurch: Macmillan Brown Centre for Pacific Studies.

Meleisea, Malama and Penelope Schoeffel Meleisea, eds. 1987. *Lagaga: A Short History of Western Samoa*. Suva: Institute of Pacific Studies and the Western Samoa Extension Centre of the University of the South Pacific.

Meller, Norman. 1969. *The Congress of Micronesia*. Honolulu: University of Hawai'i Press.

———. 1985. *Constitutionalism in Micronesia*. Laie, Hawai'i: Institute for Polynesian Studies, Brigham Young University.

Mensah, Kwaku. 1990. "Local Power-play." *West Africa* 3794:796–97.

Metge, Joan. 1976. *The Maoris of New Zealand: Rautahi*. Rev. ed. London: Routledge and Kegan Paul.

———. 1986. *In and Out of Touch: Whakamaa in Cross Cultural Context*. Wellington: Victoria University Press.

Migdal, Joel. 1988. *Strong Societies and Weak States: State-Society Relations and State Capabilities in the Third Word*. Princeton: Princeton University Press.

Miles, William F. S. 1993. "Traditional Rulers and Development Administration: Chieftaincy in Niger, Nigeria, and Vanuatu." *Studies in Comparative International Development* 28(3):31–50.

Mills, R. F. 1975. "The Reconstruction of Proto-South Sulawesi." *Bingkisan* 9: 3–32.

Minutes of the Rotuma Council. Central Archives of Fiji, Suva.

Mitchell, Timothy. 1988. *Colonising Egypt*. Cambridge: Cambridge University Press.

Moale, J. 1989. "Vanuatu's Chief." *Island Business* (Feb.):24–25.

Moyle, R. M. 1984. *The Samoan Journals of John Williams, 1830 and 1832*. Canberra: Australian National University Press.

Nakayama, Masao, and Frederick L. Ramp. 1974. *Micronesian Navigation, Island Empires, and Traditional Concepts of Ownership of the Sea*. Saipan, Mariana Islands: Congress of Micronesia.

Naramana, Richard Basil. 1987. "Elements of Culture in Hograno/Maringe, Santa Ysabel." *'O'O: Journal of Solomon Islands Studies* 1(3):41–57.

Needs, Andrew P. 1988. "New Zealand Aid and the Development of Class in Tonga." Department of Sociology, Massey University, Palmerston North.

Nooy-Palm, C. H. M. 1979. *The Sa'dan Toraja: A Study of Their Social Life and Religion*. Vol. 1. The Hague: Martinus Nijhoff.

———. 1986. *The Sa'dan Toraja: A Study of Their Social Life and Religion*. Vol. 2: *Rituals of the East and West*. Dordrecht-Holland and Cinnaminson-USA: Foris.

Norton, Robert. 1977. *Race and Politics in Fiji*. St. Lucia: University of Queensland Press.

Obeyesekere, Gananath. 1992. *The Apotheosis of Captain Cook.* Princeton: Princeton University Press, and Honolulu: Bishop Museum Press.

Oliver, D. L. 1955. *A Solomon Island Society: Kinship and Leadership Among the Siuai of Bougainville.* Cambridge, Mass.: Harvard University Press.

O'Meara, T. 1987. "Samoa: Customary Individualism." In R. Crocombe, ed., *Land Tenure in the Pacific,* pp. 74–113. Suva: University of the South Pacific.

Orange, Claudia. 1987. *The Treaty of Waitangi.* Wellington: Allen & Unwin/Port Nicholson.

Outward Letters, Rotuma District Office. Central Archives of Fiji, Suva.

Pacific Constitutions. 1986. Vol. 1, *Polynesia.* Suva: University of the South Pacific.

Paitel, Patrick. 1985. *L'Enjeu Kanak.* Paris: Éditions France-Empire.

Parliamentary Debates: Senate. 1984. *Fiji Legislative Papers.* Suva: Government Printing Office.

Patterson, Mary. 1981. "Slings and Arrows: Rituals of Status Acquisition in North Ambrym." In M. Allen, ed., *Vanuatu: Politics, Economics and Ritual in Island Melanesia,* pp. 189–236. Sydney: Academic Press.

Pawley, A. 1982. "Rubbish-Man, Commoner, Big Man, Chief? Linguistic Evidence for Hereditary Chieftainship in Proto-Oceanic Society." In J. Siikala, ed., *Oceanic Studies: Essays in Honour of Aarne A. Koskinen,* pp. 33–52. Helsinki: Finnish Anthropological Society.

Penny, Arthur. 1888. *Ten Years in Melanesia.* London: Wells, Gardner, Darton and Co.

Petersen, Glenn. 1982. *One Man Cannot Rule a Thousand: Fission in a Ponapean Chiefdom.* Ann Arbor: University of Michigan Press.

————. 1993. *Ethnicity and Interests at the 1990 Federated States of Micronesia Constitutional Convention.* Regime Change and Regime Maintenance in Asia and the Pacific, Discussion Paper Series no. 12, Research School of Pacific Studies. Canberra: Australian National University.

————. 1994. "Calm Before the Storm? The 1990 Federated States of Micronesia Constitutional Convention." *The Contemporary Pacific* 6(2):337–69.

————. Forthcoming a. "Politics in Post-War Micronesia." In R. Kiste and M. Marshall, eds., *Anthropology in American Micronesia.* Honolulu: University of Hawai'i Press.

————. Forthcoming b. "Long-term Continuities in Micronesian Political Life." In R. May, ed., *The Politics of Tradition.* Canberra: Australian National University.

Philibert, Jean-Marc. 1982. "Will Success Spoil a Middleman? The Case of Etapang, Central Vanuatu." In Rodman and Counts 1982:187–207.

————. 1986. "The Politics of Tradition: Toward a Generic Culture in Vanuatu." *Mankind* 16(1):1–12.

Pinsker, Eve C. 1981 "Constituting the Constituting of a Constitution: The 1975 Micronesian Constitutional Convention and the Genesis of 'The Micronesian Way.'" M.A. thesis, Department of Anthropology, University of Chicago.

Plant, Chris, ed. 1977. *New Hebrides: The Road to Independence.* Suva: Institute of Pacific Studies, University of the South Pacific.

Powles, Guy. 1986. "Legal Systems and Political Cultures: Competition for Political Dominance in Western Samoa." In P. Sack and Elizabeth Minchin, eds., *Legal Pluralism: Proceedings of the Canberra Law Workshop VII.* Canberra: Law Department, Research School of Social Sciences, Australian National University.

Powles, Guy, and Mere Pulea. 1988. *Pacific Courts and Legal Systems.* Suva: University of the South Pacific.

Poyer, Lin. 1992. "Defining History Across Cultures: Islander and Outsider Contrasts." *Isla* 1(1):73–89.

———. 1993. *The Ngatik Massacre: History and Identity on a Micronesian Atoll.* Washington, D.C.: Smithsonian Institution Press.

———. 1995. "Yapese Experiences of the Pacific War." *Isla* 3:223–56.

Radcliffe-Brown, A. R. 1952. "Taboo." In *Structure and Function in Primitive Society,* pp. 133–52. Reprint. New York: Free Press.

Rappaport, Joanne. 1990. *The Politics of Memory: Native Historical Interpretation in the Colombian Andes.* New York: Cambridge University Press.

Rensel, Jan. 1991. "Housing and Social Relationships on Rotuma." In A. Fatiaki, D. Fatiaki, V. Hereniko, A. Howard, I. Irava, M. Itautoka, L. Kaurasi, M. Kaurasi, T. Malo, A. Nilsen, C. Plant, J. Rensel, J. Tanu, and M. Vilsoni, *Rotuma: Hanua Pumue (Precious Land).* Suva: Institute of Pacific Studies, University of the South Pacific.

———. 1993. "The Fiji Connection: Migrant Involvement in the Economy of Rotuma." In Kerry James, ed., *Pacific Village Economies: Opportunity and Livelihood in Small Communities. Pacific Viewpoint* (special issue) 34:215–40.

———. 1994. "For Love or Money? Interhousehold Exchange and the Economy of Rotuma." Ph.D. dissertation, Department of Anthropology, University of Hawai'i.

Riesenberg, Saul. 1968. *The Native Polity of Ponape.* Washington, D.C.: Smithsonian Institution Press.

Rivers, W. H. R. 1914. *The History of Melanesian Society.* Cambridge: Cambridge University Press.

Rodman, Margaret. 1983. "Following Peace: Indigenous Pacification of a Northern New Hebridean Society." In M. Rodman and M. Cooper, eds., *The Pacification of Melanesia,* pp. 141–60. Lanham, Md.: University Press of America.

Rodman, William L. 1982. "Gaps, Bridges, and Levels of Law: Middlemen as Mediators in a Vanuatu Society." In Rodman and Counts 1982:69–95.

———. 1985. "'A Law unto Themselves': Legal Innovation in Ambae, Vanuatu." *American Ethnologist* 12:603–24.

Rodman, William L., and Dorothy Ayers Counts, eds. 1982. *Middlemen and Brokers in Oceania.* Ann Arbor: University of Michigan Press.

Routledge, David. 1985. *Matanitu: The Struggle for Power in Early Fiji.* Suva: Institute of Pacific Studies, University of the South Pacific.

Rubinstein, Robert L. 1981. "Knowledge and Political Process on Malo." In M. Allen, ed., *Vanuatu: Politics, Economics and Ritual in Island Melanesia,* pp. 135–72. Sydney: Academic Press.

Rynkiewich, Michael A. 1972. "Land Tenure Among Arno Marshallese." Ph.D. dissertation, Department of Anthropology, University of Minnesota.

Sahlins, Marshall. 1963. "Poor Man, Rich Man, Big Man, Chief: Political Types in Melanesia and Polynesia." *Comparative Studies in Society and History* 5: 285–303.

———. 1981. *Historical Metaphors and Mythical Realities*. Ann Arbor: University of Michigan Press.

———. 1985a. "Hierarchy and Humanity in Polynesia." In Antony Hooper and Judith Huntsman, eds., *Transformations of Polynesian Culture*, Memoir no. 45, pp. 195–217. Auckland: The Polynesian Society.

———. 1985b. *Islands of History*. Chicago: University of Chicago Press.

———. 1995. *How "Natives" Think: About Captain Cook, For Example*. Chicago: University of Chicago Press.

Salmond, Anne. 1975. *Hui: A Study of Maori Ceremonial Gatherings*. Wellington: Reed.

Sanders, A. J. G. M. 1983. "Chieftainship and Western Democracy in Botswana." *Journal of Contemporary African Studies* 2:365–79.

Sayes, S. A. 1976. "The Ethnohistory of Arosi, San Cristobal." M.A. thesis, University of Auckland.

Scaglion, Richard. 1996. "Chiefly Models in Papua New Guinea." *The Contemporary Pacific* 8(1):1–31.

Scarr, Deryck. 1970. "A Roko Tui for Lomaiviti: The Question of Legitimacy in the Fijian Administration, 1874–1900." *Journal of Pacific History* 5:3–31.

Schaefer, Paul D. 1977. *Confess Therefore Your Sins: Status and Sin on Kusaie*. Ann Arbor: University Microfilms.

Schneider, David M. 1984. *A Critique of the Study of Kinship*. Ann Arbor: University of Michigan Press.

Scott, James. 1990. *Domination and the Arts of Resistance: Hidden Transcripts*. New Haven, Conn. and London: Yale University Press.

Shils, Edward. 1981. *Tradition*. London: Faber & Faber.

Sissons, Jeffrey. 1993. "The Systematisation of Tradition: Maori Culture as a Strategic Resource." *Oceania* 64(2):97–116.

———. 1994. "Royal Backbone and Body Politic: Aristocratic Titles and Cook Islands Nationalism Since Self-Government." *The Contemporary Pacific* 6: 371–96.

Solomon Islands. 1972. *Recommendation 33, Paper 89, of the Governing Council Select Committee on Constitution Development*. Honiara: British Solomon Islands Protectorate.

———. 1985a. *Parliamentary Debates*. Vol. 2. Honiara: National Parliament.

———. 1985b. *Local Courts Act (Amendment)*. Honiara: National Parliament.

———. 1987. *Report of the Provincial Government Review Committee, 1986–1987*. Honiara: Ministry of Home Affairs and Provincial Government.

Somare, Michael. 1991. *Keynote Address to the Pacific Science Congress*. Honolulu, Hawai'i.

Somerville, H. T. 1897. "Ethnographical Notes in New Georgia, Solomon Islands." *Journal of the Royal Anthropological Institute* 26:357–412.

Speiser, Felix. [1923] 1991. *Ethnology of Vanuatu: An Early Twentieth Century Study*. Bathurst (NSW): Crawford House.

Spriggs, Matthew James Thomas. 1981. "Vegetable Kingdoms: Taro Irrigation and Pacific Prehistory." Ph.D. thesis, Australian National University.

Stanton, Max. 1993. "A Gathering of Saints." In G. McCall and J. Connell, eds., *A World Perspective on Pacific Islander Migration*, pp. 23–37. Sydney: Center for South Pacific Studies, University of New South Wales.

Steward, Julian. 1937. "Linguistic Distributions and Political Groups of the Great Basin Shoshoneans." *American Anthropologist* 39:625–34.

Strathern, Andrew. 1979. *Ongka: A Self Account by a New Guinea Big-Man*. London: Duckworth.

Sturtevant, William. 1983. "Tribe and State in the Sixteenth and Twentieth Centuries." In E. Tooker, ed., *The Development of Political Organization in Native North America*, pp. 3–15. Washington, D.C.: American Ethnological Society.

Sutherland, William. 1992. *Beyond the Politics of Race: An Alternative History of Fiji to 1992*. Political and Social Change Monograph no. 15. Canberra: Australian National University.

Sutton, Douglas G. 1990. "Organisation and Ontology: The Origins of the Northern Maori Chiefdom, New Zealand." *Man* 25(4):667–92.

Sykes, J. W. 1948. *Confidential Report on Rotuma*. Suva: The Secretariat, Central Archives of Fiji.

Tainui Maori Trust Board. 1988. *He Whakautu-a-Iwi ki Te Tirohanga Rangapu: A Tribal Response to Partnership Perspectives*. June 13. Ngaruawahia: Tainui Maaori Trust Board.

Talahi, 'Amanaki. 1989. *His Majesty Taufa'ahau Tupou IV of the Kingdom of Tonga*. Suva: Institute of Pacific Studies, University of the South Pacific.

Tammu, J., and H. van der Veen. 1972. *Kamus Toradja-Indonesia*. Rantepao: Jajasan Perguruan Kristen Toradja.

Theroux, Paul. 1992. *The Happy Isles of Oceania: Paddling the Pacific*. New York: Ballantine.

Thomas, Nicholas. 1989. "The Force of Ethnology: Origins and Significance of the Melanesia/Polynesia Division." *Current Anthropology* 30:27–41.

———. 1992. "The Inversion of Tradition." *American Ethnologist* 19:213–32.

———. 1994. *Colonialism's Culture*. Princeton: Princeton University Press.

Tonkinson, Robert. 1981. "Church and *Kastom* in Southeast Ambrym." In M. Allen, ed., *Vanuatu: Politics, Economics and Ritual in Island Melanesia*, pp. 237–68. Sydney: Academic Press.

———. 1982. "National Identity and the Problem of Kastom in Vanuatu." *Mankind* 13:306–15.

Toren, Christina. 1989. "Making the Present, Revealing the Past: The Mutability and Continuity of Tradition as Process. *Man* 23:696–717.

Tuti, Dudley. 1990. Speech to the Eighth Annual General Meeting of the Santa Isabel Council of Chiefs. (Notes.) Buala, Santa Isabel, May 16–19.

Ullman, Walter. 1975. *Medieval Political Thought*. Harmondsworth: Penguin.

Va'a, Leulu Felise. 1991. "The Future of Western Samoan Migration to New Zealand." Paper presented at the Pacific Science Congress Symposium on the Future of Migration in Asia and the Pacific, Honolulu, Hawai'i.

———. 1993. "Effects of Migration on Western Samoa: An Island Viewpoint." In

G. McCall and J. Connell, eds., *A World Perspective on Pacific Islander Migration*, pp. 343–57. Sydney: Center for South Pacific Studies, University of New South Wales.

van Binsbergen, Wim. 1987. "Chiefs and the State in Independent Zambia: Exploring the Zambian National Press." *Journal of Legal Pluralism and Unofficial Law* 25–26:139–93.

van Rouveroy van Nieuwall, E. A. B. 1987a. "Chef Coutumier: Un Métier difficile." *Politique Africaine* 27:19–29.

———. 1987b. "Chiefs and African States." *Journal of Legal Pluralism and Unofficial Law* 25–26:1–46.

Van Trease, Howard. 1987. *The Politics of Land in Vanuatu: From Colony to Independence*. Suva: Institute of Pacific Studies, University of the South Pacific.

Vanuatu, Republic of. 1979. *Constitution of the Republic of Vanuatu*. Port Vila: Imprimerie de Port Vila.

Vaughan, Olufemi. 1988. "Les Chefs Traditionnels Face au Pouvoir Politique." *Politique Africaine* 32:44–56.

———. 1991. "Chieftaincy Politics and Social Relations in Nigeria." *Journal of Commonwealth and Comparative Politics* 29:308–26.

Vienne, Bernard. 1984. *Gens de Motlav: Idéologie et pratique sociale en Mélanésie*. Paris: Musée de l'Homme.

Volkman, Toby. 1984. "Great Performances: Toraja Cultural Identity in the 1970s." *American Ethnologist* 11(1):152–69.

———. 1985. *Feasts of Honor: Ritual and Change in the Toraja Highlands*. Urbana and Chicago: University of Illinois Press.

———. 1990. "Visions and Revisions: Toraja Culture and the Tourist Gaze." *American Ethnologist* 17:91–110.

Wagner, Roy. 1975. *The Invention of Culture*. Chicago: University of Chicago Press.

Walker, Ranginui. 1987. *Nga Tau Tohetohe: Years of Anger*. Auckland/Harmondsworth: Penguin.

Watson-Gegeo, Karen, and Geoffrey M. White, eds. 1990. *Disentangling: Conflict Discourse in Pacific Societies*. Stanford: Stanford University Press.

Weatherbee, Donald. 1985. "Indonesia in 1984: Pancasila, Politics and Power." *Asian Survey* 25(2):187–97.

Weber, Max. 1947. *The Theory of Social and Economic Organization*. New York: Free Press.

———. 1983. "Politics as Vocation." In David Held, James Anderson, Bram Gieden, Stuart Hall, Lawrence Harris, Paul Lewis, Noel Parker, and Ben Turok, eds., *States and Societies*, pp. 111–15. Oxford: Martin Robertson.

Welchman, Henry. 1889–1908. *Diary, Missionary Life in the Melanesian Islands*. 12 vols. Canberra: National Library of Australia (microfilm m728, 805–6).

Wendt, Albert. 1973. *Sons for the Return Home*. Auckland: Longman-Paul.

Westermark, George. 1991. "Controlling Custom: Ideology and Pluralism in the Papua New Guinea Village Courts." *Legal Studies Forum* 15(2):89–102.

Whaanga, Piripi, and Tawini Rangihau. 1988. "Maori Affairs D-Day." *New Zealand Listener* (July 1–15):28–31.

White, Geoffrey M. 1991. *Identity Through History: Living Stories in a Solomon Islands Society.* Cambridge: Cambridge University Press.

————. 1992. "The Discourse of Chiefs: Notes on a Melanesian Society." *The Contemporary Pacific* 4:73–108.

White, Geoffrey M., F. Kokhonigita, and H. Pulomana. 1988. *Cheke Holo Dictionary.* Pacific Linguistics, Series C, no. 97. Canberra: Pacific Linguistics.

Wilcox, Harry. 1949. *White Stranger: Six Moons in Celebes.* London: Collins.

Williams, John. 1838. *A Narrative of Missionary Enterprises in the South Sea Islands, with Remarks upon the Natural History of the Islands, Origin, Languages, Traditions, and Usages of the Inhabitants.* London: John Snow.

Williams, Raymond. 1976. *Keywords: A Vocabulary of Society and Culture.* London: Fontana.

Wilson, Elle. 1935. *Welchman of Bugotu.* London: Society for Promoting Christian Knowledge.

Winiata, Maharaia. 1956. "Leadership in Pre-European Maori Society." *Journal of the Polynesian Society* 65(3):212–31.

Wood-Ellem, Elizabeth O. 1981. "Queen Sālote Tupou III and Tungī Mailifihi: A Study of Leadership in Twentieth Century Tonga." Ph.D. thesis, Department of History, University of Melbourne.

————. 1987. "Queen Sālote Tupou of Tonga as Tu'i Fefine." *Journal of Pacific History* 22:209–27.

Worsley, Peter. 1968. *The Trumpet Shall Sound.* New York: Schocken.

Western Pacific High Commission. 1875–1941. *Inward Correspondence, General.* Honiara: Solomon Islands National Archives.

————. 1942–54. *General Correspondence.* F. series. Honiara: Solomon Islands National Archives.

Yamamoto, Matori. 1994. "The Urbanisation of the Multiplication and Differentiation of Titles in Western Samoa." *Journal of the Polynesian Society* 103:171–202.

Yanaihara, Tadao. 1940. *Pacific Islands Under Japanese Mandate.* London: Oxford University Press.

Young, John A. 1990. "Development Education and Social Stratification in Fiji." *Practicing Anthropology* 12(1):4–5, 17.

Zeva, Ben. 1983. "Church and State on Isabel." In *Solomon Islands Politics,* pp. 133–37. Suva: Institute of Pacific Studies.

Zorgbibe, Charles. 1981. *Vanuatu: Naissance d'un etat.* Paris: Economica.

Index

In this index an "f" after a number indicates a separate reference on the next page, and an "ff" indicates separate references on the next two pages. A continuous discussion over two or more pages is indicated by a span of page numbers, e.g., "57–59." *Passim* is used for a cluster of references in close but not consecutive sequence.

Library of Congress Cataloging-in-Publication Data

Chiefs today :   traditional Pacific leadership and the postcolonial
    state / edited by Geoffrey M. White and Lamont Lindstrom.
        p.   cm. — (Contemporary issues in Asia and the Pacific)
    Includes bibliographical references and index.
    ISBN 0-8047-2849-6 (cl.) — ISBN 0-8047-2851-8 (pbk.)
      1. Oceania—Politics and government.   2. Chiefdoms—Oceania.
    I. White, Geoffrey M. (Geoffrey Miles).   II. Lindstrom, Lamont.   III. Series.
    GN663.C55   1997
    306.2'0995—dc21
                                                                        97-8986

♾ This book is printed on acid-free paper.

Original printing 1997
Last figure below indicates year of this printing:
06   05   04   03   02   01   00   99   98   97

www.ingramcontent.com/pod-product-compliance
Lightning Source LLC
Chambersburg PA
CBHW020603270326
41927CB00005B/149